Chronicle of Colonial Lima

The Diary of Josephe and Francisco Mugaburu, 1640-1697

Translated and Edited by Robert Ryal Miller

University of Oklahoma Press : Norman

By ROBERT RYAL MILLER

For Science and National Glory: The Spanish Scientific Expedition to America, 1862–1866 (Norman, 1968)
Arms Across the Border: United States Aid to Juárez during the French Intervention in Mexico (Philadelphia, 1973)
(Editor) *Chronicle of Colonial Lima: The Diary of Josephe and Francisco Mugaburu, 1640–1697* (Norman, 1975)

Library of Congress Cataloging in Publication Data

Mugaburu, Josephe de, d. 1686.
Chronicle of colonial Lima.
Written by Josephe de Mugaburu to Oct. 1686 and continued by Francisco de Mugaburu.
Includes bibliographical references.
1. Peru—History—1548–1820—Sources. 2. Lima—History—Sources. I. Mugaburu, Francisco de., b. 1647, joint author. II. Title.
F3444.M8813 1975 985'.03 73–21221
ISBN 0–8061–1134–8

 Composed and printed at Norman, Oklahoma, U.S.A., by the University of Oklahoma Press. First edition.

For Penelope

Preface

IN this first English translation of Mugaburu's diary an attempt was made to keep the wording as literal as possible in order to preserve the historical flavor of the journal. For the same reason a few words like *caballero* and *audiencia* have been left untranslated; these and several Peruvian terms are defined in the accompanying glossary. Saints' names are given in their English form, but names of convents and monasteries are in Spanish. Mugaburu must be admired more for his prolixity than his literary ability, and his style is often cumbersome or repetitious. In his manuscript there are discrepancies between dates, days of the week, and saints' days cited. To aid the reader, several redundant phrases have been eliminated, abbreviations spelled out, dates and times amplified, and occasional footnotes employed to clarify obscure passages or give additional information.

My appreciation to those who have inspired or assisted me in the preparation of this book extends to many persons. Don Carlos de Rubín y Elder and Señora Penelope González of Madrid, Spain, provided considerable translation support; both of them spent many hours checking such things as military, religious, and bullfighting terminology. Doctor Federico Kauffmann Doig, a colleague when I was a Visiting Professor at San Marcos University in Lima, introduced me to leading Peruvian historians and facilitated my entrance to archives and libraries. Señorita Graciela Sánchez Cerro, head librarian of the research division of the Biblioteca Nacional in Lima, gave generously of her time and expertise while I worked there on the diary in 1966 and 1970. My wife, Penny, drew the city plan of Lima as it appeared in mid-seventeenth century, basing it on a reconstructed map by the Peruvian engineer Juan Bromley. Encouragement for publishing the translated chronicle came from Doctor Elfrieda Lang, Curator of Manuscripts at the Lilly Library of Indiana University. I also wish to thank the University of Oklahoma Foundation and the Research Foundation at California State University, Hayward, for their timely grants.

ROBERT RYAL MILLER

Contents

Illustrations

Chronicle of Colonial Lima

The Diary of Josephe and Francisco Mugaburu, 1640-1697

Introduction

ONE of the historical treasures of Peru is a lengthy diary kept in Lima by a seventeenth-century Spanish soldier named Josephe de Mugaburu. Although many documents and printed items for the colonial period of Spanish America exist, most of them are official communications or letters from conquerors, missionaries, and merchants. Only a few colonial Latin American diaries are known to be in archives, and, of these, not one has heretofore been printed in English. Thus for the whole region of Hispanic America, and for the three centuries it was ruled by Spain, we have not had readily available any extensive firsthand account of daily life. The Mugaburu chronicle fills that void, and this particular journal is significant because it covers fifty-seven years and provides information about events and conditions in Spain's richest colony and the largest colonial city in South America.

Lima's importance stemmed from its position as capital of the viceroyalty of Peru, an area fifteen times the size of Spain. For more than two centuries the Spanish provinces from Panama to Argentina, inclusive, were governed from Lima, and all official business, mail, trade, military activities, and religious affairs were funneled through the City of the Kings. In Mugaburu's time the population of Lima averaged about thirty thousand people.* Here lived the viceroy, royal treasury officials, archbishop, heads of religious orders in Peru, and officers of the Inquisition.

Fronting on Lima's large main square, called Plaza de Armas, were offices and residences of the powerful men of church and state. On the west was the viceroy's palace, where the diarist Mugaburu was stationed as sergeant of the palace guard. The cathedral and archbishop's palace were on the north; the *cabildo* or city hall on the south; and adjacent were the jail, postoffice, courts, and important administrative agencies. Activities in this central plaza, described in Mugaburu's diary, include military parades, executions, bullfights, Indian tribal dances, religious spectacles, and official ceremonies.

Government in Spanish South America was centralized under

*Lima's population grew from 25,434 in 1614 to 37,234 in 1700; Juan Bromley and José Barbagelata, *Evolución urbana de Lima* (Lima: Editorial Lumen, 1945), pp. 65, 70.

the viceroy, a personal representative of the Spanish king. Seven years was the average term of office for a Peruvian viceroy during the seventeenth century. His chief advisers were members of the *audiencia*, an administrative council that also functioned as a supreme court and ruled during the absence of the chief executive. Mugaburu is a unique source for evidence that women governed in colonial Latin America. An entry in his diary informs us that in 1668, when the viceroy went to Upper Peru (Bolivia) to put down an Indian rebellion, he left the vicereigne in charge. During his five-month absence she exercised authority by issuing various proclamations and decrees. From his vantage point in the viceregal palace Mugaburu witnessed important events and overheard high-level conversations. Notations in his journal show the power of the viceroy when he overruled municipal elections, exiled *caballeros* whose behavior displeased him, discharged a general who failed to appear for a formation, dismissed all soldiers and sailors who were mulattos or mestizos, issued an edict that all shopkeepers had to be Spaniards and married, and intervened in the selection of church officials.

The entrance into Lima of a new viceroy occasioned elaborate celebrations lasting several days. Mugaburu's eyewitness account of these receptions are among the most colorful passages in his journal. In 1674 he wrote about the arrival of the viceroy, Count of Castellar, who entered the capital city astride a magnificent white horse, richly adorned with silver trappings. On each side, holding the bridle, were the chief magistrates of the city, dressed in crimson velvet. Companies of Spanish soldiers and military units of costumed Indians lined the parade route to the central plaza. Triumphal arches had been erected at several street intersections; the area adjacent to the one in Mercederes Street "was paved with bars of silver, the majority of which were more than 200 marks [100 pounds], which pleased His Excellency upon seeing them." The viceroy's entourage included twenty-four pages and twenty-four mulatto lackeys. For his family there were three mule-drawn carriages with six coachmen. "All wore identical livery of red, silver, and blue. Behind all this were 24 mules, covered with silk cloths bearing the coat of arms of the viceroy, and loaded with pastries. Each mule, with silver baskets and silk ropes and halters, had three large silver [escutcheon] plates with the coat of arms of His Excellency, one on the forehead and two hanging from the ears, and each mule was led by an Indian." At the plaza there were *Te Deums* in the cathedral, artillery salutes, and jousting games for the *caballeros*. On following days, while the public enjoyed bullfights and other manifestations of the *fiesta*, the viceroy and his retinue made official calls on dignitaries and visited the principal religious communities.

Mugaburu's observations clearly demonstrate that the church dominated daily life in colonial Lima. The bells of the cathedral, and those of a dozen monasteries and convents, numerous hermitages and chapels, four parishes, six hospitals, and the Inquisition, called the people to worship and announced weddings, funerals, or special services. A contemporary missionary who spent two years in Peru estimated that in 1620 there were about 1,000 men in the monasteries of that city, and 1,500 women who lived in cloistered convents.* Many clerics worked as professionals in hospitals, orphanages, schools, or as royal government officials since they were often the best educated men in the colony. Formal education, including the Royal and Pontifical University of San Marcos, was controlled by clergymen. The religious calendar designated many saint's days and holidays which were celebrated with candles and prayers in the churches and with fireworks and parades in the streets.

Diary entries relating to the church in Peru illustrate a variety of problems and historical points. Like the viceroy, the archbishop had prerogatives and wielded considerable power. He excommunicated persons who flagrantly disobeyed canon law or incurred his displeasure, and from time to time he granted indulgences to all those who attended a particular religious service or knelt in prayer when the cathedral bells pealed. In 1686, during the threat of a pirate raid, the archbishop ordered all able-bodied priests to join the army, whereupon five hundred clerics enlisted. His Grace then commissioned nine of the priests as captains, assigned fifty priests to each captain, and ordered these units to guard the convents of nuns in Lima. The unity of church and state was symbolized when the viceroy ordered an artillery salute for "Jesus Christ, captain-general of heaven and earth, and for Saint Francis Xavier, his admiral."

*Antonio Vásquez de Espinosa, *Compendium and Description of the West Indies*, trans. by Charles Upson Clark (Washington: Smithsonian Instit. Misc. Col., Vol. 102, 1942), pp. 434–41.

Conflict between church and state and within the church itself is another facet of colonial life elucidated by Mugaburu's chronicle. There were instances where criminals or those accused of a crime sought asylum in a church, but when law enforcement agents entered to arrest them, the church's role as sanctuary was violated. At that point the archbishop usually declared an interdiction for the city of Lima, suspending religious services and the sacraments until some agreement was reached between the viceroy and archbishop. Competition between secular and regular priests also generated some trouble, as did rivalry between those born in Spain and the Peruvian-born clerics.

From time to time disputes erupted in the cloisters over election of monastic officers. Mugaburu tells of a group of Franciscans who "set fire to the cell of the Father comissary because of the ill will they bore him for imposing the alternate provincial on them." The next day, when another priest was knocked down and killed in the monastery, troops were sent in to restore order, but dissention flared anew when a soldier shot one of the religious. On another occasion troops had to be dispatched to a convent when the nuns fought over the election of their mother superior. Eventually these disputes were settled, usually by intervention of the viceroy who exiled or transferred some of the active participants.

Information about secular crime and punishment also appears in the pages of Mugaburu's chronicle. There are reports about men accused of treason, rebellion, murder, petty and grand theft, bigamy, adultery, sodomy, and other crimes. Some of those convicted were fined or imprisoned; others were exiled to Chile, sent to row in the galleys, flogged, hanged, or garroted. In 1667 eight rebellious Indians "were hanged for the uprising they had planned .... After the hangings, the eight heads were removed and placed [on spikes] on the stone bridge [near the viceroy's palace]; then the victims' bodies were quartered and placed in the streets." On another date, following the murder of a Spaniard, the *audiencia* announced the following rewards for whoever disclosed the whereabouts of the suspects: "for a *caballero*, a company of soldiers in Callao; for a slave, freedom; for a free Negro or mulatto, 1,000 pesos; for an Indian, release from enforced service and tribute. For persons who concealed information, the penalty would be their life." Some policing of Lima was done by squads of soldiers who made the rounds of the city each night.

Since Mugaburu was a professional army officer, it was natural that entries in his journal often reflected military matters. Valuable historical data recorded by him include the description of an armada sent to Panama in 1685 to oppose forces under the famous English buccaneer, Henry Morgan. Besides naming and describing the seven Peruvian ships, he lists their armament: "134 pieces of brass artillery; 48 slings for fire balls; 43,563 pounds of gunpowder; 4,566 artillery balls; 10,700 pounds of fuse cord; 900 grenades; 450 fire balls; arquebuses and muskets for all the men." The 1,400 soldiers and sailors aboard were given eight months pay in advance. After battling the pirate fleet near Panama, the ships returned to Peru, but on the way one of the vessels caught fire and sank with the loss of 400 men. The continuing pirate threat led to a general call to arms of all able-bodied men between sixteen and sixty, and Mugaburu tells us who were exempted from the draft. "The warden and constable of the Holy Inquisition, all the learned [men] and the lawyers, owners and supervisors of bakeries, ordinary magistrates and those of the hall of crime, and students in *colegios* and the university." Judging from Mugaburu's diary, he spent a great deal of his army time in activities related to parades and public ceremonies.

Frequent *fiestas* in seventeenth-century Peru brought all residents of Lima together and provided entertainment for the populace. Colorful parades, fireworks, and solemn processions marked religious holidays and major events from the arrival of a new viceroy, to the birth of a prince, an Inquisition auto-da-fe, or news of a Spanish military victory. In addition to crowds of spectators, a great number of people participated as members of uniformed groups representing a parish, school group, religious confraternity, merchant or craft guild, military or governmental unit. Besides this free "theater of the street," there were formal dramatic presentations for the upper classes and members of religious communities. Plays presented in Mugaburu's time include one about King Nebuchadnezzar of Babylon; one called "The Prince of Fez"; several depicting episodes in the life of Saint Rose of Lima; another called "The Phoenix of Spain: Saint Francis of Borgia"; and a comedy entitled "Love in Lima is Fortuitous." The last-mentioned was presented in the palace, where, "after the play, all the *caballeros* and *audiencia* judges and their wives were feasted with dinner, thin wafers, much chocolate, and cold drinks."

Funerals of Spaniards, particularly those of members of the military-religious orders like the Knights of Malta, fascinated Mugaburu, and he described the elaborate ceremonies and burial etiquette of that time. Military officers were buried in their dress uniform; children were interred in white caskets, often decorated with small mirrors; palm fronds invariably accompanied the bodies of deceased virgins; coffins of nobles were covered with black velvet studded with gold nails. When a member of the royal family in Spain died, the colonists in Lima held funeral services, complete with catafalque, candles, and casket.

Other highlights in the Peruvian diary portray ceremonies in the viceroy's palace, functions at San Marcos University, arrivals and departures of armadas, pirate raids, bullfights, and hundreds of notable events. Comets were sighted and earthquakes recorded, along with the reaction of Lima's residents to them. In April of 1687, after a particularly strong tremor, one priest declared that "it was a slap from the hand of God," who was showing his displeasure, while another cleric preached that "God was most annoyed with the nefarious sin which is practiced between members of the same sex." Diary entries also provide information about dowries, marriage customs, fluctuation of prices and revaluation of currency, shipments of silver bullion to Spain, diseases and medical treatment, military recruitment and training, and the class structure.

Although Indians comprised a majority of the population and were an exotic element in the colony, Mugaburu generally ignored them and wrote mostly about the activities of Spaniards in Peru. Even when he visited the old Inca capital of Cuzco, his diary entries seldom mentioned the natives, and he never commented on their architectural monuments or other achievements. His diary is a reflection of his Iberian background, employment in the royal service, and the rigid class structure. In colonial Peru those born in Spain (*peninsulares*), were on the top of the social-political-economic ladder, and way down at the bottom were the Negro slaves. In between were Spaniards born in the New World (*creoles*), those of mixed Indian and Spanish parentage (*mestizos*), the native Indians, and free Negroes. Certain posts and occupations were open only to the privileged classes; for example merchants and high officers in church and state had to be Spaniards.

The diarist Mugaburu leaves no doubt that birth in the mother country was a definite asset for residents of colonial Peru.

A Spanish-born soldier, Don Josephe de Mugaburu y Honton, was the principal author of this Peruvian diary, compiling 95 per cent of it. He made notations about important happenings in Lima from 1640 until his death in 1686; from that date until 1697 the chronicle was continued by his son, Francisco, a clergyman trained in the Franciscan order who later became a secular chaplain. The only known biographical information about Josephe de Mugaburu is derived from the few personal references in his diary. Judging by his surname and his characteristic spelling and word usage, he was of Basque ancestry. Born in Spain in January of 1607, he served in the Spanish army in Peru for more than thirty-six years. For most of that time he was attached to the viceroy's palace guard as a sergeant, which was a higher position than that rank implies today. Mugaburu was promoted to captain in 1672 and transferred to the garrison at the port of Callao, about eight miles west of Lima. Four years later, when he retired from active military service, he spent about three years in the province of Cuzco, high in the Andes Mountains. Returning to Lima, he lived the last six years of his life in that capital city.

Some details about Mugaburu's family are contained in his diary and in appended notations of births, baptisms, and deaths. In 1636 he married Doña Jerónima de Maldonado y Flores, the widow of Don Alonzo López de Aguilar. She had two children by this first marriage: a son, Sebastián (1626–1676), who was a priest serving many years as a prebendary at the cathedral in Lima; and a daughter, Damiana (1635–1687). Damiana married Agustín de Yparraguirre in 1652; when he died six years later, she married again, but the marriage was later annulled. Ten years later in 1668 she married Captain Don Diego Pardo, governor of the province of Yauyos. Damiana was killed by falling debris in an earthquake in Lima on October 20, 1687. In addition to the two stepchildren, Sergeant Mugaburu and his wife Jerónima had eleven offspring, but only three of them lived to maturity. Of these three, José (1641–1677) and Francisco (born 1647) became priests, and Antonio (born 1656) probably did likewise. The last diary entry referring to Antonio was when he was twenty-one years old and studying in a seminary in Cuzco.

Mugaburu's other relatives in Peru included a sister, Margarita, who died in Lima in 1656, and a brother, Martín, who lived in the mining center of Potosí. When Don Martín died in 1643, he left a Negro slave boy named Dominguillo to Josephe and one thousand patacoons to the sergeant's young son, José. The diarist also mentioned several nephews in Peru and two who came from Spain with a cargo of clothing to sell. Mugaburu did not dwell on family or personal matters; he preferred to write about events in the palace or viceregal capital.

The importance of Mugaburu's diary led to its publication in Spanish. In 1917 the first edition appeared in Lima as part of a twelve-volume collection of books and documents on the history of Peru, and in 1935 the diary was reprinted in a limited edition as part of the celebrations commemorating the four-hundredth anniversary of the founding of the city of Lima. Mugaburu's original manuscript diary is now in Bloomington, Indiana, at the Lilly Library of Indiana University. Parts of it are extremely difficult to read because of ink blots and aging. Some notation in the handwritten journal were omitted from the printed Spanish accounts, neither of which contains an index. Both editions have been out of print for years, and only a few major research libraries in the United States have copies.

The primary purpose for publishing an English version of Mugaburu's chronicle is to make his comments about life in seventeenth-century Peru available to an expanded audience. A comprehensive index to topics and personalities mentioned in the journal will be useful to researchers and students of Latin American colonial life, and contemporary illustrations and maps will illuminate some points and supplement the text.

The Year 1640

Nuns of the Prado

The nuns entered the [new] convent of Nuestra Señora del Prado on Saturday, the 1st day of the month of September of the year 1640. They were five in number and came from [the nunnery of Nuestra Señora de] La Encarnación. The founder or mother superior of this cloister is Doña Angela de Iriarte [y Recalde]. With them came the vicar general, Don Juan de Cabrera, who held this position due to the vacancy left by Don Fernando Arias, archbishop of this City of the Kings.[1] Also accompanying them were Don Fernando de Sayavedra, judge of this royal *audiencia* [supreme court and viceroy's council]; Father Juan de Córdoba and Father Contreras of the Society of Jesus; and many other persons. The nuns went to the [outlying district of] El Cercado[2] with all their accompaniment to see the patron of the convent, Juan Clemente de Fuentes, who was there ill. On that day the sponsor gave them for the visit he conceded them, 18,000 patacoons [hexagonal silver dollars].[3] And being thus, as eyewitness I so subscribed it at [the City of] the Kings on the 1st of September of 1640. Said patron died on the 24th of that month of September of 1640 and was buried at the [church of] the Society of Jesus.[4]

Archbishop Don Feliciano de la Vega embarked for Mexico

[1] Lima is called City of the Kings because its site was selected by Francisco Pizarro on January 6, feast day of the Wise Men or Three Kings.

[2] The town of Santiago, better known as El Cercado from the adobe wall that surrounded it, was founded in 1568 about a mile east of the center of Lima. Its first residents were "vagabond and destitute Indians," and by 1629 the population was estimated at eight hundred Indians and eighty Negro slaves. Juan Bromley and José Barbagelata, *Evolución urbana de Lima* (Lima: Editorial Lumen, 1945), p. 59.

[3] A *patacón* (patacoon) was a hexagonal silver coin weighing one ounce Troy and equal to a silver peso (dollar) or eight *reales*; a *tostón* was worth from three to four *reales*; thirty-four *maravedís* in one *real*. A gold *doblón* (doubloon) equaled eight *escudos* or about sixteen silver pesos; a gold *ducat* equaled eleven *reales*. Antonio Vásquez de Espinosa, *Compendium and Description of the West Indies*, trans. by Charles Upson Clark (Washington: Smithsonian Instit. Misc. Col., Vol. 102, 1942), p. 839. See also Bromley, *Evolución urbana*, pp. 57–58.

[4] Burials in Lima were in vaults under churches until 1807 when a royal decree forbade the practice and a cemetery outside the city was established. Bromley, *Evolución urbana*, p. 78.

from Callao[5] on the 10th of October of 1640. (The archbishop died on the 12th of May of 1641.)

The Year 1641

Archbishop Don Pedro de Villagómez

Archbishop Don Pedro de Villagómez entered this city on the 20th of May of 1641, on the second day of Pentecost, at five in the afternoon. [Viceroy of Peru, Don Pedro de Toledo y Leyva,] the Marquis of Mancera, with his wife [Doña María Luisa de Salazar y Henríquez] and son [Don Antonio Sebastián de Toledo] were at the balcony of the palace to receive him, and there was great rejoicing and many fireworks to celebrate his entrance and reception.

News that Archbishop Don Feliciano de Vega had died reached the city on the 29th of July of 1641.

Thursday, the 8th of August of 1641, between six and seven at night, two young students came to the altar of the Virgin located at [the church of] San Pedro Nolasco, and one asked the other, "Which is the [image of the] saint that perspired the other day?" The other replied, "That is it," and looking, they saw that it perspired. With this many religious arrived and saw that it was true. It had been fifteen days since it had perspired before.

The Year 1642

On Saturday, the 20th of April of 1642, there were great festivities, bonfires, festive lights, and a race in the afternoon for all the *caballeros* [knights] and the general of Callao, son of the viceroy, Marquis of Mancera. In the evening many of the *caballeros* and the viceroy and his son, dressed in colorful attire and white plumes, walked through the streets [joyful] for the news which had arrived that day about the success of the horizontal tunnel at the [quicksilver] mine of Huancavelica [Peru].

The Year 1643

My brother Martín de Mugaburu died in Potosí on Holy Wednesday [April 1st] of 1643. He was buried on Holy Thursday in San

[5] The port of Callao is about eight miles west of Lima and is the principal entrepot for Peru.

Agustín [monastery] in Potosí. Captain Tomás de Dondiz was his executor, and he left a thousand patacoons of eight *reales* to my son [José] to become a physician when he is older, and [he left] me a young Negro [slave] named Dominguillo.

At six in the afternoon on the 17th of December of 1643, the nuns entered [the convent of] El Carmen where a great number of people were gathered. The viceroy, Marquis of Mancera, his wife and children, the *audiencia*, the archbishop, Don Pedro de Villagómez, and canons of the church were present. On this day the elderly Catalina María, who taught the young girls, took the veil. There were three nuns who came from Cartagena.

The Year 1644

[In April] a *fiesta* and novena were held in honor of Our Lady of the Rosary, the Mother of God, whose statue is located in the Rosary chapel of Santo Domingo [monastery]. She was chosen as patron saint and guardian of the armies of our king and lord, Philip IV, "the Great," may God protect him. On Sunday, the 3rd of April, after being revered for eighty years by the friars, her statue was removed from its niche and taken in procession to the cathedral. Accompanying it were [images of] a great number of saints of the same [Dominican] order, including Saint Dominic, and an angel with the words of the Hail Mary made out of many pearls and diamonds. The statue of Our Lady had more than two million jewels and pearls; such was the sight to be seen in this City of Kings. Those who preached [during] the novena were: the first day, which was Monday, the canon Zurita; Tuesday, Father Cipriano de Medina of Santo Domingo; Wednesday, Father Bustamante of San Francisco; Thursday, Father Vadillo of San Augustín; Friday, Father Carrera of La Merced; Saturday, Father Ludena of the Society of Jesus; Sunday, a father of the barefoot Trinitarians; Monday, the provincial of the Society [of Jesus]; Tuesday, Doctor Avendaño, canon of the holy church. A great number of people attended this novena and heard the predicators, all of whom preached on the same topic which was when the Mother of God was at the foot of the cross. On this topic there were many unusual items in eulogy of Our Lady of the Rosary. It was the general consensus of opinion that the Trinitarian had preached a great sermon. There were many fireworks, *Novena* and both days there were many squadrons coming and going, on foot and on horseback. The squadrons fired a great number of vollies. As general of the army, Don Antonio Sebastián de Toledo came out to see the squadron with a large retinue of battalion commander, adjutant, governor, and commissary of the cavalry,[6] as follows: battalion commander, Don Antonio de Acuña y Cabrera; adjutant, Don José Ferrer; governor of the cavalry, Don Francisco Gil Negrete; commissary, Don Ambrosio del Pulgar; aides on foot, Gaspar de Savariego and Hernando de Ribera, and many sergeants. I was one of them. The viceroy, Marquis of Mancera, and all the royal *audiencia* carried the statue. It was a day of great solemnity, and because it was thus, I so subscribed it in Lima on the 12th of April of 1644.

Saturday, the 26th of November of the year 1644, the dispatch ship arrived from Spain.

On Sunday, the 27th of this month, Doctor Don Alonso Corbacho assumed the post of canon; and on Monday, the 28th of the same month, he left [the parish of] Santa Ana after having said Mass at the main altar. Summoning all the priests, he gave a speech, and they were disheartened at his departure.

(He died on Sunday, the 5th of May of 1647, and they buried him with great ceremony on Monday, the 6th, at the cathedral of this city with the archbishop and canons in attendance.)

Church of Santa Clara

On Monday, the 28th of November of 1644, the archbishop of this city, Don Pedro de Villagómez, laid the cornerstone of the new church which was to replace the glorious Santa Clara. In a cavity of the cornerstone he placed the following coins: a large goldpiece, another of silver, another large one of copper, an ordinary patacoon, another of four *reales*, one of a single *real*, one half-*real*, and another two-*reales*.[7] On the three large coins was inscribed a memorial of our lord, [King] Philip IV, may God protect him, of His Holiness [Pope Urban VIII], of Viceroy

[6] Spanish military terminology varied through the centuries and in different parts of the empire. Here *maestro de campo* clearly refers to battalion commander, while in Spain it could mean regimental commander. Adjutant (*sargento mayor*) was an officer in charge of instruction, discipline, and distribution of funds. *Comisario de caballería* served as commissary for maintainance of the horses. José Almirante, *Diccionario militar, etimológico, histórico, technológico* (Madrid: Depósito de la Guerra, 1869).

[7] See note 3 for monetary values.

Marquis of Mancera, and of the archbishop of this city, Don Pedro de Villagómez. Present at the blessing and the Mass celebrated by the archbishop were Don Juan de Cabrero, treasurer of the church and commissary of the holy Crusade;[8] Don Fernando de Avendaño, choirmaster; and Archdeacon Zurita. Bishop Don Fray Cristóbal de la Mancha, who was to be consecrated bishop by Archbishop Villagómez on the following Wednesday, the day of Saint Andrew, was also there. There was a great gathering of people, and eight [artillery] chambers were fired within the mill, making a great noise. After blessing the church and its foundations, His Grace went to say Mass and give benediction in the new church, granting forty days indulgence to those present.

The Year 1645

On Thursday, the 26th of February of 1645, at four in the afternoon the cornerstone was laid for the *Colegio* [seminary] Santo Tomás de Aquino which was to be built in front of the water reservoir of [the church of] Santo Domingo. Viceroy Marquis of Mancera and Father Fray Juan de Arginao, provincial of said [Dominican] order, and many others were present. [Opening ceremonies were sixteen years later.] (On Sunday, the 29th of May of 1661, at five in the afternoon a procession carrying the Holy Sacrament of the altar and [a statue of] the glorious Saint Thomas went to the *colegio*, conducted by Father Meléndez of the order of Predicators, who was then vicar of the province. On this same day the religious who were to be students at this college arrived. The [viceroy] Count of Alba de Liste and all the *audiencia* also came in the procession from the city.)

Bishop Don Pedro de Ortega left the Jesuit Society for his bishopric on Friday, the 19th of May of the year 1645, after having been in the order nine months and nineteen days.

Marquis of Mancera to Huancavelica

Saturday, the 5th of August of 1645, at three in the afternoon

[8] Papal bulls of the holy Crusade were conceded to Spanish kings by various popes. These bulls, published in America every two years, permitted the selling of indulgences, or taxation, to provide funds for wars against the infidel and for the extension of the Roman Catholic faith. Although the proceeds went into the royal treasury, the *cruzada* was always regarded as an ecclesiastical tax and was collected and administered by churchmen. C. H. Haring, *The Spanish Empire in America* (New York: Harcourt, Brace & World, 1963), pp. 267–68.

Viceroy Marquis of Mancera left this city for Huancavelica to see the quicksilver works and shaft of the mine. He returned to this city from Huancavelica at the end of September of that year, 1645.

Prime Professorship The vicar general of this City of Kings, Don Domingo de Velasco, and Father Fray Juan de Ribera of the order of Saint Augustine competed for the prime professorship [theology][9] left vacant by Bishop Don Pedro de Ortega. The vicar general competed on Saturday, the 25th of November of the year 1645, and he obtained the professorate by 703 votes on Sunday, the 26th of the month. On Monday, the 27th, there was a great promenade through the city with all the clergy and *caballeros* of the city [taking part].

The Year 1646

Monday, the 10th of January, Saint Sebastian's day, by order of the vicar general, Magdalena, the daughter of my brother [in-law] Francisco de Sequera, was taken from her home to be wed, and she married within fifteen days.

The Year 1647

The Jesuit Bell The great bell which weighed 138 quintals [13,800 pounds] was hoisted to the tower of the Jesuit church on Tuesday, the 19th of February of 1647.

On the night of Sunday, the 5th of February of 1647, the Marquis of Mancera, viceroy of these kingdoms, and his son with various *caballeros* and the regiment of the city, all very gallant and with many torches, went for a stroll through the streets which were decorated with numerous festive lights. There were torches in the balconies and windows, and many ladies in carriages going through the streets. Then on the following Monday night there were fireworks in the plaza. And on this night Señor Gabriel Gómez de Sanabria died. On Wednesday there were bulls [bullfights] and great festivity and joy; these festivities were held to celebrate the good news that came from Chile and Valdivia of the peace made with the Indians.

[9] Candidates for professorial chairs (*cátedras*) in Spanish universities engage in public competition (*opposiciones*), where they are judged on their knowledge and oral exposition. In colonial Peru, professorships were designated by canonical hours as well as by subject; prime professorship (*de prima*) was an early morning class, in this case theology.

On Friday, the 20th of September of 1647, at eight in the evening news arrived [from Spain] that Our Lord had seen fit to take into His holy glory our dear prince and lord, Baltasar Carlos, on the 9th of October of the year past, 1646. Funeral services were held in this church, the cathedral of [the City of] Kings on the afternoon of the 10th of October of 1647. The cortege went from the palace to the cathedral. Friday morning was a repetition of the previous day, and [the procession] left in the following order:

Death of Prince Don Baltasar

The first to appear with his large black mourning cloak was Captain Don Francisco de Izásaga, as captain of the arquebuses of the guard company of this kingdom; then all his soldiers with the same cloaks; followed by the *consulado* [merchant guild] with its ministers at the front; followed by [representatives from] three *colegios*, Santo Toribio, San Martín and the Colegio Real; followed by the [Royal and Pontifical] University [of San Marcos] with its beadles;[10] which were followed by the secretaries of the offices of judicial fines and the deceased, and others related to these offices with their ministers; followed by the relators[11] of the royal *audiencia*; followed by the *caballeros* of the [military-] religious orders;[12] followed by the *cabildo* [city council]. Behind the king at arms[13] were the chancellor, the royal *audiencia* with His Excellency, the Marquis of Mancera, then his household with its royal chaplains and commissioners; and then the company of lances with its captain, Don Francisco Barba, with which the procession came to an end.

In all there were one hundred and forty-six [mourners in] cloaks so long they dragged on the ground. They left by the main door of the palace and went directly to the cathedral entering by way of the baptistry. The retinue passed ostentatiously through a

[10] The Royal and Pontifical University of San Marcos in Lima, Peru, was founded by royal decree in 1551. Beadles were university ceremonial officers who carried a mace in processions.

[11] A relator is a lawyer who prepares briefs of laws, decrees, and proceedings for high courts of justice.

[12] Modeled on the Knights Templars, four important military-religious orders developed in Spain, primarily in connection with the Christian wars against the Moslems. The oldest order was the Caballeros (Knights) of Calatrava, founded in 1158; the others were Santiago, Alcántara, and Montesa. Some Spaniards were members of the Knights of Malta, also known as Caballeros de San Juan de Jerusalén.

[13] King at arms (*reyes de armas*) was a position held by a *caballero* who had charge of arranging ceremonies and maintaining registers of nobility.

wide avenue formed by a large number of the battalion of this city who turned out with their arms. The battalion commander in charge was Don Antonio Mogollón de Ribera; the sergeant [major], Don José Ferrer; the adjutants, Don Gaspar de Savariego and Andrés de Murgia. There were twelve sergeants among whom I, Josephe de Mugaburu, was one. Four companies on horseback also turned out with their captains. Ambrosio del Pulgar, commissary of the cavalry, was in command with his aide, Luis de Aresti.

The catafalque was very sumptuous with many interesting details, numerous candles, and symbols. Archbishop Don Pedro de Villagómez sang the Mass and the Very Reverend Father Pedro de Valverde of the Augustinian order preached at length and very well. On this day an official carpenter by the name of Santiago, a mulatto, fell from the height of the catafalque while walking on a strap as he was lighting the candles. His arms and legs were broken, but he was not killed. And because all this is true, as eyewitness I so wrote it.

On this occasion the viceroy [Marquis] of Mancera, in deference to the gentlemen of the religious orders, ordered the house arrest of royal officials and several aldermen for the disrespect they showed at the cathedral in arising from their seats. Those placed under house arrest were the accountant Bartolomé Astete y Ulloa; the royal official Pedro de Jaraba; another by the name of Caballón; also a royal official awaiting new assignment; the *regidores* [city councilors] Alonso de Paredes, Bartolomé de Azaña, Felipe de Mieses, Doctor Avendaño; and others. And this occurred on the same day as the funeral services, Friday, the 11th of October of the year 1647.

Captain Alonzo de Paredes and the councilor [Bartolomé de] Azaña paid the fine of 500 pesos; Captain Alonso de Paredes was exiled to Ica, and Azaña to Huánuco; the royal officials were fined 300 pesos and the other aldermen 200 pesos.

Dispatch Ship from Spain

Another dispatch ship arrived from Spain [via Panama] on Sunday, the 20th of October of 1647, at the time of the annual *fiesta* celebrated for the name of Mary.[14] The procession of Santo Do-

[14] The *fiesta* for the name of Mary is celebrated on September 12, but a number of times Mugaburu gives an October date; perhaps he confused it with the feast day for the divine motherhood of Mary, October 11th. Mary's immaculate conception is celebrated on December 8, her nativity on September 8, and

mingo [church] set out in great splendor headed by eleven maidens chosen by lot, and there was a great squadron formed in the plaza with much artillery and great solemnity.

At dawn of Monday, the 21st of the same month, Francisco de Madarriaga, prior of the *consulado*, died without having confessed [his sins], and he was buried at [the church of] San Francisco.

This dispatch ship brought the news that our king and lord, Philip IV, was to wed a cousin in Germany, and that the galleons of silver sent to Spain in charge of Don Pedro de Ursúa arrived at Cádiz in forty-five days [from Panama].

Consecration

On Sunday, the 17th of November of 1647, the archbishop of this City of Kings, Don Pedro de Villagómez, consecrated Fray Juan de Auidras as bishop of Santa Cruz de la Sierra.

And on this day the ship *San Juan de Pimocha* arrived from Chile with the adjutant of Valdivia, Hernando de Ribera, as well as Captain Gabriel de Lequina and other captains. On the following Tuesday, which was the 19th of the month, there was a great earthquake which lasted more than four *credos* [minutes], and by the grace of God it caused no harm. It was at nine-thirty in the morning.

Then the following Thursday there was a great rumbling at midnight and it seemed that the whole city would collapse, whereupon everyone went out into the streets at that hour. In many sectors [the presence of] Our Lord Jesus Christ was felt.

The Year 1648

Lieutenant Bernabel López died of dropsy on Friday night, the 6th of March, 1648, and he was buried on Saturday, the 7th of that month and year, in Holy Christ Chapel of San Agustín [church].

On this same day Doctor Peronio, nicknamed Navarra, died and was buried at the [church of San José de las Monjas] Descalzas.

Juan Bautista Loza died this same day, and he was buried in San Francisco [monastery].

Tuesday, the 12th of May of 1648, [my brother-in-law] Francisco de Sequera was wounded in the hand. (He died on Tuesday, the 18th of December of 1663.)

her assumption on August 15. *New Catholic Encyclopedia* (15 vols., New York: McGraw-Hill, 1967), IX, 211–12.

General Francisco Mexía died on Sunday, the 12th of July of 1648, and he was buried in the convent of Our Lady of Mercedes on the following Monday. Viceroy Marquis of Mancera, the royal *audiencia*, and the secular and ecclesiastic councils attended the funeral which was one of the most solemn funerals held in Lima.

Ambassador The ambassador of the [new viceroy] Count of Salvatierra entered this city at five in the afternoon on Tuesday, the 5th of August of 1648, with great applause and ceremony. [He rode] between the two justices, Alvaro de los Ríos and Ordoño de Zamudio. On Tuesday, the 11th of August, there was bullfighting in honor of his arrival.

Brother of the Viceroy Monday, at eight in the evening [Don Alvaro Sarmiento de Sotomayor,] brother of His Excellency the [new] viceroy, Count of Salvatierra, arrived in this city with a great retinue. Don Antonio de Toledo, son of the Marquis of Mancera, and the Marquis of Baydes went outside the city to receive him. This was Monday, the 24th of August of 1648, the day of the glorious Saint Bartholomew.

The [new viceroy, Don García Sarmiento de Sotomayor,] Count of Salvatierra, arrived at the port of Callao at five in the afternoon on Friday, the 28th of August of the year 1648, the day of Saint Augustine. Many pieces of artillery were fired in royal gun salutes. On the following Saturday at four in the afternoon he disembarked from the ship, and for a second time gun salutes were fired from land and sea.

On the afternoon of Sunday, the 30th of the same month, the [outgoing viceroy] Marquis of Mancera went to visit Callao with many *caballeros* who accompanied him from this city. The Marquis went by mule from the palace to the *chácara* [rural estate] of Don Fernando Bravo, and from there to Callao by carriage. Tuesday, the 1st of September of that year, at four in the afternoon the Marquis of Mancera left the palace amidst great applause and a retinue of *caballeros* and all the judges, and he went to reside in the house of Doctor Salazar, justice of the court of this city, adjacent to [the convent of] La Concepción. On this day an infantry company arrived from Callao with thirty-four men under Captain Don Diego de la Portilla. On the following Wednesday the Count of Salvatierra arrived from Callao at seven in the evening to visit the Marquis of Mancera. There was a great exchange of courtesies between the two gentlemen who sat facing each other; however the count sat under the *dosel* [canopy] and the marquis outside it. After a long while they left for the room of the marchioness where polite compliments were exchanged between the count and the marchioness; the marquis left and waited outside while the count paid his visit. After taking his farewell of the marchioness he went with the marquis to the patio of the house where the marquis had had the carriage of the count outfitted with six mules and two coachmen. Then he departed for Callao with his brother, Don Alvaro, and Don José Yzasi de Enríques, who accompanied the count because His Majesty so requested, may God protect him, and because he was captain of the guard of His Excellency.

Sunday, the 6th of that month, the marquis and marchioness went with their household to the rural estate of Don Francisco Bravo which is near Callao, and they dined there. Later in the afternoon they went to Callao to visit the Count and Countess of Salvatierra, where they received a splendid gun salute upon entering and leaving. They visited until the hour of the *Ave María* [dusk] and from there returned to the same *chácara* to spend the night.

They remained until Tuesday, the 8th of the month, when the Count and Countess of Salvatierra arrived at the same *chácara* for a visit with the other viceroy and his wife. That same night the Marquis and Marchioness of Mancera went to Lima.

My captain, Alonso de Pales, died suddenly at midnight on Thursday, the 10th of September of the year 1647, day of the glorious Saint Nicholas [of Tolentino]. He was buried the following Friday at [the church of] San Marcelo, in the vault. Memorial funeral rites were held on the 15th of the month. It was such a deplorable death, there not having been another such sudden death in all the city, that it astounded everyone.

Wednesday, the 16th of the month, at five in the afternoon the proclamations of the king, our lord, were made public in the plaza of this city. Amidst much applause they were carried by the Count of Salvatierra accompanied by the ordinary justices.

Don Pedro Jaraba, commissioner and royal official of this city, died abruptly on the night of Monday, the 20th of September of the year 1648. He was buried at [the church of] San Francisco in the chapel of Saint [Francis] Solano.

Entrance of the Viceroy On Saturday, the 19th of September, [the count] left Callao, and without stopping at any *chácara* he went directly to the hermitage of Nuestra Señora de Monserrat, while the countess came to the palace where she slept.

On Sunday, the 20th of that month, on the eve of the day of the apostle Saint Matthew [the new viceroy] entered Lima under a canopy. Several troops of Indians went to [the hermitage of] Monserrat as well as numerous infantrymen on duty, along with two captains, Don Marcos de Lucio and Don Francisco de Flores, and with Colonel Don Antonio de Mogollón y Ribera. Not having continued to the university as had the city councilmen, they did not pass before His Excellency. They took his oath and then he rode on horseback under the *pallium* [canopy], as was the custom, with the aldermen as *pallium* bearers, and the justices holding the reins of the horse. At the bronze marble [memorial stone] they showered him with many flowers and silver. And in Mercaderes Street there was another arch where they also showered him with many flowers and with silver. All the area encompassed by the arch was paved with ingots of silver; there were almost 300 bars of silver.

There was also a squadron in the plaza with many people present, and the company guard of the Marquis of Mancera turned out. The palace company did not go out into the plaza because they always flanked inside until His Excellency entered. Ten pieces of artillery in the plaza fired three times after his entrance into the palace, which was at dusk.

On Tuesday, the 28th of the month, he called on the gentlemen of the Inquisition.

On Wednesday he went to visit the monastery of Santo Domingo; he called on the father provincial and visited there at great length. He then went to [the monastery of] San Francisco where they received him with the cross raised and a canopy. He visited the cell of the commissary general and, after having prayed, visited all of the cloister.

On Thursday, the 1st of October, he visited the other religious orders in the same way, with which he concluded his official calls.

On Tuesday, the 6th of the same month, the Marquis of Mancera with his son Don Antonio de Toledo, and Don Bartolomé de Salazar, justice of the court, went to visit the Viscount of Portillo, Don Agustín Sarmiento de Sotomayor.

At dusk on the same day the Count of Salvatierra with Don Andrés de Vilela, president of this royal *audiencia*, also went to visit the viscount, and there were many offerings on the part of the Count of Salvatierra, who treated him as his second cousin.

On the night of Thursday, the 15th of the month of October, the Count of Salvatierra presented his brother, Don Alvaro, as his lieutenant, with the staff of command of general of Callao, first rendering with great solemnity the honors that such cases require. Present were Battalion Commander Don Antonio Mogollón de Ribera, Adjutant Don José Ferrer, and many captains of the battalion of this city in units with their cavalrymen. Many *caballeros* of this city were also present. Don José de Cáceres, as secretary of the government of this City of Kings, read the titles of all the favors granted by the viceroy.

The Armada

The armada left Callao for Tierra Firme [Panama or northern South America] with the treasure of His Majesty on Thursday, the 29th of October 1648. It was the first that the Count of Salvatierra personally dispatched, and it left under the command of General Melchor Polar and Admiral Don Juan de Quesada, treasurer of the royal funds. On the sixth day of navigation General Melchor Polo died and [his body] was cast to sea.

Royal Celebrations

On Thursday, the 17th of December of 1648, there were royal celebrations wherein many *caballeros* of this city appeared in grand uniforms, something very spectacular and much admired because of the high cost of livery. There were also *cañas* [jousting games] and the bulls were the bravest ever run in the Plaza [de Armas] of Lima.[15]

On Tuesday, the 22nd of this month, there were bulls, and the same *caballeros* came out in great splendor to the plaza for [jousting] games of *alcancías*. There were many that pricked the bulls with a *garrocha* [iron-pointed pole]. On both days Don Lucas de Almeida came out with many of these pointed weapons, and he used them much to the satisfaction of those who were watching, because there were many *caballeros* in the plaza who had come from all over the kingdom upon the arrival of the Count of Salvatierra.

[15] Bullfights were held in the public plazas until 1768 when Lima's first bullring, Plaza de Acho, was built. Bromley, *Evolución urbana*, p. 72.

Dispatch Ship Thursday, the 31st of December of 1648, the dispatch ship arrived at this city bearing news of the arrival of the galleons [from Spain] at Panama, and it brought some letters which said that the Marquis of Mancera would be going to Mexico as viceroy.

Damiana, my [step-] daughter, was selected by lot for the sodality of the Pure and Immaculate Conception of Our Lady at [the church of] San Francisco on Monday, the 30th of November of 1648, day of the glorious Apostle Saint Andrew. She came out in the procession the 8th of December of that year with eleven other maidens, which made a total of twelve. The sponsor who took her by the hand was Martín Velasco, twenty-fourth of the sodality, and the superior was Juan López de Utrera. She has a dowry of 450 patacoons [pesos] for such time as she enters the state of matrimony or the religious life. My daughter came out in the lots drawn the second year after I had made the petition; the day she appeared [in the procession] she was thirteen years, two months and eleven days old.

In the year 1648 I gave Matheo de Zamacola seven hundred patacoons to take to Tierra Firme [Panama]; he will use them for my account. The contract was executed before Martín de Ochandiano, public notary, and a comrade of Zamacola was secondary trustee.

The Year 1649

Wednesday, the 17th of February of 1649, first day of Lent, the Count of Salvatierra issued a proclamation that all the Portuguese with armed ships in this sea [Pacific Ocean] should sell them within three months under penalty of losing them; and that they should not own them themselves nor through a third person, under penalty of two thousand pesos for the one having it, and for the Portuguese, loss of his possessions; and that within three days they should surrender their arms.

Tuesday, the 5th of January of 1649, the dispatch boat arrived from Spain bringing confirmation that the Marquis of Mancera had been appointed viceroy of Mexico. The Count of Salvatierra then went to the house of the marquis to congratulate him, whereupon great courtesies were exchanged. Neither of the viceroys sat in the ceremonial dais, but outside it, and they remained there for a long while during which compliments were paid to the marquis by all the *caballeros* of this city. Immediately afterwards the marquis went to [the church of] Santo Domingo to give thanks to Our Lord and the Virgin of the Rosary.

At the end of March 1649 the galleons and the fleet would leave [Spain] for Tierra Firme [Panama] to pick up the silver which had been sent there from this city on the 29th of October of last year, 1648.

Squadron and Procession

[Holy] Thursday, the 25th of March of 1649, the day of the Incarnation of Our Lord Jesus Christ, a very solemn procession was held in retaliation for what the Jews did in Quito to Our Savior, which was to disparage the Holy Sacrament of the altar, may it be forever praised. This procession was held in this city of Lima as though it were the day of Corpus [Christi] with the Holy Sacrament uncovered. It was taken out of the cathedral to [the church of] Santo Domingo, and from there to [the church of] San Agustín, and returned to the cathedral by way of Plateros Street where there were many interesting altars. A squadron was formed in the main plaza; those who failed to attend this formation were fined six pesos which they paid without exception.

Armada for Arica

Saturday, the 1st of May of 1649, the armada headed by General Martín de Samalbide left for Arica [Peru].

Controller Medina

On Saturday, the 8th of the present month, the controller Juan de Medina of Avila left the royal jail of the court, where he had been held on a charge formulated by the Marquis of Mancera.

Father Fray Juan Durán, Franciscan commissary general, died on Monday, the 5th of July of the year 1649, and he was buried the following Wednesday. A large crowd attended, and his body was carried by all the prelates of the monasteries. The viceroy, Count of Salvatierra, and the *audiencia* were present at the burial.

Father Fray Alonso Velázquez, provincial of the Franciscan order, died Saturday, the 10th of the month of July of the year 1649, and he was buried Monday, the 12th of the month, with the same grandeur as the commissary general and in the same manner. Tuesday, the 13th of the same month, they elected Very Reverend Father Olloscos, who had been provincial before, as provincial and vice-commissary.

Consecration of Zurita Señor Zurita was consecrated as bishop on Sunday, the 11th of July of the year 1649, by the archbishop of this city, Don Pedro de Villagómez.

Tuesday, the 13th of July of 1649, the vicar general of the Mercedarian order entered this city.

On Wednesday, the 14th of this month, the greatest atrocity in the world occurred in this city. A Negro of the Terranova tribe killed a Negress of his same tribe with a kitchen machete, chopping her body into pieces. Then he wounded the licentiate Isidro, a priest, eleven times, all fatal blows, and cut the fingers off his hands, leaving him for dead. He then entered another house and killed an Indian man and woman. He wounded the owner of the house, his wife, and a twelve-year-old child, inflicting three large wounds on the young girl. En route to the corral he met another Indian woman and split her head open, leaving her seriously injured. Then the Negro climbed to the rooftops with a halberd in his hand which he had seized from a man whom he hit in the left arm with the machete, inflicting a large wound. While he was on the rooftops a great number of people went up there but they were not able to kill him. On the rooftops he killed a mestizo blacksmith before the latter had time to confess, running the halberd through his body four times, and with the machete he split his head spilling his brains. And in all this fracas, quite beside himself, was Juan Pascual, a minister of justice. Not being able to catch him [the Negro], they brought a security guard, and with the shot fired he did not fall, but with another discharge which José Vejete fired in his face, he fell on the rooftops where they captured him. While they were tying him up, the roof caved in with all the people. They took him to the city jail where he asked for confession, and after having confessed, the Negro died. Then the judge, Don José de Mendoza, had him hung in the porticoes of the city council where he was left until the afternoon. In the afternoon the justice ordered that he be dragged through the usual streets; they dragged his body on the ground as far as the Islas drainage ditch where he had committed the crime, and from there they took him to the plaza where they prepared a noose and hung him for twenty-four hours. The judge then ordered that they have him quartered, and they placed his head and his hands where he had committed the crime.

[Captain Francisco Gutiérrez de] Coca died on Tuesday, the

3rd of August of 1649, and was buried at nine in the morning, on the 4th of the month, Saint Dominic's day, in the Jesuit church. He received an ostentatious burial with the viceroy and *audiencia* in attendance. The *caballeros* of the [military-] religious orders, of whom he was one in the order of Santiago, carried his body from the house. The ceremonies being over, the same *caballeros* wanted to take the deceased to the vault, but the viceroy ordered the justices to the court and the [*audiencia*] judges to carry him.

Sunday, August 8, 1649, a Chinaman employed as a workman killed a Spanish superintendent and two Negroes; it was not possible to prevent it.

The Holy Lignun Crusis

On Sunday, the 19th of September of 1649, the great relic of the holy *lignuncrusis* [fragment of authentic cross of Jesus] which His Holiness donated to this holy church was placed in the cathedral. It had been brought by the Count of Salvatierra, viceroy of these kingdoms, and it was carried in a very solemn procession from the monastery of San Francisco to the cathedral, in which the religious orders, the councils of this city, the viceroy, and the *audiencia* participated. They also brought out six white banners with green crosses which were carried by six priests named by the archbishop as *visitadores* to visit all the archbishopric and preach the faith of Our Lord Jesus Christ to the Indians and do away with their idolatry, and to punish such [idolatrous] Indians.

On this day it was announced that the celebrations which His Holiness had ordered eliminated were not to be observed. And this day Father Fray Blas de Acosta of the order of Predicators gave a sermon at the cathedral.

Procession

Sunday, the 17th of October of the year 1649, a holy crucifix was taken in great solemnity from [the church of] San Agustín to that of La Encarnación. It was the greatest procession ever held in this city, with [statues of] all the saints of that [Augustinian] order adorned as for the procession of Corpus [Christi] which the convent of San Agustín celebrates with great splendor. All the streets and all the altars along the way were decked with hangings. The Count of Salvatierra, viceroy of these kingdoms, all the *audiencia*, and a great number of infantry preceded the procession, and a squadron was formed at the small Encarnación plaza.

The Year 1650

Governor for Chile The governor for Chile, Don Antonio de Cabrera, left Callao on Saturday, the 26th of March of the year 1650.

On Saturday, the 2nd of April of the year 1650, the Marquis of Mancera left this city for Callao with a great following of persons and with the Count of Salvatierra accompanying him. All the [military] people on duty sallied forth, and a squadron was formed at the small plaza of Santiago. Other people formed a line along both sides of the street below [the Mercedarian Recollect] Belén. The marchioness also went along in a carriage with her son and daughter; and the count accompanied them to the street below Belén.

Armada The armada left for Tierra Firme [Panama] on Holy Monday, the 11th of April of the year 1650, in which the Marquis of Mancera with his entire family left for Spain. This armada carried the silver of almost two years, which was more than twelve million [pesos].

On Wednesday, April 27, 1650, my son Marcos began school, and he was eleven years old.

Tallow Candles It was on Thursday, the 28th of April of the year 1650, when the tallow candles were brought to the *cabildo* [city council]. They were sold in a line from the galleries to the plaza at one *real* apiece, quite an improper thing for a government such as that of this city. The ordinary justices were Felipe de Mieses and José Delgadillo.

My *comadre*, Juana de Cárdenas, died on Tuesday, May 31, 1650, and the following day she was buried in Holy Christ chapel of San Agustín church. It was a very ostentatious burial. José, the husband of Juana de Cárdenas, and my *compadre*, died at eleven fifteen on the night of October 23, 1650. On the 24th he was buried in the same chapel with his wife.

On Sunday, the 25th of September of 1650, Magdalena de Seguira committed suicide. On this day her husband brought her bruised body to my house. He left [my house 3½ months later] at six in the evening of Tuesday, 10th of January, 1651.

On Tuesday, the 11th of October of 1650, the dispatch boat arrived from Spain bringing much news.

Sunday, the 16th of October of 1650, the licentiate Don Pedro de Espina took on the habit of Santiago in the royal chapel of the palace. His sponsor was the Marquis of Baydes, and the Count of Salvatierra conferred on him the title of *caballero*. As it was the custom for a prior or provincial of San Agustín to attend, a prebend of this holy convent, who also belonged to the order of Santiago, was present. There were also a great number of *caballeros* there.

My sister-in-law María left on Wednesday, the 19th of October, 1650, after having stayed eight years in my house [sheltered] for God's sake.

Wednesday, the 14th of December, 1650, a colloquium was held in the old church of the Jesuit Society. There were more than forty children who came from Callao. The Count of Salvatierra, viceroy of these kingdoms, and the countess were present, as well as all the *audiencia*, the judges, and a great assembly of people.

The Year 1651

Tuesday, the 17th of April of 1651, my son Marcos passed to *Medianos* [the grammar school class in syntax], having been in *Menores* [third class] for six months.

Armada

The armada left the port of Callao for Tierra Firme with the treasure of His Majesty and of private individuals on Saturday, the 23rd of September of the year 1651. The inquisitor Gaytán left in this armada.

The Plaza Fountain

Wednesday, the 7th of December of 1651, the large base of the bronze fountain was installed in the plaza. New water pipes had been started a year ago for the fountain, and the work was finished the 7th of September of 1651. The water flowed on Friday, the 8th of the month, but when it began it did not flow from the four lions nor from the two fountain troughs facing the palace. Later they were repaired, and when the Count of Salvatierra came from Callao after dispatching the armada of the year 1651, water was flowing through all the figures.

The Year 1652

Justices Don José Delgadillo and Don Francisco de la Cueva, *caballero* of the order of Calatrava, were chosen ordinary *alcaldes*; the election of these justices was done at the palace due to the illness of the viceroy. On the 6th of January, the feast of the Epiphany, while the viceroy Count of Salvatierra was at Surco, the dispatch boat arrived from Spain with eleven boxes. The boxes were placed under guard pending the arrival of His Excellency from Surco the following day. [Orders for] the suspension of Don Andrés de Vilela, judge of this royal *audiencia*, arrived, and also [orders to the effect] that an amount of silver be collected from Antonio Fajardo and Antonio Ruiz de Osarcoaga, who were formerly consuls.

Doña Magdalena Sarmiento de Sotomayor, wife of Don Federico Flores, died on Monday, the 15th of January of 1652. She was buried Tuesday, the 16th of the month, at the convent of Nuestra Señora de las Mercedes.

Señor Francisco de Godoy was consecrated as bishop of Guamanga [Huamanga] on Sunday, the 21st of January of 1652. This was arranged by the archbishop of this city, Don Pedro de Villagómez.

Devaluation of Silver An edict was proclaimed through the city that the patacoons issued in 1649 would have a value or circulate at seven and a half *reales*, and those that had been issued at the time of the Marquis of Mancera, at six *reales*.[16] This proclamation was ordered by the Count of Salvatierra at eleven-thirty on Wednesday, the 31st of January of 1652, following many sessions with the *audiencia*. All the ordinary *alcaldes*, the chief bailiffs of this city, and Don Pedro de Quesada, a notary of this royal *audiencia*, were present at this proclamation.

Marriage of Damiana On Thursday, the 29th of February of 1652, articles of marriage were drawn up for my [step-]daughter Damiana by the royal notary of His Majesty, Don José del Corro. The dowry was eight thousand pesos.

My [step-] daughter Damiana was married to Agustín de Yparraguirre on Friday, the 1st of March of 1652. Licentiate

[16] See note 3 for monetary values.

Pedro Flores Marmolejo, a presbyter, father superior, and administrator of the nuns of the convent of La Concepción of this city, performed the ceremony. The witnesses were a brother of the licentiate Pedro Flores Marmolejo, Captain Don Jaime Maldonado, and Jerónimo Muñoz. The license was granted by the *bachiller* Francisco Pulido, priest of the parish of Santa Ana. And on this day I gave him seven hundred pesos for the minor daughter.

The Armada

On Wednesday, the 2nd of August, the day of Saint Augustine, the armada for the year 1652 left the port of Callao for Tierra Firme. It was under General Don Baltasar Pardo de Figueroa and Admiral Don Francisco de Sosa.

Monetary Restrictions

On Friday, the 13th of September of 1652, at eleven-thirty noon the viceroy, Count of Salvatierra, gave orders that from that hour hence patacoons of six *reales* were not to circulate, nor the three and four *reales* [coins], except for the patacoons restamped at six and a half *reales*, and the four *reales* restamped at three and three-fourths, and the *reales* of two and one and a half which could circulate until the end of May of 1653. As this proclamation was taking place the earth suffered a slight earthquake. The palace soldiers had just been paid in patacoons of six *reales* when it was announced that they could not circulate nor could anyone receive them, and because I was caught with ninety-seven pesos' worth of six-*real* patacoons from the pay that I had received, I so subscribe it in Lima, the 13th of September of 1652.

In the month of October, 1652, my son, Josephe de Mugaburu, entered Santa Toribio *colegio* [secondary school]. He left the *colegio* on Monday, June 21, 1655.

The Year 1653

Dispatch Boat from Spain

Friday, the 28th of February, the dispatch boat arrived at this city from Spain with news that Catalonia had surrendered to His Majesty, may God protect him, the king and our lord, Philip IV, after having been in revolt from 1640 until the 13th of September of 1652 when the prince, Señor Don Juan of Austria, son of the king, our lord Philip IV, surrounded the city of Barcelona with a great number of men. Upon finding themselves surrounded by the son of the king they surrendered, whereupon our king and lord looked upon them as his vassals, deserving great punishment.

My son Marcos advanced to the University on April 20th, 1653; he will have three years of canon law and Spanish grammar.

Departure of the Armada

Friday, the 22nd of August of 1653, at four in the afternoon the armada left for Panama with the treasure of His Majesty and of private individuals with Admiral Don Francisco de Sosa in command. His lieutenant, Don Francisco de Solís, was in charge of the consort [second ship of an armada] due to the surrender of the staff of command by Don Baltasar Pardo de Figueroa. The Count of Salvatierra, viceroy of these kingdoms, having discovered a great quantity of silver ingots and sprue cones in the storeroom of General Don Baltasar Pardo aboard the flagship which was due to leave shortly for Tierra Firme, placed Don Baltasar Pardo in prison with four soldiers on guard until a decision arrived from Spain.

Ban on Silver Ingots and Sprues

Friday, the 29th of August of the year 1653, a ban was placed on silver ingots and sprues, stipulating that no one could set these aside nor make ingots to take to Spain or any other place under penalty of losing all their property and being exiled from the kingdom. For the silversmith, brazier or blacksmith, or any other person that cast them, [punishment would be] two hundred lashes and four years in the galleys, and large rewards [were promised] for those who gave notice of these diversions.

Ban Regarding Negroes and Mulattoes

Friday, the 5th of September of this year, the proclamation was issued that no mulatto, Negro, nor zambo could carry a sword, dagger, knife, or any other arms either by day or by night, even though accompanying his masters, under penalty of one hundred lashes and four years in the galleys and a fine of fifty patacoons for his master, without exception for any person, ecclesiastic or secular. This ban was proclaimed through the government, and immediately thereafter the Marquis of Baydes and Señor Don Alvaro de Luna, brother of the viceroy, Count of Salvatierra, ordered that the justices and other persons of the municipality confiscate the swords of their lackeys, and that no one refuse.

The Year 1654

Trip to Mexico

Thursday, the 14th day of May of 1654, the [feast] day of the Ascension of Our Lord Jesus Christ, at five in the afternoon the ship *Santiago* left Callao for Acapulco, [Mexico]. It was dispatched by the viceroy, Count of Salvatierra, to bring [Don Luis Henríquez de Guzmán,] the Count of Alba de Liste y Villaflor, who was coming as viceroy of this kingdom of Peru. The ship sailed with Andrés de Aguilar as admiral and Don Francisco de Paz, chief overseer of the palace of the Count of Salvatierra, as ambassador and adjutant of the fifty infantrymen who were aboard.

The lawsuit of Agustín de Yparraguirre [Mugaburu's son-in-law] and Alonzo de Zervantes was continued in the [notary's] office of Martín de Ochandiano. Don Alonzo de Zervantes left the city jail as a result of the visit by the [*audiencia*] president and *oidores* who were making a general visit on the holiday of the Holy Spirit. He was on bail and gave as guarantors Captain Andrés de Caravajal, Francisco de Montes de Oca, Enrique de la Nebera, Josephe de la Berrera, and a confectioner. The bail was posted on May 30, 1654.

Sunday, the 18th of October of 1654, at seven in the evening the armada left for Spain [via Panama] with the royal treasure of His Majesty and private individuals, with 13,060,000 patacoons, which were registered. The flagship was commanded by General Don Francisco de Sosa, and Lieutenant Don Francisco de Solís was in charge of the consort vessel. The Marquis of Baydes, who had been governor of Chile, boarded the consort with his sons and all his family, bound for Spain. The lieutenant went in charge of the consort because Admiral Andrés de Aguilar had gone with another ship to Acapulco for the Count of Alba de Liste who had been named viceroy of Peru.

Sunday, the 15th of November of the year 1654, news arrived that the flagship that had left for Tierra Firme with the royal treasure of His Majesty and individuals had been lost when it struck bottom at Punta de Carnero y Chanduy, fourteen leagues below [south of] Guayaquil, between Chanduy and Punta del Carnero.

Funeral for the Mother of the Countess

Monday, the 16th of November of 1654, funeral services were held for the mother of the Countess of Salvatierra in the cathedral of this City of Kings, where an impressive and grandiose catafalque was prepared with many details worthy of note. The Count of Salvatierra went by carriage from the palace to the cathedral with all the *audiencia* judges and a great retinue of the council and all the *caballeros* of this city. The archbishop of the city, Doctor Don Pedro de Villagómez, said the Mass, and Señor Don Vasco de Contreras, treasurer of this holy church, gave the sermon.

Feast of the Immaculate Conception

Tuesday, the 8th of December, the day of the Pure and Immaculate Conception of Mary, Our Lady conceived without original sin, this city celebrated the great *fiesta* at the cathedral, the whole city attending. Archbishop Don Pedro de Villagómez said the pontifical Mass. In his sermon, Father Fray Gonzalo de Herrero, presently the Franciscan provincial, extolled the purity of Mary, Our Lady. The viceroy, Count of Salvatierra, was present with all the *audiencia*. After the sermon was finished all voted to guard and defend [the doctrine of] the pure and immaculate conception of Our Lady, without original sin; the archbishop was in charge of the voting. The first to vote was the ecclesiastic council, then the viceroy, followed by the royal *audiencia*, and then the secular council. In the afternoon there was a procession around the plaza where there were five [temporary] altars, and there was much to be seen. A statue of Our Lady of the Immaculate Conception was carried in the procession. Such a celebration had never been seen before. On this day the city voted that the Immaculate Conception of Mary be its patron saint even though Saint Elizabeth had been the patron saint for many years, and that every year the celebration and procession would be held. This was Tuesday, the 8th of December of 1654, to the honor and glory of the Virgin, Our Lady conceived without original sin. Amen. Jesus.

The Year 1655

Arrival of the New Viceroy

The Count of Alba de Liste arrived from Mexico at Paita [Peru] on Sunday, the 3rd of January of the year 1655. He arrived at Callao on the 8th of February, whereupon he was given a grand gun salute from land and sea. He did not disembark until Tuesday, the 9th of the month, which was Shrove Tuesday. On Thursday, the 11th of the month, at six in the afternoon the Count of Alba de Liste went from Callao to call on the Countess of Salvatierra, the Count [of Salvatierra] having already welcomed His Excellency upon his disembarking at Callao. The Count of Alba de Liste came accompanied by his son. There were a great number of people at Callao where there was much regalia, and during Monday and Tuesday more than one hundred and eighty pieces of artillery were fired.

My son Marcos, at the age of fifteen years and nine months, died at eight in the evening of January 18, 1655. He was buried in the principal chapel of Santa Ana [parish] alongside his two other brothers, Juan Felix and Juan Sebastián. It was a very grand interment for my beloved son.

My nephew Josephe de Zamorro died on Saturday, February 13, 1655, and he was buried on Sunday, the first day of Lent, in La Merced [convent].

Entrance of the Viceroy

Tuesday, the 23rd of February, [the new viceroy] went from Callao to [the hermitage of] Monserrate where he remained that night. At five in the afternoon of Wednesday the 24th, day of the glorious apostle Saint Matthew, with great public approval he entered this city under a canopy. The *alcaldes* were Don Yñigo López de Zúñiga and Don Felipe de Mieses, magistrate of this city.

My friend Ensign Juan López de Villa died on Saturday, March 13, 1655, and he was buried on Sunday in Santa Ana [parish].

Dispatch Boat from Spain

On the 19th of August of 1655 it was announced that the armada for Panama would depart from the port of Callao on the 20th of September. On the 5th of that month the dispatch boat arrived from Spain in which His Majesty, Philip IV, may God protect him, sent instructions to the viceroy, Count of Alba de Liste, to remit to Spain a million [pesos] in silver. And for this he sent a galleon to Puerto Bello [Panama] in charge of an adjutant with forty infantrymen and thirty-six pieces of artillery.

The viceroy dispatched the million [pesos] in the flagship from this Southern Sea [Pacific Ocean] on Saturday, the 18th of September of this year, with Admiral Andrés Aguilar in charge. The armada was delayed.

Earthquake of the Year 1655

Saturday, the 13th of November of the year 1655, at three in the afternoon there was the greatest earthquake so far felt in the major part of Lima. It occurred while I, Sergeant Josephe de Mugaburu, was standing guard on the *Santiago*, royal consort ship of this sea, which carried forty-six pieces of artillery. There were eighty-three men on board destined to go as aid to the kingdom of Chile along with the other infantrymen who on this occasion were weighing anchor to leave Lima. These eighty-three men were criminals sentenced to the galleys. Aboard ship I was in charge of sixteen infantrymen with whom I guarded the prisoners. The ship made such a noise that it seemed it wanted to throw off the bulkhead brackets and burst into pieces. I saw a large section of the island in the bay [San Lorenzo Island] break loose and fall into the ocean. The dust clouds formed were so thick that the island could not be seen for quite a while. Returning later to the town of Callao, I saw the chapel and dome of the Jesuit church of that port caved in. Many houses also collapsed, whereupon all the inhabitants moved into the plazas and the streets to sleep.

It caused great damage to all the houses in Lima. Only a married woman, sister-in-law of Don Toribio de la Vega, and a Negress were killed. But the houses were uninhabitable for many days, so that all the people went out into the plazas and streets, the large patios and gardens, and *chácaras*. In the space of three days there were more than a hundred tremors, and everyone trembled [with fear] at what had never been perceived in this city. For a period of fifteen days the churches were open day and night with the Holy Sacrament uncovered. In the main plaza there were three pulpits where the predicators preached without stopping, in competition; as one descended another went up. In the main plaza alone twenty sermons were preached in one day, and there were [services] in the other small plazas and churches. It was something that cannot be imagined.

Processions for the Earthquake

Three [processions] started out from the cathedral with all the religious orders, Viceroy Count of Alba de Liste and his *audiencia*, and Archbishop Don Pedro de Villagómez with his canons. Many penitents took part. Another procession went forth at midnight with the religious of the Franciscan order performing great acts of penitence. All the religious were without cowls, barefoot, and their bodies covered with ashes. Another procession then set forth with the miraculous statue of Our Lady of Copacabana, traveling from the church of San Lázaro to the cathedral where there were many penances. On Friday, the 26th of the month, another procession with all the merchants went from the Mercedarian monastery to the cathedral, bringing forth the [image of the] Mother of God, [Our Lady] of Mercy, which had never been taken out of the church, [a statue of] Saint Dominic, and another figure. There were eight hundred persons participating and doing great penances. The superior of this sodality was Pedro de Molino. All the Augustinian priests went barefoot, giving what food they had for themselves to the poor in the prisons. And so it was for two days, Friday and Saturday. It should be noted that in all these penances the majority of those doing public penance were women, [penances] as unusual as any ever seen. As of today, Saturday, the 27th of the month, there have been one hundred and fifteen tremors.

In the afternoon of this day, Saturday the 27th of the present month [November], a procession set out from the cathedral proceeding around the plaza where there were seven altars of devotion. The [image of the] Visitation of Saint Elizabeth was brought out, and more than a thousand persons of all classes did penance: men, women, and children, Indian men and women, Negroes and Negresses, and mulatto men and women.

At this time the Count of Alba de Liste, viceroy of these kingdoms, was [living] in his patio, and he slept there. The Count of Salvatierra, who was no longer viceroy, with the countess, the adjutant his secretary, and all his family were in the garden of the monastery of San Francisco of this city, where the friars had opened a small door for them leading to Milagro Street.

People for Chile

Friday, the 26th of November of 1655, Don Pedro Porcel de Casanare left the port of Callao for Chile to take up his post as governor, sent by the viceroy, Count of Alba de Liste, for whom he had been captain of the guard. He left with three ships carrying three hundred and fifty men with their weapons, muskets, and arquebuses, for aid to that kingdom. He went so that Don Antonio de Cabrera y Acuña, who was governor of that kingdom for His Majesty, could retire. The Indians in that kingdom had revolted and taken over everything, and his [the governor's] forces had lost.

Tuesday, the 7th of December of 1655, on the eve of the Pure

Vote for the Virgin Mary

and Immaculate Conception, the *audiencia* and ecclesiastical and secular council voted to observe her feast day by fasting, and to defend her purity. They named her patron saint of all the kingdom, and that day there were many festivities.

Proclamation of the Armada

[Proclamation of the armada] was made public on Thursday, the 30th of December of 1655, for the end of January of 1656. On that same afternoon the decree was proclaimed that the patacoons of six and a half *reales*, and the *tostónes* of three and a half *cuartillos* would circulate for eight months from the first of January of 1656 until the end of August of that year.[17] On this day the viceroy, Count of Alba de Liste, and the *oidores* [*audiencia* judges] convened three times. It was not possible to find any way to exchange a restamped peso.

The Year 1656

A decree was proclaimed on the 29th of January of this year, that due to certain problems the armada would be detained in the interests of the royal service of His Majesty.

Chapel of San Francisco

The main chapel of the Franciscan monastery collapsed on Friday, the 4th of February of the year 1656, at eleven-thirty in the morning. Our Lord was served, and no one was injured as the church was closed. The religious were about to leave for the church to give thanks after eating. The pillar of the pulpit gave way and completely caved in with more than half of the chapel of the Immaculate Conception, as well as a large piece of the ceiling over the door leading to the cloister.

Chaplaincy of Domingo de Barambio

Wednesday, the 1st of March of 1656, Domingo de Barambio established a chaplaincy of one thousand pesos capital so that his brother, Pedro de Barambio, could serve [as chaplain], with the stipulation that he say ten Masses each year, receiving ten pesos as alms for each Mass. Upon the death of his brother, the chaplaincy would go to a young boy named Martín, whom he was raising in his house; and after him my son José, who today is fifteen years old, more or less; and after them it would fall to the Magdalena Recollect of the order of Predicators. It is understood that after his brother, the other chaplains should say twenty Masses each

[17] See note 3 for monetary values.

year, and the alms for each Mass should be twenty *reales*. The bond or contract was executed before Martín de Ochandiano, notary public of this City of the Kings, on said day and year.

On Tuesday, the 10th of April of the year 1656, the viceroy, Count of Alba de Liste, sent additional aid to Chile. There were three hundred men with those who came from the town of Potosí under Captain Don Nicolás Ibáñez de Zavala. Don Francisco Coronado went as captain and chief, which [post] he had held once before in the kingdom of Chile.

Don Pedro de Meneses, judge of the royal *audiencia*, died at midnight on Wednesday, the 17th of May of 1656. He was buried at [the monastery of] Nuestra Señora de la Merced on Friday, the 19th of the month.

Wednesday, the 17th of May of 1656, Agustín de Yparraguirre and my daughter Damiana left my house to live in the apartment that was Aguada's. They had been with me and my wife Doña Jerónima since they were married, which was on Thursday, February 29th, 1652, until they moved out to live in the lodgings mentioned above. On Monday, the 26th of June of 1656, he went to the mines from his house without saying goodbye to me nor his mother, nor his wife. [He died about two years later.]

My sister Margarita died on Saturday, the 2nd of July of 1656, and she was buried in the Remedios chapel of La Merced convent. The illness began on Friday and lasted twenty-four hours.

The accountant Francisco de Arbestayn died on Sunday, the 10th of July of 1656, and he was buried in the Belen recollect. He died after three days [of illness].

Saturday, the 5th of August of the year 1656, a proclamation was issued that the armada should leave for Tierra Firme on the 24th of the month.

A decree was proclaimed on Monday, the 7th of August of this year, that patacoons would circulate throughout the kingdom at seven *reales*, and the *tostones* at three and three-fourths *reales* until the end of April of the year 1657, by order of the viceroy, Count of Alba de Liste y Villaflor.[18]

The 8th of September of 1656, day of the nativity of Our Lady, the consort vessel *Santiago* left the port of Callao for Tierra Firme. It went alone without the flagship, and with only the treasure of His Majesty, without any silver of private individuals

[18] See note 3 for monetary values.

on board, nor passengers for Spain. Don Francisco de Vitoria, aide of the viceroy, Count of Alba de Liste, went as admiral and general chief of the command ship.

Fiestas for the Immaculate Conception

Celebrations for the Immaculate Conception, which this city of Lima holds, began on Saturday, the 14th of October of 1656. That night there were splendid fireworks. Then, on the following Sunday there was a pontifical Mass by the archbishop, Don Pedro de Villagómez; the sermon was delivered by Father Fray Bartolomé Badillo of the order of Saint Augustine. In the afternoon there was a great procession around the plaza where there were large altars; the viceroy, Count of Alba de Liste, and all the *audiencia* attended.

On Saturday, the 21st of the month, the merchants began their celebrations. That night, there were the greatest fireworks ever seen in this city. The fireworks were brought into the plaza at five in the afternoon along the street from the [stone] bridge. The first [of the fireworks floats] to be entered was a serpent with seven heads, very impressive to see, on a cart drawn by two mules and with four Negroes in livery. The second represented the fountain in the plaza, and [entered] in the same manner. The third was a horse with two savages, artfully elaborated. The fourth was another serpent with an angel on top, in the same fashion. The fifth, a tree with Adam and Eve and a serpent with the apple tree. The sixth, another carriage with the image of the Immaculate Conception, [entered] in the same way. All the floats moved along on wheeled vehicles to the music of drums and bugles; it was a night of unforgettable fireworks.

On the following Sunday there was a great sermon and procession around the church, and they brought out the [image of the] Holy Virgin of the Immaculate Conception, "La *Chapetona*,"[19] which is in [the church of] San Francisco. There was a pontifical Mass with the viceroy and the gentlemen of the *audiencia* present.

That night around the plaza and fountain there were torches of tar and pitch, and the entrances of all the surrounding streets were closed off so that carriages could not enter. Some members of the troops were burned and many injured by the fires both in the plaza and in the streets leading off from the plaza due to the size of the fireworks, which cost a thousand patacoons. The prior

[19] *La chapetona* was a nickname for a newly-arrived European female in America; often translated as "tenderfoot."

and the consuls were: prior, Don Juan de Céspedes; consuls, Don Juan Domingo de Lea, and Baltasar de Avila y Frias.

On Monday, the 23rd of the month, Don Baltasar de Pardo and [blank] went to the Alameda [park] where they fought a duel. Don Baltasar de Pardo wounded the other man with a sword thrust; he later recovered from his wound.

The sergeants on duty started their rounds on Friday, the 3rd of November of 1656, two each night with eight men, natives of the city. (And it lasted until Tuesday, the 17th of January of 1657, by order of the viceroy, Count of Alba de Liste. Sergeant Pedro Carrasco Becerra and I, Josephe de Mugaburu, made the rounds together.)

Thursday, the 26th of the month, another man was killed at the same place [Alameda] without [time for] confession.

Monday, the 20th of November, Captain Juan de Urdanegui and Don Gaspar de Lopilente went to fight at the same place, and Captain Urdanegui was wounded seriously.

Bullfights and Cañas

On Wednesday, the 22nd of the month, there were bullfights and games of *cañas* in the plaza of the city. There were very brave bulls, and there were haltered bulls ridden bareback that caused much gaiety.

On the afternoon of Thursday, the 23rd of the month, four thieves were hanged in front of the side door of the [convent of] La Encarnación. [There were] two mulattoes, one zambo, and a Negro who stole from a shopkeeper.

Saturday, the 25th of the month, there were bulls in the merchants' plaza. There were thirty bulls, the best that have been run in this plaza. The *caballeros* also came out for games of *alcancías*. The *alcaldes* at this time were Don Luis de Sandoval and Don Juan de Salmerón. The fountain was adorned with flowers, and six highly-decorated carriages showered the plaza with flowers. There were many *caballeros* who gave spear thrusts, and there were dummies to divert the bulls' attention in the plaza; one was inside a barrel, and a bull with a thrust of his horns got them stuck in the barrel. Eighty boards of food were brought in through the plaza and distributed to the spectators in the galleries, and they cast food out the windows to the people in the bleachers. It was something worth seeing. All this celebration was in honor of the Pure and Immaculate Conception of Our Lady.

Celebration of the Silversmiths

On Saturday, the 9th of December of 1656, the silversmiths offered a great celebration in honor of the Pure and Immaculate Conception of the Mother of God. At six in the afternoon eight carriages, well decorated with branches of flowers and plants, entered the plaza strewing many flowers. Behind these carriages there was a large sailing ship float with many young men and sailors. On entering the plaza three pieces [of artillery] fired a gun salute. One of the floats carried a lion over a globe of the world representing the king of Spain, Philip IV, may God protect him, and an image of the Immaculate Conception, an unsheathed sword defending her purity. Behind it another very large carriage depicting Fame and three seated nymphs entered the plaza, a sight worth seeing. Behind this float there was another, very large and very costly, carrying a phoenix bird representing the Virgin, and within, many angels singing their eulogies. These carriages went around the plaza twice, and upon exiting, the ship fired as it does at sea when seeking help upon being moored on a shoal in shallow water. Within a short time the ship was rent to pieces in the plaza, this being carefully done. There were very brave bulls run, and *caballeros* who ran the bulls in the plaza. There were also *alcancías* and spear thrust games, with which the gayest afternoon the town had ever seen came to an end. The commissaries were Pedro Gonzáles and Juan de Melgar.

The University Masquerade

Thursday, the 14th of December of that year [1656], the university came out in masquerade with six large carriages for the celebration of the Immaculate Conception of the Mother of God. More than one thousand five hundred persons turned out, a thousand with great splendor and elegantly dressed and five hundred in outlandish attire. Because it was so good, the viceroy ordered that it come out a second day, Friday, and it went to the convent of Santa Clara, where His Excellency, the Count of Alba de Liste, was.

Negro Fiestas

Tuesday, the 19th of the month, the creole [American born] Negroes fought bulls in the plaza. There were spear and wood-chopping contests. A merry afternoon.

Saturday night, the 23rd of the month, the blacksmiths and tailors sponsored a great fireworks display: a castle and four galleons built over four pairs of carriages filled with fireworks that enveloped the castle; something worth seeing.

On the following Sunday there was a pontifical Mass, sermon, and procession inside the cathedral. With this the celebrations came to an end.

The Year 1657

Señor Don Gabriel Gómez de Sanabria, [member] of the royal *audiencia* of Lima, died on the night of February 25, 1657.

The papal bulls were made public on Sunday, the 29th of April of 1657. The delay was due to the fact that the bulls had not arrived from Spain; they finally came in the dispatch boat which His Majesty, may God protect him, dispatched for the sole purpose of bringing the bulls.

Decree about Restamped Silver

A decree was proclaimed on Monday, the 30th of April of 1657, at six in the afternoon in which His Excellency the Count of Alba de Liste, viceroy of this kingdom, ordered that the restamped patacoons having a value of seven and a half *reales* and the *tostón* valued at three and three-fourths *reales* should not be cast, and that none should circulate except for patacoons and *tostones* [stamped] with two columns, as of the 1st of May of this year. Since I was one of the sergeants of the battalion, I went on the proclamation of this decree. The decree further stated that in Chile an additional year's time should be given before it should be enforced in that kingdom because they did not have the facilities either to melt or cast bars; and that no person should take restamped silver to that kingdom under penalty of having it confiscated along with the ship in which it was carried as well as any slaves and munitions. A [guilty] captain and other persons who were accomplices would receive six years exile to the fortress of Valdivia.

Bernabel de Honton y Mugaburu died in his house on May 9th of 1657.

My friend Pedro de Orbe died on Friday, the 1st of June of 1657, and he was buried on Saturday, the 2nd, in the vault of Our Lady of Aranzazú.

Sunday, the 17th of June, 1657, Lieutenant Azaña, Sergeant José de la Aberruza, and two corporals, José de Cuéllar and Diego Gómez were stripped of the palace company flag for allowing a man to escape who was in prison in the guard corps of this city by order of the viceroy, Count of Alba de Liste, and his remaining in prison was in the interest of His Majesty. On the same day His Excellency ordered that the lieutenant, the sergeant, and the corporals be imprisoned on the barge, where they were taken by Captain Mármol and two soldiers on horseback. His Excellency gave the flag to José Vejete and the halberd to the squadron corporal, Francisco de Soria.

Armada Sails for Panama

Saturday, the 28th of July of 1657, the flagship and the consort left for Panama with Don Enrique the son of the viceroy, Count of Alba de Liste, as general, and Don Francisco de Vitoria as admiral. Don Antonio de Leiva, Count of Monza, and Francisco Fernández de Avila with his wife and daughter left for Spain in this armada.

Tuesday, the 7th of August of 1657, the Count of Alba de Liste was godfather for a daughter of Captain Don Juan Ramírez, who was his royal standard bearer upon his entrance into the city. The newly born was the granddaughter of Captain Don Jorge de Ribera, and she was christened in the church of Santa Ana. Don Juan de Cabrera, *caballero* of the order of Santiago and commissary general of the Holy Crusade of all these kingdoms of Peru, baptized and annointed her.

Death of Father Urraca

Father Fray Pedro Urraca of the Mercedarian order died on Tuesday, the 7th of August of 1657, at seven in the evening, and he was buried Thursday, the 9th of the month. The viceroy, Count of Alba de Liste, the *audiencia*, the secular and ecclesiastic councils, and all the people of this city attended as he was a holy man. He was laid out at the foot of the altar of Saint Peter Nolasco so that it would be known that he was a sanctified man. Memorial funeral services were held on Monday, the 13th of this month of August of the year 1657.

Death of Captain Idiáquez

Don José de Idiáquez, former magistrate of Conchucos and Cuzco and captain of the guard of the Count of Salvatierra, ex-viceroy of Peru, died Sunday, the 29th of July of 1657. He was buried at the church of San Francisco.

On the 20th of October of 1657 the prime professorship of this royal university of Lima, for which Don Diego de Vergara and instructor Fray Juan de Robera of the order of Saint Augustine competed, was obtained by the instructor by virtue of eighty extra votes and his qualifications. *Prime Professorship of Theology*

The Year 1658

On Friday, the 13th of April of the year 1658, [my son-in-law] Agustín de Yparraguirre died at his sugar mill "Nuevo Potosí" located at Pachachaca. He died suddenly and without leaving a will.

On Friday, the 26th of April of 1658, my daughter Damiana [widow of Agustín de Yparraguirre] married Francisco del Ribero. Señor Francisco Pulido, the priest of the parish of Santa Ana, performed the ceremony. [Three and a half years later] on Friday, the 2nd of September of 1661, Francisco del Ribero left my house for the mines of Nuevo Potosí, and this marriage was declared annulled by two decisions made in [the church court at] Huamanga, according to the writs in my possession.

Don Alvaro de Luna, brother of the Count of Salvatierra who had been viceroy of this kingdom of Peru, died on Thursday, the 9th of May of the year 1658. He was buried Friday at eleven in the morning at the monastery of San Francisco of this city, with the viceroy, Count of Alba de Liste, and all the tribunals present. It was a burial of much grandeur. *Death of Señor Don Alvaro de Luna*

A dispatch arrived from Buenos Aires on the last day of Pentecost, Tuesday, the 11th of June of 1658. It brought news of the birth of the prince, heir to the throne of Spain, on the eve of [the day of] Saint Andrew of the year 1657, and that he was named Philip Andrew, "the Prosperous." *Dispatch via Buenos Aires*

On Friday, the 5th of July of 1658, Don [blank] de Valverde, who brought the dispatch from Spain, entered this city and was received in Lima as an ambassador. With all the accompaniment of the *caballeros* of this city and the secular council, he entered between the two *alcaldes* who were Don Gabriel de Vega and Don Antonio de Bravo. On the night of his arrival there were great bonfires and festive lights. The viceroy, Count of Alba de Liste, *Ambassador* furnished his own lackeys and the horse on which he entered, and he was lodged in the room of his [the count's] secretary, Orejón, which His Excellency had ordered prepared for his accommodation.

Armada Sails for Panama

On the 8th of September of 1658 the armada left for Panama with the treasure of His Majesty and private individuals, with Don Enrique, the son of the viceroy, as general, and Francisco de Vitoria as admiral.

A dispatch arrived at this city from Spain with news that the fleet and galleons had arrived at Puerto Bello, [Panama, from Spain] on the 26th of September of this year. It had been four years since a fleet or galleons had arrived.

On Sunday, the 3rd of November, the viceroy, Count of Alba de Liste, went to Pachachaca to rest and enjoy himself, accompanied by his son Señor Don Juan and numerous *caballeros*. He remained three days, and there were bullfights. He returned on the following Wednesday.

Prime Professorship of Theology

Saturday, the 23rd of November of 1658, Father Fray Pedro de Córdoba was awarded the prime professorship of theology. The candidates were the canon Vergara and Father Maestro Fray Juan Báez, a Mercedarian.

Death of the Franciscan Commissary

Sunday, the 24th of the month, the Very Reverend Father Fray Francisco de Borja, Franciscan commissary general, died. He was buried the following Monday, with the viceroy and all the *audiencia* in attendance. He was carried by all the prelates of all the religious orders.

The Year 1659

Wounds Inflicted by Felipe Mieses

At one in the afternoon on Tuesday, the 25th of March of 1659, day of the Annunciation of Our Lady, a lackey of the viceroy, Count of Alba, killed his father-in-law who was a halberdier. [The victim died] without confession.

On this same day at eight in the evening Felipe de Mieses, alderman and chief controller of this city, and his son wounded his son-in-law. Two such occurrences as these had never before taken place in one day.

The Franciscan commissary general, Father Fray Gabriel de Guilléstegui, entered and was received into this city on Saturday, the 29th of March of the year 1659.

Death of the Count of Salvatierra

The Count of Salvatierra, who had been viceroy of this kingdom of Peru, died at two in the morning of Wednesday, the 25th of June of the year 1659. At that hour the bells of the cathedral of this City of Kings tolled, followed by all [those of] the churches and convents. He was buried on the following Friday in the afternoon with the same grandeur and splendor as the day that he was received as viceroy in this city. The body was laid out in the house where he died, which was at the home of his brother Don Alvaro de Luna. All the walls were hung with brocade with the mourning draperies underneath. When the body was removed, the brocades were dropped leaving the walls draped with black flannel cloth. The body was in a coffin of black velvet trimmed with golden nails and golden handrails. He was dressed in rich colorful attire with his white cape of the order of Santiago, white boots and golden spurs, his hat on, and with his captain general's command staff. His beard was newly cropped and his mustache turned up. The cushioning of the bier was of green brocade with the raised design in gold.

At four in the afternoon the present viceroy, the Count of Alba de Liste, left the palace with all his *audiencia* and his two guard companies, lances and arquebuses. With all this retinue he went to where the body reposed. Behind His Excellency followed Archbishop Don Pedro de Villagómez with all his canons and clerics. Also, three tall crosses were brought from the cathedral and the churches of San Sebastián and Santa Ana.

While the responsory for the dead was being chanted, two squadrons of two lines were formed facing each other in the plaza of Lima, one end at the cathedral and the other at the palace. Captain Don Francisco de Solís, who at present is captain of the palace guard, came out armed along with his company and a large segment of [the company] of lances and arquebuses, marching as follows. First were the mercenary cavalry soldiers, behind them the cavalry company of arquebuses of the royal guard, and behind them Captain Francisco de Solís with the above-mentioned men and four flags. Then came all the religious orders, followed by all the tribunals, and following them the body of the deceased carried by the [*audiencia*] president and the *oidores* to the first stop, which was at the cross in the plaza next to the cathedral. Seven pieces of artillery were fired; then the flags of the squadron which had been prepared for this occasion were brought forth from the center of the formation and were lowered. At the next stop, which was at the corner of the archbishop's [palace], another seven pieces of artillery were fired and the other flags which were in the squadron repeated the same ceremony, and at the third halt at the *chasque* [post office] corner, another seven pieces of artillery were fired.

The burial procession then went towards the bridge and past the fish market to the monastery of San Francisco. Following the body was a horse with pared hooves and covered with a long [black] funeral train which dragged more than twelve yards behind. The entire family of the deceased count, the secular and ecclesiastic council, all the *audiencia* with the viceroy and the two gentlemen, his children, followed behind the body. Later all these persons gathered at the small plaza of San Francisco and there they were incorporated into another small group where they remained until eight at night when the ceremonies were over. It was striking to see the people who gathered to witness the funeral.

On the following Saturday the viceroy and the *audiencia* with all the family went to the Mass held in the presence of the body.

A novena of nine days was held at [the church of] San Francisco in the novitiate chapel with all of the family attending. There must have been as many as twenty men with their long funeral robes and caps [present] to hear the Mass sung every day in the presence of the body, with its vigil. The following day memorial funeral rites were held at which His Excellency, the city [council], and all the ecclesiastic council attended. Mass was said by Don Juan de Cabrera, dean of this holy church, and the sermon was given by Father Aráoz of the order of Saint Francis, his [the deceased's] confessor. The catafalque was impressive in its curious and artistic detail offering much to see with its many lights, sonnets, and symbols.

The Galleon

Wednesday, the 9th of July of 1659, a galleon was put to sea; it was one of the two that the Count of Chinchón [Luis Jerónimo Fernández de Cabrera, Viceroy of Peru, 1629–1639] had ordered to be built. The viceroy, Count of Alba de Liste, his two sons, and the whole city of Lima attended the launching, and five pieces of artillery were fired when Mass was said.

The Controller Izu

The controller, Don Juan Fermín de Izu, died and was buried in the cathedral. The viceroy did not attend the burial because he was in Callao, but His Excellency did attend the [subsequent] memorial rites.

Celebration for the Prince

Monday, the 1st of September of 1659, celebrations for the birth of our prince began. The viceroy, Count of Alba de Liste, his two sons, and the chief bailiff of the court, Don Melchor Malo, took part, the four of them setting out in a group. His Excellency appeared very gallant with twenty lackeys all in scarlet, and he brought out four midgets. His Excellency jousted at *cañas* with his son Don Juan Enríquez; and [the other son] Don Enrique with the chief bailiff, Don Melchor [Malo]. Twenty-four *caballeros* in six groups promenaded; it was all quite imposing with extraordinary livery and the horses very well adorned, so that the plaza of Lima seemed like a garden of flowers. There were many *caballeros* fighting bulls on horseback, and very brave bulls; many *caballeros* were tumbled. It was an afternoon of much merriment and gaiety.

On the following Monday, the 8th of the month, the two *alcaldes*, Don Gabriel Vega and Don Antonio Bravo, went forth with all the rest of the *caballeros* except for the viceroy and his two sons. Don Melchor Malo came out in attire that was wondrous to behold and with twenty lackeys bearing maces, never before seen in this plaza. There were bulls and *alcancías*, etcetera, and *caballeros* who came out to fight very brave bulls from horseback, and *caballeros* tumbled by the bulls. It was an afternoon of much laughter and merriment.

Saturday, the 13th of the month [September], the notaries had their bullfight celebration with very brave bulls, but the fighting was not solely on horseback. The eve of that day, the 12th, there were three very good demonstrations of fireworks and great festive lights imaginatively contrived, such as never before used in this plaza.

Wine Merchants and Grocers

Monday, the 29th of the month [September], the wine merchants and grocers set up a fountain of wine, and the wine flowed from ten in the morning until prayertime [sunset] without stopping. There was much to see. There were many drunks, Indians and Negroes. After the Angelus they began putting on the festive lights of the castle which they had [built] across from the palace. That same night there were four very good pieces of fireworks. After the fireworks a bull came out with a pack saddle and an artifice of fireworks on its horns; and it was run that night, with which that celebration terminated.

On Tuesday, the 30th of the month, at three in the afternoon they began to run bulls, and at four o'clock twelve men, well disguised as Turks and very well ornamented, entered on finely-trapped horses, each one with his page dressed in the same manner. After making a tour around the plaza they entered their castle. Then two galleons [floats] entered the plaza from the street of the wine shops. They were well made, looking like those of Spain with their prisoners rowing, and circling the plaza they attacked the castle and forced its surrender, throwing the Turks into the two galleons. They put our [Spanish] flags on the castle, and then the two galleons left [the plaza] from where they had entered. There was *lanzada* bullfighting,[20] and bulls were run the rest of the afternoon. The whole afternoon was a very enjoyable occasion.

Bullfights

There was bullfighting. That afternoon there was an acrobat on a rope, and at five in the afternoon the tightrope walker glided from the upper tower to the plaza, beyond the fountain.

Death of the Alcalde, *Don Antonio Bravo*

Wednesday, the 29th of October of the year 1659, at eleven in the morning near the bull pen which closed off the plaza, Don Antonio Bravo, an ordinary *alcalde*, had words with Captain Don Luis de Rojas. [Later] Don Luis took out his sword and killed the justice, who died instantly, falling down the stairs of the *cabildo* where he was caught by the custodian. Many people arrived, mulattoes, and other classes of people who turned on said Luis de Rojas. This occurred upstairs in the corridor of the *cabildo*.

On Friday, the 7th of November, the aforementioned celebra-

[20] *Lanzada* is an old form of bullfighting where the *torero* kneels on the ground awaiting the charge of the bull with a lance imbedded in the ground and inclined toward the bull, so that charging forward it would be run through by the lance.

tion continued. A carriage with all kinds of acrobatic equipment was brought out, and from the tower of the cathedral they launched four [papier-mache] figures filled with pigeons.

Death of the Countess of Alba

Sunday, the 16th of November, news arrived by *chasque* [post runner] from Quito that the Countess of Alba de Liste, vicereine of Peru, had died in Madrid. Memorial funeral rites for the vicereine were held at the monastery of Santo Domingo on Thursday, the 27th of November of the year 1659, and were attended by the viceroy, his son, all the *audiencia*, the secular council, and tribunals all with long sweeping mourning cloaks. A catafalque was made with great artistry and curious detail, and there were one thousand three hundred candles each weighing a pound. The sermon at these funeral rites was given by the Very Reverend Father Fray Juan de Rivera of the order of Saint Augustine, bishop-elect of Santa Cruz de la Sierra, [the rites] ending at two-thirty in the afternoon.

Celebration of the Artists

Tuesday, the 2nd of December of that year, the painters, sculptors, and carpenters held their celebration for [the birth of] our prince. There was a parade of floats, ludicrous and witty, with four carriages bearing the "four elements;" another three with very comic figures; [another with] figures of all the viceroys who had governed this kingdom; then eight costumed Incas; followed by a very large figure carrying the world on his shoulders and with veins of silver and gold, offering it all to the prince; and then [representations of] all the eminent artists that ever existed. Behind all this was another carriage which caused much admiration when seen; it was fourteen yards high, ten wide, and eighteen long, artistically made with large columns by Ascencio de Salas, great architect and sculptor. On top rode the prince, who was represented by the son of Don José González, and all who looked at him marveled that he moved along with such majesty. There were very brave bulls the rest of the afternoon, with which the day came to a close. Everyone was pleased to have seen such an extraordinary and majestic event.

Silversmiths and other Crafts

On Friday, the 29th of December, the silversmiths, joined by other craftsmen, held their celebration in which they brought nine carriages [floats] out to the plaza. Each one represented a kingdom, offering the prince the treasures of each kingdom. All the grandees of Spain were represented, in their image, very well dressed and with much regalia; and also all the guard of His Majesty: Teutonic, German, and Spanish, with captains of the guard, all very splendid. There were bulls that same afternoon, and four who came out as grandees of Castile fought on horseback; a very merry afternoon with much to see.

The Indians

On Tuesday, the 23rd of the month, the Indians held their *fiesta*, for which they built a fort in the plaza. The Inca king appeared and fought with two other kings until he conquered them and took over the fort. Then the three kings, with dignity, offered the keys to the [Spanish] prince who was portrayed on a float. Then [representatives of] all the Indians of this kingdom came out to the plaza, each in his native dress. There were more than two thousand. The plaza appeared to be covered with a variety of flowers as all the Indians were elaborately costumed and with much finery. There were bulls that afternoon, and the Indians came out to spear the bulls. It was a joyful *fiesta* for everyone, and it is said that they [the Indians] were the best of all, with which the celebrations ended.

Murder by Don Cristóbal de Hijar

Wednesday, the 31st of December of 1659, at five in the morning Don Cristóbal de Hijar y Mendoza killed his wife Doña María Hurtado de Mendoza.

The Year 1660

Ordinary Justices

Thursday, the 1st of January of 1660, the viceroy, Count of Alba de Liste, was in Callao where he sent for his regiment. There he made a selection of *alcaldes*; Don Gabriel de Castilla and Don José Delgadillo were appointed.

Monday, the 26th of July of 1660, Doctor Juan Merino, presbyter, who for many years was chief collector of this archbishopric of Lima, died. He was buried at the monastery of Santo Domingo of this city because he had professed in that order. The collectorship was given to the presbyter Don Juan de la Barrera, son of the attorney Don Gabriel de la Barrera.

Wednesday, the 28th of said month [July] of the year 1660, the armada left for Spain [via Panama] with Don Enrique, son of the Count of Alba de Liste, viceroy of these kingdoms, as general. The Countess of Salvatierra embarked on the command ship with all her [household] people for Spain, taking the remains of the count, her husband, who had died on Wednesday, the 25th of June of the year 1659. The admiral was Cristóbal de Armello. *Departure of the Armada for Spain*

When the countess left her house to embark, she was carried in a sedan chair by two Spanish lackeys; and the viceroy, Count of Alba de Liste, placed his hand on one side of the chair, and on the other side, Don Juan Enríquez, his son. In addition, Archbishop Don Pedro de Villagómez, all the *oidores* of this royal *audiencia*, and all the nobility of the *caballeros* of this city accompanied her as far as the wooden pier. After their excellencies had embarked, thirty pieces of artillery were fired, and the tender was decked in mourning. At two in the afternoon of the same day the armada set sail, and a great number of pieces of artillery were again fired; at which point His Excellency returned to Lima.

Sunday, the 1st of August of 1660, at nine at night there was a great earthquake, so sudden that everyone in the city said it was greater than the one of the 3rd of November of the year 1655. That same night there were three more tremors, but not as great. Our Lord was served in that no harm was done. *Earthquake*

Don Antonio de Villagómez, who was the governor of Huancavelica, died there within twelve days after having reached the town and taken charge. His uncle, Archbishop Don Pedro de Villagómez, held funeral rites and a pontifical Mass in this City of Kings on Monday, the 23rd of August of 1660, which were attended by the viceroy, Count of Alba de Liste, the *audiencia*, all the religious orders, and the *caballeros* of the city. *Death of Don Antonio de Villagómez*

At dawn on Thursday, the 16th of December of 1660, my son José went to the curacy of Tapo, near Huánuco, with his cousin Don Antonio Flores, who is the parish priest of Tapo. That same dawn there was an earthquake. *My Son José*

Tuesday, the 21st of December of 1660, day of the glorious apostle Saint Thomas, two aldermen were expelled from the cathedral of this City of Kings. *Expulsion of Aldermen from the Church*

His Excellency exiled the *alcaldes* for several years, and he suspended Don José Delgadillo and Don Gabriel de Castilla for one month. Don Bartolomé de Azaña was exiled five leagues from this city. He named as interim justices Don Alonso de la Cueva and Don José de Mendoza y Castilla. (On the last day of the year he returned their staffs to Don José Delgadillo and Don Gabriel de Castilla.)

This same day [December 21] in the afternoon and the following Wednesday there were processions because the volcano [Pichincha] at Quito had erupted on Saint Simon's day, the 28th of October. Although the regiment was not present at any of the processions, the viceroy, Count of Alba de Liste, and the royal *audiencia*, Archbishop Don Pedro de Villagómez and his council, and the people of the city took part. The first day the procession went from the cathedral to [the churches of] Santo Domingo, San Agustín, and La Merced; the second day to San Francisco, La Concepción, and to the Society of Jesus.

The Year 1661

Justices

Saturday, the 1st of January of 1661, Don Alonso de la Cueva and Don Sebastián de Navarrete, *caballero* of the order of Calatrava, were elected *alcaldes*.

Consecration of the Bishop of Huamanga

Sunday, the 1st of March of 1661, day of the apostles Saint Philip and Saint James, at four in the morning the illustrious archbishop of this city, Don Pedro de Villagómez, consecrated Bishop Don Fray Cipriano de Medina as bishop of Huamanga. He was consecrated even though the night before it had been agreed to notify the archbishop not to consecrate the bishop, but the notification did not reach him because he was inside the monastery of San Francisco, where he consecrated him at the above-mentioned hour. At nine in the morning the bishop went with great solemnity in procession from the monastery to the cathedral where he performed high Mass and the sermon alone, without the archbishop. At that time the viceroy and *oidores* entered, as a group.

Excommunication of the Alcaldes

Tuesday, the 15th of March of 1661, Don Francisco de Pastrana, *regidor* [alderman] of this city, was sent to prison by the gentlemen of the Inquisition. That same day they excommunicated the *alcaldes*, who were at that time Don Alonso de la Cueva and

Don Sebastián de Navarrete, *caballero* of the order of Alcántara. Don Francisco Pastrana was imprisoned in the penitence house.

The Alcaldes

Alcaldes Don Sebastián de Navarrete and Don Alonso de la Cueva received their staffs of office again on Saturday, the 9th of May of that year. They were without staffs two and a half months. Don Sebastián de Navarrete paid one thousand ordinary pesos fine, and Don Alonso de la Cueva one thousand assayed pesos, with which the staffs were returned to the justices.

People for Chile

Friday, the 18th of March of 1661, additional help of three hundred men was sent to the kingdom of Chile. They went in a large ship under Captain Farfallada.

News of the Arrival of the Viceroy at Paita

Friday, the 6th of May of 1661, news came about the arrival of the fleet and galleons [in Panama], and that [Don Diego Benavides] the Count of Santisteban, was arriving as viceroy of Peru. Sunday night, the 29th of the month, adjutant Diego de Ulloa brought news from Paita that the [new] viceroy had arrived at Paita and requested the Count of Alba to dispatch provisions and seamen to enable him to continue his trip to Peru.

Departure of the Ship to Paita for His Excellency

Monday, the 30th of the month, the escort vessel, companion ship of that which comes from Panama to Paita, left the port of Callao with seamen and soldiers and a great quantity of provisions as well as many gifts sent by the Count of Alba de Liste.

Admiral Don Cristóbal de Olmello

As soon as the news from Paita arrived, General Don Juan Enríquez, general of Callao and son of the viceroy, dispatched the ship within one day with Cristóbal de Olmello, native of Portugalete in the [Spanish] province of Vizcaya, as admiral. Don Diego de Ulloa, captain of the guard of the Count of Alba de Liste, also went on this ship.

News of the Count of Santisteban

Thursday, the 9th of June of this year, at seven in the evening the ambassador of the Count of Santisteban, who had arrived that night from the rural estate of Don Bartolomé de Azaña, went with a large retinue to see the viceroy, Count of Alba. The viceroy offered him a seat, and the viceroy and Don Juan de Cabrera, dean of the church in Lima, and the ambassador were seated. They talked for an hour, then he returned to the same *chácara*.

Entrance of the Ambassador The following Friday at five in the afternoon the aforementioned ambassador entered amidst great applause of people of this city. He was accompanied by, and went between, the two ordinary *alcaldes* of this city, Don Alonso de la Cueva and Don Sebastián de Navarrete of the order of Calatrava. The ambassador was of the order of Alcántara, and he was resplendent in beautiful attire embroidered in color, with boots and a black hat with a band of diamonds. He appeared with four lackeys dressed in red, two Spanish servants, and a young boy, all on horseback. Entering from the bridge, he went to the corner of the city prison chapel, then proceeded along the street past Santo Domingo [monastery], and along Mantas Street to the plaza where there were a great number of carriages with ladies. He went directly to the palace of His Excellency. When he came out, he went with the same accompaniment to the house of Don Juan de Cabrera, dean of the church, where he was lodged. The ambassador's name was Juan de Urrea y Viveros, and he was a native of Pamplona, in Navarra, [Spain,] and related [to the new viceroy]. On this day, Friday, when he gave the embassage to the Count of Alba, the latter did not offer a seat to the ambassador. Until that day an ambassador had not entered this city so resplendent and amidst such applause.

Proclamation Saturday, the 11th of the month, the Count of Alba de Liste sent forth a proclamation so that all would know that the squadron was to be formed on the day of the reception of the Count of Santisteban in this city. All the lancers and arquebusiers of the guard of this kingdom who failed to appear would each be fined thirty pesos and ten days in prison; the infantry on duty, six pesos and four days in prison; and the cavalry on duty and at the *chácaras*, eight pesos and ten days in prison. All [absentees] would be fined with no exceptions made for any person.

Bullfights Tuesday, the 14th of this month of June, there was a running of the bulls for the entrance of the ambassador.

Tuesday, the 28th of June of 1661, on the eve of Saint Peter's day, at five in the afternoon the viceroy, Count of Alba de Liste,

Viceroy's Departure from the Palace

left the palace with a great contingent of *caballeros*, members of the university, and all the tribunals, for the house of Doctor Don Bartolomé Salazar, *oidor* of this royal *audiencia* and president-designate of [the *audiencia* of Charcas at] Chuquisaca [Upper Peru]. The count made a farewell bow upon leaving the palace and went directly without detours to the house where he was to reside.

Tuesday, the 12th of July of the year 1661, at ten in the morning General Don Juan Enríquez with many *caballeros* left this city for Chancay to welcome the Count of Santisteban. Don Juan de Cabrera, dean of this holy church of Lima, also set out on the same day with many splendidly-attired people for the same purpose.

Count of Santisteban at the Chácara

Wednesday, the 20th of the month, the Count and Countess of Santisteban [Doña de Silva y Manrique] arrived at the *chácara* of Don Sancho de Castro, where they and the great number of people following them were received. That day they had left the *chácara* of Doctor Avendaño which is in Chuquitanta, and they came upriver as far as the ravines of the rural estate of Zamudio. The count was in one sedan-chair and the countess in another; they did not alight until reaching the *chácara*. Then the count came by mule to where the Count of Alba de Liste and all the *audiencia* awaited him. They left Paita on the 6th of June and arrived at this city on the 20th of July, the count and countess having come by land. On the same day the flagship and the consort left Paita; the latter arrived at the port of Callao the same day that the viceroy came to this city, the 20th of July, but the flagship had not appeared.

This same day a ship arrived from Chile with news that the three hundred men that the Count of Alba de Liste had sent as support, and that left from Callao the 18th of March of this year, had arrived.

The following Thursday the Count of Santisteban went to the *chácara* of the Count of Alba de Liste and his two sons, Don Juan Enríquez and Don Enrique. He went in a small carriage they call a *voladora* to speak with the Count of Alba de Liste. The two men visited more than two hours, from twelve until two in the afternoon.

Staff of General to Don Manuel de Benavides

Sunday, the 24th of the month of July of 1661, the staff of command of general of land and sea of the port of Callao was presented to Don Manuel Benavides, twelve years of age, son of the Count of Santisteban. This was a courtesy extended by the Count of Alba de Liste, transferring it from his son Don Juan Enríquez, who was presently general. He presented it on this day with a squadron formed in the plaza of Callao. Don Tomás Pardo was battalion commander for the king, our lord. The entire squadron fired, and fifty pieces of artillery were also fired from all the forts and from [ships at] sea. There was a great crowd of people, all very resplendent, and many servants of the Count of Santisteban. To all those with the [new] commander, General Don Enrique, who was a maritime general, gave a banquet at his house where there were many things to be seen.

Visit to the Palace

Tuesday, the 26th of the month of July, Saint Anne's day, at one in the afternoon the Count and Countess of Santisteban came from the *chácara* to see the palace and arrange for their lodgings. Having arrived at the palace, the countess did not want to leave again, nor did the count, and they immediately sent to the *chácara* for all of their family. Such a thing had never been seen in this kingdom, that the viceroy and vicereine should sleep in the palace before they were [officially] received.

Entrance of the Flagship

Friday, the 29th of the month, the flagship entered the port of Callao, damaged by a great storm during which the consort was lost sight of. The admiral was Don Cristóbal de Olmello.

Entrance of the Viceroy in Lima

Saturday, the 30th of the month of July of the year 1661, a workday on which there had never been a previous entrance by a viceroy in Peru, the Count of Santisteban entered under a canopy, to take charge. The ordinary *alcaldes* were Don Sebastián de Navarrete, *caballero* of the order of Calatrava, and Don Alonso de la Cueva. There were impressive events, and a formation in the plaza in front of the cathedral with all the men of the battalion. There were twelve infantry companies under Colonel Don Francisco de Valverde, *caballero* of the order of Santiago, as well as all the cavalry companies and their commissary general, Don Ambrosio del Pulgar. The two companies of the battalion went to the arch. The Count of Alba de Liste watched the entrance of the viceroy from a balcony on the corner of Mercaderes Street which looks down the whole street to beyond [the hospital of] Espíritu Santo.

At the Jesuit Church

Sunday, the 31st of the month, day of the glorious Saint Ignatius, the count secretly went to the Jesuit church, where the viceroys [Counts] of Alba and Santisteban met privately in a gallery. [Don Fray Juan de Almoguera,] the bishop of Arequipa and a former predicator of His Majesty and friar of the order of the Holy Trinity, who had just arrived from Spain, gave the sermon that day in the church. The archbishop of this city, Don Pedro de Villagómez, also attended.

Monday morning, the 1st of August of the year 1661, the Count of Santisteban went publicly to the cathedral with all the retinue of the *oidores* and the *cabildo*. Canon Calvo gave the sermon on this day.

Trip of the Viceroys to Callao

Thursday morning, the 11th of the month, the viceroys of Alba and Santisteban went to Callao where artillery was fired from land and sea at their entrance and departure. And this day the Count of Alba gave a dinner for the Count of Santisteban and all his family. They returned to Lima together the same day in the carriage of the Count of Alba.

Ban on Swords with Needle Points

Monday, the 22nd of the month, the Count of Santisteban issued a proclamation that no person of any class could carry a sword with needle points, under penalty of one hundred pesos for the first offense, and two hundred for the second; and that no sword-cutler put these needles on the scabbards, under penalty of one hundred pesos, and another hundred for any smith that made them, and two years [exile] in Chile.

Negroes, Mulattoes and Indians

Nor could a sword, dagger, nor any arm of any other nature be carried by a mulatto, Negro, or Indian, even though they be free, unless they were officials on active duty such as captains, lieutenants, aides, and sergeants. And it is understood they must be wearing their insignias; otherwise there would be a penalty of fifty patacoons which would have to be paid by their masters, and two hundred lashes and two years in the galleys. And he ordered that this be inviolably executed and these two bans transmitted to the government.

Proclamation on Diversions and the Residencia

Tuesday, the 23rd of the month of August, a proclamation was issued banning the diversion of silver and gold sprue cones under penalty of loss of all their possessions for anyone who did this. This same day the *residencia*[21] of the Count of Alba de Liste was proclaimed, to be supervised by the *oidor*, Don Juan de Erretuerta, who came to this *audiencia* of Lima from Charcas.

Commander's Staff to Don Francisco de la Cueva

Thursday, the 22nd of September of 1661, at six in the afternoon the staff of command of regiment commander of the battalion of this city was presented to Don Francisco de la Cueva, *caballero* of the order of Calatrava. It was presented to him in the guard chamber of this city by General Don Manuel Benavides, son of the Count of Santisteban, viceroy of these kingdoms, with great applause from the *caballeros* of this city. Don Tomás Pardo, commander of the regiment of Callao, had held the staff of command for two years since the death of Don Antonio Mogollón who had previously held the post.

Two Viceroys in the Chapel of the Desamparados

Friday, the 23rd of this month and year, the two viceroys, the Count of Santisteban and the Count of Alba, were together in the chapel of the Desamparados where Father Castillo of the Society of Jesus gave an illustration of the vindications of Our Lord Jesus Christ. Both sat together on a ceremonial bench; the Count of Alba de Liste was to the right of the Count of Santisteban, the viceroy who presently governs this kingdom.

Provincial Father Juan Meléndez

The 22nd of July of the year 1661, Father Maestro Fray Juan Meléndez became Dominican provincial as a result of the legal proceedings held with Father Fray Juan Moreno, prior of the Recollect, upon the death of Father Fray Juan López who was [then] provincial and who had died a year and four months before

21 At the end of their term of office, Spanish administrators in America had to undergo a *residencia* or inquest into their conduct in office during which all persons with grievances or complaints could present them. A viceroy's *residencia* was limited to six months. The normal term of office for a viceroy was three years, later changed to five, but it could be altered by the king. Annual salary of Peruvian viceroys in the seventeenth century was 30,000 ducats (41,250 pesos). Edward Gaylord Bourne, *Spain in America, 1750–1780* (New York: Barnes and Noble, 1962), pp. 230–31.

completing the provincialate. Having indicated that the chapter meeting should be held at the Recollect, Father Meléndez, being prior of the father house, claimed that in his position as father superior he should be provincial vicar. And it was accorded that the post and [corresponding] visit to all the province be given to him. The bishop of Huamanga had ousted him from the monastery of Santo Domingo in great dishonor more than six months ago. At this time news arrived that his superior had postponed the chapter meeting for another year so that meetings of the religious orders of Saint Augustine and Saint Dominic would not coincide in this city. Named as first preference for vicar general in place of Father Fray Juan López was Father Maestro Huerta. Inasmuch as they had elected Maestro Meléndez as provincial on the above mentioned date, he did not want to obey the manifests of his religious superior, and he legally protested in sessions lasting more than a month. An agreement was reached on Friday, the 2nd of September of that year, that the commands of the superior of the order be obeyed. Many friars left the monastery of Santo Domingo because they did not wish to obey Father Maestro Meléndez; a number of them were at the monastery of San Francisco. Many religious had been castigated before the news was announced that obedience should be given to Father Maestro Huerta.

Saturday, the third of the month, all the religious of Santo Domingo went in procession to [the church of] San Francisco, and they carried the bishop of Huamanga, Father Cipriano de Medina, in another procession back to [the monastery of] Santo Domingo, with great applause. If the day of his consecration was great, this day was even greater. He said a pontifical Mass in the church of his order, Santo Domingo.

The following Sunday there were many horse races in the street, and bullfights. And at all this Father Meléndez did not appear, nor did he wish to give obedience to Father Maestro Huerta.

Alderman Don Francisco de Pastrana, after having been imprisoned in the penitence jail and in his house for five and a half months, was released on Monday, the 5th of September of 1661. He paid two thousand pesos for guards and another thousand pesos as punishment imposed on him by the inquisitors.

Professorship of Scripture The professorship held by Canon Vergara that was left vacant at his death was given to Maestro [Juan] Báez of the order of Our Lady of Mercy in convocation [of the faculty] because there were no competitors for the professorship. He took possession of this professorship on Monday, the 12th of September of the year 1671.

The nones professorship[22] that had been held by Father Maestro Fray Juan Báez was given in convocation to Doctor Don Diego de Salazar on Friday, the 23rd of the month of September of 1661.

Companies for Chile On the 20th of September of the year 1661, sixteen [military] companies left to contract people from all the districts of this kingdom of Peru and take them to the kingdom of Chile by [order of] the viceroy, Count of Santisteban. The names of the captains are recorded in their entirety:

Captain Don Julián Baca, for Saña
Captain Don Pedro Angulo, for Puno
Captain Don Francisco Villavicencio, for Huancavelica
Captain Don Nicolás Perez de León, for Cuzco
Captain Don Felipe de Lorenzana, for Quito
Captain Don Vicente Palomino, for Quito
Captain Don Luis de Perea, servant of His Excellency, for Quito
Captain Don Juan de la Barrera, for Arequipa
Captain Don P. Cattenas, for Cailloma
Captain Don Juan Pitta, for Potosí
Captain Don Andrés González, servant of the Count of Santisteban, for Cajamarca
Captain Don Manuel Grande de los Cobos, for Lima
Captain Don Fernando de Córdoba, for Lima
Captain Don Domingo de Amezcua, for Lima
Captain Don José de Luzuriaga, for Lima
Captain Don Diego López de Ulloa, for Nuevo Potosí
Captain Don José de Velasco, for Pisco
Captain Don Rafael Gil, for the city of La Paz
Captain Don Francisco Alonso, son of the secretary, for Paraguay
Captain Don Juan Antonio de Peredo, son of the governor, in Lima

[22] *Nones* is one of the canonical devotions recited between noon and three in the afternoon; hence professorship of subject (Scripture) taught at that hour. See note 9.

On Sunday, the 2nd of October of 1661, at nine at night, Señor Don García Carrillo de Alderete, *caballero* of the order of Santiago and *oidor* of this royal *audiencia*, died. At five in the afternoon on the 4th of the month, day of the glorious Saint Francis, he was buried in his [order's] monastery with a great number of persons present, including the viceroy, Count of Santisteban, and all the *oidores*. Also present in the congregation was the Count of Alba de Liste who had been viceroy of this kingdom. Memorial funeral rites were held the following Friday in the church of San Francisco with the same attendance listed above.

Death of Don García Carillo

Sunday, the 9th of this month and year, the *fiesta* for the name of Mary [her divine motherhood][23] was celebrated with the accustomed solemnity of a military formation and procession in the afternoon. Many persons turned out for the formation, and the Count of Santisteban with the royal council were in the procession. The vicereine with her ladies were at the corner windows of the palace. Some distance away the Count of Alba with his two sons and all his family watched the passing of the procession of this celebration.

Fiesta *for Mary*

Monday, the 10th of October, Captain Domingo de Amezcua set up his flag in Lima to get emigrants for the kingdom of Chile.

Wednesday, the 18th of the month of October of 1661, the Count of Alba and his two sons, went to Pachacámac for an eight day vacation. [On his return] the Count of Santisteban went out to meet him at the outskirts of the city on the custodian's *chácara* located past Huaquilla.

Count of Alba's Trip to Pachacámac

Sunday, the 23rd of the month of October, the two companies of this city, the palace guard with Captain Don Pedro de Mendoza and the guard company of the Count of Alba with Captain Don Enrique, son of the Count of Alba, went to Callao to pass muster. The Count of Santisteban, viceroy of these kingdoms, was present at the muster.

Muster-roll of October 23rd

The 26th of the month, salaries were suspended for the captains and all the officers of the Negro and mulatto companies. From the six companies they formerly constituted, three of mulattoes and

Reformation of the Negro and Mulatto Companies

[23] See note 14 for Mary's *fiesta* dates.

three of Negroes, they were reduced to two companies and assigned to two peace officers of the government.

The Battalion Commander and the Adjutant

From the remaining salaries which had been given to these companies of Negroes and mulattoes, that is to the captains, one hundred pesos a month were given to the battalion commander of this city, Don Francisco de la Cueva, and to Domingo de Albizu who had just been made adjutant for Callao.

Procession of the Jesuit Saints

Saturday, the 29th of October of 1661, at four in the afternoon a very large procession came out from the Jesuit church for the honor and glory of Saint Ignatius Loyola [whose statue was brought forth] first; followed by twelve biers richly adorned, carrying the bones of forty-eight martyrs. All the illustrious of the city turned out with great riches and pearls, and more than fifty small boys dressed as angels. This procession set forth from the Jesuit church going by way of Melchor Malo Street to the cathedral. Then it crossed the plaza diagonally, [and went] from the palace to the Dominican convent, and from there to [the church of] San Agustín, and back home along Plateros Street. It was accompanied by the archbishop, Don Pedro de Villagómez, with all the canons and clerics, and the viceroy, Count of Santisteban, with the secular council and the royal *audiencia*. The Count of Alba watched from the balconies of the canon, Don Esteban Ibarra.

Captain Don Pedro de Mendoza's Company

Captain Don Pedro de Mendoza's company, which was on guard at the palace, marched in the procession with Lieutenant Don Gil de Benavides and Sergeant Alonso del Pino.

That same night there were great fireworks displays in the same company. The following Sunday there was a pontifical Mass by His Grace, Don Pedro de Villagómez; on that day Canon Calvo delivered the sermon. This celebration lasted three days until All Saints' Day with the same grandeur as on the first day.

Don Antonio de Peredo, Governor of Chile

Sunday, the 30th of the month at eight at night, Don Antonio de Peredo, who was formerly governor of Jaén de Bracamoros, arrived at this city. He had been appointed governor of Chile, a favor granted him by the Count of Santisteban. He was received by Agustín de Huruña in his [the viceroy's] stead, who put him up in the house next to that of General Don Antonio de Morga.

Cornerstone of the Free Negro Hospital of Saint Bartholomew

Saturday, the 5th of November of 1661, at five in the afternoon the cornerstone for the hospital wards was placed in the foundations which were laid in the garden. In the stone they put some coins that circulate this year in the time of the king, our lord, Philip IV, may God protect him. On this day the Count of Santisteban, viceroy of these kingdoms, and the archbishop of this city, Don Pedro de Villagómez in pontifical garb, and Don Juan de Cabrera, dean of the holy church of Lima, were present at the blessing of the [hospital] church. Señor Francisco Tijeros was presently superintendent of this Saint Bartholomew hospital for free Negroes. There was a great crowd of people there. (The day that the church [hospital] was completed was the 24th of August of the year 1684, when the viceroy, Duke of la Palata, and Archbishop de Liñán were present. The religious of San Agustín [monastery] sang.)

Captains for Chile

Monday, the 22nd of November, at four in the afternoon another five flags were hoisted in this city to the same end [recruitment for Chile] by: Captain Don Angel de Peredo; Captain Don Pedro de Mendoza, presently captain of the palace company, who had the second flag with his same company officers, Lieutenant Don Gil de Benavides and Sergeant Alonso del Pino; Captain Don Manuel Grande de los Cobos; Captain Don Fernando de Córdova; and Captain Don Juan López de Luzuriaga.

Staff as Governor of Chile to Don Angel de Peredo

Thursday, the 8th of December of 1661, the day of the Pure and Immaculate Conception of the Mother of God, at one in the afternoon after having left the cathedral the Count of Santisteban, viceroy of these kingdoms, presented the staff of command as captain general for the kingdom of Chile to Don Angel de Peredo. This took place in the great hall of the palace in the presence of a large number of people. The governor made a fine appearance dressed entirely in suede, wearing breeches and doublet without a cloak, and with large boots and spurs in the style of Flanders. All the captains in this city were present.

This same day His Excellency ordered that a guard be placed at the house of the governor; thirty soldiers and a corporal went from the company of Captain Domingo de Amezcua.

Death of Captain Don Rafael Gil

Saturday, the 31st of the month of December, the last day of the year 1661, a special messenger arrived from the city of La Paz [Upper Peru or Bolivia] with news of the murder in that city of the *corregidor* [governor] and magistrate, and of Captain Rafael Gil and his sergeant, José de Campusano. [The assassins were] some mestizos who rebelled at the captain's imprisonment of another mestizo for service in Chile. The captain and sergeant were recruiting in that city. After having killed them, [the villains] sacked the houses of the *corregidor* and magistrate, who was called Vaca, and committed many other wrongdoings. As a result, the viceroy, Count of Santisteban, and *oidores* met to deliberate the problem.

The Year 1662

On the first day of the year 1662 another special messenger arrived from Puno [Peru] with news that more than two hundred men had banded together [in revolt. The core was] the one hundred men contracted in Puno who already had been assigned positions in Chile and who fled with more than two thousand Indians who joined this seditious group.

Later, news arrived that the *corregidor* of Puno, Juan de Erquimigo, and the other *corregidores* had caught many of these mestizos and had them hanged; the group had been dispersed and [the rebellion] was ended.

Prisoners for Chile

Wednesday, the 15th of March of 1662, at ten at night they started to make arrests for Chile. That night *alcaldes* Don José de Vega and Don Gabriel de Castilla, and the chief constable of the city and the one of the court, and Don Bartolomé de Azaña, justice of the rural police, all with their subordinates and each one on his own, went out that night and made many arrests. In the morning His Excellency, the Count of Santisteban, ordered that they [the prisoners] be taken to Callao. Later he had them return from La Legua to justify the cause of some [of the arrests]. Those arrested without cause he ordered released, and the others he ordered to be taken to the consort vessel where there were more than three hundred men who had come in their companies from different parts of the kingdom.

Saturday, the 19th of March of 1662, at one at night on the eve of Saint Joseph's day, the Countess of Santisteban gave birth to a baby girl [named Josefa].

Childbirth of the Countess of Santisteban

Alonso del Pino died on Monday, the 27th of March of the year 1662, at seven at night. For a year and seven months he had been a sergeant in the palace company of Don Pedro de Mendoza of this city.

Death of Sergeant Alonso del Pino

Due to his death, they promoted Juan [blank] of this city from the ranks to sergeant.

[He died] on Saturday, the 8th of the month of April 1662, and was buried Sunday morning, the first day of Easter in [the church of] San Francisco.

Death of Don Diego de la Presa

At five in the afternoon of Monday, the 10th of April of 1662, the second day of Easter, he left the port of Callao with two ships for the kingdom of Chile where he took succor of more than four hundred men. His son Don Juan Antonio de Peredo also went; and for the men he had designated as captains for this expedition, I refer to a previous entry where all their names are listed.

Governor Don Angel de Peredo Leaves for Chile

Father Fray Pedro Córdoba of the order of Saint Augustine, prime professor of theology in the University of Lima, died on Wednesday, the 12th of April of 1662, at seven in the morning. He was buried in his monastery the same day at eight in the evening. The Count of Santisteban, viceroy of these kingdoms, and all the gentlemen of the royal *audiencia*, and all the religious of the monasteries were present. All the people with horses [*caballeros*] of this city were also present. He had held the professorship from the 23rd of November of the year 1658 until the day he died, which was three years, four months, and eighteen days.

Death of Father Fray Pedro de Córdoba

Saturday, the 15th of April of the year 1662, at seven in the morning the bells of all the city began to ring the interdiction. It lasted until noon of the following day, Sunday, when it was ordered that Alonso Meléndez be returned to the church. He had killed his wife without any cause and had sought asylum in the church of the hospital of Santa Ana, from where they [government officials] had taken him. He was condemned by the magis-

Interdiction Which Lasted a Day and a Half

trate to be hanged and *encubado* [cast at sea in a barrel].[24] He appealed to the hall of crime, and because he proved that he was an *hidalgo* [a gentleman], they condemned him to be beheaded from the back and *encubado*. The scaffold was already erected in front of the palace next to the fountain, and there were many meetings as to whether the church was valid [asylum] or not. The interdiction lasted until Thursday at midday when an agreement was reached. He had killed his wife on Friday, the 24th of March of 1662, exactly at twelve noon.

Baptism of the Daughter of the Count

Friday, the 21st of April of the year 1662, at five in the afternoon the baby daughter of the Count of Santisteban, viceroy of these kingdoms, was baptized at the cathedral of this city. The baptism was attended by the most elite, and they appeared with their golden chains. She was baptized by the archbishop of this city, Don Pedro de Villagómez. The godfather of the baby Josefa was Father Fray Alfonso de Valdivia, a Franciscan lay father, and the godmother was the other young daughter of the Count of Santisteban, called Doña Teresa, who must have been around three years old. The Count of Santisteban with all the royal *audiencia* were in the cathedral in front of the baptistry until she was christened.

The Count of Alba and his Children

The Count of Alba and his two sons Don Juan and Don Enrique, and all the *caballeros* of Lima, walked from the palace to the cathedral in front of the two sedan chairs in which the two little girls rode, each with her palace lady of honor. Then the friar godfather carried the infant girl in his arms, Don Enrique carrying the godmother, from the door of the Holy Sacrament, where the ceremonial seat of the archbishop was located, to the baptismal font. The Count of Alba and Señor Don Juan preceded them. Following the christening, the Count of Alba gave some doubloons[25] for the offering. After the archbishop had said the Gospel, Señor Don Juan Enríquez picked up the newly christened child in his arms, and Señor Don Enrique [lifted] the godmother, and

24 The interdiction, or suspension of divine services, was declared because government officials had violated the ecclesiastical right of asylum. *Encubado* was a form of capital punishment where the condemned was placed in a barrel, sometimes with a live chicken or snake, and then cast into a sea or lake. It was usually reserved for patricides.

25 A *doblón* (doubloon) was an old Spanish gold coin equal to about seventeen silver pesos in 1650; see monetary values, note 3.

carrying them, put them in their sedan chairs turning them over to their ladies. All the accompaniment went ahead, as before, with the Count of Alba and his two sons on foot next to the sedan chairs, and the godfather behind, between the provincial and guardian of the monastery of San Francisco of this city, because the godfather was the cook at the monastery infirmary. The two little girls went together in their chairs through the plaza where the infantry company of the palace and the infantry guard of the Count of Alba formed a line from the door of the cathedral to the palace. Because there was only one flag, the palace flag was lowered in salute to them.

The Baptismal Font of the Church

The baptismal font as well as the whole chapel was adorned with hangings. It was exquisitely decorated in a manner never before seen, designed so that where the hangings came together there were golden fountains and basins. There was such a crowd of people that one could neither enter the church nor walk through the plaza. Within the baptistry there was an ornate bed with bedstead and curtains all green, edged in gold, and with exquisite mattresses, pillows and spreads. May God make a saint of the recently christened little girl called Doña Josefa.

When they brought her from the palace to the church, the count took her in his arms and turned her over to the godfather, Fray Alfonso de Valdivia, Franciscan lay brother, a virtuous man who led a good life.

Death of Francisco González Mauricio

Saturday, the 6th of May of 1662, at three in the afternoon Francisco González Mauricio fell from a balcony to the street. He was a porter who had come from Spain, and he had married in Seville. He died without leaving a will, and everything was confiscated by the Court for the Deceased.

Aid of Two Hundred Men for Chile

Monday, the 15th of May of 1662, a ship left the port of Callao with two hundred men as succor for the kingdom of Chile. Captain Tiberio, who had been a soldier of that kingdom for many years, went in charge of these men.

Residencia *of the Count of Alba*

Tuesday, the 16th of the month of May, the *residencia* of the Count of Alba was made public, confirming him as a good governor and a good judge. That same day there was great rejoicing in the whole city, and all the *caballeros* of this city hastened to the street where he resided. And there were bullfights. In the balconies were the viceroys, the Count of Santisteban and the Count of Alba, with the rest of the *caballeros*, and they passed many platters of food from the balconies to the street. That same night there were numerous festive lights and bonfires in celebration of the admirable outcome of the *residencia* of His Excellency.

The Sergeants

The sergeants began to make their rounds on Sunday, the 21st of November of 1661, by order of the viceroy, Count of Santisteban.

Later His Excellency ordered that three regular sergeants should be on duty, each one with twelve soldiers. Six patrols went out each night under three duty sergeants and three palace reserves to make the rounds of the entire city. Each one had six men; all the soldiers were on active duty. This second time the rounds began was on Sunday, the 25th of June of 1662. The patrols sallied from the palace guardhouse and were dispatched by the adjutant, Don Juan de Arnedo.

Proclamation of the Armada of 1662

Friday, the 1st of September of the year 1662, it was proclaimed that the armada would sail for Tierra Firme on the 20th of the month.

Father Mosquera Died

[He died] Tuesday, the 12th of September of the year 1662, at ten in the morning, and was buried that same afternoon in his monastery, San Agustín. He had not even been sick in bed two days, but had a serious attack of a high adynamic fever in the stomach. Before he died, his aunt, Doña Jerónima, entered the infirmary of San Agustín. To approve her entry, a chapter meeting was held. Father Maestro Lagunilla was prior.

Second Proclamation of the Armada

Wednesday, the 20th of the month, another edict was issued for the armada to leave the port of Callao for Panama on the 10th of October of the year 1662 without fail. On the 21st of September the Count of Alba with his two sons and many followers went to see his lodgings where he was to embark.

Death of a Prince, Birth of Another

Friday, the 29th of the month of September, news arrived [from Spain] about the death of our prince and lord, and how a week after his death another was born and named Don Carlos José.

On Saturday, the 7th of October of 1662, the ambassador who brought this news was received. Sunday, the 8th of the month, a *fiesta* for Mary was held. Tuesday, the 10th of the month, the royal decree of His Majesty was read and posted in the four corners of the plaza. [It said] that the city should hold great celebrations and demonstrations of rejoicing [for the birth of a prince].

Masquerade of the Count of Santisteban

Saturday, the 14th of the month, a great masquerade was held where the viceroy, Count of Santisteban, his son, and fifty more *caballeros* of the city promenaded. They appeared with great splendor, which could not have been surpassed even at court, and with more than six hundred pages, all with very expensive livery. They walked through the city, past all the convents of friars and nuns as far as Santa Clara, and from there they returned to the plaza by way of the [convent of San José de las Monjas] Descalzas. It ended at twelve at night. The only [religious] place they did not go was to Santa Catalina. The masquerade took four hours to walk through the city, and His Excellency walked throughout until it was over.

Bulls

Wednesday, the 18th of October of 1662, bulls were run for the ambassador who brought the news of the birth of our Prince Don Carlos José.

Consecration of the Bishop of Trujillo

Sunday, the 22nd of the month of October, the Very Reverend Father, Fray Juan de la Calle, who was presently vicar general of the Mercedarian order, was consecrated bishop of Trujillo. The archbishop of this City of Kings, Don Pedro de Villagómez, consecrated him in the church of Santo Domingo, where the Count of Santisteban and the vicereine, his wife, and also the Count of Alba de Liste, and all the *caballeros* of this city were present. With a great number of people they walked in procession that morning from the house of the archbishop to [the church of] Santo Domingo.

The Habit of Santiago to Pedro Carassa

Saturday, the 28th of the month, day of the holy apostles Simon and Judas, the habit of Santiago was bestowed on Don Pedro Rodríquez Carassa in the monastery of San Agustín, with the Count of Santisteban present. The Count of Alba, wearing his cloak, sat with the *caballeros* of his order on a plain bench. Following His Excellency was Don Antonio de Acuña y Cabrera, who had been governor of the kingdom of Chile, followed by all the *caballeros* of the order of Alcántara. A court magistrate and the revenue official of the royal *audiencia* put on his [Pedro Rodríguez Carassa's] spurs. His sponsor was Don Andrés de Vilela, president of the royal *audiencia.* Afterwards the viceroy took him to the palace in his carriage. There were a great many people at the church.

My Son Francisco Received by the Franciscans

Thursday, the 9th of November of 1662, they accepted my son, Francisco de Mugaburu y Honton, as religious chorister. That same day he remained at the monastery with two others who entered as choristers, and others as lay brothers.

Sunday, at four in the afternoon on the 12th of the month, [eve of the] day of the glorious Saint James, they bestowed habits on my son and another two [boys] as choristers, and one as a lay brother. That same afternoon Father Fray Bartolomé, whom they call Colunas, professed [adherence to the Order of Saint Francis]. The provincial, Fray Diego de Andrada, was the one who accepted them all. On the day he received the habit my son Francisco de Mugaburu y Honton was fifteen years and seven months old.

Fiesta *of Our Lady*

This same day they began to celebrate the *fiesta* of the Presentation of the Virgin Mary, and Father Felipe de Paz of the Society of Jesus preached in the cathedral.

Play for the Count of Alba

This same day, the 12th of November, the Count of Alba de Liste, who had been viceroy of this kingdom, went to the Corral de las Comedias[26] to see the play. There were many people and they passed a great quantity of food from the balconies to those watching the play. He gave one thousand pesos to the actors.

Friday, the 17th of the month of November, at four in the afternoon the Countess of Santisteban went to Callao in the litter of the archbishop of this city. The Count of Alba and his two sons, dressed in black, accompanied her as far as the Recollect [Nuestra Señora de Belén]. The viceroy went in the carriage.

[26] In the sixteenth century, dramatic representations in Lima were held in courtyards of the churches, but beginning in 1604 they were presented in a building at the corner of San Bartolomé and Sacramentos de Santa Ana. The theater was known as the "Corral de las Comedias." Bromley, *Evolución urbana,* pp. 22–23. See also Guillermo Lohmann Villena, *El arte dramático en Lima durante el virreinato* (Madrid: Estades, 1945).

The Count of Alba Departs for Callao

Thursday, the 22nd of November of 1662, at five in the afternoon, the Count of Alba de Liste, who had been viceroy of this kingdom, left for Callao with all the accompaniment of the city, and the tribunals, and the Count of Santisteban, present viceroy of this kingdom. Both set forth with their standard bearers, and in the small plaza of San Diego they formed a front of flags, whereupon they lowered the flags toward him. Afterwards, within that same hour, the Count of Alba returned again to the house where he was residing, which is that of *oidor* Don Bartolomé de Salazar.

Mail from Spain

Friday, the 25th of the said month and year, the mail arrived from Spain, and it went to Callao because His Excellency was there.

Departure of the Armada from Callao

Saturday, at four in the afternoon, the Count of Alba de Liste went to Callao with all his household and a great accompaniment of *caballeros* and other people of this city. As soon as he arrived, at the hour of evening prayer, they fired all the artillery that there was in that fortress. He stayed at the port of Callao until Saturday, the 2nd of December of the year 1662, when at four in the afternoon the armada set sail for Tierra Firme. Aboard were the Count of Alba, who had been viceroy of this kingdom, and his two sons Don Juan and Don Enrique. He was accompanied as far as the ship by the viceroy, Count of Santisteban, Archbishop Don Pedro de Villagómez, and the gentlemen of the royal *audiencia*. All the artillery of Callao was fired three times.

Procession of the Pure and Immaculate Conception

Friday, the 8th of December of the year 1662, at four in the afternoon, after a novena had been celebrated at [the church of] San Francisco and the Holy Sacrament had been uncovered for eight days, there was a procession. It went from San Francisco to the bridge, and from there along Hierro Viejo [Palace] Street to the plaza, and past the dry goods stores to the corner of Don Diego de Carbajal, and from there to Milagro [Street]. In these blocks there were beautifully decorated altars for the Immaculate Conception of Our Lady. Leading the procession was [a statue of] Saint Francis with a blue flag in his hand and a banner which said "Mary, conceived without stain of original sin." Following him were twelve [statues of] male and female saints of his [Franciscan] order, very well adorned. Behind all those saints went the [image of the] patriarch, Saint Dominic, and following him were twelve maidens who had been chosen by lot by this sodality. They went with their sponsors, and behind these maidens went the [statue of] the Immaculate Conception of the Mother of God. At the end was the Holy Sacrament of the altar, may it be praised forever. It was carried by the father provincial of the order of Saint Francis, Father Fray Diego de Adrada. [And then followed] the Count of Santisteban, the royal *audiencia*, the secular *cabildo*, all the religious orders, and the people; [a procession] such as never before seen. All this was owing to the purity and immaculateness of Our Lady, conceived without original sin.[27]

Thursday, the 21st of the month, there was a large procession at the Jesuit church which went around the block where there were very fine [temporary] altars.

The Sermon at Santo Domingo

Friday, the 22nd of December of 1662, the notaries of [the church of] Santo Domingo held the celebration of the Immaculate Conception of the Virgin Mary, Our Lady, conceived without original sin. That same afternoon the father prior of that monastery, Father Fray Domingo de Cabrera, gave the sermon. He gave the first part of the sermon lukewarmly, eulogizing first the Holy Sacrament of the altar, and then he stopped. Immediately all the listeners said, "And the Pure and Immaculate Conception of the Virgin Mary, Our Lady conceived without original sin," and the priest said, "And I so say and confirm it." Although it came from his lips, it was said tepidly, and at the end of the sermon he said it the same way. In the procession that went through the cloister and the Veracruz chapel there were almost no Dominican friars, but all the laymen went, shouting throughout the procession, "Without original sin."

At eight o'clock that same night, Friday, the 22nd of the month, some four or six lay brothers set out with several schoolboys, each with two tallow candles, chanting through the streets, "The Virgin was conceived without original sin." A short time later from an Indian tailor, they confiscated an image of the Immaculate Con-

[27] The doctrine that Mary was immaculately conceived, although supported by many church fathers for centuries, did not become dogma until 1854 when Pope Pius IX defined it as "of faith" in the Bull *Ineffabilus Deus*. *New Catholic Encyclopedia*, VII, 381.

ception painted on canvas, which they later presented to Doctor [José de] Reyes who was going by on his mule. Within less than a half hour more than four thousand lights had joined the procession, people of all types, each one with candle in hand, and all chanting in a loud voice, "The Virgin was conceived without original sin." The crowd kept growing in such a way that it totaled more than ten thousand persons. Upon entering the plaza the bells sounded in the cathedral and then in all the churches of Lima. That night the procession went through the streets until daybreak, and at dawn they stopped at the monastery of San Francisco. During this time the bells in Santo Domingo did not peal or move, though the crowd of people went twice to the corner [where the church was located], which was something never before seen in this kingdom.

On Saturday afternoon, the 23rd of the month, at four o'clock, a procession left from [the church of] San Francisco with the same figure as the previous night, under a canopy, and went around the plaza and entered the cathedral where all the ecclesiastic council was. And there they said their litanies. From there it went to the Jesuit Society [church] with a great multitude of people chanting, "Without original sin."

Pedro de Molino

Saturday, the 23rd of the month, at eight at night, another procession departed from the house of my friend Pedro de Molino. They had a large statue of the Immaculate Conception and filed through the whole city accompanied by the merchants, almost all of them with banners and blue ribbons.

Sounding of the Bells in Santo Domingo

That same night, after having walked until two in the morning, the referred-to procession went to [the church of] Santo Domingo where the whole [religious] community awaited with candles in hand, the cross high, and the door open. The bells pealed many times, and all the people of the city were happy. If they had not been, it would have weighed heavily on the Dominican Fathers. And for this, every night processions go forth from every house for devotion.

Procession from Santa Ana

Wednesday, the 27th of December, the third day of Christmas, the procession for the Pure and Immaculate Conception of Our Lady set out from the church of Santa Ana, and went from there to La Caridad [hospital], to La Concepción [convent], and to the Society of Jesus [church]. From there it moved to Mercaderes Street, then to the plaza and across to the corner of the Archbishop's [palace], then back along the street of the Franciscan church, and from there as far as [the convent of] Santa Clara, then back home. There were a great many well-dressed people with many candles. This procession dazzled the city.

Procession from San Sebastián

It took place on Thursday, the 28th of the month, with many lights and many persons. That same night the house of Pedro de Murúa, street merchant, caught fire, and a twelve-year old son of his was burned to death. The following day they buried him in [the church of] San Francisco.

Convention of the City Priests

Friday, the 29th of the month, a convention of all the priests of the city left the cathedral in a colorful procession. Under a canopy they carried the statue of Our Lady of the Immaculate Conception. All the priests wore surplices and walked throughout the city with torches in hand chanting, "Without original sin." It was something spectacular and worth seeing.

Saturday, the 30th of the month, another procession went from the convent of the nuns of Santa Catalina, with a galleon [float] drawn by four mules, very brightly decorated, and many children on it dressed as angels. They carried [an image of] Our Lady followed by all the lineage of Our Lady. It was done in much taste, and with that the year 1662 ended.

The Year 1663

The Dominican Preacher

Monday, the 1st day of the new year of 1663, it happened that when a Dominican father went to preach in the cathedral of this city, after the salutation he said only, "Praised be the Holy Sacrament of the Altar," and stopped. Whereupon all the canons and all the people listening said in a loud voice, "And the Virgin Mary, conceived without stain of original sin." The predicator did not want to say it, so they made him descend from the pulpit, and they continued with the high Mass. This preacher said that his prelate had ordered him not to say it, and that he was a student and under orders. Since the vice-prebend, the licentiate Portachuelo, did not support him, the people who were present in the church wanted to set upon this predicator, and he left the cathedral very upset.

Procession of Mulattoes

This same day, a colorful procession of mulattoes left the cathedral and went throughout the city. On the same day, another procession of dark-skinned people set out from the hospital of Saint Bartholomew, and also went all over the city accompanied by many people.

Three Kings' Day Masquerade

Saturday, the 6th of January of 1663, at eight at night there was a masquerade with much outlandish mockery. Four floats appeared depicting four highly-adorned pontiffs with their cardinals, floats bearing nuns of all the convents of this city, and another cart portraying our king and lord, Philip IV, and the prince, and behind all this, another float with [images of] the Mother of God and numerous angels chanting, "Without original sin." They were followed by all the *caballeros* of all the orders, all very resplendent, and the three Wise Men and a number of Turks, all very well dressed. It was something quite worth seeing, and it was repeated Sunday at four in the afternoon.

Procession from San Lázaro

Monday, the 8th of the month, a procession of dark-skinned people started out from [the church of] San Lázaro. They were all dressed as figures of the Old Testament, from Adam to Joseph, with their costumes depicting the ancient dress worn at that time.

Procession of Caballeros *of Santiago*

Sunday, the 14th of January, a very resplendent procession left the monastery of San Agustín with all the [images of the] saints of the order very well adorned, and the [statue of the] apostle Saint James on horseback. All the *caballeros* of the order of Santiago, and the viceroy, Count of Santisteban, all with their cloaks, walked in the procession chanting, "Without original sin." The Holy Sacrament of the altar, may it be praised forever, was also carried in the procession behind the [image of the] Holy Virgin. There were four [temporary] altars, three of them the best that have been set up in this city of Lima; the first altar in the street intersection at [the monastery of] San Agustín, with four façades; the second at the entrance of Plateros Street, excellently done; the third on the street which forms a corner with the prison chapel at the bridge, admirably contrived with much art; and the fourth altar at the door of [the monastery of] Santo Domingo. The procession passed from San Agustín to the first altar, and from there along Mercaderes Street to the corner of the prison chapel, and from there to Santo Domingo, and from there back home. There was nothing so impressive to see as this celebration for the Pure and Immaculate Conception of Our Lady which was held on this day.

Placement of Our Lady of Solitude

Friday afternoon, the 26th of January of 1663, [the statue of] Our Lady of Solitude was placed in her new chapel with a very ostentatious procession which went around the four streets where there were four excellent altars. The viceroy and the royal *audiencia* and a great group of *caballeros* went in the procession, lighting the way for the Holy Sacrament of the altar.

Masquerade of Colegio *San Martín*

Saturday, the 27th of the current [month and year], a grandiose comic masquerade was launched from the *Colegio* San Martín. An impressive array of illustrious persons of this city were depicted with their rich attire and jewels. There were many floats, much illumination, and it was all very impressive.

Procession from La Merced

Monday, the 29th of the month, the day of the patriarch Saint Peter Nolasco, a large procession set out from [the monastery of] Nuestra Señora de la Merced, where a cart was brought forth drawn by little angels, with the [image of the] Pure and Immaculate Conception of Our Lady on her throne. There were also many figures from the Old Testament, all richly adorned with many jewels, and all the *caballeros* of the order of Redemption of the Captives appeared as prisoners with golden chains and valuable jewels. Behind them were all the *caballeros* of the orders of Alcántara and Calatrava. There were as many as eleven or twelve *caballeros* who went with the viceroy. And there were four very expensive altars. The one at the corner of the post office was covered with mirrors from top to bottom; it was quite a sight. In the center was a large statue of Our Lady, and at her feet a large serpent, and there was a tree with apples, and below, Adam and Eve. Of all the celebrations up to this day, this was the best one held. Of the *caballeros*, the following were missing: Don Alvaro de Navamuel, *caballero* of Alcántara; Don Luis de Mendoza, *caballero* of Calatrava; and Don Pedro Calderón, of Calatrava.

Bulls and Plays

Tuesday, the 30th of January, bulls were run in the small plaza of San Francisco. Wednesday, the 31st of the month, and Thursday, the 1st of February, there were plays on both days at the door of Our Lady of Solitude [chapel]. Saturday, the 3rd, the day of Saint Blase, there were also bulls in this small plaza, and the viceroy and vicereine watched them both days from some balconies.

Procession of San Juan de Dios

Saturday, the 10th of March, the fathers of [the monastery of] San Juan de Dios held a large procession in praise of the Mother of God. There were four altars done with great imagination, and the procession went around four blocks. The Mercedarian provincial brought out the Holy Sacrament, may it be praised forever, and His Excellency was present with all the gentlemen of the *audiencia.*

Dispatch Boat from Chile

Monday, the 16th of April, Don Juan Antonio de Peredo, *caballero* of the order of Calatrava, son of the governor of Chile, Don Antonio de Peredo, arrived from Chile with news that the Indians of the kingdom of Chile had come to peace terms similar to those pledged to Señor Don Francisco Lazo, and that they had received missionaries and were being baptized. At this news there was great rejoicing and festive lights in this city.

Squadron

Sunday, the 29th of April of the year 1663, a review squadron was formed with only the twelve companies of the battalion of this city. Monday, the 30th of the month of April, the duty companies of the guard began to enter the palace. The first was the company of Captain Don José Tamayo y Mendoza; and they are on guard twenty-four hours.

The Mounted Companies

Tuesday, the 1st of May of the year 1663, the eight mounted companies, four from the city and the other four from the rural estates, went to the plaza to pass muster. The son of the Count of Santisteban, Señor Don Manuel de Benavides, as general of the cavalry, and his lieutenant, Don Melchor Malo de Molina, came out [for the review].

Ban on Mules

Wednesday, the 2nd of the month, the decree was proclaimed that no one should go about on a mule but on horseback, under penalty of forfeiting the mule for war costs and any other [punishment] that His Excellency might order.

Another Proclamation

Friday, the 4th of the month, another proclamation was issued in which His Excellency ordered that a month would be granted in which to find horses on which to ride, and with heavy penalties [for disobedience thereafter].

Death of the Dominican Prior

Friday, the 4th of the month of May, the Dominican father prior, Domingo de Cabrera, died and was buried on the following Saturday. He was presently prior of the large monastery of this city.

Death of the Provincial of Santo Domingo

Sunday, the 6th of May of 1663, Father Maestro Fray Francisco de Huerta, who was presently Dominican provincial, died. He was buried on the following Monday with great ostentation, and the Count of Santisteban and all the royal *audiencia* were present at his burial.

Tuesday, the 8th of the month, His Excellency went to Ancón by sea, returning overland the following day.

Decree to Pass Review

Saturday, the 12th of May, an edict was issued decreeing that all those who were in the quarters of the four companies pass muster. The one under Captain Don Pedro de Córdoba, another under Don José Tamayo, another under Captain Izquierdo, [and] the other under Don Luis de Sandoval, [would muster] on Monday the 14th of the month, the second day of Pentecost; and four companies on the following day, Tuesday; and the other four on Holy Trinity Sunday. His Excellency was present, and he placed his chair against the door of the hall of arms in the palace.

Death of Father Fray Francisco de Buenaventura

Monday, the 14th of May of 1663, Father Fray Francisco de Buenaventura died. He was commissary of Jerusalem of the Franciscan order, a servant of God, who was much revered in this city of Lima.

Ban on Soldiers of Callao

Wednesday, the 17th of the month, His Excellency issued a proclamation that no soldier registered in the royal books as holding a post [in Callao] could come to Lima without permission of His Excellency and the battalion commander, Don Tomás Pardo, under penalty of four years in Valdivia.

Fray Juan Martínez of the Franciscan order died Wednesday, the 16th of May of 1663, at two in the afternoon. He was known by another name, "El Chuncho," [the name of a tribe of Peruvian Indians]. [He was] a holy father, and was known in the whole city for his good life and great penitence, and it was he who asked [for donations] for the maintenance of the sick Franciscan fathers. He was buried the following Thursday amidst great praise from the people. Four canons of the holy Church and *caballeros* of various orders carried the body. At the church there was a great turmoil of people who went to see him and they removed two of his habits as relics. After twenty-four hours he had a very good appearance, as though he were alive, and he gave forth a very penetrating and pleasant aroma, which consoled all those who kissed his hand and the holy habit of Saint Francis.

Death of Father Fray Juan Martínez

Tuesday, the 6th of November of 1663, which was a workday, there was a military formation in the plaza of this city of Lima, for which more than eleven hundred men turned out. At the center was the fountain, and in the fountain were the [company] flags. There were thirteen companies that mustered that afternoon. It was the first time that all the silversmiths came out in their guild; the captain of their company was Captain Juan de Beingolea. All the public and royal scribes also came out in a body; all appeared in great splendor. That same afternoon His Excellency, the Count of Santisteban, came out accompanied by all the *caballeros* of this city, and made a tour of the plaza, and then placed himself in front of the squadron where the flags were lowered towards him. Then with all the *caballeros* and the eight mounted companies, the four of the city and the four of the *chácaras*, and with Señor Don Manuel de Benavides, his son and lieutenant general, acting as guide, he went to the convent of the barefoot nuns of San José to give thanks to Our Lord Jesus Christ as an act of gratitude for the health and years completed by our prince Joseph Charles of Austria. None of the gentlemen *oidores* nor the battalion commander, Don Francisco de la Cueva, *caballero* of the order of Calatrava, went with His Excellency. The formation was organized by the adjutant, Gaspar de Savariego, and Don Juan de Arnedo, and it was disbanded by Sergeant Josephe de Mugaburu, in accordance with military regulations. After the squadron was disbanded there were great festive lights and many fireworks worth seeing.

The Formation

This same day the pulley [for the gibbet] was set up in the plaza for those who had evaded the formation.

Death of Doña Francisco Aguilar

Doña Francisca de Aguilar died Sunday, the 18th of November of 1663, at nine-thirty in the morning in this city in the house of her brother the prebend. She was the wife of Don Juan Bautista de Rueda and sister of the prebend Don Sebastián de Aguilar. The same day they took the deceased to Callao in a carriage drawn by four mules so that she could be buried there in her native town.

Profession of my Son Francisco

Monday, the 19th of November of 1663, day of the glorious Saint Elizabeth, Queen of Hungary, at five in the afternoon my son Fray Francisco professed along with three others who took vows as choristers, and another as lay brother. They were five in all; the five had received their [Franciscan] habits jointly on Thursday, the 9th of November of the year 1662. Father Fray Carlos Blanderas was instructor of the novices, and Father Fray Francisco Delgado was the local father superior of the monastery who professed them. That afternoon many people attended including the secular *cabildo* and a great number of *caballeros*, and also Don Manuel de Benavides, son of the Count of Santisteban, viceroy of these kingdoms. Also present were my two nephews, Don Esteban de Legorburu and Don Pedro de Legorburu, who had arrived from Spain with a cargo of clothing [to sell].

Proclamation of a General Auto-da-fé

Monday, the 3rd of December of 1663, at four in the afternoon it was proclaimed by the Holy Office [Inquisition] of this city, that on the 23rd of January of 1664, day of the glorious Saint Alphonso, a general auto-da fé[28] would be held in the main plaza of this city. Many officers of the Inquisition appeared with their staffs and insignias, and behind all of them, Don Pedro López de Gárate, *caballero* of the order of Santiago and chief bailiff of the Holy Office. At his side was the licentiate Farias, secretary of that holy tribunal.

Ban Regarding Mulattoes, Negroes, and Indians

Saturday, the 15th of the month of December, His Excellency, the Count of Santisteban, issued an edict proclaiming that no Indian, mulatto, or Negro carry a sword, dagger, knife, or machete, under penalty of two years in the galleys, and if he were a

[28] *Auto-da-fé* was the ceremony accompanying the pronouncement of judgment by the Inquisition, followed by the carrying out of sentences passed; hence the punishment or execution of a heretic.

slave, payment of one hundred pesos by his master to the agent who caught him and two years in the galleys. Only those who were presently military officers such as captains, ensigns, aides, and sergeants of said companies of Indians, mulattoes and Negroes could carry them. It was also proclaimed that no Spaniard could carry a sword with a needlepoint. For [non-complying] *caballeros* of the religious orders, the fine would be one hundred pesos and one month in one of the forts of Callao, for everyone else, one hundred pesos fine and one month in prison in the public jail of this city.

Death of my Brother-In-Law, Francisco de Sequera

Francisco de Sequera, my brother-in-law, died Tuesday, the 18th of this month of December of the year 1663, and the following Wednesday he was buried in the vault of Saint Raymond at the monastery of Nuestra Señora de la Merced.

The Year 1664

Auto-da-fé

At five in the afternoon of Tuesday, the 22nd of January, a procession led by Father Barbarán, presently provincial of the Dominican monastery, left from the Holy Office [Inquisition] for the platform of the Holy Cross. The banner was carried by Don Manuel de Benavides, son of the Count of Santisteban, viceroy of these kingdoms. At his side went Don Baltasar Pardo, and Gabriel de Castilla, *caballeros* of the order of Santiago. All the religious orders took part, and the fathers of the Society [of Jesus] were mixed with the collegiates of San Martín. Their going out in a group had never been seen before. That same night we of the companies were quartered. There were thirteen [companies], the number of this city, with those of the silversmiths and their captain, Juan de Beingolea, who walked in the procession, and those who were to be punished. And thus when four o'clock Wednesday morning struck, three companies remained in the small plaza of the Holy Office, one of Captain Don Pedro de Córdoba, the other of Don Luís de Sandoval, and the other of Captain Fernando Izquierdo. That of Beingolea, which is the one of the silversmiths, went with all the penitents, and with the other three formed a squadron in the small plaza, which was Wednesday the 23rd of January. Then the convicted were brought out. One was burned [at the stake], two were burned in effigy, three were wearing sanbenitos [pentitent tunics],[29] one for having married twice. There were four friars, and others who had been witches. In all, twenty-one were sentenced.

After all the convicted had come out of the Holy Office, His Excellency the Count of Santisteban arrived with all the accompaniment of *caballeros* and all the guards of lances and arquebuses. Then the gentlemen inquisitors came forth, the senior [member] Don Cristóbal de Castilla, and the other, Don Alvaro de Ibarra, with the viceroy between them; and the standard bearer brought Don Alvaro de Ibarra, as newest inquisitor, to the platform. The chief bailiff was Don Pedro López de Gárate. There was great discord regarding the seating of the captains of the battalion and the mercenaries of Callao, resulting in His Excellency's ordering that they be seated alternately. First seated was the battalion commander of Lima, Don Francisco de la Cueva, *caballero* of the order of Calatrava; then Lieutenant General Don Francisco de Valverde, *caballero* of the order of Santiago; then Sergeant Major Domingo de Albizu; then Sergeant Major Don Pedro de Mendoza y Toledo, who was captain of the palace guard; then Captain Don José Tamayo, the senior captain of this battalion [of Lima]; and then another mercenary of Callao; and in this manner all were seated. We quartered ourselves, all of the companies, in the palace until the auto [da-fé] was over, which must have been four in the afternoon, and a squadron was formed again until His Excellency returned from the Holy Office. Neither the viceroy, the inquisitors, nor the *oidores* took time out to eat, nor did they eat the whole day.

At four in the afternoon the reading of the sentences was over, and the viceroy between the two inquisitors and all the retinue returned to the Holy Inquisition. Then the viceroy returned to the palace. The squadron having been until that time in the plaza, His Excellency ordered that it be disbanded, and it was.

Floggings by the Holy Office

Thursday, the 24th of the month, the witches were flogged, as was the Jewish doctor, but not his wife. This was at five in the afternoon.

[29] Spanish Inquisition penitents, on being reconciled to the church, wore a *sambenito* (from St. Benedict of Nursia) resembling a scapular; it was yellow with a large red cross in front and back. Those impenitents who were condemned wore a similar tunic but it was black and decorated with flames and devils.

Garrote

Monday, the 10th of March of 1664, at four in the afternoon Antonio Ordóñez, who it is said was captain of the regular cavalry of the city of Santiago de Chile, and who had been condemned to be executed by garrote in the plaza of this city of Lima for having killed a woman, was taken out of the court prison. By decree of the viceroy, Count of Santisteban, he was turned over to Gaspar de Savariego, adjutant of this corps of the battalion, who with a part of the soldiers of the palace company took him on foot from the prison. He was dressed in mourning. Upon being strangled by the garrote, they cut off his right hand and placed it where the crime was committed.

Articles of Marriage

Thursday, the 8th of May of the year 1664, a dowry document was drawn up for Juana de Alanda. It was for eight hundred pesos: the three hundred that her father had left her, which were given by Captain Martín Sánchez de Aranzamendi who had them in his care, and five hundred pesos which her [future] husband donated. These articles of marriage were drawn up by Juan de Espinoza, public scribe, this same day and year in this City of Kings.

Earthquake at Pisco and Ica

At four thirty on the dawn of Monday, the 12th of May of 1664, an earthquake ravaged Ica and Pisco, wherein many people, young and old, died. Nine of the eleven religious at the Franciscan monastery in the town of Ica died. [Killed] in the Augustinian monastery were the secretary of the Augustinian father provincial, Father Fray Pedro de Tóvar, who had gone to visit the province, and also two young boys and a Negro whom he had brought as his servants. [The provincial] escaped with great difficulty. In Pisco the cathedral collapsed as did some houses in the town.

Processions

Three processions were held with the [statue of] Holy Christ of the Desamparados [church]. The last one was with [penitent] blood.[30] Bearing [the statue of] the Holy Christ and the image of Our Lady of the Desamparados, it went from the church of the Desamparados to the cathedral, to the Society of Jesus, to the convent of La Concepción, to San Francisco [church], and from there back to Desamparados, the whole city accompanying and

[30] *Penitentes*, as religious fanatics, scourge or flog themselves until they shed blood.

illuminating [the way]. The viceroy and the gentlemen of the royal *audiencia* and *cabildo* took part. This last procession was on Saturday, the 7th of June of 1664, at four in the afternoon.

Death of Fiscal *Don Nicolás Polanco*

The *fiscal* [royal treasury official] Don Nicolás Polanco died at one in the morning of Tuesday, July 15, 1664. On Thursday at eleven they buried him at the *colegio* of San Ildefonso, which belongs to the order of Saint Augustine. Upon taking him to be buried, [a dispute arose] at the first funeral stop. The senior accountants of the tribunal of accounts, having carried him thus far wished to continue carrying him, but the present *alcaldes*, Don Bartolomé de Azaña, *caballero* of the order of Santiago, and Don Amador de Caberra, said that it corresponded to the *cabildo* of the city to carry the body. At this Don Tomás Barreto came forth and had words with Don Andrés de Miesei, chief accountant, and they drew their swords, and there was a great uproar. The viceroy, Count of Santisteban, who was present, and the gentlemen of the royal *audiencia* ordered that Don Andrés Miesei be imprisoned at the guard company, and he was taken there by the chief bailiff of the court, Don Melchor Malo, the other being taken to the city hall. They remained there one afternoon, and then were placed under house arrest; and His Excellency ordered them exiled and each fined two thousand pesos for the irreverence [committed]. They requested clemency.

Imprisonment of Father Iporre

Thursday, the 16th of July of the year 1664, His Excellency ordered that Fray [Cristóbal] de Iporre be taken from the hermitage of Nuestra Señora de Monserrate of this City of Kings because he was upsetting the religious of Santo Domingo who were to hold their chapter meeting on the 24th of that month. At ten at night, by order of His Excellency, Sergeant Major Domingo de Albizu went with thirty soldiers to Monserrate and brought him in a carriage to the house of Señor Don Alonso de Herrera, secretary of the viceroy, Count of Santisteban. The [church] father slept in the bed of the secretary that night, and at four in the morning the sergeant major with four soldiers took him in His Excellency's carriage and put him aboard the consort ship.

Saturday, the 19th of July of 1664, at five in the afternoon after the litanies had been sung and the rosary said for Our Lady, with the whole community of the religious of Santo Domingo present, and the church filled with people kneeling, Father Barbarán, prelate of the Dominican monastery, came forward with many prominent religious of the order. Placing themselves at the main altar, all the religious said in a loud voice, "Blessed and praised be the Most Holy Sacrament of the altar and the Virgin Mary, Our Lady, conceived without original sin from the moment of her conception." Whereupon all the city solemnly rejoiced and was filled with gladness.

Dominicans Chanted "Without Original Sin"

Thursday, the 24th of July of the year 1664, Father Fray Juan de Barbarán Lazcano was elected Dominican provincial, with which the fathers were pleased.

The Provincial, Father Barbarán

Tuesday, the 29th of July of the year 1664, the fathers of [the monastery of] Santo Domingo in this City of Kings celebrated the Pure and Immaculate Conception of Our Lady. The provincial was Father Maestro Fray Juan de Barbarán Lazcana; and the Very Reverend Father Fray [blank] gave the sermon about the immaculate conception of Our Lady.

Procession of the Dominican Fathers

The following Wednesday there was a great procession through the streets and plazas of this city. [A statue of] Saint Dominic was carried on a gilded wooden litter; [an image of] the Virgin of The Conception from [the church of] Santo Domingo was on a silver litter; all the religious order chanting, "Without original sin." Archbishop Don Pedro de Villagómez went in pontifical attire, and the *cabildo* appeared [in the procession] where all the nobility of this city gathered to illuminate [with candles] the Most Holy Virgin. The statue was from the Franciscan monastery, and the following Thursday it was taken in procession back to San Francisco [church].

Doña Juana de Acevedo died Thursday, the 28th of August of the year 1664, day of the glorious Saint Augustine, at twelve midnight. At eleven on Saturday, the 30th of the month, she was buried at [the church of] Santa Ana.

Death of Doña Juana de Acevedo

The Very Reverend Father Maestro Fray Juan de Valenzuela was elected provincial of the Mercedarian [order] on Saturday, the 30th of August of the year 1664, at seven in the morning.

Mercedarian Provincial

Visitador *of the Royal* Audiencia

Monday, the 8th of September of 1664, at five in the afternoon the *visitador* [royal inspector] Don Juan Cornejo, *fiscal* of the Council of the Indies, entered this city in his carriage along with those [members] of his household, without any reception. He entered the palace through the garden gate and spoke with the viceroy, Count of Santisteban. In a short while he left and went to his residence, and within an hour the viceroy returned the visit, departing after a brief time. His Excellency ordered that a guard of twenty soldiers be placed at the house where he would reside, called the house of Lorca's widow, which was adjacent to the cathedral.

Friday, the 12th of the month, at four in the afternoon [the *visitador*] came to the council hall of the palace with a great following of people in carriages. Captain Don Juan de Beingolea's company, which is of the silversmith's guild, was lined up in the plaza. From the gate to inside the palace was the mercenary company of which Don Pedro de Mendoza is captain. Within an hour he departed in the same manner as he had come, and he went to his house.

Tuesday, the 30th of September, they published the decrees which he brought from His Majesty for the said official visit.

Exile of Colmenares

Saturday, the 24th of September of the year 1664, by resolution of the royal *audiencia* and the express decree of His Excellency the Count of Santisteban, viceroy of these kingdoms, Don Francisco de Colmenares, royal official of the royal funds of His Majesty, left the court prison of this city to comply with his exile to Pisco, resulting from his having quarreled in the *audiencia* with a cleric and the present *visitador*, Don Juan Cornejo.

Dispatch Ship from Spain

The dispatch ship from Spain arrived at this city on Friday, the 26th of September of the year 1664, at eight at night. [It brought the appointments of] Don Sancho Pardo, dean of Trujillo, as bishop of Panama; and for canons of the holy church of Lima: the prebends Don Juan de Montalvo and Don Juan Zegarra; Doctor Don José de Avila; and Doctor Don Juan Hurtado, curate of Chancay. All the replaced dignitaries proceeded to relocate.

Fiscal Protector

Thursday, the 2nd of October, Doctor Don Diego Pinelo, prime professor as was his predecessor, was received as district fiscal protector of this royal *audiencia*.

Blessing of the Church of San Francisco

Thursday, the 2nd of October of the year 1664, at ten in the morning the archbishop of this city, Don Pedro de Villagómez, blessed the new church of San Francisco, after which His Grace said Mass. To all who attended the Mass he granted forty-five days indulgence.

The Procession

Friday, the 3rd of the month, at four in the afternoon [the statue of] Saint Francis was taken from its church to the plaza with all the saints of the [Franciscan] order. There it awaited [the statue of] Saint Dominic, and the two were taken together to the cathedral. With great solemnity and with all the accompaniment of his *cabildo*, the archbishop brought the Holy Sacrament, may it be forever praised, to the new church of San Francisco where it was deposited that afternoon. Everyone attended the vespers, the archbishop, his *cabildo*, and all the people of this city. That night there were many fireworks.

The following Saturday, day of the glorious Saint Francis, Archbishop Don Pedro de Villagómez celebrated a sung pontifical Mass. And this day the father superior of the [Franciscan] monastery, Fray Francisco Delgado, gave the sermon. The viceroy and all the *audiencia* were present; and this day there was no Dominican friar [preaching.] Sunday, the 5th of the month, the father superior, Fray Francisco Delgado, said Mass at the high altar, and the lector, Father Fray Pedro Guerra of that monastery, gave the sermon. On Monday there was sung Mass and there was no sermon.

Procession through the Four Streets

Tuesday, the 7th of the month, the prior of Santo Domingo celebrated a sung Mass; the father superior of [the monastery of Nuestra Señora de los Angeles] the Descalzos of this city, called Picón, gave the sermon, which was attended by the viceroy and all the *audiencia* and *cabildo* of the city. At four in the afternoon of this day, Tuesday, the procession passed by the four streets where the four altars were [located]; they were better than any heretofore seen in this city. [Images of] all the saints of the Franciscan order were so adorned as to cause admiration. Five days after the procession was over [the statue of] Saint Dominic was brought to [the church of] San Francisco, and in the company of all the [images of Franciscan] saints, taken to the plaza of Santo Domingo. All the street entrances were closed off so that neither carriages, horses, nor mules could enter, even into the small plaza. There were three nights of great fireworks. The number of people that turned out was so great that it was necessary to bring the infantry company from the palace with goads to hold back the people and let the procession pass. This was about evening prayer time. In this procession the Holy Sacrament was not taken through the streets but just the [statues of] saints of the order and Saint Dominic and Saint Francis, and the Mother of God of the Immaculate Conception, who went behind all the saints.

Proclamation about the Armada

Wednesday, the 12th of November of 1664, at eleven o'clock midday, a proclamation was issued that the armada would leave on the 20th of the month, and a royal decree of His Majesty, may God protect him, was read wherein [it was stipulated that] all the stevedores who were from Castile, and all the merchants of that kingdom, should embark for Tierra Firme. Monday, the 17th of the month, another proclamation was issued in which His Excellency, the Count of Santisteban, ordered that all the Spanish merchants embark by the 25th of the month under penalty of two thousand pesos each, and that this proclamation would serve as confirmation that each one was personally notified of this edict.

Armada Left for Panama

Wednesday, the 10th of December of the year 1664, at ten in the morning the flagship and consort vessel, with another ship sailing under their convoy, left the port of Callao for Tierra Firme with Don José de Alzamora as general and Don Juan de Luza, *caballero* of the order of Santiago, as admiral. Considerable treasure went with these ships, more than fourteen million [pesos]. May God bring them safely to harbor and to the defense of our most holy law of Jesus Christ! The viceroy, Count of Santisteban, attended the dispatching of the armada in Callao, where he remained more than twenty days with all his family.

Prime Professorship of Law

Doctor Don Gregorio de Rojas, Doctor Don José Dávila, canon of the holy church of this City of Kings, and Doctor Don José de Reyes, all three eminent men and great academicians, competed for the prime professorship of law which Don Diego Pinelo had left vacant. With a plurality of forty-five votes, Doctor Don José de Reyes won it on Tuesday, the 23rd of December of the year 1664, with such acclaim from people of all classes as never before seen in this city. The 22nd of the month, which was when he lectured [for the competition], was exactly two years from the time that Doctor Reyes had gone forth that night with a great concurrence of people chanting through the streets, "The Virgin was conceived without original sin."

The Year 1665

Founding of a Chaplaincy by Don Pedro López

Tuesday, the 10th of March of the year 1665, Doctor Don Pedro López de Gárate, *caballero* of the order of Santiago and chief constable of the Holy Tribunal of the Inquisition, established a chaplaincy with two thousand pesos principal, giving a hundred pesos each year. This was levied against a house he owned facing the one in which he lived, which, from the corner of Don Diego de la Presa, was toward San Francisco de Paula. It was stipulated that one Mass be said each week, either Saturday or Sunday, in [the church of] Santa Clara, but should the chaplain leave this city and be accommodated elsewhere, he may say the Mass wherever located. This [chaplaincy] was bestowed on my son, the *bachiller* José de Mugaburu. The endowment or contract was drawn up by Juan de Sandóval, public scribe, on the day, month and year mentioned above.

Saturday, the 21st of March of the year 1665, on the eve of Passion Sunday, the illustrious gentleman, Don Pedro de Villagómez, archbishop of this city, conferred holy orders in the main sacristy of this holy church. Four were ordained to say Mass, nine as deacons, and among them Doctor Don José de Avila, canon of this holy church; for sub-deacons, four, and among them my son the *bachiller* José de Mugaburu as chaplain, chosen by Señor Don Pedro de Gárate, *caballero* of the order of Santiago and chief constable of the Holy Office, and Captain Don Bartolomé Maldonado, with [an endowed chaplaincy of] one thousand pesos as principal, which are fifty pesos [annually] on his two houses.

Holy Saturday, which was the 4th of April of 1665, he [my son] was ordained as deacon in the holy orders conferred by Archbishop Don Pedro de Villagómez, archbishop of this City of Kings, in the chapel of his palace.

Tuesday, the 21st of April of 1665, at eleven in the morning a proclamation was issued by the Count of Santisteban, viceroy of

Ban Regarding Mulatto and Negro Women

these kingdoms of Peru, passed in the court of justice, that no mulatto woman, nor Negro woman, free or slave, wear woolen cloth, nor any cloth of silk, nor lace of gold, silver, black or white. Penalty for the first offense was confiscation of everything, and for the second time, one hundred lashes. Free women [violators] were to be exiled fifty leagues from this city, and slaves confined in the house of their master with severe punishment. Responsibility for the execution of this [order] was given to the criminal judges and the *alcaldes* and to Captain Bartolomé de Azaña, *caballero* of the order of Santiago and *alcalde* of the brotherhood.

Thursday, the 30th of April of the year 1665, my nephews, Don Antonio de Legorburu and his brother Don Pedro, and their comrade Juan Bautista de Olazábal left from the port of Callao for Arica on the ship named *San Juan de Dios* of which Manuel R. Farfalladas, Junior, was proprietor. They took with them the cargo of clothing from Castile to sell in Potosí and other regions.

Habit of Santiago

Friday, at four in the afternoon of the 1st of May of the year 1665, the day of Saints Philip and James, the habit of Santiago was bestowed on my *compadre*, Captain Pedro Merino de Heredia, in the church of the convent of La Encarnación of this City of Kings. The viceroy of these kingdoms, Count of Santisteban, and the dazzling *caballeros* of this city were present. That same afternoon there was a general formation in the main plaza of this city, with a great fireworks display.

Consecration of the Bishop of Panama

Sunday, the 17th of May of the year 1665, Doctor Don Sancho Pardo, formerly dean of Trujillo, was consecrated as bishop of Panama by the archbishop of this city, Don Pedro de Villagómez. The viceroy of these kingdoms, Count of Santisteban, and all the gentlemen of the royal *audiencia* and *cabildos* of this city with all its illustrious [members] were present. (News of his [the bishop's] death in Panama on the 13th of January of the year 1670 reached this city of Lima on the first of May of 1670.)

Franciscan Commissary General

Tuesday, the 19th of May of 1665, the Franciscan father commissary, Father Miguel de Molina, entered this city at nine in the morning with a great number of persons accompanying him, including all the *cabildo* of the city. At that hour he entered the palace between two alcaldes, Don Juan de la Celda and Don

Tomás Barreto, to see the viceroy, Count of Santisteban. Later he was received at [the church of] San Francisco with cross held high and all the community of San Francisco as well as that of Santo Domingo present. (He died Saturday, the 12th of March of the year 1667, at five in the afternoon and was buried the following Sunday at twelve noon. The gentlemen *oidores* who governed in the absence of a viceroy were present at the burial.)

Prime Professorship

Wednesday, the 20th of May of the year 1665, Maestro Báez, friar of the Mercedarian order, obtained the prime professorship of theology by a margin of eighty-five votes. Other contenders were Maestro Ulloa of the order of Saint Augustine and Doctor Don Diego de Salazar.

Nuns Depart for Chuquisaca

Thursday, the 21st of May of the year 1665, at six in the morning three nuns departed from the convent of Our Lady of Carmen of this City of Kings to found another convent in Chuquisaca [also called La Plata or Sucre, Bolivia]. With them went a secular maiden to take the veil there. This convent was founded there by the present archbishop of La Plata [Upper Peru], the Very Reverend Illustrious Archbishop Villarroel. On the morning that they left, the archbishop of this City of Kings, Don Pedro de Villagómez, accompanied them outside the city, and there was a great crowd of people at their departure from the convent. (News of the death of the [La Plata] archbishop arrived by *chasque* on Sunday, the 20th of November of the year 1663.)

Saturday, the 30th of May of 1665, on the eve of the Holy Trinity, in the holy orders conferred by the bishop of Panama, Don Sancho Pardo, in the church of the convent of the nuns of Santa Catalina of this city, he ordained my son, the *bachiller* José de Mugaburu, for Mass. My son Francisco de Mugaburu, of the order of Saint Francis, was also ordained to the fourth degree. There were seven ordained as priests, five deacons, eighteen subdeacons, and fifty-two in all. The others were of four degrees and tonsure, friars, and students. This same day the *bachiller* Francisco del Molino, son of my *compadre* Pedro del Molino, was ordained as deacon.

Sunday, the 21st of June of the year 1665, the large bell called "La Agonía" was hoisted up [to the belfry] of [the church of] Santa Ana. Brother Francisco, head nurse of the hospital, had ordered it to be made with the alms he solicited, and he was the one who undertook the cost of putting it in its place, which he did with his diligence in asking for charity.

First Mass of My Son José

My son, the *bachiller* José de Mugaburu, sang his first Mass in the church of the convent of Santa Clara of this city on Thursday, the 24th of June of the year 1665, day of the glorious Saint John the Baptist. His altar patron was Doctor Don Sebastián de Aguilar, prebend of this holy church. This day there were a great number of people in the church and many invited to eat at my home. Three tables were spread at which twenty men ate at a time, ecclesiastics and seculars, and a corresponding number of ladies [ate] in the bedroom. There was enough for everyone, thanks be to God.

Vicar of Santo Domingo

Thursday, the 1st of October of the year 1665, [the Dominicans] received as vicar general Father Fray Pedro de Quevedo of the order of Santo Domingo and they removed Father Fray Juan de Barbarán, who was presently vicar, due to orders which had arrived from the commander in chief in Spain, sent by Father Fray Martín Meléndez. (News was received that the vicar died outside this city on the 8th of August of 1666.)

Removal of Nuns from El Prado

Monday, the 12th of October of the year 1665, at eight in the evening the canon Balcázar, the secretary of the archbishop, his superintendent, and other chaplains, removed nine nuns of the black veil from the convent of Nuestra Señora del Prado. It was determined that the vows they had taken were invalid because they had not agreed to observe the ruling of the pious Mariana. Of these nine nuns, one was left at the convent of Santa Clara at her request, another at la Concepción, and seven at la Encarnación.

The following day the same canon removed another two of the white veil who also chose to be taken to la Encarnación. Thus, of the thirty-three religious who were at the convent, eleven left, as mentioned. Twenty-two remained at this convent of Nuestra Señora del Prado to observe the ruling and newly-imposed conditions.

Regrettable Incident of Don Juan de Esquivel

Tuesday, the 17th of November of the year 1665, at four in the afternoon Don Juan de Esquivel was found dead and hanging from a rope in the window of his room. This was a room in the house of his sister, Doña María de Esquivel, and was the house for which Pedro de Saldías had hewed the stones, next to the convent of [San José de las Monjas] Descalzas. On that day his sister and the other people of the house had gone to the theater where [the play] "*La Mujer de Per-Ibánez*" was being presented. The whole city of Lima was upset by such an event, the young man being [only] twenty-one years of age. He used to go about resplendent on a bedecked mule and with three servants. Everyone in his house said that he was demented. After things were arranged with the archbishop and his provisor and the learned men, he was buried in the cathedral of this city on Thursday, the 19th of the month, with great attendance and splendor. The dean and *cabildo* of this holy church, and the secular *cabildo* attended his funeral.

Circulation of the Bull of His Holiness

Thursday, the 26th of November, at four in the afternoon the [Papal] Bull sent by His Majesty to the archbishop of this city, Señor Don Pedro de Villagómez, was circulated through the city with the brilliant accompaniment of all the sacerdotal clergy of this city and the *caballeros*. It was to publicize the [doctrine of the] Conception of Mary, Our Lady Conceived without Original Sin, and [to petition] that the priests pray with their *otava*[31] [prayer book], and also that men as well as women say the minor service of the "Mother of God," ordered by the highest pontiff.

Death of Archbishop Villarroel

Sunday, the 29th of this month, news arrived by the *chasque* from Potosí that the archbishop of Chuquisaca, Don Fray Gaspar de Villarroel of the order of Saint Augustine, had died.

My Son José Departs Lima for Cuzco

On the morning of Monday, the 7th of December of 1665, my son the *bachiller* José de Mugaburu, presbyter, left this city of Lima for Cuzco, in the company of many *caballeros* who were going there. He went at the request of his cousin, the Very Reverend Father Fray Buenaventura de Honton, at present the Franciscan provincial of the province of San Francisco de los Charcas. He departed resplendent and very well prepared for all of his needs.

Procession of the Immaculate Conception

Tuesday, the 8th of December of the year 1665, the procession left the cathedral of this City of Kings at four in the afternoon and went past Santo Domingo to Mantas Street, and ended at

[31] *Otava* or *octava* was a small book containing the prayers for eight days.

the plaza and cathedral. All the brotherhoods of the city with their [images of] saints came out, as on the day of Corpus [Christi], and all the religious orders and all the clergy were there. [The statue of] the Virgin Mary of the Immaculate Conception and the Holy Sacrament were on beautiful litters carried by the viceroy and the gentlemen of the royal *audiencia* and the ecclesiastic and secular *cabildos*. That afternoon all the city attended the procession; this celebration in the cathedral lasted eight days, with great solemnity. All the tribunals held their celebration.

Assassination of Ignacio Santoyo

That same day, Tuesday, the 8th of December of 1665, Ignacio Santoyo was killed in his own home at the side of his mother.

Celebration of the Otava [*8-day* fiesta]

On the afternoon of Tuesday, the 15th of December, a very splendid procession left from the cathedral going around the plaza in the same manner as on Tuesday, the 8th of the month. It was without the [images of] saints of the sodalities but with their banners and with [a statue of] the Holy Virgin and everything pertaining to her day, and the Holy Sacrament, which was carried by the archbishop, Don Pedro de Villagómez. The son of the Count of Santisteban, Don Manuel de Benavides, scattered roses on the ground in the path of the Holy Sacrament, and the large silver tray was carried by Don Francisco de la Cueva, *caballero* of the order of Calatrava and battalion commander of this city and captain of the guard of the viceroy, Count of Santisteban. This celebration was offered by the vicereine, and on this morning Father Maestro Marín of the Mercedarian order gave the sermon in the cathedral.

The Year 1666

Ordinary Alcaldes

Friday, the first day of the new year of 1666, the election of the ordinary *alcaldes* of this city was held in the palace because the viceroy, Count of Santisteban, was ailing with gout. For *alcaldes* the *cabildo* elected Don Gabriel de Castilla and Don Juan de la Presa, *regidor* of this City of Kings and senior scribe of the South Sea [Pacific Ocean]. When His Excellency saw the votes he said, "The gentlemen of the *cabildo* have elected good *alcaldes* in Señor Don Gabriel de Castilla and Don José de Mendoza y Castilla," who had been presented for justices. Don Juan de la Presa was not mentioned.[32]

Election of Prior and Consuls

Monday, the 4th of this month and year, one hundred and fifty-two circulars were distributed recommending the election of Captain Agustín de Iturrizaga for consul.

Tuesday, the 5th of the month, Don Pedro de Zorilla, *caballero* of the order of Alcántara, being present at the election in the house of the *consulado* [merchant guild], was elected consul without his aspiring to it, nor being on the list of thirty candidates. Felipe de Zavala was [also] elected consul.

Parade of the Flag

This same afternoon the flag was carried in parade by the royal ensign Don José de Zúñiga, son-in-law of Bolsa de Hierro. He was in mourning [attire] with black ribbons, but the horse was not. The following Wednesday he went forth in full dress with many plumes and marched at the side of Señor Don Francisco Sarmiento, senior *oidor*. [These formations were] due to the fact that the viceroy was ill with gout, from which he was suffering.

Auto-da-fé at La Caridad

At eight in the morning of Tuesday, the 16th of February of 1666, seven convicted persons were taken from the Holy Inquisition to the church of La Caridad. Three were women censored for being sorceresses and superstitious; one was the one who played the harp in the theater; one for being married twice; another was a lay friar of the order of Saint Augustine of the province of Quito, censored for having given confession to Indians and taking alms for saying Mass, and he did not know how to read or write; two Judaizing Jews; and one heretic who had been brought forth in the *auto* of 1664. No one was flogged; only the three women were [publicly] shamed that same morning after the reading of the sentences. The remainder were exiled. Present were a great number of people, religious of all the orders, and the gentlemen of the Inquisition: Señor Don Cristóbal de Castilla, head inquisitor, Señor Doctor Don Alvaro de Ibarra, and Señor Doctor Don Juan de Huerta. With the execution of the sentences, and having walked the witches through the streets, Pedro López de Gárate, *caballero*

[32] The *cabildo* is often cited as the one democratic institution in colonial Spanish America, but as Mugaburu indicates, the viceroy sometimes disregarded the election and appointed *alcaldes*.

of the order of Santiago, was elected chief constable of the Holy Tribunal.

This *auto* was held at the church of La Caridad because the church of Santo Domingo was without a roof and they were making a dome of plaster and cane.

Death of the Count of Santisteban

The Count of Santisteban [the present viceroy] died on Wednesday, the 17th of March of 1666, at six in the morning; others say at ten at night, but at six in the morning the cathedral [bells] gave the signal. At that same hour an order was sent from the *visitador* of this royal *audiencia*, Don Juan Cornejo, *fiscal* of the royal Council of the Indies, with his chief constable and secretary and others, to the house of Señor Don Francisco Sarmiento, *oidor* of the royal *audiencia*, wherein he was notified of a royal decree of His Majesty that he was not to leave his house, under penalty of four thousand pesos to the treasury of His Majesty. That decree had not been disclosed before for certain reasons; and Señor Don Bernardo de Iturrizarra, senior *oidor* of this royal *audiencia*, was immediately received as governor.

The Count of Santisteban governed this kingdom four years, seven months, and sixteen days. His burial was Thursday afternoon, the 18th of the month, and there was much [pomp] to be seen. There were four gun salutes at the four funeral halts in the plaza; one, in front of the door of the palace where they fired nine rounds [of artillery]; another at the corner of the archbishop's palace, where another nine were fired; another at the cross of the cathedral; and the other in Mercaderes Street. In all they fired thirty-six rounds. Going along Mantas Street, [the procession] returned to Santo Domingo [church], where there were two other halts, but at these they did not fire.

The Battalion Commander

At the head of the cortege went Colonel Don Francisco de la Cueva, *caballero* of the order of Calatrava and battalion commander of this city, dragging a pike, followed by two captains of the battalion with a large segment of the troops of arquebuses and pikes, with six flags dragging. A large squadron formed in the plaza where there were many members of the battalion. The colleges, tribunals, and *encomenderos*[33] [grantees of Indian tribute] all went in order [by rank] as was customary, and all with long black cloaks. The [*audiencia*] president and *oidores* followed.

Señor Don Manuel de Benavides, son of the deceased viceroy, walked between Don Bernardo de Iturrizarra and the *visitador.*

Mass in the Presence of the Body

Saturday, the 20th of the month, Archbishop Don Pedro de Villagómez with his canons went to the Mass in the presence of the body. He went in his carriage to [the church of] Santo Domingo. Later all the others came out of the palace wearing their funeral cloaks in the same manner as on the day of the burial, except for the president and *oidores* who wore their mourning togas.

Funeral Services

Wednesday, the 31st of March of the year 1666, memorial funeral services for the deceased viceroy were held at Santo Domingo [church], where [members of] all the religious orders and recollects went to sing the Mass and responsory. The catafalque reached to the ceiling and was very elaborate, of great architecture, and on which there were eight hundred candles. At ten in the morning all the mourners left the palace: the [deceased viceroy's] family, the *consulado*, the university, and the *cabildo* of the city, and Señor Don Manuel, son of the viceroy, with his cloak dragging, [walked] between the *visitador* and Don Bernardo de Iturrizarra. The gentlemen of the *audiencia* did not wear long black cloaks, but the *encomenderos* appeared with their cloaks dragging. The members of the company on duty formed a line from the palace to Santo Domingo [church]. The company of the silversmiths, with its captain Don Juan de Beingolea, was in front. The palace company, which is the mercenary one, with its captain, Don Pedro de Mendoza, went as rearguard, the flags dragging. On this day the sermon and responsories ended at two in the afternoon. They [the mourners] returned in the same manner to the palace. Later, funeral services were held at San Agustín and San Francisco [churches].

First Proclamation of Señor Iturrizarra

Wednesday, the 7th of April of 1666, at eleven in the morning [Governor Iturrizarra] issued a proclamation [stipulating] that all those [military men] receiving a salary from His Majesty should go to the port of Callao on Saturday the 10th to pass

[33] An *encomendero* was an individual who for distinguished service received a royal grant of the tribute and/or labor of Indians within a certain boundary, with the duty of protecting and Christianizing them.

muster. The palace company, of which Don Pedro de Mendoza y Toledo was captain, went the following Thursday. On that day Captain Don Juan de Beingolea with his company of silversmiths entered on guard at the palace, and until Monday, when the other [company] whose captain was Francisco Ruíz [de la Cueva] returned from Callao, other companies of this battalion of Lima served on guard in the palace.

Friday, the 9th of the month, Señor Don Bernardo de Iturrizarra, dressed in black without a cape and with his staff of command, went to Callao, where the corps battalion commander of Callao, Don Tomás Pardo, received him with a squadron in the main plaza, and they lowered all the flags toward him. His Lordship ordered the squadron to open and close formation, and all the pieces [of artillery] of the [sea] wall were thereupon immediately fired. He left for Callao with a great retinue of *caballeros* and captains who followed him.

Saturday, the 10th of the month, all the infantry and seamen passed muster, and he remained in Callao until Tuesday, the 15th of the month.

Monday, the 12th of April, the company of Captain Francisco Ruíz de la Cueva of that city came from Callao to enter on guard in this palace of Lima.

Death of Sergeant Major Domingo de Albizu

Wednesday, 5th of May, the sergeant major Domingo de Albizu left his house for Surco to convalesce. He died the following Thursday at six in the morning in the town of Surco at the house of Doña Francisca de Coca. That day they brought his body to Lima.

Friday, the 7th of the month, at six in the afternoon he was buried in his uniform at the monastery of San Francisco. He was buried without any ceremony, not in a vault but as a private individual.

Imprisonment of Don César

Thursday, the 20th of May of 1666, Doctor Don César [de Bandier] was imprisoned by the Holy Office. Monday, the 24th of the month, his four mules were sold in the plaza of this city in the presence of the receiver of the Holy Office, canon Don Esteban de Ibarra, the chief constable, Don García de Hijar y Mendoza, and secretary Don Pedro de Olarte.

Death of Captain Francisco de Jaúregui

Captain Francisco de Jaúregui died without making a will. Being rather burdened with business matters he left power of attorney to the accountant Domingo de Barrambio, Captain Pedro de Echevarría, Martín de Iturraín, and to another friend. All his property and other items were immediately attached by the Court of the Deceased. He died at dawn on the 6th of July of 1666 and was buried in the Recollect of the Magdalena, in the chapel of Our Lady of the Rosary.

Death of Doña Magdalena de Urrutia

Doña Magdalena de Urrutia died intestate, and without being able to receive the sacraments. At the time of her death she was the legitimate wife of Don Andrés de Vilela, former president of this royal *audiencia*. She was found dead at dawn on Wednesday, the 14th of July of the year 1666, and was buried with great ostentation on Thursday, the 15th of the month, in the monastery of San Francisco.

News of the Death of the King

Saturday, the 24th of July of the year 1666, on the eve of Saint James, a dispatch ship arrived at this city bringing news of the death of the king, our lord, Philip IV, "the Great," on the 17th of September of the year 1665. He died from a blood hemorrhage which lasted five days until his death. There was also news that the archbishop of Toledo and other kings and potentates were dead, and that the pontiff was in the last days of his life. [We learned] how our lady the queen was governing with four grandees and the president of Castile until our prince and lord Charles II, King of Spain and of everything else belonging to him as legitimate heir of our King Philip IV his father, reaches the age of fourteen years.

Monday, the 26th of the month, the day of Saint Ann, the cathedral of this city gave the signal, tolling the large bell one hundred times, whereupon all the monasteries and churches of this city rang their bells from two in the afternoon until prayertime [sunset].

Wednesday, the 1st of September, a proclamation was issued at four in the afternoon by the [*audiencia*] president and *oidores*, who were Don Bernardo de Iturrizarra, Don Bartolomé de Salazar, Don Pedro González de Guzmán, Don Fernando de Velasco, and Don Francisco de Mejía, that due to the death of our king and lord Philip IV, and for the great loss and grief felt in the entire kingdom, everyone, men and women, should dress in mourning within three days in accordance with the position and means of each one. And these gentlemen ordered that this proclamation be circulated because they governed upon the death of the Count of Santisteban, who had been viceroy of these kingdoms.

For the execution of this proclamation the following went forth, heralded by six clarions: all the ministers of justice; the two ordinary *alcaldes*; the chief constable of the city, Don Nicolás de Torres; the *alcalde*, Don Gabriel de Castilla; Don José de Mendoza y Castilla; and the secretary of the *cabildo*, Francisco de Cárdenas. All were dressed in mourning indicating great sorrow. At the same hour that the proclamation was being heralded in the plaza, thirty pieces of artillery were fired at the port of Callao, which were heard as if they were being fired in the plaza of Lima, causing profound feeling.

Second Dispatch Ship

Friday, the 10th of September of the year 1666, at five in the afternoon a dispatch ship from Spain arrived at this city, bearing the royal decree of the queen, our lady, ordering that the *visitador* discontinue his visit and embark for Spain. This decree was presented to him by the two scribes of the chamber on Monday, the 3rd of this month and year.

Tuesday, the 14th of September, by order of the president and *oidores* who governed upon the death of the Viceroy Count of Santisteban, the *oidor* Don Francisco Sarmiento was notified of this [decree] after having been exiled at Pachacámac for six months by the *visitador*. And [the *visitador*] having come to this city, the president and *oidores* notified him through the two scribes of the chamber not to enter the *audiencia* and to prepare himself to depart for Spain on the first galleons to leave the port of Callao.

That same day Juan de Padilla, senior *alcalde* of the hall of crime, was notified not to enter therein, but to embark for Mexico, otherwise he would receive no salary.

Funeral Rites for Our King and Lord, Don Philip IV

Thursday, the 16th of September, and Friday, the 17th, funeral rites for our king and lord were held in the cathedral of this city with as much solemnity and grandeur as that which could have been celebrated in the court of our king and lord [in Spain]. A wooden palisade was constructed from the palace to the cathedral, around the plaza past the [place of the] scribes to the Perdón door of the cathedral. Five companies of the battalion with Colonel Don Francisco de la Cueva and his five captains sallied forth; each company was composed of one hundred men dressed in mourning. The order in which they appeared was the same as in the funeral services for the prince. Two hundred fifty-four persons came out dressed in mourning with long black funeral cloaks. Don Bernardo de Iturrizarra did not appear at these services as he was sick in bed. Don Bartolomé de Salazar officiated as president, and on his left went Don Manuel, son of the Count of Santisteban. In Callao, an artillery piece was fired each hour. In these [two] days two thousand six hundred and thirty-one pounds of [candle] wax were used, which makes 26 quintals, one arroba, and eleven pounds, not counting what was given to each religious order that came to the cathedral to say Mass and a responsory. There were one hundred candles weighing a pound each for every religious order, and to the parishes, for the same [reason], fifty candles weighing a pound each.

The day of the funeral services, which was Thursday afternoon, the first to go inside the palisaded enclosure were the four religious orders with all their communities, crosses [held] high, [and] with [the statues of] Saint Dominic, Saint Francis, Saint Augustine, and Our Lady of Ransom [Merced]. Behind Archbishop Don Pedro de Villagómez, who was wearing a sombrero over a clergyman's cap and a long train, and following all the religious orders, were all the [secular] clergy in surplices, totaling more than four hundred priests; and then the prebends and canons with their long cloaks of black taffeta. Then followed Colonel Don Francisco de la Cueva and his captains, and then all the rest referred to and recorded on folio sixty-two [of Mugaburu's diary] that went to the burial of Prince Don Baltasar. A large catafalque which reached to the ceiling was constructed in the cathedral. It was of great architecture and interesting detail with space for more than three thousand candles where the referred-to wax was placed and consumed. All the church was hung with drapings of black damask with Sevillian gold coins, and the four pillars in front of the chorus in black damask and rich colored fabrics. All the ceiling or dome of the cathedral was covered with black buckram. It was all such [a wonder] that there was nothing [better] left to see. It was complete.

The following day, Friday, the 17th of the month of September, neither the archbishop nor his clergy, nor the religious orders went to the enclosure, only the secular clergy. During the whole day, all the religious orders held their sung Mass with responsory, and each order was given one hundred candles of a pound each; and all the parishes did likewise and were given fifty candles of a pound each for every parish and the priest and his clergy. This same day Archbishop Don Pedro de Villagómez said the pontifical Mass, and the canon Palma gave the sermon. They left the church at two in the afternoon.

Monday, the 27th of the month of September of the year 1666, at the church of the convent of the Sisters of the Concepción of this city, a very elaborate and ostentatious catafalque was constructed, where a great number of lighted candles were placed. In the middle of the catafalque there was a large world globe on which there was a figure of our king and lord, very much in his likeness, with his crown of gold, and in his hands a column, and on the column a gold chalice. The church was decorated all around with drapings of damask and rich colored fabrics, and all replete with a thousand sonnets.

The Inquisitors

Monday evening all the Inquisition officials and their servants came forth, and all the consultors and classifiers, accountant, and secretaries, and then the chief constable of this Holy Tribunal, Don García de Hijar y Mendoza, *caballero* of the order of Santiago, with the banner of the green cross [Inquisition symbol]. At the end were the three gentlemen of the Inquisition, Señor Don Cristóbal de Castilla, Señor Don Alvaro de Ibarra, and Señor Huerta with their sombreros over their clerical caps. They wore very long cloaks of black Holland cloth, dragging the ground, and all the rest also wore their long cloaks of heavy flannel. All the street entrances were closed. This evening they set out at eight at night.

They appeared the following day in the same order. Inquisitor Don Cristóbal de Castilla said the high Mass; Father Maestro Fray Francisco Messía of the Mercedarian order, the Gospel; and the sermon was given this day by Father Avendaño of the Society of Jesus. There were six choruses of music, three of seculars and three of nuns. This day they left at the end of the services, at two in the afternoon.

Acclamation of Our King and Lord Charles II

Sunday, the 17th of October of the year 1666, was when the acclamation of our king and lord Charles II, may God protect this name many years, was celebrated.

The throne where the portrait of our king and lord was placed was impressive. It was set up next to the door of the palace, on the left as one enters from the plaza. There was much to see in the tableau, where there were many large figures, and the Inca and Coya [Indian empress] offering our king and lord, with great reverence, an imperial crown, and the Coya, one of laurel. The two *alcaldes*, Don Gabriel de Castilla and Don José de Mendoza y Castilla, the chief constable of the city, Don A. de Torres, and Don Bartolomé de Azaña removed the portrait from the council hall. In the plaza there was a large formation of Spaniards made up of more than a thousand men with twelve captains and eight cavalry companies with their captains, the four of the city and the four of rural estates, and another two squadrons of Indians. All were formed by the adjutant Gaspar de Savariego and his battalion commander, Don Francisco de la Cueva y Guzmán, *caballero* of the order of Calatrava, and Sergeant Josephe de Mugaburu. There were also ten pieces of artillery with their shelters, and two very well decorated carts were set up in the plaza by Lieutenant General Don Miguel de las Cuevas, with his captain, artillery sergeant, and artillerymen.

Musket and Artillery Charge

A simultaneous charge [of artillery and muskets] was fired at the same time that the portrait appeared in the plaza, which caused great admiration. The shouts and acclamations were, "Long live the King our Lord!"

Transfer of the Flag

After the royal standard was brought from the *cabildo* amidst the illustrious accompaniment of the city council and a great number of *caballeros*, the royal ensign Don José de Zúñiga, who appeared gallantly attired and with many lackeys and orderlies, surrendered the royal standard to Señor Don Bernardo de Iturrizarra, senior *oidor* and president, [as well as] governor and captain general on the death of the viceroy Count of Santisteban. The king at arms thrice saying, "Hear ye, hear ye, hear ye," the president said three times in a loud voice, "Castile, Leon, and Peru for the king our lord Don Carlos II, may he live many years!" Whereupon the flag of His Lordship was lowered three times and everyone exclaimed, "*Viva, viva, viva,* may he live for many years!" After this he returned the flag to the royal ensign, who returned the courtesies of His Lordship and left with the flag, putting it in the center of the stage. The king at arms again requested silence three times, then the royal ensign repeated in a loud voice the same words, "Castile, Leon, and Peru for the king our lord Don Carlos II, may he live many years!" Then the squadron rendered the same musket and artillery salute. This ceremony on the stage being over, the due reverences having been paid to His Majesty, all descended and mounted their horses, and the royal ensign returned with the flag to face the portrait of our king. He performed three reverences, lowering the flag three times, and continued to the halls of the *cabildo* where he hung the flag in its regular place, accompanied by two of the senior councilmen, and the king at arms. All the retinue and the citizens returned there, and upon lowering the portrait of His Majesty, the last artillery and musket salute was given, and the portrait was placed in the room from which they took it. Then everyone accompanied the royal *audiencia*, all [of whom were] on horseback, to the cathedral to offer thanks. They sang the *Te Deum laudamus* and the customary prayers for such ceremonies. After leaving the cathedral, all the royal *audiencia* circled the plaza until they reached the palace. Then the squadron was disbanded, which was after the [evening] prayer.

Then two company battalions, the one of Captain Don José Tamayo, and the other of Captain Don Pedro de Córdova and his sergeant Josephe de Mugaburu, went out [as honor guard] in attendance of the royal flag which was to remain eight days in the *cabildo*. At eight in the evening the two *alcaldes* indicated that the two companies should withdraw, with which the event terminated.

Proclamation Regarding the Armada

Saturday, the 20th of November of the year 1666, at five in the afternoon a proclamation was issued that the armada for Panama was to depart Wednesday, the 24th of the month. It was issued by the president and *oidores* who governed upon the death of the viceroy. This proclamation was signed by the licentiate Don Bernardo de Iturrizarra, Don Bartolomé de Salazar, Don Francisco de Velasco y Gamboa, and Don Diego Cristóbal Mejía. One hundred merchants were named in the proclamation, ten for

Spain and the rest for Tierra Firme. The first one named was Juan Zorrilla de la Gándara for Spain, and the others followed; something that had never before been done. There was a penalty of two thousand pesos for each one named if they had not embarked by the 24th of the month; one thousand pesos would be added to the distribution of the gentlemen of the royal Council of the Indies, the other thousand for the expenses incurred in the funeral rites for our king and lord Philip IV.

Departure of the Armada

Friday, the 10th of December of 1666, the armada left the port of Callao for Panama with the treasure of His Majesty, may the Lord protect him, and of individuals. This day there were more than twenty million [pesos] just in bars of silver and *reales*, which was more than had ever been sent from the time of the discovery of Peru to the present day.

The Countess of Santisteban

The Countess of Santisteban, widow of the [ex-viceroy] count, and all her family also sailed in this armada. She left the palace in Lima at ten in the morning of Thursday, the 9th of the month, with much accompaniment, and she arrived at the port of Callao at one in the afternoon. At two o'clock she embarked from her carriage, which had gone right up to the dock. That night with all her people she slept on board.

The *visitador* Don Juan Cornejo with all his family embarked in this same armada. He had been in this city two years, two months and two days, until the day when the armada set sail.

This armada left at one in the afternoon. The flagship and consort vessel set sail along with two merchant ships, the one of Captain Pedro de Chavarría, and the other of the son of Captain Manuel Rodríquez, upon which there were many merchants, well invested [with capital]. Don Manuel de Benavides went as general of this armada as far as Panama, and Don Juan de Ala as admiral. Don José de Alzamora also went on the consort to come back on the return trip as general.

Proclamation of the Papal Bull

Sunday, the 12th of December of the year 1666, the [papal] bull of the Holy Crusade was made public. Present at the proclamation were all the gentlemen of the royal *audiencia*; Señor Don Bernardo de Iturrizarra as president and captain general was in the first seat with his pillow at his feet. His Lordship arose from his chair, and accompanied by the canons and ordinary *alcaldes*, ascended the main altar of San Francisco [church]. He, alone, kissed the Holy Bull, then the other gentlemen followed him two by two. From San Francisco the procession went with the accompaniment of all the religious orders and the whole city to the cathedral. After the Holy Bull was placed on the main altar, the commissary of the Holy Crusade, Señor Don Juan de Cabrera, went down and sat in his purple velvet chair. Señor Don Bernardo de Iturrizarra [was] in the first place, and in the second, the commissary general Don Juan de Cabrera; then followed Don Andrés de Vilela and Señor Don Sebastián de Alcocer as guests since they were retired. Then followed the remaining gentlemen. On this day Father Juan Laynes of the Franciscan order gave the sermon in the cathedral.

Indian Rebellion Thursday, the 16th of December of the year 1666, eighth day [of the fiesta] of the Immaculate Conception of Our Lady, the iniquity of the Indians who wanted to stage an uprising in this city and kill all the Spaniards was discovered. They planned to set fires in many parts of the city and release the water from the large canal of Santa Clara.

Staff of General Wednesday, the 22nd of December of 1666, Don Baltasar Pardo of the order of Santiago took possession [of the staff] as general of Callao. On this day he went to be received at Callao, and at the reception there was a formation in the port plaza, and many pieces of artillery were fired. He went with many *caballeros*, and he sent four trumpeters ahead of him.

Men to Guachipa Friday, the 31st of December, at eight at night three hundred men went with General Don Baltasar Pardo to the hills of Oropesa, Guachipa, and other parts as a result of a dispatch that was received indicating that more than three thousand Indians were gathering in that region for [an uprising on] the night of the eve of the Epiphany. That same night the captain of the silversmiths, Juan de Beingolea, was on guard, and his whole company and the one of the cavalry on duty in this city all went out on horseback and hired mules. They returned Saturday, the 1st of January, at nine in the morning without having come across nor seen anything for which they went in search [rebellious Indians].

The Year 1667

Saturday, the 5th of February of the year 1667, at eight at night Presa, *regidor* of this city, and Don José de Torres y Zúñiga were elected ordinary *alcaldes*. *The New Year*

Wednesday, the 5th of the present [month], Captain Juan de Beingolea was elected prior of the merchant guild, and Cosme de Ascurra, consul. *Prior and Consuls*

At midnight on Monday, the 3rd of January of 1667, Don Pedro Bohorques was executed by garrote in the court prison. At dawn on Tuesday his body was hung in the plaza and his head cut off and placed on the bridge.[34] *Garrote for Don Pedro Bohórquez*

Monday, the 21st of January of 1667, eight Indians were hanged for the uprising they had planned, and three Indians were punished with ten years in the galleys. Many others were also sent to the galleys. After the hangings, the eight heads were removed and placed on the bridge, and they [their bodies] were quartered and placed in the streets. This justice was done on Monday, in the afternoon, with the whole city gathering at the plaza. The duty company of Saint Lazarus that was on guard that afternoon was utilized in the plaza, and ten men from the other companies went with lances to assist until justice was rendered. *Eight Indians Hanged*

(The battalion companies had been in their quarters from the 17th of December of 1666 until the 4th of February of the year 1667. They began guard duty at the palace as of Friday, the 17th of December of the year 1666.)

Saturday, the 5th of February of the year 1667, at eight at night a pistol shot was fired at Don Sebastián de Navarrete while he was traveling in his carriage. The bullet struck him in the right hand causing great pain. He was fired on near Ensign Estacio's gate. *Pistol Shot at Don Sebastián de Navarrete*

Bishop Don Vasco de Contreras, the bishop who came from Popayán to serve in Huamanga, died in this City of Kings on

[34] Pedro de Bohorques was a Spanish soldier who tried to establish an Indian kingdom in the Andes with himself as king. See Constantino Bayle, S.J., "Historia peregrina de un Inca andaluz," *De Razón y Fé* (Madrid, 1927).

Death of Bishop Contreras

Wednesday, the 2nd of March, at eleven-thirty in the morning. He was buried in this cathedral Thursday afternoon, the 3rd of March of 1667.

Father Fray Cristóbal de Contreras was received as or elected as Franciscan commissary general on Wednesday, the 23rd of March of 1667, and the election was held at the Recollect. He was secretary to Father Fray Miguel de Molina, commissary general of San Francisco. The election was approved by the whole order.

Colonel Francisco de la Cueva

Thursday, the 21st of July of 1667, Colonel Don Francisco de la Cueva, *caballero* of the order of Santiago, who was battalion commander of the Lima battalion, went to Callao with General Don Baltasar Pardo, *caballero* of the order of Santiago and a great following of *caballeros*. That same afternoon the company that Don Antonio de Silva had in Callao was given to Colonel Don Francisco de la Cueva by Don Baltasar Pardo so that he would be battalion commander of the presidio of Callao.

Jesuit Bell

The large bell of the Society of Jesus, said to weigh two hundred and twenty quintals [hundredweights] and cast by a brother of the Society called Father Pedro Suárez, was hoisted [to the belfry] on Saturday, the 16th of July of the year 1667, exactly at twelve noon. Archbishop Don Pedro de Villagómez blessed it before it was positioned.

Dominican Provincial

Sunday, the 24th of July of the year 1667, the Very Reverend Father Fray Juan González was elected provincial of Santo Domingo [monastery] to the gratification of the entire order. Monday, the day of Saint James, he came, as is customary, to [the monastery of] San Francisco with all corresponding accompaniment.

My *compadre* Pedro de Molino died Saturday, the 31st of July of the year 1667, at seven-thirty in the morning. He was buried Sunday, the 31st of the month, in his monastery as an Augustinian friar, in a vault of that cloister where the Holy Virgin of the [Immaculate] Conception is located.

Saturday, the 13th of August of the year 1667, Don Alonso Bravo, chief accountant of the tribunal of accounts, took on the habit of the order of Alcántara in Monserrate [hermitage].

The dispatch ship, bearing news of the arrival at Panama of the [new] viceroy, Count of Lemos, reached this city Saturday, the 6th of August of the year 1667. It was brought by Captain Nicolás Serrano. *Dispatch Ship from Panama*

Thursday, the 18th of August of the year 1667, Don Juan de Urdanegui joined the order of Santiago at the monastery of San Agustín amidst great applause of the *caballeros*. There were twenty-six gentlemen of his order present. His sponsor was General Don Baltasar Pardo de Figueroa.

The battalion commander of Callao, Don Tomás Pardo, died on Friday, the 26th of August of the year 1667, at two in the afternoon. He was buried Saturday, the 27th, at the monastery of San Francisco of that port of Callao. On the day they took him to be buried, his company went with the body from his house to the main plaza where there was a formation of the presidio companies. [The cortege] passed in review in front of the formation. There were four funeral halts, and at the end of the responsory at each stop a piece of artillery was fired in his honor. They returned by way of the street that goes from Santo Domingo to the monastery of San Francisco, accompanied by a great number of people from this city of Lima. At this time Don Baltasar Pardo de Figueroa was general of Callao. *Death of the Callao Battalion Commander*

Don Francisco de Valverde, *caballero* of the order of Santiago and lieutenant of the battalion commander, died at dawn on Monday, the 12th of September of the year 1667. He was buried at the Society of Jesus [monastery] on Tuesday morning. The entire city, the *caballeros*, ecclesiastic and secular *cabildos*, all the gentlemen of the royal *audiencia*, and up to forty infantrymen of the two companies who were at that moment preparing to leave, attended his burial. There were no flags but only presentation of arms. *Death of Don Francisco de Valverde*

Wednesday, the 28th of September of this year, a soldier on horseback arrived with information that His Excellency the Count of Lemos had arrived at Paita [Peru] on the 14th of the month, and that he planned to leave that port by sea on Sunday, the 25th of this month and year. He was bringing with him as a prisoner aboard the flagship the [*audiencia*] president of Panama, Don Juan de Guzmán.

Auto-da-Fé On Saturday morning, the 8th of October of the year 1667, an auto-da-fé was held in the church of the Holy Office wherein four [persons] were sentenced. [One was Doctor] Don César [de Bandier, or Nicolás Legras], the physician brought [to Peru] by the viceroy Count of Santisteban, and the greatest heretic known in these times. [Born in France in 1600,] he was the son of a Christian father and mother, and was a priest. Later he married in Rome and from there went to Constantinople, where he became a great herb doctor and cured the sultan of Turkey. He traveled all over the world, and in this city cured many and killed many more. He was a physician at the royal hospital of Santa Ana of this City of Kings; while he was curing he killed more than two thousand Indians. And he was a doctor of this royal university, a doctor of medicine. This so-and-so denied the immortality of the soul, and his errors were worse than Luther, Arius, Mohammed, or any of the sectarians. He was of such a type that he went up to paintings of the crucified and dying Jesus Christ and one of the Virgin of Solitude, and he said to the holy Virgin, "Why is that [female] liar crying for a son that has deceived the world?" There were so many insults and blasphemies and dishonest words that he said to the holy Virgin, that I do not write them for the great horror and scandal they cause to Christian hearers. They were so bad that in relating his wickedness and evil deeds [at the Inquisition], all those who heard became riled up, and if the gentlemen of the Inquisition had not ordered that no more be read, they would have killed him right in the chapel of the Holy Office. The sentence was to wear a sanbenito, life imprisonment, and exile from these kingdoms of Peru. He went to the Inquisition of Seville to serve out his sentence.

The following day, Sunday, the 9th of October, more than two thousand souls awaited in the event they brought him out to the cathedral to hear Mass, and with determination, young and old [awaited] to stone him to death. But the gentlemen [of the Inquisition] knowing that there was such a tumult, ordered that neither he nor the other two go out to hear Mass. His nephew [Luis Bandier or Luis Legras] was as great a heretic as he. They gave him the same sentence and took him to the Society of Jesus [monastery].

[The third penitent sentenced by the Inquisition was the Carmelite Friar César Pasani Beniboli, a native of Modena, Italy.] He was a great heretic, and being a priest said Mass, this dishonest and lascivious dog. While relating his evil doings, he said that in a certain city [La Paz, Upper Peru] he had carnally known more than three hundred and sixty women, and in a convent of nuns had committed many sacrileges. They brought him prisoner [from the mines of Puno] en route to Buenos Aires by way of Chile. They gave him the same sentence and took him to the Franciscan monastery of this city.

The Carmelite Friar

Friday, the 14th of October of the year 1667, at four in the afternoon the Holy Sacrament was carried out of the chapel of the Holy Office in the hands of the chief inquisitor, Don Cristóbal de Castilla, whose acolytes were two somber Dominican friars. The first two poles of the canopy were carried by the canons, the others by the prelates of the religious orders, and the insignia by the vicar of Santo Domingo. The same image of the [Virgin of] Solitude and the Holy Christ, towards which the heretic dog [Don César de Bandier] directed so many insults, were brought out in the procession. The image was carried by the clerical priests, and the Holy Christ by four grave religious of the Dominican order.

Procession of the Gentlemen of the Inquisition

From the Inquisition to Santo Domingo [church] all the streets were swept and sprinkled, the ground full of flowers; balconies and windows were hung with great display. All the religious orders and the Society of Jesus attended with lighted candles in their hands. In this procession there were almost eighty students dressed as angels, all very well costumed, [as well as] all the secular priests, *caballeros*, and residents with their lighted torches. The Holy Sacrament was uncovered during the entire procession.

The following Saturday at Santo Domingo [church] there was rejoicing. Head inquisitor Don Cristóbal de Castilla said Mass. On this day Father Maestro Fray Meléndez of the Dominican order gave the sermon in praise of the Virgin. The other two inquisitors, Don Alvaro de Ibarra and Don Juan de la Huerta, participated in the Mass and the procession with their candles in hand. All the [Inquisition] officers attended these two days with their insignias on their chests. The banner of the faith was carried by Señor Don García de Híjar y Mendoza, *caballero* of the order of Santiago and chief constable of the Holy Office.

The inquisitors told Archbishop Don Pedro de Villagómez

that His Grace should order and instruct where the two images of Jesus Christ and his Holy Mother of the Solitude should be placed. His Grace chose the convent of Nuestra Señora del Prado.

The Archbishop to Santo Domingo

On the afternoon of Saturday, the 15th of October, the archbishop went in full regalia and with his canons and clergy from the cathedral to the church of Santo Domingo. They returned in procession to the cathedral with the Holy Sacrament, carried by the archbishop, and the two images of Jesus Christ and his Holy Mother of the Solitude. The main altar was draped as on the day of the Corpus [Christi]. The Holy Sacrament was uncovered Sunday, Monday, and Tuesday. There was great rejoicing. The canon Balcázar delivered the sermon on Tuesday morning in vindication of the Holy Virgin of the Solitude.

Procession of the Archbishop

Tuesday, the 18th of this month and year, at four in the afternoon a magnificent procession set forth from the cathedral to the convent of the Sisters of [Nuestra Señora] del Prado. The Holy Sacrament was borne by the archbishop accompanied by his canons and more than eight hundred clerics in surplices with lighted candles in their hands, and all the religious orders in like manner. All the sodalities were present as on the day of Corpus [Christi], and many little [children costumed as] angels followed strewing flowers. The streets from the cathedral to the Prado [convent] were swept and sprinkled and the ground full of flowers. The balconies and windows were full of drapings, and [there were] many altars. The two images of Jesus Christ and his Holy Mother of the Solitude went at the head [of the procession]. Stopping at an altar in front of the main door of the convent of [San José de las Monjas] Descalzas, at the station of the Holy Sacrament six nuns of this convent came out—one was the abbess, another the prioress, two who seemed to be professed [nuns], and two lay sisters—carrying silver trays, strewing flowers. My son, Antonio de Mugaburu, eleven years of age and made up as an angel, very richly dressed, with a long-stemmed lily a yard long in his hand and a silver tray filled with flowers, went in front of the little nuns. Behind them was another child dressed as a cleric with surplice, biretta, and a candle in his hands, representing a chaplain. The whole city thought it [the procession] was very good and the archbishop and all the clergy were proud that it had turned out so well. All the city, men and women, the secular *cabildo*, the president and *oidores*, with all the accompaniment of the cavalry, participated in the procession. At all the street entrances [there were] infantry soldiers; thus no carriages could enter the streets through which the procession passed. At the [hour of the] Ave María [the procession] arrived at [the convent of] Nuestra Señora del Prado, where His Grace gave his benediction, putting the Holy Sacrament in its place, and the Holy Christ at the right side of the main altar and his Holy Mother on the other side. The novena lasted nine days with great rejoicing. His Grace granted indulgences to all persons who attended that church and prayed there what they felt in devotion and applied it to the vindication of the Holy Virgin of Solitude, and there were great sermons on this same topic.

Reception of the Saints

From [Nuestra Señora] del Prado to El Carmen [convent] the two images of Jesus Christ and his Holy Mother were awaited by [images of] the apostle James, Saint Joachim with Our Lady, Saint Joseph, Saint Augustine, Saint Michael and many other saints, and the giants [large papier-mache figures] of the day of Corpus [Christi], and many dances. From the small plaza of the Inquisition to the Prado [convent] there were many altars, all filled with arches and many [artificial] clouds filled with doves and birds. There was much happiness and consolation for all Christians; another day of such rejoicing had not been seen in Lima.

Arrival of the Ambassador of the Count of Lemos

Sunday, the 23rd of October, at five in the afternoon Don Jacinto Romero Caamano, ambassador of [Don Pedro Fernández de Castro] the Count of Lemos who was coming as viceroy of these kingdoms of Peru, entered this city. Because of the death of the viceroy Count of Santisteban, the *oidores* received him in the council hall with the ceremonial throne and table removed. The ambassador spoke to them of His Excellency, and all the *oidores* were there: Señor Don Bernardo de Iturrizarra as president and captain general, Señor Don Bartolomé de Salazar, Señor Don Pedro Guemes, Señor Don Fernando de Velasco, Señor Don Diego Cristóbal Messía, and Señor Don Juan de Munive. They seated the ambassador next to the president. With charming eloquence he gave a lengthy account of the viceroy, his parents and grandparents, and of all his ancestry. Don Bernardo de Iturrizarra gave him lodgings next to his house in the small plaza of San Diego, and he was accompanied by all the regiment and cavalry of this city.

He entered [the city] between the two *alcaldes*, Don Juan de la Presa and Don José de Torres y Zúñiga.

Procession to the Holy Office

Friday, the 28th of October of the year 1667, at four in the afternoon the procession in retaliation for insults by the heretic Don César [de Bandier] to the Holy Mary of Solitude left the chapel of La Soledad. The holy image of La Soledad with its beautiful and costly litter appeared in the procession. The battalion commander of this city, Don Francisco de la Cueva, *caballero* of the order of Calatrava, accompanied by all the *caballeros* of this city with burning torches in their hands, carried the banner before this image. A statue of the crucified Holy Christ followed, accompanied and lighted by many men and women, and at the end was the Holy Sacrament carried by the commissary general, Father Cristóbal de Contreras. At the head [of the procession] went all the friars of San Francisco, barefoot, and those of Guadalupe, with flaming torches in hand. And there was magnificent music preceding the images and the Holy Sacrament. The procession left the chapel and proceeded down the street of the archbishop's [palace], went around the entire plaza and entered the cathedral, going up to the main altar where they deposited the Holy Sacrament. There they sang and all the canons came forth to receive it and burn incense. Then the procession went up the street as far as a block from La Concepción [convent] and circled around the chapel of La Soledad. The canons accompanied the procession up to the cathedral, and then took leave. There was a novena in the chapel of La Soledad with the Holy Sacrament uncovered. And there was tremendous rejoicing.

Wednesday, the 2nd of November of 1667, bulls were run for the ambassador of the Count of Lemos.

Death of Lieutenant Juan Azáldegui

Wednesday, the 9th of November of the year 1667, at midday the [*audiencia*] president Don Bernardo de Iturrizarra with a squadron of cavalry soldiers was going in his carriage towards Callao to see if the consort ship in which the Count of Lemos was arriving had anchored. In the side street named Juan Simón he told the captain of the hall of arms of this city, who was Nicolás

Pérez de León, to halt the cavalry troops that went ahead. They halted and fell in behind his carriage. The aforementioned Nicolás Pérez said to Lieutenant Juan de Azáldegui with superiority, "Halt and do not pass ahead," as though it were he who had ordered it, without mentioning that the president had told him to do so. And the lieutenant replied, "Your Honor doesn't have to order anything, I know what I have to do and I understand it better than Your Honor." With this, words ensued and Nicolás Pérez de León took out his sword and thrust it into Lieutenant Juan de Azáldegui, who immediately fell down dead, without having been able to confess [his sins]. This was at the step of president Don Bernardo de Iturrizarra's carriage. The soldiers of that same troop seized Pérez in the act, and the president ordered that he be taken prisoner to the court prison. Don Lucas de Almeida, being the adjutant of the troops, and to whom it corresponded to accompany the soldiers, did not go [back to Lima]; instead he took over [the captain's post] and went to Callao. (Don Lucas de Almeida, adjutant of this cavalry troop, died on the 10th of December of the year 1667.)

Arrival of the Count of Lemos at Callao

Wednesday, the 9th of November of the year 1667, at three in the morning the consort ship fired a piece of artillery at some distance from the island [of San Lorenzo] and at four in the morning the shot was answered from the port of Callao with three pieces of artillery, which were heard in this city. As anxious as everyone was, all became excited and rushed to Callao to watch the ship's arrival. At twelve noon it started approaching the island and came all sails set facing the river of Callao, and there made a turn towards the sea. With this turn and another it made before anchoring, which must have been around seven at night, more than two hundred pieces [of artillery] were fired from land, the forts, and the ship *San Francisco Solano* which was anchored in the port, functioning as consort. The vessel in which His Excellency came fired nine pieces. His Excellency slept on board the ship that night. There were many boats with all the *caballeros* of this city, but they did not reach the ship until it anchored.

Day of the Landing

Thursday, the 10th of November of the year 1667, at five in the morning after the countersign was given, a military salute was fired with all the artillery of that port. Thereupon the sea wall was immediately filled with men and women, and it looked like a garden of flowers with the variety of mantillas and costly clothing that had been worn for the occasion, by the men as well as the women. Another such entrance of a viceroy had never before been seen.

Disembarkation of the Viceroy

From early morning until he disembarked, which was at eleven, thirty-six boats and small craft filled with men and women circled the ship. To disembark the viceroy, vicereine, and all the family, there was a very large raft with a canopy of taffeta, and a dais with six velvet pillows and a chair of the same for the viceroy. More than one hundred persons came in the raft pulled by two small boats with six rowers each. After [the crew] shouted farewell, the raft pulled away and the warship fired nine pieces of artillery. The salute was returned from land with all the pieces of artillery as before.

This raft arrived at another larger one awaiting at the shore edge with two sedan chairs, one of green velvet, where the duenna sat with a baby son of the viceroy. The other sedan chair of rich fabric trimmed with gold studs, very costly, was the one in which the vicereine sat with another child she brought, a very little girl. Upon touching land the viceroy went ahead, uncovered [in full view without a canopy], looking at the sea wall where he had seen such a variety of gala attire and ladies. Everyone welcomed and cheered him, and with handkerchiefs in hand gave the acclamatory cry [Long live the viceroy]. The viceroy showed them many courtesies as he went along, and the vicereine took out her handkerchief and did likewise to those that were cheering them.

There were also three carriages at the shore, and all the duennas and ladies that she brought entered them and went to the palace.

Presentation of the Staff and Keys

At the same seaport, General Don Baltasar Pardo de Figueroa, who was presently general, presented him the keys on a golden tray and a staff of command worth more than four thousand pesos, with golden tips and many diamonds. Captain Francisco de la Cueva with his company, and Captain Don Pedro de Mendoza with his, formed a line up to the main plaza [of Callao] where there was a gathering of many people.

Upon disembarking, His Excellency and the vicereine went straight to the cathedral of Callao and heard Mass which was said for them by the vicar of that church. The viceroy was very pleased at having seen the church, and when he came out of it he went up to stand in front of the squadron that was awaiting him, and they lowered the flags towards him. Then he went to his [Callao] palace.

Visit of the Archbishop

As soon as he had gone to the palace, the archbishop of this city, Don Pedro de Villagómez, paid him a visit, and he came out as far as the stairs to receive him. Upon kissing the hand of the archbishop he humbled himself greatly; by very little more he would have touched his knee to the ground, and he took his hands and kissed him many times. And upon leaving he accompanied him to the same stairway.

Fireworks

That same night a variety of fireworks and many innovations had been prepared.

The first departure from the palace of Callao was with the vicereine on Saturday, the 12th, when they went to the Franciscan monastery to hear the *Salve Regina* [Hail Holy Queen].

The following Sunday they disembarked the Holy Christ [image] from the warship, and in wanting to take it to the monastery of San Agustín of that port there was a controversy between the prior of the monastery of Lima, Father Jerónimo de Urrutia, and the vicar of Callao as to whether it should be adorned to enter the church of San Agustín of that port. To avoid any incidents the viceroy ordered that it be taken to the main church of that port, where it was placed. The following Monday the Count of Lemos and Archbishop Don Pedro de Villagómez were present at the Mass in that church. That day the vicar of Callao chanted the Mass.

The Staff of General

Monday, the 14th of the month, at two in the afternoon the Marquis of Naval-Morquende [also spelled Navamorquende] was given the command staff as general of land and sea in the presence of all the people attending from this city of Lima, and a squadron was formed. The former general, who was Don Baltasar Pardo de Figueroa, presented it [the staff] to the new general.

Tuesday, the 15th of the month, there were bullfights at Callao.

Wednesday, the 16th, [the viceroy] left Callao under a canopy

Arrival at Lima to see the *chácara* of Don Sancho Castro where he was to stay. From there he came under cover in a carriage to Lima exactly at twelve noon, and he entered the palace by way of the garden gate, where he viewed everything. After eating there, he returned to Callao at four in the afternoon.

Review in Callao Thursday, the 17th of the month, [the Count of Lemos] passed review of the men of the infantry, artillerymen, and seamen. He ordered the elimination of more than one hundred and thirty positions of sailors, soldiers and artillerymen who were, or appeared to be, mestizos or mulattoes. And he ordered that only five hundred positions for soldiers should remain, and these should all be [for] Spaniards. He also ordered that accounts be settled for all that was due to everyone, dead and dismissed, by the 16th of this month of November.

That same day, Thursday, the 17th of the month, the last to pass in review were the men of the galley. Upon calling for General Don Sebastián de Navarrete, he was not found present. His Excellency asked why the general did not appear, and the royal treasury officials replied, "Sir, as he draws a salary from His Majesty [the King], the decree [about his post] is not in these books but in the portfolio containing the ones of perforated paper." He ordered that it be brought, and as soon as it was read to him, he ordered that there should be marked on the margin of the decree, a favor granted him by the *oidores*, that the post was eliminated as being ridiculous, and because he had not complied with the obligation he had as [galley] general, and because his captain general was becalmed on the consort vessel four leagues away in view of Callao, but he did not go with the galley to haul in the ship to port. And so he ordered that the matter be closed and that he [Navarrete] hold nothing more than the title of royal official. At this the inspector general replied that in order that this be recorded for all time, His Excellency would have to sign, upon which he immediately took the pen and signed "Count of Lemos" at the bottom of the abovementioned [decree], with which the matter was settled.

Saturday, the 19th of the month, he went from Callao with the vicereine and all his family to the *chácara* of Don Sancho de Castro where he remained Saturday, Sunday, and Monday until noon. The *chácara* was elaborately decorated with a thousand marvels.

That same day he granted General Don José de Alzamora [the post of] general of the cavalry of this kingdom.

The flagship arrived at the port of Callao on Tuesday, the 22nd of November of 1667.

Reception of the Viceroy

Monday, the 21st of November of 1667, day of the Presentation of Our Lady, His Excellency the Count of Lemos [officially] entered this city and was received as viceroy.

On this day he was received as viceroy, under a canopy, by the two ordinary *alcaldes*, Don Juan de la Presa and Don José de Torres y Zúñiga, and all the *regidores* dressed in crimson-colored fabric. Holding the bridle, the two *alcaldes* led the horse that the viceroy rode; it was a white horse with the saddle and adornments all very richly trimmed in silver. The viceroy was dressed in dove-like cloth all embroidered in gold, and he came with a group up to the palace entrance. He was accompanied by all the tribunals, university [officials], two battalion companies of this city, the one of Captain Don Luis de Sandóval, and the other of Captain Don Agustín de la Cueva, two companies of lances and arquebuses of this kingdom, and that of the Cañarí Indians.

Two Arches

All the balconies and windows by which His Excellency passed were draped with banners and filled with ladies. At the entrance of Mercaderes Street near the door of the *consulado* there was a magnificent and costly arch, which was worth seeing. There was another very tall arch of fine architecture at the intersection near the end of the same street. This arch, top to bottom, inside and outside, was filled with platters, vessels, and trays all in white and gilded silver, which were very artful, costly, and interesting. All the hollows of the arch were laid with more than five hundred and fifty bars of silver; each bar weighed more than two hundred marks.[35]

The Vicereine Rides through the Streets

From all the windows [spectators] threw them many flowers and roses. From a balcony, the vicereine watched the procession of the viceroy, then she and the duennas and ladies that she brought in her household went through the streets where the viceroy had passed. Accompanied by a large retinue of *caballeros*, the vicereine

[35] A mark (*marco*) was a unit of weight used for gold and silver; it was about half a pound.

rode in a sedan chair and the rest of her family in carriages. She arrived at the cathedral where the archbishop and canons received her with the *Te Deum laudamus* and organ music. In a short while the viceroy arrived at the cathedral and they received him in the same manner.

There were twelve pieces of artillery in the plaza and they fired three times. In a formation made up of many infantrymen, there were twelve companies, and they fired a military salute three times. The Marquis of Naval-Morquende was at the front of the formation as general, and Don Francisco de la Cueva as battalion commander.

There were also eight companies on horseback, four from this city and four rural ones, with their general, Don José de Alzamora, and Lieutenant Don Melchor Malo de Molina, chief constable of the court of this city. All were so very splendid that they could appear before His Majesty [the King], may the Lord protect him and we see him reach old age.

The vicereine in her sedan chair left with her family from another door of the cathedral, and they went to the palace by way of the garden gate.

His Excellency, with all the accompaniment, came back out of the church and mounted his horse, and the twelve flags that were brought forth to the front of the squadron were lowered towards him. Then he went to the palace and stood in the windows and watched the companies on horseback and all those of the infantry. At prayertime [sunset] he went inside.

This squadron was formed by the adjutant Gaspar de Savariego and Sergeant Josephe de Mugaburu with the other sergeants.

Wednesday, the 23rd of the month, the vicereine went to the *fiesta* at [the Augustinian Recollect of Nuestra Señora del] Guía. She traveled in a sedan chair with a great accompaniment of *caballeros* of this city, all of whom went on foot.

First Visit of His Excellency

Thursday, the 24th of the month, His Excellency went to visit the archbishop at his house.

Friday, the 25th of the month, he went to the *audiencia* of the *oidores* and sat with them wearing a black taffeta cap on his head; the *oidores* all had their heads uncovered.

Saturday, the 26th of the month, he went to the cathedral with all the *audiencia* and those of the *cabildo*. On this day Archbishop

Don Pedro de Villagómez held a pontifical Mass, and the doctor and canon of the cathedral of this City of Kings, Doctor Don Jerónimo Hurtado, gave a wonderful sermon. The viceroy Count of Lemos sent the preacher a lengthy note of gratitude.

This same day, in the morning, he sent orders to the prelates of the convents to hold three sung Masses [praying] that he would succeed in governing well. The first was Saturday, the 26th of the month, at La Santísima Tridinad; the second on Sunday, at the Santísimo Sacramento; the third, Monday, at the Pura y Limpia Concepción.

Saturday, the 26th of the month, he visited the nuns of [Nuestra Señora del] Carmen where he stayed all afternoon.

Proclamation regarding Pistols

Thursday, the 1st of December of the year 1667, a decree was announced with kettledrums, in which the two *alcaldes* of the court, two ordinary *alcaldes*, and two constables of the court and of the city participated. It [stipulated] that no person, whatever his rank or position, dare have in his house or carry with him a pocket pistol, pistol, or arquebus that measured less than a yard, under penalty of losing half of his possessions and exile from this kingdom for life.

Squadron and Procession

On the morning of Thursday, the 8th, day of the Pure and Immaculate Conception, there was a great celebration in the cathedral of this city, in which the viceroy, Count of Lemos, and all the city participated. There was a pontifical Mass chanted by Archbishop Don Pedro de Villagómez. Father Oserín of the Franciscan order gave the sermon. In the afternoon there was a great procession. It went to the Dominican and Augustinian churches, and from there it returned to the plaza by way of Mercaderes Street. There were two squadrons, one in front of the cathedral, another in front of the palace. The one at the palace turned and placed itself in front of the small street through which the procession came. Once the procession had passed, this same squadron returned to the front of the palace where it had first formed, until the viceroy returned to the palace. He brought the image of Our Lady to his royal chapel.

On this day of the Virgin, the cavalry soldiers made an altar where they placed [a statue of] the Holy Virgin of the Immaculate Conception.

This day the viceroy, being very devoted to her, wore on his chest a large rosette made of diamonds with [an image of] the [Immaculate] Conception on it.

Ban on Negroes and Mulattoes

Saturday, the 10th of December of the year 1667, at eleven in the morning the viceroy Count of Lemos ordered the proclamation of three bans on the same day. [The first was] that no mulatto woman, Negress, or *zamba*, freed or slave, without exception, wear a dress of silk, nor trimming of gold or silver, nor black trim of silk or linen. The penalty for anyone caught would be the loss of everything; the second time it would be the same with a fifty peso fine; and the third, two hundred lashes and eight years exile.

The second ban was that no Indian, mulatto, or zambo carry a sword, dagger, knife, or machete. [Penalty for] those caught with these or any other arms would be, for the first offense, a fine paid by his master of fifty patacoons to the official who arrested him with these arms. Only captains, ensigns, adjutants, and sergeants could carry them during the day while wearing the insignia of the post they occupied. After seven o'clock in the evening all were forbidden to carry them at night, even while wearing their insignias. For the first offense they would be relieved of their post, on the second, fined one hundred patacoons, and on the third, exiled to Valdivia.

The third ban was that no one carry a long sword, nor one with a needlepoint. If they were noblemen, on the first offense they would be fined two hundred patacoons; and for the others [not noblemen] loss of arms, fifty patacoons, and twenty days in prison. The sword makers and blacksmiths who made long sheathes and blacksmiths who made needlepoints for swords would receive two hundred lashes. These bans were to be observed inviolably.

Ban on Meat, Bread, Candles

Wednesday, the 14th of the month, a proclamation was issued that no mulatto sell meat in a plaza or street, under penalty of one hundred lashes, and any meat vendor that sold it at more than the established price, two hundred lashes, and to the supplier who permitted it, five hundred patacoons. And for the baker who sold bread weighing less than the established weight, for the first offense, two hundred patacoons [fine]. And for the candle maker who made tallow candles, the same penalty. For the grocer who sold bread and candles that were not of the proper weight, fifty patacoons for the first offense; and if they sold wine by measuring cups, another fifty patacoons and two years exile unless the measuring cups were officially stamped [as to exact weight or content]. For those who went on the roads and took away the provisions that the Indians brought to the city, one hundred pesos for the first offense, and two hundred for the second and exile fifty leagues from Lima.

That day the company of Colonel Don Francisco de la Cueva, who is battalion commander of that city, came from Callao with fifty soldiers. On that same day the one [company] that was in the palace under command of Don Gaspar de Mancilla, left.

Galley Criminals

That same Wednesday, the 14th of December, all the criminals came in wagons from the galleys at Callao with their shackles, and they were put in the prisons by order of His Excellency. As of this day, the galleys and the officials in charge were eliminated, and he ordered that these criminals be taken to the quicksilver mine of Huancavelica.

Sunday, the 18th of the month, by order of His Excellency, these criminals were taken to Callao to wait embarkation for Chincha, and from there they would be taken [overland] to Huancavelica.

Imprisonment of the Mulattoes

Monday, the 19th of the month, more than twenty-six mulattoes were arrested, and all were shot in the prison of this city by order of His Excellency.

Visit to the Prisons

Saturday, the 24th of December, just before Christmas, His Excellency visited the prisons. All who were justly imprisoned he ordered to be processed for [exile to] Chile. On the same day, following visits to the two prisons, His Excellency dined with the *oidores*, without the vicereine.

That same afternoon His Excellency ordered that Don Juan de Céspedes, Don Clemente Villavicenio, and Captain Pedro de Chavarría be called in for certain affairs, and His Excellency ordered that all their possessions be confiscated.

Novena at La Concepción

His Excellency ordered that a novena be held at the convent of the nuns of La Concepción of this city for devotion to the Immaculate Holy Virgin, for his success [in governing as viceroy], and for the health of our king and lord Charles II, and the queen, our lady, and the propitious state of all their kingdoms.

His Excellency and all the *oidores* and the archbishop attended the Mass and sermon each day without missing a single day. The first day, Wednesday the 28th of December, there was a pontifical Mass. The sermon was given by the canon Don Jerónimo Hurtado; the second day, Thursday the 29th, by Father Fray Bartolomé de Llevaneras, prior of Monserrate; the third, Friday, by Fray Nicolás Ramírez of Santo Domingo; the fourth, Saturday the 31st, by Father Fray Diego de Herrera of San Francisco; the fifth, 1st of January, by Father Fray Luis de Lemus of San Agustín; the sixth, Monday the 2nd, by Father Maestro Fray Juan Baes of La Merced; Tuesday the 3rd by Father Fray Rodrigo de Valdés of the Society of Jesus; Wednesday the 4th, by Father Jacinto de Andrade of the order of San Jerónimo.

Saturday, the 31st of December of the year 1667, the lookout [ship] arrived from Chile with news that the governor of that kingdom had ordered that the [treasury] inspector of that kingdom be garroted. The reason will be made known later.

The Year 1668

Sunday, the 1st of January of the year 1668, Don Bartolomé de Azaña and Don Iñigo de Zúñiga y Torres were chosen *alcaldes*.

Seven Months Pay

Monday, the 9th of January of 1668, His Excellency went to Callao and was present for the seven months' [salary] payment to the infantry, which [still] left one year in arrears. He remained in Callao until the 12th day of the month. At this payment three soldiers were taken from each company to go to Chile with the Marquis of Naval-Morquende, who was governor of that kingdom.

Monday, the 16th of the month, the seven months' [salaries] were paid in Lima, leaving the year 1667 due, to all the duty sergeants of this city and to the company that was on guard at the palace. This [company] was under Colonel Don Francisco de la Cueva, battalion commander of this city. Viceroy Count of Lemos was not present at the payment as it was the day of Saint Marcel and His Excellency went to the church of that name. Present for this payment was the general, Marquis of Naval-Morquende, governor-elect of Chile.

The said payment of the seven months' [salary] and the muster took place in the upper corridor of the palace on Monday, January 16, 1668.

The Hanging

His Excellency, Count of Lemos, ordered that those condemned to hang be taken to the small plaza of Santa Ana. The first to be hanged were a mullato and a Negro [convicted] as thieves; justice was dealt to them on Thursday, the 12th of January of the year 1668.

Saturday, the 21st of that month and year, dawn found Nicolás Rondón hanged in this small plaza for three deaths [for which he was responsible]. That same night they had garroted him in the court prison by order of His Excellency. The adjutant and other mounted soldiers had taken him from the hospital of Saint Bartholomew, which was the one for Negroes.

Saturday, the 21st of January of the year 1668, a proclamation was issued that mutton should be sold by weight; two pounds and four ounces for one *real*; four pounds and a half, for two *reales*; and nine pounds for four *reales*. That same day they began to sell meat at the above mentioned prices, by order of His Excellency the Count of Lemos.

Consecration of the Bishop

Sunday, the 22nd of January of the year 1668, Don Fray Martín de Montalvo, a religious of the Augustinian order who came from Spain assigned as bishop of Chuquiago, was consecrated. The archbishop of this city, Don Pedro de Villagómez, consecrated him, and the Count of Lemos, viceroy of these kingdoms of Peru, was present. Six *caballeros* served [Mass at the consecration], three of the order of Santiago and three of the order of Calatrava, and also the Marquis of Naval-Morquende, the governor who is going to Chile.

At four in the afternoon of Tuesday, the 24th of January of the year 1668, the viceroy Count of Lemos personally visited all the wholesale meat markets to see if what His Excellency had ordered was being carried out. The last one he visited was the market of Huaquilla. The ordinary *alcalde* Don Iñigo de Zúñiga also came with His Excellency.

The Company Flag

Wednesday, the 25th, the flag of Captain Don Bernardo de Ayala, secretary of the Marquis who was going to Chile as governor, was blessed in [the church of] Santo Domingo. More than one hundred and forty men of this company paraded, both active and inactive captains, ensigns, and sergeants. It turned out very splendidly. The captain of the *Coletos* [buff coats] and former fortress commander of Valdivia was chosen as lance groom. Lieutenant General Don Felipe Romana and the sergeant major, who were both on active duty, officiated as sergeants. At eleven o'clock of that day the viceroy with the *oidores* went to the windows of the council hall where they were all meeting to watch the company pass in review.

The Very Reverend Father Fray Gaspar Vadillo, Mercedarian vicar general, died on Friday morning, which was the 27th of this current month and year.

Governor for Chile

Saturday, the 4th of February of the year 1668, at four in the afternoon the Marquis of Naval-Morquende left the port of Callao for [his post as] governor of Chile, by order of His Excellency, the Count of Lemos, viceroy of this kingdom. The Marquis took with him four hundred soldiers, all youthful and splendid. The *oidor* Don Lope de Munive also went along as *visitador* to that kingdom, taking with him as his scribe Francisco Muñoz.

Sunday, the 5th of the month, at three in the afternoon another ship left the port of Callao with the governor for Valdivia, servant of the viceroy, and it also took many soldiers and splendid young men to that post. On this ship went Sergeant Juan Manuel, Sergeant Juan de Morales, and another soldier ordered to exile for six years at half salary for not having properly followed the orders they had been given to guard the house of a goldsmith.

Orphan Boys

Wednesday, the 8th of February of the year 1668, the viceroy sent six orphan boys to the port of Callao to serve as orderlies on the ships of His Majesty. They would receive a salary from the king, our lord, and learn to be seamen.

Sunday, the 12th of the month, a sung Mass was celebrated at the chapel of the hospital of Saint Bartholomew; Dean Don Juan de Cabrera chanted the Mass at the main altar.

Saturday, the 18th of the month, memorial funeral services for His Excellency the Count of Alba de Liste, who had been viceroy of this kingdom of Peru, were held at the monastery of San Francisco. Present were His Excellency the Count of Lemos, viceroy of these kingdoms, and all the *oidores* and the [*audiencia*] president, as well as all the illustrious *caballeros* of this City of Kings. Father Jaramillo gave the sermon and the Reverend Father Maestro, Commissary Cristóbal de Contreras, said Mass. All the religious orders were present.

Funeral Services of the Count of Alba

That same day, Saturday, battalion commander Don Francisco de la Cueva went to Callao to witness his infantry company in that city pass review.

On Sunday morning, the 19th of the month, all the companies passed review, and all the soldiers of all the companies in this review were assigned to Puno. At this review His Excellency was not present, but [in his stead] Colonel Don Antonio Ordóñez, *caballero* of the order of Santiago. Those who did not turn out for the muster had their posts abolished, some for desertion and others for not being present at the muster.

At the same review the adjutant Pedro Carrasco Becerra was demoted from captain for four days. At new orders the staff of command as aide to the general battalion commander was granted to him to go with His Excellency to Puno with the infantry already indicated. This new favor was granted him by His Excellency for his post as captain.

The canon magistrate of this cathedral of Lima, Don Jerónimo Hurtado de Aguila, died on Friday, the 2nd of March. He had been made canon only two years ago, and he left an estate of one hundred thousand patacoons. May God keep him in His holy glory.

Saturday, the 24th of March of the year 1668, on the eve of Palm Sunday, my son the *bachiller* José de Mugaburu was sent as an interim [priest] to the collative parish of Caicai in Cuzco [province] by Bishop Don Bernardo de Izaguirre.

A Negro Escapes Hanging

Wednesday, the 7th of March of the year 1668, at five in the afternoon a Negro about to be hanged for thievery was taken to the plaza of Santa Ana where the scaffold was located. Upon being assisted by a Dominican father to better face death, and while he was in an act of contrition, a soldier named Pablo arrived at this small plaza on horseback and shouted that the hanging be suspended. The people present clamored for pardon. The hangman, with all this clamoring, removed the two nooses from the neck of the condemned man who descended [the scaffold], entered the church of Santa Ana, and escaped. (This Negro who had escaped the noose was caught and hanged in the large plaza on Monday, the 18th of February of 1669.)

Saint Francis of Paula

Saturday, the 7th of April of the year 1668, at five in the afternoon [the statue of] Saint Francis of Paula was removed from the monastery of San Agustín of this city, where it had been for a long time, and was taken in procession with great solemnity to its original home. All the streets were hung with decorations. The accompaniment was made up of the whole community of the religious of the monastery of San Agustín, the viceroy, Count of Lemos, all the *oidores*, and the entire city with all the nobility.

Sunday, the 22nd of April of that month and year, the ordinary *alcalde* of this city, and the *caballeros* and servants of the viceroy, Count of Lemos, ran the ring[36] [jousting] in front of the palace.

Marriage of my Daughter

Wednesday, the 25th of April, day of the glorious apostle Saint James, at four in the afternoon my [step-]daughter Damiana de Aguilar y Mugaburu was married to Captain Don Diego Pardo, a nephew of the former battalion commander of Callao, Don Tomás Pardo. Her brother, the prebendary Don Sebastián de Aguilar, married them. Captain Alonso Luján, Don Fernando Bravo, and the licentiate Vadillo were present. The articles of marriage were [signed] this day before Don Bartolomé Maldonado, royal notary.

Beheading of Posadas y Torres

At one in the afternoon on Friday, the 11th of May, a platform a yard and a half high, with a tall pole at the foot of which was a chair, was set up next to the fountain in the plaza of this city. On a mule decked in black, Don Sebastián Posadas y Torres was brought out from the court prison and beheaded for having killed a priest at a vineyard estate in Pisco.

The day he was beheaded was exactly four years since the priest had died. The day he killed him was the 11th of May of the year 1664, and on the 12th of that month there was an earthquake in Pisco and Ica which destroyed the whole town and killed many people.

36 *Correr la sortija* was a jousting or tilting exercise where charging mounted men tried to put the point of a lance through a ring hanging from a ribbon.

Saturday, the 26th of May of the year 1668, a proclamation was issued that everyone [military and *caballeros*] carry wide swords, and not rapiers, under penalty of demotion and six months exile to Valdivia for officers or soldiers, and for the other *caballeros* and persons, two years in Valdivia, without any possibility of revoking the penalty.

Garrote for Sánchez

Monday, the 28th of the month, Salvador Sánchez, a white man dressed in black, was taken on foot from the court prison and tied to a pole on a small platform next to the fountain. He was garroted because he had killed a Negro that had killed his brother Tomás Sánchez, a white man.

Thursday, the 31st of May of the year 1668, holy day of Corpus Christi, the Count of Lemos appeared at the cathedral in a colored suit trimmed in silver, with a lace Vandyke collar, without a cape and carrying his captain general's staff. He was present at the conversion of the wine [to the blood of Christ] and walked the whole procession. This day there was a pontifical Mass held by Archbishop Don Pedro de Villagómez. His Grace did not walk in the procession, and the canon Don Juan de Rojas carried the Holy Sacrament in his hands throughout the whole procession.

Also without capes were: Don Melchor Malo; the battalion commander of this city, Don Francisco de la Cueva; the battalion commander of Callao, Don Antonio Ordóñez; Lieutenant General Don Felipe de Romana; and all the other servants of His Excellency.

Litigation of Salcedo

Saturday, the 2nd of June of the year 1668, at twelve midnight a warrant was issued from the [council] hall to notify [Gaspar de] Salcedo and [Juan de] Salazar to go to Puno to answer charges [against them] and that they name a counselor and attorney there to defend their cause. At that hour Salcedo began to shout, asking for justice and not wanting to get dressed, until the viceroy, Count of Lemos, entered the room where he was prisoner. With good arguments he encouraged Salcedo to get dressed and go to Puno, [assuring him] that he would be justly treated. At nine that day, Sunday, Salazar and Salcedo left the palace by way of the garden gate where His Excellency had had a carriage prepared for the two of them. They entered it and were taken to Callao by Lieutenant General Don Felipe Romana and eight cavalry soldiers. At the port the two left the carriage and were taken in a boat that had been provided by the consort vessel and immediately embarked on the warship.

Embarkation of the Viceroy

That same Sunday, the 3rd of the month, the Count of Lemos left the palace around four in the afternoon to go to Callao [and then to Puno] with a great retinue of *oidores*, comptrollers, and many *caballeros*. First he entered the cathedral, where the Holy Sacrament was uncovered, to pray, and after a long while he left the church with all his accompaniment and went to Callao. As soon as he arrived he was given a grand military salute by the artillery.

On Monday, the 4th, the soldiers going to Puno were given four months' pay. They had previously received another four months' pay.

That same day, Monday, His Excellency embarked with all his people, and because a north wind rose the vessel could not leave the port. His Excellency stayed on the consort that night and Tuesday.

Wednesday the 6th, since the same wind was blowing, he disembarked and came that night to Lima and slept in the palace.

His Excellency Sets Sail

Thursday, the 7th of the month, the eighth day of Corpus [Christi], His Excellency returned to Callao in a carriage, and at twelve noon that day the consort vessel hoisted anchor, set sail, and left the port of Callao [for Islay]. May God guide him safely and return him. [The viceroy went to the region of Puno to put down a rebellion there.][37] The vicereine remained [in Lima] as governor.

Saturday, the 16th of June of the year 1668, and Monday the 18th, a proclamation was issued against the French. Anyone being French, as well as anyone having news of them, must declare it, also declaring any companies and haciendas known to belong to them in this kingdom as well as Tierra Firme, Mexico, and in Spain and France, under penalty of being [considered] traitors to the royal crown and the other punishments indicated.

This proclamation was issued at the order of the vicereine, Countess of Lemos, by the authority vested in her to act as gover-

[37] For details on the rebellion in Puno, Peru, see Jorge Basadre, *El Conde de Lemos y su tiempo* (Lima: Editorial Huascarán, 1945), pp. 81–108.

nor by the Count of Lemos as viceroy and captain general of these kingdoms when His Excellency embarked for the port of Islay.[38] The royal decree was from His Majesty, may God protect him, issued the 12th of June of the year 1667. And Her Excellency, in her position as governor of these kingdoms, by virtue of this royal decree ordered that the proclamation be issued that all Frenchmen declare themselves.

Wednesday, the 4th of July of the year 1668, the ship named *San Juan de Dios* arrived at the port of Callao bringing news that the Marquis of Naval-Morquende had been received in Santiago de Chile as governor of that kingdom, and that Don Francisco de Meneses, former governor of that kingdom, had been imprisoned.

The Vicereine Leaves the Palace

Thursday, the 5th of the month, the Countess of Lemos went from the palace to the cathedral to attend a sung Mass with the Holy Sacrament uncovered. As she was in advanced pregnancy, she went in her sedan chair and was accompanied by the *oidores*, *alcaldes* of the court, comptrollers, and the secular *cabildo*. The Mass was sung by the canon Balcázar as an act of thanksgiving for the successful results in the kingdom of Chile. The vicereine governed this kingdom while the viceroy Count of Lemos went to the upper provinces of Arequipa and Puno. On this occasion, the vicereine was given the pax[39] and incensed, and they also gave her the missal to kiss after the holy Gospel [was read].

The Countess Gives Birth

By dawn of Wednesday, the 11th of July of the year 1668, the Countess of Lemos, who presently governed in the absence of the viceroy, Count of Lemos, who was on a voyage to the port of Islay and Arequipa, had given birth to a son.

Monday, the 23rd of July of the year 1668, at four in the afternoon the infant son of the Count of Lemos, viceroy of these kingdoms, was christened. [He was named Don Salvador Francisco de Borja Fernández de Castro y Portugal.] His Excellency at this time was in Arequipa. The godfather of the child was Father Castillo of the Society of Jesus, and the archbishop of this city, Don Pedro de Villagómez, applied the water and chrism. There was a great accompaniment of *caballeros*, all with gold chains and

[38] This example of a woman governing the Viceroyalty of Peru is unique. Normally the *audiencia* or its president, or occasionally some male royal official, governed during the absence or following the death of the viceroy.

[39] The pax (*paz*) is a tablet bearing a figure or symbol of Christ, the Virgin Mary, or a saint, which is given to people to kiss during a Mass; an osculatorium.

large jewels on their chests. The following Tuesday there were roped bulls in the plaza, and horse races by many *caballeros* wearing golden chains. All the servants of His Excellency [also] wore [gold] chains.

My Son, Father Francisco

Friday, the 3rd of August of the year 1668, at nine in the morning the Very Reverend Father and vice-commissary general, Fray Cristóbal de Contreras, left this city for that of Cuzco by way of the plains. He took with him to Cuzco my son, Father Fray Francisco, at the request of the father provincial of that province, who was presently Fray Buenaventura de Honton, my nephew, a barefoot religious of the Franciscan order of that province. He [Francisco] would also visit his brother the licentiate Don José de Mugaburu, who was the interim priest at the town of Caicai. My son went very well accommodated with Father [Cristóbal de Contreras] during the whole trip.

My Daughter Damiana

Sunday, the 6th of August of the year 1668, at ten in the morning Colonel Don Diego Pardo left this city for his office as *corregidor* at Yauyos with his wife Doña Damiana de Aguilar y Mugaburu, my [step-] daughter. That office was given to him by the Count of Lemos, viceroy of these kingdoms, at the beginning of this year of 1668. The day they left I accompanied them as far as the farm of the Mercedarian fathers. All their household effects were left at my home for safekeeping.

News of the Capture of Puerto Bello

Friday, the 31st of August of the year 1668, at ten at night the dispatch ship arrived from Panama with news that the English enemy had captured Puerto Bello [Portobelo, Panama] on the 11th of July with a large fishing boat, two frigates, and twelve canoes, landing their men and taking everyone prisoner.

Aid Sent by the Vicereine

Within six days she [the vicereine] sent aid from this city in the form of men, silver, and artillery as well as provisions necessary for war, and many other things which are so numerous I refer to the paper attached to this sheet [since disappeared] in which it can be seen that nothing was missing. The brevity [of time in which this aid was prepared and sent] had neither been done nor heard of in our times, and [it was done] with the assistance, soliciting, and supervision of the present battalion commander of Callao, Don Antonio Ordóñez, *caballero* of the order of Santiago.

Saturday, the 22nd of September of the year 1668, at twelve noon the Countess of Lemos issued a decree that street vendors not be allowed unless they were one of the forty street vendors registered by the government, paying the half annate [required of official vendors]. Any others who were found selling would be imprisoned with a fine of fifty patacoons and two years at the [Indian] war in Chile, and they would remain in prison until they could embark for that kingdom. *Ban on Vendors*

At four in the afternoon of Thursday, the 27th of September of the year 1668, day of the glorious Saints Cosmas and Damian, the cornerstone for the convalescent home for Indians was laid. Located beyond Cercado, it was called [Nuestra Señora del] Carmen convelscent home for natives, and Don Diego de Aguilar was majordomo. Many persons from this city of Lima were present.

Saturday, the 20th of October of the year 1668, at eight at night the dispatch ship arrived at this city from Panama with news that the pirate English enemy had left Puerto Bello after having been in port a month and two days, and after the pillaging they did at Puerto Bello which was considerable. The residents of Panama [City] gave them [ransom of] one hundred thousand pesos; 60,000 in patacoons and 40,000 in wrought silver. They left without damaging or taking anything from the fort nor all the houses of that port [Panama City], and they freed the prisoners they had captured. On the night that the dispatch ship arrived at this city there was a great pealing of bells and many fireworks. The following day there was a pontifical Mass, and at night a small masquerade of *caballeros* around the plaza. *Dispatch Ship from Puerto Bello*

At five in the afternoon of Sunday, the 28th of October of the year 1668, day of the glorious apostles Saints Simon and Judas Thaddaeus, a procession left the monastery of Nuestra Señora del Carmen for the hermitage of the previously mentioned convalescent home for natives above El Cercado. The [statue of the] Mother of God was taken in the procession accompanied by [those of] Saint Joachim, the aspostle Saint James, and Saint Theresa. The secular *cabildo* and many clerics with surplices and candles in hand accompanied the procession as did the whole city. There were giant figures and many dances in it [the procession].

Execution of Salcedo

Tuesday, the 30th of October of the year 1668, at eleven in the morning it was proclaimed that the Count of Lemos had ordered that José de Salcedo be beheaded and quartered as a traitor, and that all his possessions be confiscated for His Majesty, may God protect him, which were more than four hundred thousand pesos in bars [of silver] and *reales* and the value of his mines. All persons with whom he had [business] dealings either in deposits or contracts should turn them over within four days under penalty of losing their lives and [being proclaimed] traitors of His Majesty. Justice was done to José de Salcedo at Puno on the 11th of October of that year of 1668, and the proclamation came from there, [issued] by the Count and dated the 12th of that month and year.

Decree on Wax

Wednesday, the 31st of October of the year 1668, a proclamation was issued in this city that no one having cakes of crude wax could sell them at more than one hundred and forty pesos a quintal, under penalty of four thousand pesos fine. Those who denounced violators would receive one third, the rest would go to the council of His Majesty. [It also declared] that wax makers must sell finished wax at twelve *reales* a pound, under penalty of one hundred pesos fine for the first offense. This proclamation was ordered by the Countess of Lemos.

They wrote from the city of Cuzco that the Count of Lemos, coming from Puno where he had done justice to José de Salcedo and other complices in that city on the 11th of October, had arrived at Cuzco on the 24th of October of the year 1668.

While in Cuzco, the Count of Lemos granted my son, the *bachiller* Don José de Mugaburu, the collative parish of Yanaoca, Don Bernardo de Izaguirre being bishop at that time, the 3rd of November of the year 1668. His nomination was immediately sent to that town, and he competed for this parish with fifteen opponents, [specialists] of the [Quechua Indian] language.

Arrival of the Viceroy

Sunday, the 2nd of November of the year 1668, the escort ship arrived at the port of Callao, anchoring at two in the afternoon. Aboard it was the Court of Lemos who had been in Cuzco, Puno, and Arequipa for five months minus five days all told. The following Monday he came to Lima with a great number of people who accompanied him.

In another ship he brought as prisoners from Arequipa: General Antonio Buitrón Anaya, the two Trejo brothers, and another, Don Esteban Ramírez. His Excellency ordered that they be put in the court prison in chains. Don Esteban Ramírez was notified that he was sentenced to ten years at Valdivia, followed by exile from the kingdom of Peru for the rest of his life, under penalty of losing his life if he disobeyed.

Celebration of the Immaculate Conception

On the afternoon of Friday, the 7th of December of the year 1668, the statue of Our Lady of the Pure and Immaculate Conception was brought in procession from the royal chapel of the palace to the cathedral. His Excellency and all the gentlemen were present, and they attended the vespers.

On the morning of Saturday, the 8th, His Excellency with the president, *oidores*, and secular *cabildo* attended the Mass and sermon, and in the afternoon a procession was held that went from the cathedral to [the monasteries of] Santo Domingo and San Agustín, returning to the plaza. The viceroy carried the banner [of the Virgin] the whole time, without releasing it, until they reached the cathedral. That afternoon two squadrons made up of many persons were formed in the plaza.

Masquerade of the Sergeants

Thursday, the 13th of December of the year 1668, at eight at night a masquerade was held in honor of the viceroy by the sergeants and lieutenants of the cavalry of this city. They set out from the small plaza of the Inquisition, went to the main plaza and along Mercaderes Street and Plateros Street to the Society of Jesus, and returned to the same small plaza from where they started, and ended there. More than three hundred personages were represented [in masquerade].

The Papal Bull

Sunday, the 16th of said month and year, the holy bull [affirming the beatification of Rose of Lima] was made public, and all the religious orders, the viceroy Count of Lemos, and all the tribunals walked in the procession from San Francisco [church] to the cathedral. This day was the first that Don Esteban de Ibarra, magisterial canon of this holy church and delegate of the pope in these kingdoms, took over [his post] at the cathedral. This day Father Fray Juan Laines of the order of Saint Francis gave the sermon.

Monday, the 17th of December of the year 1668, at eleven in the morning Juan Cisternas was hanged, according to the proclamation for being seditious and for having been caught in many robberies and murders in Laicacota.

Saturday, the 29th of December of the year 1668, there were bulls run and *cañas* games in the plaza of Lima. The viceroy, Count of Lemos, and the vicereine went to the corridors of the *cabildo* with all of the *audiencia* to watch them.

On the afternoon of Sunday, the 30th of the month, His Excellency with the Countess of Lemos went to see the archbishop at his *chácara*, and then they went to the *chácara* of the inquisitor, Don Alvaro de Ibarra. That night their excellencies slept there, and Monday, the 31st of the month, returned to their palace.

The Year 1669

The Alcaldes

Tuesday, the first day of the new year 1669, Don Diego de Carbajal, *caballero* of the order of Calatrava and postmaster general of all the kingdom, and Don Alvaro de Navalmuel Villar de Fuentes, *caballero* of the order of Alcántara, were elected ordinary *alcaldes* of this city. The viceroy, Count of Lemos, chose them without their having aspired to be *alcaldes*. [Names of] those who had aspired were left in the ballot box.[40]

News from Spain

Wednesday, the 16th of January of the year 1669, day of Saint Marcel, the dispatches from Spain arrived at this city of Lima. They brought news that peace had been made with Portugal; that the second son of the Duke of Braganza had been crowned king [of Portugal]; that peace had also been made with France; and that the Count of Lemos had been fined twelve thousand pesos for having removed Don Juan Pérez de Guzmán from his *audiencia* presidency in Panama and for having brought him prisoner to the port of Callao.

The House of Saint Rose

Sunday, the 24th of February, of the year 1669, the day of the apostle Saint Matthew, two religious of [the monastery of] Santo Domingo held a sung Mass at the house where the glorious Holy

[40] See note 32 above about the viceroy's intervention in *cabildo* elections.

Mary of the Rose [Saint Rose of Lima] was born.[41] From that day the house has been held in great veneration.

Saturday, the 23rd of March of the year 1669, at three in the afternoon the flagship and consort left the port of Callao with only the treasure of His Majesty and without any merchant of Castile or of this city having embarked for Panama. Don Juan de Urdanegui of the order of Santiago went as general, and Don Francisco Benítez as admiral. Viceroy Count of Lemos stayed in Callao until they set sail. In this armada went [Inquisition prisoners] Don César [Bandier], his nephew, and the Carmelite friar, each wearing a sanbenito.

Edict on Amnesty

Monday, the 25th of March, an edict was issued regarding all those who had committed a transgression of the law in the Puno affair. Those who had committed an offense would be granted amnesty, but this did not cover those who were presently held prisoners.

Ban On Tonsures

Wednesday, the 27th of the month, a proclamation was issued by the viceroy that no mulatto woman, *zamba*, or Negress wear a tonsure like the clerics. Penalty for the first offense was having their heads and eyebrows shaved, and for the second offense, one hundred lashes and a month in jail. For Spanish women, at the first offense [a fine of] one hundred pesos, and twice that amount for the second time.

Decree on Wax

Thursday, the 28th of the month, a proclamation was issued that in the processions of the mulattoes, Negroes, and zambos during Holy Week, no more than fifty candles be carried by each sodality, under penalty of losing the wax conceded for the Holy Sacrament of the church from which the procession set forth. And no dinners were to be held after the procession, under penalty of forfeiting all that was found at such dinners to be given to the poor in the prisons.

[41] Saint Rose of Lima (1586–1617), the first saint from the New World, was born in Lima and baptized with the name of Isabel Flores de Oliva but called Rose because of her beauty. A member of the Third Order of St. Dominic, she wore a crown of thorns under her veil and a crown of roses over it. In her family home she established an infirmary where she cared for destitute children and old people. Her devotion and good works led to her beatification in 1668 and canonization three years later; her feast day is August 30. *New Catholic Encyclopedia*, XII, 673–74.

Those who were found dining [would receive] one month in prison.

Celebration for Saint Rose

Monday, the 29th of April of the year 1669, at four in the afternoon the viceroy, Count of Lemos, left the palace for the church of Santo Domingo with a jewel of great worth on his chest. He was accompanied by the *oidores*, secular *cabildo*, and the servants of the viceroy with their chains of gold and jewels. At that hour the papal bull [beatifying Rose of Lima] was brought in procession under a pallium to the cathedral. With great applause and veneration it was carried by the very reverend father provincial vicar, who presently was Father Fray Bernardo de Carrasco, and accompanied by all the religious orders. The archbishop of this city, Don Pedro de Villagómez, received it at the door of the cathedral. The statue of Saint Rose from Santo Domingo [church] was on a silver litter. After solemn vespers were held at the cathedral, the papal bull was read aloud from the pulpit, following which the statue was uncovered. In this procession the statues of Saint Dominic and Saint Catherine of Sena were brought out.

Celebration for Saint Rose

On the morning of Tuesday, the 30th of April of the year 1669, a pontifical Mass and sermon were held at the cathedral with the attendance of the viceroy with all the above named. In the afternoon twelve pieces of artillery were brought out in the plaza and fired three times.

There were three fine squadrons made up of many persons splendidly attired, and the battalion commander of this city, Don Francisco de la Cueva, *caballero* of the order of Calatrava, was on a white horse. The squadron was formed by the adjutants Gaspar Savariego and Roque Rosales, and Sergeant Josephe de Mugaburu and other sergeants.

The procession left the cathedral with [the statues of] all the saints as well as the patriarchs of all the sodalities and went around the palace and the *cabildo*, where there were two altars. Then it went by way of Mercaderes Street to [the monasteries of] San Agustín and Santo Domingo. The viceroy carried the banner of the saint [Rose] and appeared in shirt sleeves dressed in a colored suit and with his staff as captain general. All the city was very happy.

Adoration of the Holy Sacrament

Sunday, the 5th of May of the year 1669, the archbishop of this city publicly announced at the cathedral the great indulgences that would be gained by those who, upon hearing the pealing of the large bell at the raising of the Holy Sacrament, knelt to the ground wherever they were and worshipped Our Lord.

Death of Don Francisco Mejía Carbajal

Doctor Don Francisco Mejía Carbajal died on Wednesday, the 15th of May of 1669. He was buried Thursday, the 16th of the month, at the church of Santa Ana where he had currently been priest.

That same day Wednesday, the 15th of May, day of the glorious Saint Isidore, "tiller of the soil," my friend Mateo Pérez Labrador died. He was buried on Thursday, the 16th, in the chapel of La Soledad, where he was superintendent of that sodality.

The commissary general of the order of San Francisco, the Very Reverend Father Fray Luis de Zervela, entered this city on Friday, the 28th of June of the year 1669, at eleven at night. At that hour he went to the palace where he spoke with the viceroy, Count of Lemos, and then he went quietly to his monastery.

Cornerstone of Desamparados Church

Saturday, the 29th of June of the year 1669, day of Saint Peter, at five in the afternoon the cornerstone was laid in the area acquired for the enlargement of the church of the Desamparados. Father Castillo of the Society of Jesus is in charge of the said church and all the priests of the Society were there together with their provincial and rector. The viceroy, Count of Lemos, was the one who carried the cornerstone. All the *oidores*, chief comptrollers, many *caballeros*, and a great number of people were also present.

Death of Captain Pedro de Chavarría

Captain Pedro de Chavarría died Sunday, the 7th of July of the year 1669, at five in the afternoon. He was buried at the monastery of San Francisco on Monday, the 8th of the month, at the [hour of the] Ave Maria. He named as executor and guardian of his estate the comptroller Domingo de Barambio, his great friend.

Armada for Panama

Monday, the 8th of July of the year 1669, at three in the afternoon five ships left the port of Callao for Panama with Spanish merchants and those of this kingdom [destined] to make purchases at Puerto Bello. These ships carried more than sixteen million pesos in patacoons and bars, and the viceroy, Count of Lemos, dispatched them personally. He was at Callao from Wednesday, the 3rd of the month, until the 8th, and he did not return to Lima until they had set sail.

My nephews, Don Antonio and Don Pedro de Legorburu, embarked for Spain going as far as Panama on Don Pedro López de Gárate's ship named *La Guía*. May God grant them a good voyage, and that the silver reach Spain safely for the defense of the faith of Our Lord Jesus Christ!

The Hanging of a Zamba

Friday, the 12th of July of the year 1669, the gentlemen of the [court of] crime ordered the hanging of a mulatto woman or *zamba* because she tried to kill her mistress by putting mercury chloride in some fried eggs. God was served in that her mistress did not die. She was hanged on this day at eleven thirty in the morning.

Ensign José de Villanueva Killed

Saturday, the 13th of July of the year 1669, José de Villanueva, a royal scribe, was killed. The one who killed him was Don Juan Francisco Maldonado, known by another name as "*mayorazgo*" [oldest son]. He killed him over an argument they had during a game. The dead man was killed at the place where he lived, adjacent to La Trinidad [church].

Election of the Augustinian Provincial

Saturday, the 20th of July, at ten in the morning the Count of Lemos, viceroy of these kingdoms, went to the monastery of San Agustín of this City of Kings for the election of the provincial. He went with fifty soldiers, twenty of whom came from Callao with Colonel Don Antonio Ordóñez, *caballero* of the order of Santiago. At ten that night, the viceroy, wanting to settle the very great differences that arose among the religious who had a vote, did not receive cooperation from Father Maestro Fray Diego de Urrutia, the present provincial, nor the Father counselor Melchor Beláustegui. At that same hour he had them exiled, sending them to the port of Callao to be embarked. They went in the carriage of the viceroy with the above-mentioned colonel and eight mounted soldiers. That same night Father Fray Francisco Lagunillas was chosen provincial.

Dominican Provincial

Wednesday, the 24th of July of the year 1669, at ten in the morning very quietly and peacefully, without anything out of the ordinary, the Very Reverend Father Hernando Carrasco was chosen provincial of the Dominican order. The following day, day of the apostle Saint James, he went in procession to the monastery of San Francisco where he sang high Mass, then he returned to his monastery.

Death of Doctor Cristóbal de Saavedra

Wednesday, the 31st of July of the year 1669, the dispatch ship arrived from San Mateo de Huanchos with the news that my friend Father Fray Cristóbal de Saavedra, priest and vicar of that town, had become suddenly ill and had emitted a great amount of blood from his mouth. The following Thursday, the 1st of August of that year, they buried him in his church in that town. Before dying he made a codicil witnessed by the *corregidor* and royal officials.

Franciscan Provincial

Sunday, the 4th of August, in the afternoon the commissary general of San Francisco went with the fathers who were to vote to the Alameda Recollect of this city. At three in the morning of the following Monday they began to call for Father Fray Francisco Franco who was in the main convent, very quiet, without having aspired to be provincial. All the votes were given to him because of his seniority, and he was elected provincial. At nine in the morning he came to the palace with his counselors to speak with the Count of Lemos, viceroy of these kingdoms, after which he returned to the Recollect.

Tuesday, the 6th of the month, day of the Transfiguration of the Lord, the Franciscan provincial went to [the church of] Santo Domingo, where he held a sung Mass. Traveling to and from [the church], the commissary general, Fray Luis de Zervela, walked at his right.

Remittance for the Indians of Yanaoca

Wednesday, the 7th of August of the year 1669, I obtained the covering letter and remittance for the Indians of Yanaoca, where my son the *bachiller* José de Mugaburu was priest. It was based on the last reappraisement which was made of that town in the year 1662. I sent it to him by *chasque*.

That same day the tribunal of accounts of this city took note of the testimony of the royal officials of Cuzco, sent to me by my son, that he paid at that treasury through Doctor Don Diego de Honton, one hundred and nineteen pesos of his monthly salary and contributions of his parish [recorded] in the perforated book of half annates.

Later, on Thursday the 8th of the month, the royal officials in charge of the treasury and in whose care the book of half annates was entrusted, took record of it. That same day, before Jerónimo Maldonado, royal scribe of those funds, I cancelled the contract in which I was guarantor for my son for that money, whereupon they released me [from my word of guaranty] and the notation was stricken from the injunction brought by Isidro, bailiff of the said treasury.

Wednesday, the 7th of this month and year, a funeral service for my *compadre* was given at [the church of] Santa Clara by his sister, Doña María de Saavedra. There was great solemnity and many Masses were said, and on this day the Mass was sung by the canon Balcázar.

Thursday, the 8th, Doña María de Urdanivia, nun of that [Santa Clara] convent had another memorial service held, with great solemnity, and many Masses said. The high Mass was sung by the canon Calvo. At the responsory there were twenty-four priests in surplices, holding lighted candles.

Edict About Shopkeepers

Friday, the 9th of August of the year 1669, at five in the afternoon a proclamation was issued at this plaza that no one could be a shopkeeper nor have a general store unless they were married. Six days were given by the government [to comply with the ruling]. Later the Count of Lemos, viceroy of these kingdoms, giving fifteen days leeway, ordered that no mulatto, Negro, or mestizo be a shopkeeper, under penalty of five hundred pesos, and that the Spanish [storekeepers] either marry or give up their stores.

Canon Don Sebastián de Aguilar

Canon Don Sebastián de Aguilar, who was a prebend of this holy church of Lima, received notice of his appointment as canon of the church of Trujillo due to the death of canon Zapata of that church. He bade farewell to the chorus of canons of Lima on Wednesday, the 14th of August of the year 1669. That same day he went to Callao with all of his household, taking his sister Doña Tomasa and all his nephews, and embarked for Trujillo.

The Fiesta *of Saint Rose*

Sunday, the 18th of August of the year 1669, a proclamation was issued by the *alcaldes* Don Diego de Carbajal and Don Alvaro de Villafuerte, ordinary *alcaldes* of this city, and by the magistrate and the regiment, that this same night bonfires and illuminations be erected throughout the city for the [proposed] canonization of Holy Mary of the Rose [Saint Rose of Lima].[42] She was chosen as patron of this city by the viceroy, Count of Lemos, the royal council, and by the holy Inquisition and the Holy Crusade, all voting her patron saint of this noble and loyal city of Lima. [The proclamation stipulated] that all the guilds hold their celebrations on the novenary [ninth day of the feast of Saint Rose]. That same Sunday afternoon, the 18th of that month and year, the archbishop and canons in their chorus capes and all the clergy with surplices went in procession to the monastery of Santo Domingo to vespers.

That same night the viceroy, Count of Lemos, was in the chorus with the religious of Santo Domingo [monastery] at matins [vespers] until they were over. It was later than ten at night when he returned to the palace.

Monday, the 19th, the archbishop returned to [the church of] Santo Domingo and said a pontifical Mass; Doctor Calvo, canon of this holy church, gave the sermon. A great number of people attended the celebration: the viceroy and gentlemen of the royal *audiencia*, the comptrollers, and the secular *cabildo*; and [they sat] in the same arrangement as the previous afternoon at vespers. The ceiling of the cloister of Santo Domingo was exquisitely hung with decorations. There were many interesting things to see, tables laid out with all kinds of food, and gardens. The octave [for Rose's feast day] lasted eight days, and each order went every day to hold its celebration from vespers until the following day, continuing until the sung Mass and sermon in eulogy of Saint Rose was held. The statue of Saint Ignatius Loyola with the accompaniment of all the fathers of the [Jesuit] Society was brought in procession on the last day, and it was accompanied from the church of Santo Domingo by an infantry company which consisted of a great number of soldiers on call in addition to the palace company. That was Sunday, the 25th of August of the year 1669. Monday, the 26th, the Society of Jesus held their celebration, and that morning Father Barraza gave the sermon.

On Monday afternoon there was a very large formation, and that same afternoon the viceroy departed from the palace dressed

[42] See note 41 for Saint Rose of Lima and her feast day.

The Viceroy Sallies Forth

in color and in shirt sleeves. With the banner of Saint Rose in his hand, he went on horseback through the streets that the procession was to pass. Later he came out on foot in the procession with this banner, and he carried it the whole time until returning to the monastery of Santo Domingo. [The procession] started out from there and went to San Agustín, then by way of Mercaderes Street to the plaza where the squadron was [formed]. Accompanying him in their holy glory were [images of] all the saints of the order of Santo Domingo, [Saint Dominic] being the first, followed by Saint Ignatius, and then five angels, the five with their saints. Behind them was Saint Francis followed by [a banner with] the words of the Ave Maria, then all the saints, and the clergy of all the religious orders with their surplices, and at the end [the statue of] Saint Rose. When it arrived in front of the squadron, the front of flags parted whereupon the saint [the statue of Saint Rose] entered. Three charges of arquebuses, muskets, and small cannons were fired instead of the six pieces of artillery that were not fired because the vicereine, who was at the windows of the palace, was pregnant and very close to the time of giving birth. All the flags were fluttered and lowered simultaneously towards the [statue of the] saint, which remained there for a long while. It was a great consolation for this city, from which much pleasure was derived.

Arrival of the Dispatch Ship from Spain

The dispatch ship from Spain arrived at this city bringing the [papal] bull of His Holiness, on Friday, the 23rd of August of the years 1669, which was the day of celebration of the octave of the feast day of Saint Rose, patron saint of all this kingdom. This same day celebrations were being held in her honor. It was on this day [52] years ago that the favored saint had died, may she pray to Our Lord for all those who have been her devotees, and in particular for those of this city who so greatly celebrated her canonization.

Favor Granted to Don Alvaro de Ibarra

On this same dispatch ship that arrived at this city on the 23rd of August there was a royal letter in which His Majesty, may God protect him, granted Don Alvaro de Ibarra the favor of senior *oidor* and *visitador* of the royal *audiencia*; and upon completion of his visit, the post of *oidor* of the Council of the Indies [in Spain]. On Monday, the 2nd of September of that year, there were horse races by *caballeros* along his street.

The Unfortunate Death of Don Félix de Aguero

Dawn of Sunday, the 1st of September of the year 1669, found Don José Félix de Aguero [dead]. The first word to come from his house at dawn was that he had hanged himself from a water storage rack. Later, word circulated that he had choked from phlegm. May Our Lord pardon his sins, as he had been very demented for some time.

Monday, the 2nd of the month, at eleven in the morning he was buried in his chapel at Santo Domingo [church] with [the attendance of] the dean and the ecclesiastic and secular *cabildo* and all the *caballeros* of the city. Don Juan de Céspedes went to the funeral with the minor son of the deceased because the first born, son-in-law of Céspedes, was ill and for this reason could not go.

Second Childbirth of the Countess of Lemos

By dawn of Thursday, the 18th of September, the Countess of Lemos of this City of Kings had given birth [to a daughter].

That same day the dispatch boat arrived from Panama with news that a fleet of galleons was in Cartagena, having arrived at that port on the 14th of June of the year 1669.

Reception of Don Alvaro de Ibarra

At ten in the morning on Friday, the 20th of said month, with great solemnity and the applause of all the *caballeros* of this city, Señor Don Alvaro de Ibarra was received as [*audiencia*] president, senior *oidor*, and *visitador*. There were many arches over the decorated streets, and flags hung from balconies and windows. Such a display had never been seen in this city.

Consecration of the Bishop of Huamanga

Sunday, the 29th of September of the year 1669, day of the archangel Saint Michael, Señor Don Cristóbal de Castilla [y Zamora],[43] who was presently high inquisitor of this city of Lima, was consecrated bishop of Huamanga by the archbishop of this city, Don Pedro de Villagómez. Present [at the consecration] on this day were the viceroy, Count of Lemos, the royal *audiencia*, the secular *cabildo*, and all the nobility of this city.

Baptism of the Child of the Count of Lemos

Tuesday, the first of October of the year 1669, at five in the afternoon, the baby daughter of the viceroy, Count of Lemos, was

[43] Don Cristóbal de Castilla y Zamora was an illegitimate son of King Philip IV of Spain. Manuel de Mendiburu, *Diccionario histórico-biográfico del Perú* (11 vols., Lima: Imprenta "Enrique Palacios," 1931–34), IV, 89–90.

baptized in this cathedral of Lima with very great solemnity, attended by all the nobility of this city. Señor Don Pedro de Villagómez, archbishop of this city, annointed her with oil and chrism and sprinkled water on her. The godfather was Father Castillo of the Society of Jesus, and the godmother, the oldest daughter of the viceroy. His Excellency was present with all the *oidores*. Many persons attended, and she was given the name of Rose [Rosa Francisca de Castro y Portugal].

Celebration of Saint Rose at Santa Ana

Sunday, the 20th of October of the year 1669, commenced the eight day celebration of the parish of Santa Ana for the feast of Saint Rose. On each of the eight days there was a great celebration and a sermon. The viceroy, Count of Lemos, attended the afternoon of the first day. That afternoon Father Maestro Fray Juan Baes, of the Mercedarian, preached, and there were four sermons.

Nieces of the Prebendary Aguilar

Saturday, the 26th of October of the year 1669, at five in the afternoon the two nieces of the prebendary Don Sebastián de Aguilar entered the convent of Nuestra Señora del Prado as nuns. The youngest one left the convent within two days.

On the morning of Saturday, the 26th of the month, there was a Mass and sermon with the attendance of Señor Don Cristóbal de Castilla, bishop of Huamanga, and the Count of Lemos, viceroy of these kingdoms. On Sunday morning, the 27th of the month, there was a Mass and sermon which was preached by Father Maestro Marín of the Mercedarian order. In the afternoon there was a solemn procession with a great number of [images of] saints, and they brought the statue of Saint Philip of Neri from San Pedro [church] with a surplice and a candle in his hand, and [the statue of] Saint Rose who went behind all the saints, and the Holy Sacrament which was carried by the canon Don José Dávila. The procession went through the same streets as those usually taken for the celebration of Corpus [Christi].

Captain Moreno's Company

An infantry company also appeared with eighty-seven soldiers, all very resplendent, the majority of whom were on inactive duty. There was also a fountain of wine that flowed from noon until night.

The Vicereine Goes to Mass After Childbirth

Monday, the 4th of November of the year 1669, at eleven in the morning the Countess of Lemos went to the cathedral of this city to attend a [thanksgiving] Mass for the birth of her child. She was dressed in white, [went] in a sedan chair, and the viceroy in gala attire went in a group with all the *oidores* and the secular *cabildo*. Mass was sung by Canon Calvo.

In the afternoon the viceroy appeared on a white horse and ran three races in the barricaded area set up for that purpose, and he ran doubles with Don Manuel de Andrade, who was his secretary for correspondence. The viceroy and his companion set out from the palace with their faces half covered with black lace.

Death of the Mercedarian Provincial

Tuesday, the 5th of November of the year 1669, at eight at night Fray Miguel de Salazar, present provincial of La Merced [monastery] died. He was buried the following Wednesday at three in the afternoon. The entire ecclesiastic council with all its canons was present because his brother-in-law, called Miguel de Medrano, was the present treasurer of the cathedral.

The Certificate of Father Fray Juan Macías

Sunday, the 10th of November of the year 1669, at twelve noon there was a pontifical Mass said by Don Pedro de Villagómez, archbishop of this city. After the sermon given by Father Maestro Toro, regent of studies of the Dominican order, at the time of the offertory [Fray Juan Marcías] read the certificate for beatification [of Rose of Lima] sent by His Holiness [requesting] that the head sacristan of the cathedral, the licentiate [blank], collect the necessary information. The viceroy, Count of Lemos, all the *oidores*, and all the city were present.

The Viceroy Goes to the Corral de la Comedia

Wednesday, the 13th of November of the year 1669, at three in the afternoon the presently governing viceroy, Count of Lemos, and the vicereine with her eldest daughter and son went to the theater to see the play about Saint Rose, done with much finesse. With His Excellency went all the *oidores* and Señor Don Alvaro de Ibarra, president and *visitador* of this royal *audiencia*. The three *alcaldes* of the court were seated in the theater on three chairs, and the viceroy, vicereine, and all the *oidores* in the box which they had enlarged to accommodate them all. The viceroy said that he wanted this [the seating arrangement] to be an example for subsequent viceroys.

Bullfights for Saint Rose

Saturday, the 16th of November of the year 1669, bulls were run in the small plaza of Santa Ana for the celebration of Saint Rose of Holy Mary. In the middle of the small plaza there was a greased topmast of the admiral's ship with prizes placed at the top: four pairs of silk stockings, one pound of ribbons of all colors, and a purse with three hundred pesos for anyone who climbed up. No one managed to reach it.

That same afternoon the viceroy, Count of Lemos, and the vicereine and all the *oidores* watched the bulls from the balcony of [house of] the canon Don Luis Zegarra. [The canon] gave gifts to the viceroy and many to the countess and the *oidores*; and the canon also threw silver from the windows. At this point the bells of Santa Ana pealed for the silver that the canon had thrown, which everyone considered a great favor on his part to show such generosity.

The second bulls were [run] Wednesday, the 20th of November of the year 1669, in the same small plaza of Santa Ana.

Death of the Chambermaid of the Countess of Lemos

The chambermaid of the Countess of Lemos, called Mariana, died Thursday, the 12th of December of the year 1669. She was buried at eleven in the morning on Friday, the 13th, at Santo Domingo [church]. The Count of Lemos went to her funeral wearing a long taffeta cape, as did all the *oidores* with their president, Señor Don Alvaro de Ibarra, and the secular *cabildo*, all dressed in mourning. The archbishop was in the church in his seat, and the dean and ecclesiastic *cabildo* attended. The deceased was carried by members of the Dominican order, in which Doña Mariana had a son.

Death of a Strangled Boy

Saturday night, the 21st of December, day of the apostle Saint Thomas, they found [the body of] a boy of about eight or nine years of age, in the side street of Juan Simón, naked and barefoot, who had been strangled with the ribbon of his hat. It was later determined that another boy of eighteen years of age, a relative, had committed that crime.

Bulls for Saint Rose

Monday, the 23rd of this month and year, bulls were run at the *fiesta* for Saint Rose, and the viceroy, Count of Lemos, and the vicereine went to the *cabildo* to see the bulls. That day no *caballero* came out into the plaza, only the Marquis of Villar with his lieutenant to clear the plaza with two hundred duty soldiers of this city. All the plaza was cleared without any person of any kind remaining therein, and the bull pen and the plaza encircled by boards, as is done in Madrid. That afternoon a soldier ran on horseback in front of the bull, and gave three turns [around the plaza].

Release of General Antonio Buitrón

Wednesday, the first day of Advent of the year 1669, at twelve noon General Antonio Buitrón and Colonel Juan Núñez de Aya left the court prison of this city, upon decree of the viceroy, Count of Lemos, after having been imprisoned fourteen months. To the royal ensign, Don Martín de Gareca, who was under house arrest, His Excellency granted city arrest which included five leagues beyond the city.

Departure of the Count for Villa

Friday, Christmas day of the year 1669, at three in the afternoon the viceroy, Count of Lemos, and the countess went in their carriage drawn by six mules, the two of them going alone to Villa, the ranch of the fathers of the Society of Jesus. Their eldest daughter and eldest son, along with a duenna and six ladies, went in another carriage drawn by six mules. All the [palace] gentlemen and Don Felipe Romana [went] on their mules.

Tuesday, the 31st of December of the year 1669, the Count and Countess of Lemos and Don Alvaro de Ibarra returned from Villa after five days of rest.

The Year 1670

No Election of Alcaldes

Wednesday, the first day of the new year of 1670. On this New Year's Day there was no election of ordinary *alcaldes*. (Thursday, the ninth, the *alcaldes* were elected as they appear below).

Departure of the Viceroy for the Chácara

Thursday, the 2nd of January of the year 1670, at nine in the morning the viceroy, Count of Lemos, without a cape and dressed in color, and the vicereine went to the *chácara* of Don Alvaro de Ibarra. They went in the same way and with the same servants and ladies as on the trip to Villa.

Monday, the 6th of the month, the new battalion commander for Callao, sent from Spain by His Majesty, entered this city.

Bulls and Cañas *in which His Excellency Ran*

Wednesday, the 8th of the month, there was a running of bulls and *cañas* jousting. The Count of Lemos ran a race from the corner of the archbishop's [palace] to the *cabildo* with Don Alvaro Navamuel, *caballero* of the order of Alcántara, who was a former ordinary *alcalde*. The other *caballeros* followed them, and then they raced around the plaza in a circle. The plaza was well sprinkled, clean and completely empty of any people, and all surrounded with boards as in Madrid. Six highly decorated gray mules appeared carrying the canes and bearing the arms of His Excellency, and the Indians that led them were colorfully dressed in their headdresses. They entered the plaza with drums, followed by the pages and then His Excellency. They [the *caballeros*] raced from one corner to the other, hurling canes, and the viceroy galloped with his escadrille. Later, on picking them up, they all started off at a gallop from the fountain to the palace. This event ended with two bullfights, with which the evening came to a close. At the *cabildo*, under the canopy, there was a portrait of our king and lord Don Carlos II, and above it one of Saint Rose.

Election of the Ordinary Alcaldes

Thursday, the 9th of January of the year 1670, Don Martín de Zavala, *caballero* of the order of Santiago and comptroller of the Holy Crusade, and Don Francisco Mejía Ramón were elected ordinary *alcaldes* of this city of Lima.

On this day Mass was said in the royal chapel of the palace.

The Corregidor *of Cuzco*

On the night of Friday, the 10th, the *corregidor* of Cuzco [a member] of the Order of San Juan [de Jerusalén, or Knights of Malta],[44] said to be a natural son of the Duke of Medina Sidonia, entered this city.

Sent to Valdivia

Monday, the 13th, His Excellency ordered that Don Francisco Colmenares, royal official of this city, be escorted by six mounted soldiers to Callao [enroute to Chile as inspector]. Lieutenant General Don Felipe Romana took him as far as Callao to embark him on the ship there on which Don Antonio de Montoya of the order of Santiago, former *corregidor* of Arica for His Majesty, was going as governor of that post [Valdivia].

Thursday, the 16th of January of the year 1670, the dispatch boat arrived at this city with thirteen boxes [of correspondence]

[44] See note 12 for Spanish military-religious orders.

which the galleons had brought from Spain. This dispatch ship came loaded with commercial goods for Callao, something that had never occurred before. It was brought by Don Francisco de Castro, who had sailed in charge of this ship with six pieces of artillery and four merchant vessels that left with supplies in July of the year 1669.

Dispatches from Spain

This ship brought [notification] that Señor Don Blas de Aguinaga was [named] auxiliary bishop of this city with a retainer for his position. Archbishop Don Pedro de Villagómez was to give him three hundred pesos each month for his income and at the end of the year it should be adjusted to four thousand pesos taking into account the three hundred every month.

This dispatch ship also brought news that Fray Gabriel de Guilléstegui, bishop of Paraguay, was coming as bishop of Cuzco, and that the Very Reverend Father Maestro Fray Juan de Iturrizarra was going as bishop to Paraguay.

Bishop for Cuzco

There was also news in this dispatch ship that the Very Reverend Father Maestro Loyola of the order of Saint Augustine was [appointed] bishop of Concepción, Chile.

Doctor [Don Juan] de Rojas, former canon of the city of Cuzco, also became prebendary of this cathedral of Lima and was received in this holy metropolitan church in Lima on Friday, the 17th of January, of the year 1670.

[Orders arrived] that all the posts that had been sold since the year 1624 be relinquished and an accounting be made of all the salaries that had been drawn.

Saturday, the 25th of January of the year 1670, at eleven in the morning an edict was proclaimed with war drums by order of the viceroy, Count of Lemos, and by royal decree sent by the queen, our lady, dated the 22nd of September of the year 1667 in Madrid, and countersigned by her cabinet minister, and by the Council of the Indies. [It decreed] that all Indians, male and female, young and old, be free and at liberty to go to their lands without anyone hindering them, with the same penalty given [offenders] for bothering free persons. For those who had trafficked in such slaves subsequent to the day of the referred-to decree [be it known that] their [the slaves'] rights would be upheld against those who sold them.

Decree that the Indians be Free

The Governor of Chile

Sunday, the 26th of the month, at eight at night the ship destined for Valdivia left the port of Callao with the governor of that post, Don Antonio de Montoya, *caballero* of the order of Santiago and ex-*corregidor* of Arica. Don Francisco Colmenares also left on this trip as inspector of the royal funds, and Sergeant Espinosa with twenty more men as soldiers for that post.

Third Bullfights for the Feast of Saint Rose

Monday, the 27th of January of the year 1670, bulls were run in this plaza. The viceroy went all around the plaza in his carriage with the *oidores*, and with the *alcaldes* on horseback beside the carriage. Then he went to his seat at the *cabildo* where the countess and his oldest son were.

More than two hundred battalion soldiers in shirt sleeves came out to clear the plaza with highly sharpened pikes. Along with their sergeants they looked very handsome.

Following this, four dapper *caballeros* entered the plaza with their pages and spears. One was Don Luís de Sandoval, who gave a spear thrust to a very brave bull that [responded by] injuring the horse, and he left the plaza. The second was Don Manuel de Andrade, correspondence secretary of His Excellency. He gave very good spear thrusts, and he took out the broadsword from his belt and cut the bull to pieces. The third was Don Diego Manrique, who battled well with the bull and ran the brute through the neck with the spear, producing a favorable reaction [from everyone]. The fourth was the very handsome Don Cristóbal de Llanos who serves in a post as royal official, and he used the spear very skillfully. At his first attempt to place the spear his hat dropped to the ground, and he took out the broadsword from his belt and killed the bull. The second [bull] he engaged very well, thrusting the spear up to the middle of the handle in the back of the neck. The third time, he toppled another ferocious bull bewildering it, and his assistants finished killing it. He was cheered on this last thrust by the viceroy and vicereine, and the whole city shouted acclaim, all waving their handkerchieves. It was the best afternoon seen in *fiestas* in this plaza, with which the celebrations finished. Night approached and everyone was very content.

Departure of the Viceroy for La Calera

Wednesday, the 27th of January of the year 1670, the viceroy, Count of Lemos, and the vicereine with all of the family went to the Franciscan lime quarry where they were entertained by the commissary general Father Fray Luis de Zervela, and the lay brothers of the same order put on a play for them. Their Excellencies returned that same night to their palace.

Departure of His Excellency for Callao

Monday, the 3rd of February, day of Saint Blase, the viceroy, Count of Lemos, went to Callao, without anyone's knowledge, [everyone] thinking he was going to Magdalena [Recollect]. Upon arriving at the port of Callao he ordered a review [of the troops], and eliminated the posts of various soldiers who did not appear at the time His Excellency held muster.

Death of the Governor of Chile

Friday, the 7th of February of the year 1670, Don Antonio de Cabrera, *caballero* of the order of Santiago and former governor of the kingdom of Chile, died. He was buried Saturday the 8th at the cathedral of Lima, in his chapel. The viceroy, Count of Lemos, and the gentlemen of the royal *audiencia*, secular and ecclesiastic *cabildos*, and all the nobility of this city attended the funeral. He was buried as a private *caballero*.[45]

Death of Licentiate Carbajal

Licentiate Don Diego de Carbajal, head chaplain of the San José convent of barefoot nuns of this city, died Saturday, the 8th of February, at two in the morning. He was buried on the afternoon of Sunday, the 9th, in his church with the attendance of all of the order and the priests.

Death of Doctor Alonso Coronado

At four in the afternoon of Tuesday, the 11th of the month, during a discussion at San Martín [*colegio*, Doctor Alonso Coronado] was struck with such a great pain that he could not continue, and he left the *colegio*. At the corner, after having confessed a couple of words to a priest of the Society of Jesus, he expired on the spot.

Departure of the Viceroy for the Chácara *of Ibarra*

Wednesday, the 12th, the viceroy and vicereine with their family went to the *chácara* of Señor Don Alvaro de Ibarra and remained there until Tuesday, the 18th of February, which was the Tuesday before Lent. That same afternoon at five the viceroy went to the public festivity at the Jesuit Church and from there went to the palace.

[45] *Enterrado como caballero particular* means he was buried in a private tomb, not in the general vault of his military-religious order of Santiago.

Death of Don Pedro López de Gárate

Señor Don Pedro López de Gárate died at four in the afternoon of Shrove Tuesday which was the 18th of February of 1670. On Wednesday, the first day of Lent, at five in the afternoon he was buried at the Magdalena Recollect, next to the very venerable Father Fray Juan Macías. His executor and holder of his assets was Captain Martín de Iturraín.

General Proclamation

Saturday, the 1st of March of the year 1670, a proclamation was issued by the Count of Lemos relating to all the decrees that the Count of Santisteban had issued from the year 1662 until the above-mentioned day, in addition to those the Count of Lemos had issued. These referred to meat, bread, fish, candles, and other provisions, swords with needlepoints, and on the tonsures and dress of mulatto women and Negresses. There were many other things included in this decree, with grave penalties for those who disobeyed, and [stipulating] that every year, a day after the election of the ordinary *alcaldes*, this proclamation [of viceregal decrees] be published without any errors. It was so ordered and proclaimed by the viceroy, Count of Lemos, on that day.

Death of the Bishop of Panama

On the afternoon of Saturday, the 1st of March of the year 1670, the dispatch boat arrived from Panama with news of the death of the bishop of that city, Señor Don Sancho Pardo, and [news of] many other persons who had gone to make purchases in Tierra Firme.

At four in the morning of Wednesday, the 12th of March of the year 1670, the goldsmith Pedro de Valdés, steward in charge of the Holy Sacrament [chapel] of the cathedral of Lima, having held that post for many years, died. He was buried the following Thursday in the vault of the Holy Sacrament chapel of the cathedral. At this time work on the new cathedral was quite advanced. The son-in-law of the deceased was Don Felipe Romana, lieutenant general and personal attendant of the Count of Lemos. His Excellency and the secular *cabildo* were present at the funeral services on Saturday, the 15th of this month and year. After the Mass and other services were over His Excellency accompanied the bereaved ones as far as the house of the deceased.

House of Las Amparadas

Wednesday, the 19th of March of the year 1670, day of the glorious Saint Joseph, at five in the afternoon a procession set forth from the royal chapel of the palace with images of the Immaculate Conception of Our Lady, conceived without original sin, and the glorious archangel Saint Michael. The viceroy, Count of Lemos, carried the banner from the palace to the house where it was deposited, called *Las Amparadas* [the sheltered women]. All the *caballeros*, noblemen, and individuals walked in the procession carrying lighted candles which they provided. There were also more than one hundred men of the battalion of this city with their firearms and lances, added to the mercenary company that is at the palace. There were three days of celebration with a sung Mass and sermon by the fathers of the Society of Jesus. It was Father Castillo who arranged for this cloister for single women who had been maids for the honor and glory of Our Lord.

Arrival of the Governor of Chile

Saturday, the 22nd of March, at five in the afternoon the Marquis of Naval-Morquende, who came from Chile where he was governor of that kingdom, arrived at the palace to see the viceroy, Count of Lemos. He had come at the call of His Excellency, and he stayed at the palace, living there as before and had his meals with their excellencies.

New Governor for Chile

Señor Don Juan Enríquez, the new governor for the kingdom of Chile sent by our lady, ruler, and queen, arrived at this city of Lima on Wednesday, the 26th of March of the year 1670, after the Ave Marias, with an impressive accompaniment. He entered [the palace] to speak with the viceroy, Count of Lemos. On this occasion the two brothers of the governor were in the city as the viceroy had asked them to come down from the city of Cuzco. One was choirmaster of the church of Cuzco and a member of the order of Calatrava, as was the other brother; the governor was of the order of Santiago. (Governor Don Juan Enríquez took his leave of the viceroy, Count of Lemos, on Saturday, the 20th of September of the year 1670, and went to Callao the same day with the Marquís of Naval-Morquende, in the carriage of the Marquís.)

Closing of the Churches on Holy Thursday

Thursday, the 3rd of April of the year 1670, was the sacred day of Holy Thursday. By order of the viceroy, Count of Lemos, and the archbishop, Don Pedro Villagómez, all the churches of this city were ordered closed at ten in the evening and they were not to open until five in the morning of Good Friday; and it was so done.

A proclamation was likewise issued by the viceroy, Count of Lemos, that at nine thirty that same night of Holy Thursday the curfew bell be tolled, and that at ten at night all the women retire to their homes. It was so carried out, something that had never before been seen in this city of Lima.

Death of the Archbishop of Charcas

Holy Friday, the 4th of April, the mail arrived from Cuzco bearing word of the death in Cuzco of the archbishop-designate of Charcas, Don Bernardo de Izaguirre, the present bishop of Cuzco, who was preparing to go to Charcas. He died after four days [of illness]. He was buried in the Society of Jesus [church] of that city of Cuzco the 18th of May of the year 1670. May God keep him in His holy glory.

Fall of Don Bartolomé de Salazar

Wednesday, the 23rd of April of the year 1670, Doctor Don Bartolomé de Salazar, *oidor* of the royal *audiencia*, went to hear Mass at the palace chapel. At eight in the morning, while descending the small steps of the chapel he slipped and broke his leg in two places. (He died on the 16th of July of that year.)

Death of Doña Teresa Avalos

At noon on Sunday, the 27th of this month and year, Doña Teresa de Avalos y Toledo died. She was the widow of Don Juan Manrique who had been killed by his Negro [slave] seventeen years ago, the present age of her son.

Procession to Las Amparadas *Church*

At four in the afternoon of Wednesday, the 28th of May of the year 1670, [the image of] the Holy Virgin, the Immaculate Conception of Our Lady, was taken from the palace chapel and joined by [statues of] four highly-adorned angels, the archangel Saint Michael, Saint Joseph, and Saint Rose. The Holy Sacrament was taken from the cathedral, carried by the precentor Palma with all the canons illuminating [the way]. The viceroy, Count of Lemos, carried the banner accompanied by all the *oidores* and the regiment. And the [statues of] Saint Ignatius and Saint Francis of Borja were brought forth from the Society of Jesus to the church of *Las Amparadas* where Our Lord, in the form of the Holy Sacrament, was deposited. The infantry company of the palace came out [for the occasion] and all the same men were also [members] of the battalion. There were six pieces of artillery in the plaza, but only twelve small cannons were fired. The whole city was present at the procession.

My Son Francisco Ordained

On the eve of Holy Trinity Sunday [June 1st] of the year 1670, with permission of his prelate the [Franciscan] father provincial, Francisco Franco, my son Francisco was ordained to say Mass. [This was] in Arequipa, and the bishop of that city ordained him. He sang his first Mass in the Santa Clara convent of nuns in the city of Cuzco on Thursday, June 10th, day of the seven martyrs. His sponsor at the altar was the guardian of his college, and his other sponsor was Doctor Don Diego de Honton, his cousin. A great number of people attended that day, and the doctor took all of them to his house for dinner. There were bullfights, horse races, and festivities.

The Statue of Saint Rose from Rome

Sunday, the 15th of June of the year 1670, the Count of Lemos left this city for Callao at seven in the morning without cape and dressed in color, with his staff of captain general [in hand]. As soon as he arrived at the port all the artillery began to fire from the ships and from land, and His Excellency ordered that it be fired three times at the disembarkation of the large statue of Saint Rose which came from Rome. When His Excellency returned [to Lima] in the afternoon, he went to the theater where the countess was attending the play which had been presented at the cathedral for the Corpus [Christi] *fiesta.*

The Statue of Saint Rose Comes to Lima

Friday, the 20th of June of the year 1670, they [the people of Callao] took her [the statue of Saint Rose] at six in the morning from the port of Callao and brought her as far as the royal chapel of the palace without anyone else carrying her. All the women of that port, married and single, came on foot with lit candles in their hands, some wearing cloaks and others with mantillas. They crossed all the canals full of water, of which there were many, without stopping for anything, [even though] they had shoes and stockings on.

The Infantry

The infantry of Callao with their arms and their battalion commander and sergeant major also went in accompaniment, carrying [the statue] when their turn came. The viceroy sent orders to La Legua that the sergeant major return from there to Callao to guard that port, as it had remained without anyone, and the battalion commander came to this city of Lima guiding the infantry on foot, as mentioned.

The Mule Cart On the road above La Legua they met the mules [and cart] of the viceroy that were going to bring the holy figure of Rose, and the people carrying it stoned the mules, and if they had not belonged to the viceroy would have killed them. The whole troop came with the statue along Naranjos Road.

The Recollect of Belén When they arrived at the Recollect of Belén, all the religious came out with cross held high wanting to carry the [statue of the] saint, but those carrying it from Callao did not consent. They followed with their cross and the religious community.

San Juan de Dios The fathers of San Juan de Dios did the same as above, and they were [also] not permitted [to carry the statue], and they followed with their cross.

Those of the Monastery of La Merced The religious of the main monastery of La Merced did likewise, and they also were not permitted, so they followed with all three crosses held high, and the three communities went right up to the royal chapel. The rejoicing and contentment with which the people of Callao came was so great that the whole city cheered them. That same night there were bonfires throughout the city and candles in the windows and in the streets.

Death of Bishop Aguinaga Señor Don Blas de Aguinaga, schoolmaster of this holy church of Lima and elected auxiliary bishop of this archbishopric, died after two days of hemorrhaging. He was buried in the cathedral on the 25th of July of the year 1670. The Count of Lemos, viceroy of these kingdoms, all the gentlemen of the *audiencia*, the secular and ecclesiastic *cabildos*, the archbishop, Don Pedro de Villagómez, and all the nobility of this city were present at his funeral.

Acrobat in the Palace Sunday, the 13th of July of the year 1670, at five in the afternoon an acrobat danced on the tightrope and did many somersaults of the high rope. He glided from the roof to the patio in front of the guard corps where the infantry was, and there did somersaults. The viceroy, Count of Lemos, and the vicereine with the [*audiencia*] president, Don Alvaro de Ibarra, and the *oidores* were watching from the high corridor. That same afternoon a great number of people were there.

Death of the Blessed Isabel de Jesús

Monday, the 14th of July of the year 1670, the Blessed Isabel de Jesús of the order of Saint Agustíne, died. It had been thirty-six years since she had professed to that order, and she died at the age of seventy, a spinster. That same day they took her to be buried at the monastery of San Agustín and placed her in the anteroom of the sacristy until Tuesday, the 15th of the month, during which time everyone went to see her, and she had a very good appearance. Archbishop Don Pedro de Villagómez with all his *cabildo*, the viceroy, Count of Lemos, all the gentlemen of the royal *audiencia*, the secular *cabildo*, and all the nobility of this city of Lima attended her funeral as she was a great servant of God. She was buried as a virgin with a coronet in the vault of Pedro del Molino, where they deposited her body. The vault is in the cloister of that monastery at the foot of the altar of the Pure and Immaculate Conception of Our Lady, where she is deposited until her time [of reckoning].

(Memorial services in her honor were held on Wednesday the 13th of August of the year 1670 at San Agustín [Church]. Father Ocón of the Augustinian order gave the sermon. Present at the services were the viceroy, Count of Lemos, the *oidores* and the secular *cabildo*, and a very great number of persons, so many that they did not fit in the church.)

Death of Señor Don Bartolomé de Salazar

Wednesday, the 16th of July of the year 1670, at eleven in the morning Doctor Don Bartolomé de Salazar, *oidor* of this royal *audiencia* of Lima, died. He was buried the following Thursday at the convent of the nuns, I mean in their church of La Concepción. The viceroy, Count of Lemos, gentlemen of the royal *audiencia* and ecclesiastic and secular *cabildos*, and all the *caballeros* of this city went to the burial.

The Holy Sacrament to the Convalescent Home

At four in the afternoon of Friday, the 25th of July of the year 1670, day of the glorious Saint James, patron of all the Spains, the holy sacrament was taken from the church of Cercado [Indian village] to Nuestra Señora del Carmen convalescent home for natives. It was carried by the present father provincial of the Society of Jesus and accompanied by music, [statues of] many saints, Archbishop Don Pedro de Villagómez, as well as a great number of people. The procession went along the street that leads directly to the hospital. That same afternoon the holy sacrament was placed in that chapel, may it be praised forever and ever, in Christ, Amen.

Repair of the Two Canals of My Street

Wednesday, the 30th of July of the year 1670, repairs were finished on the two canals with their bridges [on my street behind Santa Ana church] which had been ordered by Captain Antonio Campos, *regidor* of this city of Lima, and who was then water commissioner. All the other canals were repaired at the order of the viceroy, Count of Lemos, and charged to the excise tax which was being levied at this time.

Lassoed Bulls

Thursday, the 31st of July of the year 1670, there were horse races by *caballeros* in the plaza in honor of the birthday of the Countess of Lemos. After the races bulls were lassoed, and a bull charged the *caballero* Don Agustín de Bracamonte, who had been president of [the *audiencia* of] Panama, and knocked him to the ground causing him to lose his beribboned hat. There was great perseverance on the part of the *caballeros* and the Marquis of Naval-Morquende, who had been governor of Chile, who entered the plaza together and had a hand at the bull. So did the governor who was going to Chile, Señor Don Juan Enríquez, *caballero* of the order of Santiago, and his brother. There were many enthusiastic pursuits that afternoon until the bull was killed, and there were many injured and wounded in the head, and much to see.

That same night a play was held at the palace by the servants and soldiers of His Excellency.

Aid of People for Panama

Thursday, the 18th of August of the year 1670, the tender of His Excellency left the port of Callao for that of Panama with aid of more than one hundred soldiers that the viceroy, Count of Lemos, sent for Panama and Porto Bello with Captain Pantoja as chief of the ship and men. The son of Bola de Herro went on this occasion, sent by His Excellency.

Formation for Saint Rose

Tuesday, the 26th of August of the year 1670, [the statue of] Saint Rose which had been taken there from the royal chapel on the afternoon of the day before, was carried in procession from the cathedral of Lima. There were solemn vespers with the viceroy and the gentlemen of the *audiencia* in attendance, as well as a great crowd of people. On the morning of that day a pontifical Mass and sermon were given. In the afternoon she [the statue of Saint Rose] was taken in procession to [the church of] Santo Domingo. There were four squadrons in the plaza, and the procession went from the main door [called the door of] *Perdón* [Forgiveness] up to the corner of Mercaderes Street, and from there to the corner of the chapel of the city prison, then from there the procession went directly to Santo Domingo. The viceroy, Count of Lemos, carried the banner throughout the whole procession. Eight companies on horseback, four city and four rural, came out into the plaza. The Marquís of Naval-Morquende appeared as general, very gallant and dressed in colored attire, well embellished, and he was on a very handsome horse belonging to the viceroy, all decorated with colored ribbons. The afternoon was worth seeing.

Death of Comptroller Gabriel de Erazo

Gabriel de Erazo, salaried comptroller, died on Saturday, the 30th of August of the year 1670. He was buried at six in the afternoon of Sunday, the 31st of this month and year, in the monastery of San Francisco.

Death of Don Francisco de Arano

Sunday, the 31st of August of the year 1670, Don Francisco de Arano, *caballero* of the order of Calatrava, died soon after having made a will. The fathers of the Society of Jesus took his body to the novitiate of the Society, and on the afternoon of Monday, the 1st of September, they buried him in the church of the novitiate of the Society of Jesus.

Masquerade that Went Out from San Marcelo

Monday, the 8th of September of the year 1670, at four in the afternoon the masquerade celebrated by the parish of San Marcelo of this city of Lima set out from that parish. There were three splendid floats brought forth which the parish had prepared with humor, and many [that were] very attractive. On the last float was a child of about ten years of age representing our king and lord. The viceroy, Count of Lemos, the Countess, and all the gentlemen *oidores* and many people were at the palace balconies to watch this masquerade pass.

Play of King Nebuchadnezzar

Wednesday, the 10th of September, day of the glorious Saint Nicholas of Tolentino, the Count of Lemos, viceroy of these kingdoms, and the Countess with their children and family, and the *oidores*, went to the theater where the play about King Nebuchadnezzar was being given with great staging. There were also many people of the city there. King Nabuco was played by the actor Fernando de Silva who was very good.

Prayers in the New College of Corazón de Jesús

Tuesday, the 16th of September of the year 1670, at four in the afternoon the viceroy, Count of Lemos, and all the *oidores*, and a great number of people [consisting] of *caballeros* and religious of all the orders, were present at the prayers said in Latin that same afternoon by Father Juan de Giocochea, schoolmaster of the senior students.

The following Wednesday the [religious] father of the junior students spoke to the archbishop and all the canons. On Thursday he addressed the entire university which was present with the rector, Doctor Juan de Zamudio, and where the stateliness of the university was to be seen. All the halls were richly decorated on all three days.

Monday, the 22nd of the month, the teachers read to the students in the new halls. That same day my son, Don Antonio de Mugaburu, inaugurated his lecture hall and sharply criticized all the students of the senior hall who lost their collegiate sash.[46] He was a senior student by order of his teacher, Father Juan de Goicochea, and he was currently studies monitor.

Masquerade at Callao

Saturday, the 20th of September, at nine at night a masquerade for Saint Rose was held in Callao that was quite worth seeing. Everyone from this city of Lima was present at that port [of Callao]. Also present were the Marquis of Naval-Morquende, and the governor, Don Juan Enríquez, who was embarking to govern in Chile, and [later] he went aboard ship.

Departure of the Ship for Chile

At four in the afternoon of Thursday, the 25th of September of the year 1670, the ship set sail carrying Don Juan Enríquez, governor for the kingdom of Chile, [having been] named by the queen, our lady and governor of all the Spains. The governor left and did not take any recruits, nor did he take regulars. Ensign Astor, whom His Excellency had imprisoned at the court prison of this city, went with His Lordship.

Friday, the 26th of September of the year 1670, at three in the afternoon the Count and Countess of Lemos left the palace for the

[46] *Banda* was a sash worn by collegiates, with different colors for various disciplines (medicine, law, etc.) and levels. In this sentence Mugaburu may have meant that the students lost the right to wear their sash.

Departure of the Count of Lemos for San Juan

hacienda called San Juan, belonging to the fathers of the Society of Jesus, where they stayed and slept that night.

On the morning of Saturday, the 27th of the month, His Excellency went from San Juan to the cascades of Surco. On the sandy part of the beach the *corregidor* of Cercado had prepared a house with a hall, parlor, bedroom, and service rooms for a reception where they awaited their excellencies, and the corregidor gave a luncheon. The viceroy on muleback and the Countess in a sedan chair went quite a way to see the small waterfalls, which pleased them very much. In the evening they returned to San Juan to sleep there that night.

Monday, the 29th of the month, day of the archangel Saint Michael, he [the viceroy] went to the shelter called Taboada, which is [in] the small plain of Pachacámac, where there was another country house. Many deer were chased with hounds over the plain by the postmaster general and Don Baltasar Pardo.

Death of General Francisco de Vitoria

General Don Francisco de Vitoria died on Monday, the 29th of September of the year 1670. He was buried the following Tuesday at the church of the novitiates of the Society of Jesus of this city of Lima.

Death of the Comptroller Ordóñez

The reappraisement comptroller, Don Jerónimo Ordóñez, died on Monday, the 29th of the month, the day of the archangel Saint Michael. He was buried at Santo Domingo [church] at twelve noon on Tuesday, the 30th, his saint's day, Saint Jerome.

Return of the Viceroy from San Juan

Tuesday, the 30th of the month, at seven at night the viceroy and the countess and all the rest of their family returned to this city from San Juan.

Thursday, the 3rd of October of the year 1670, the viceroy, Count of Lemos, went with the *oidores* and the countess with her ladies to the theater to see another play about Saint Rose that the licentiate Urbaido dedicated to His Excellency.

My *compadre* Jacinto de Acosta died Thursday, the 30th of October of the year 1670, at eight at night. He was buried on Friday, the 31st, at eight at night at the church of Santa Ana.

Bulls and Races in the Plaza

Thursday, the 6th of November of the year 1670, bulls were run in the plaza. The Marquis of Naval-Morquende with the two ordinary *alcaldes* and many very resplendent *caballeros* all on horseback [were present]. There was a barricade from the corner of the prison chapel to that of the archbishop's [palace]. The viceroy, Count of Lemos, rode on horseback through the plaza. In the evening there was a great play [given] at the palace. All was in honor of the birthday of our king and lord, Joseph Charles of Austria [Charles II], may God protect him many years.

Edict Concerning Peddlers

Thursday, the 27th of November of the year 1670, the viceroy, Count of Lemos, ordered the proclamation of the royal decree received from our queen and governor dated the 24th of September of the year 1668. [It ordered] that no peddler could wander through the streets selling, under penalty of losing all that he was found with and exile of ten leagues from this city. For a second offense, the same and four years [exile] in Chile. Nor could any Indian, mulatto, or Negro, [peddle] under penalty of one hundred lashes and losing all they were found with, and on the second offense, two hundred lashes.

Auto-da-fé at the Chapel of the Holy Inquisition

Tuesday, the 2nd of December of the year 1670, there was an auto-da-fé in the chapel of the holy Inquisition. The Count and Countess of Lemos attended, watching it from the rostrum of the chapel. A great number of people from the city, and all the religious orders [attended]. The licentiate Francisco de Frías, presbyter, was punished with sanbenito as a very great heretic. Also punished were a Negro, a mulatto, another *mestizo*, and a Spaniard, each one for marrying twice, and a mulatto woman for being a sorceress. That same day the five received two hundred lashes. Inquisitor Huerta and the treasury official attended this ceremony at the Inquisition.

Departure of Don Diego Pardo for Callao

Don Diego Pardo with his wife Doña Damiana [Mugaburu's step-daughter] went to live in Callao, and they left this city for that port Saturday, the 6th of December of the year 1670. He went with all his family.

Feast of the Pure and Immaculate Conception

On the afternoon of Monday, the 8th of December of the year 1670, a large squadron was formed in the plaza of this city. At four in the afternoon a procession left the cathedral and went to Santo Domingo [church], where there was a magnificent altar of the Augustinian fathers in the middle of the other street. From the corner which they call Valladolid, it came to the plaza, and at the steps of the cathedral there was another altar of the fathers of the Society of Jesus. All the religious and all the illustrious of this city came out [for the procession]. The viceroy went forth dressed in color and without a cape, and throughout the procession carried the banner in his hands, without releasing it. The tassels were held by the *visitador*, Don Esteban de Ibarra, and Don Andrés de Vilela.

Monday, the 15th of the month, there was another procession for the octave of Our Lady, and throughout the eight days sermons were given by great preachers. At five in the afternoon another procession went around the plaza with the same image of Our Lady of the Pure and Immaculate Conception and in the same order as above, the viceroy, Count of Lemos, carrying the flag, and dressed in black, with the abovementioned gentlemen and all the religious orders. There were three altars; [one] on the corner of [the street of] Jamón at the university, from where the procession started out. Another altar [was] at the entrance of Mercaderes Street, and another altar at the *cabildo*. All three were excellent. This afternoon there was no formation, and the whole plaza was hung with decorations and was very attractive.

Procession of the Relics of Saint Faustus

Sunday, the 21st of December of 1670, at five in the afternoon a procession went from the cathedral to Santo Domingo [church] to deposit the relics of Saint Faustus who had died as a holy martyr in Rome fourteen hundred years ago.[47] His Holiness [the pope] had sent them to the *cabildo* and regiment of this city of Lima, with a pontifical indulgence, and they were to be placed in the Holy Cross chapel of the monastery of Santo Domingo in this city of Lima.

Death of the Maiden Doña Florencia de Medina

Doña Florencia de Medina, a maiden thirty-four years of age, died at five in the afternoon of Thursday, the 25th of December, the first day of Christmas. On Friday, the second day of Christmas, she was buried in the parish of San Sebastián in the vault of the Holy Christ chapel. Her body was placed in a sealed coffin, as it was so ordered by the priests, one of whom was Doctor Mejía

[47] Mugaburu probably was referring to Saint Faustinus who was martyred in Rome about 302 A.D.; his feast day is July 27. See Charles G. Herbermann, *et al.*, editors, *The Catholic Encyclopedia* (16 vols., New York: Robert Appleton, 1907–1914), XIV, 3–4.

and the other, the licentiate Sarmiento, because all held the deceased in veneration as having good habits and being very virtuous. She was buried [as a virgin] with wreathes and palm,[48] and the priests buried her gratis. There were many priests in surplices [in attendance], and all the music [choir] of the cathedral of this city of Lima, and a very large accompaniment of illustrious people at her burial.

The Year 1671

Election of the Alcaldes

Thursday, the 1st day of the new year of 1671, Don García de Híjar y Mendoza, Junior, and Antonio del Campo, *regidor* of this city, were elected ordinary *alcaldes* of this city of Lima.

Funeral Rites for Flora

Tuesday, the 13th of January of the year 1671, funeral rites for the deceased Flora [Florencia de Medina] were held at San Sebastián [parish church] with music and a sung Mass. There were thirty Masses said for her the same day; twenty charity Masses paid for by Captain Jacinto de Vargas, and ten more commissioned by the sodality of the brotherhood of San Sebastián where she was buried.

News From Chile About the Enemy

Friday, the 23rd of January of the year 1671, a dispatch ship arrived at this city with news that twelve enemy ships had been seen in Valdivia, [Chile]. The 14th of February of this year another dispatch ship arrived with the report that there was only one ship that had arrived in those parts, damaged and off course, and the tender that accompanied it had disappeared in the storm that caught them in the Strait [of Magellan].

News of the Capture of Chagres

Tuesday, the 24th of February of the year 1671, the dispatch ship arrived from Panama with news that the English enemy [pirates under Henry Morgan] had captured the stronghold of the Chagres River fort, and that they had killed and beheaded more than two hundred slaves.[49] [Panama's *audiencia*] president, Don Juan Pérez de Guzmán, sent a request for help to the Count of Lemos.

48 Interring a palm with the deceased was a Spanish burial practice reserved for virgins.

49 Alexander O. Exquemelin, a pirate under Henry Morgan, gives an eyewitness account of the 1670 raid on Panama in his book, recently re-translated

Aid to Panama

Wednesday, the 4th of March of the year 1671, he sent two ships to Panama with three hundred men—two hundred Spaniards and one hundred mulattoes and Negroes. Hernando de Ribera went as battalion commander and chief of these men.

Second Aid for Panama

Monday, the 23rd of March of the year 1671, at four in the afternoon five ships left the port of Callao with one thousand six hundred and fifteen men for aid to Panama. Don Francisco Baños de Herrera went as chief of all the men. There were four colonels; and one of them was my *compadre* Don Antonio Buitrón y Mojica.

Third Aid sent to Panama

Saturday, the 4th of April of the year 1671, at four in the afternoon the royal flagship of this Southern Sea left the port of Callao with thirty-two pieces of artillery and another auxiliary ship with more than five hundred men as aid to Panama. There were three companies of mulattoes which made up the more than five hundred men.

Procession of the Rosary

Monday, the 20th of April, at four in the afternoon the communities of all the religious orders, the [cathedral] dean and *cabildo* with all the clergy, the viceroy with all the gentlemen of the royal *audiencia* and the secular *cabildo* came out in procession along the portals of Sombreros Street to the corner of the *cabildo*. From there it went to Santo Domingo [church] from where a very solemn procession set forth with [the statues of] Saint Dominic and the Most Holy Mother of God, [Our Lady] of the Rosary. This procession went from Santo Domingo to Mantas Street, then to the corner of the *cabildo* and past the palace to the cathedral. The litter of the Virgin was carried throughout the whole procession by the viceroy, Count of Lemos, and Señor Don Andrés de Vilela and all the other gentlemen of the royal *audiencia*. All types of people, friars, clerics, seculars, and women were saying the Rosary aloud throughout the procession. Such a multitude of people praying to Our Lord through the intercession of His Holy Mother for a successful outcome at Panama had never before been seen.

Arrival of Four Pirates at Callao

Thursday, the 23rd of April of the year 1671, at eight at night

from the Dutch and published as *The Buccaneers of America* (Baltimore: Penguin Books, 1969).

there arrived at this city an Englishman who disembarked at the point of [San Lorenzo] Island off Callao. He was brought to this city in a carriage, and the other three [pirates] arrived at twelve the same night on mules. All the sergeants of the mercenary companies of Callao came as guards. Friday, the 24th of this month, the ship in which they came, called the *Troy*, was lost in the bay of this port near Bocanegra.

News that the English had Left Panama

Sunday, the 26th of April of said year, the dispatch ship arrived at this city with news that the English had gone from Panama [City] to Cruces and had captured some of the religious of the Society of Jesus, La Merced, and San Juan de Dios, and asked fifteen thousand *pesos* ransom for them. The day they left [Panama] was the 7th of March of that year, and the help that His Excellency had dispatched for that kingdom of Panama had not arrived. The two Englishmen [in Lima] were named John and Charles Henry; the others [pirates] were a German and a mulatto born at San Lúcar de Barrameda [Spain].

Return of Our Lady of the Rosary to Her Church

At the end of the novena on Wednesday, the 29th of April, at five in the afternoon the holy statue of [Our Lady of] the Rosary was returned in a very solemn procession to the cathedral.

Death of the Marquis of Naval-Morquende

The Marquis of Naval-Morquende died at seven in the morning of Thursday, the 30th of April of the year 1671. He was buried Friday, the 1st of May, at twelve noon in the cathedral. All the duty soldiers of this city and seven companies of merchants came out with their arms. There were four military formations around the plaza. Commander of the merchants' corps was Captain Juan de Beingolea with his sergeant major, Captain Francisco de Alduaín; the sergeant major of the battalion regiment was Don Julián Corbera; and the adjutants, Gaspar de Savariego and Roque Rosales.

Funeral Rites for the Marquis of Naval-Morquende

Friday, the 8th of May, his memorial funeral rites were held at the cathedral of this city with all solemnity and the accompaniment of the viceroy and all the nobility of this city.

Saturday, the 7th of May of the year 1671, day of the Ascencion of the Lord, exactly at noon Doña Magdalena de Medina, the wife of my nephew, Juan Chamorro, died at the hospital of La Caridad. She was buried in the hospital church of La Caridad on Friday, the 8th of this month and year, with a sung Mass, vigil, and responsory. The priest of the parish of San Sebastián [officiated].

Death of Doña Magdalena de Medina

Tuesday, the 12th of May, news arrived from Panama that the enemy had gone from there and had burned all the houses where they had stayed and had captured the fathers of the Society of Jesus at one of the rivers of Panama. The fathers had embarked on a ship that they owned with all of the goods and wealth they possessed. This was the ship that the Englishmen found at the cross currents of Panama, and they boarded it with pieces of artillery and their men, and went through all the islands [in it]. They took with them as prisoners all the people [Jesuits] that they captured there and other religious of [the order of] La Merced and San Juan de Dios, and many families of men and women.

Departure of the Enemy from Panama

Señor Don Pedro de Villagómez, archbishop of this city of Lima, who began to govern this holy church Monday, the 20th of May of 1641, and who ruled this holy cathedral of Lima thirty years minus eight days, died between five and six in the afternoon of Wednesday, the 13th of May of the year 1671. He was buried on the afternoon of Friday, the 15th, in the cathedral of this city, and his burial was the most grandiose that has been held. His body was taken around the plaza, where they held eight funeral stops, and his body was placed on [each of] the eight platforms which had been built at the halting places. The Count of Lemos, all the *audiencia*, the regiment, as well as all the nobility of this city accompanied the body.

Death of Archbishop Don Pedro de Villagómez

Monday, the 18th of May, the second day of Pentecost, His Excellency the Count of Lemos received news from the president of Quito [*audiencia*] that dispatches from Spain were coming by way of the kingdom, [of New Granada] since Panama was captured by the enemy. There was [news of] the canonization of Saint Rose, Saint Francis of Borja, Saint Luis Beltrán, and Saint Peter of Alcántara; and Don Juan de Lara, parish priest of Madrid, was coming as bishop of the city of Cuzco.

News of the Canonizations of the Saints

It was Saturday, the 24th of January of the year 1671, when

Removal of Quarters Ban

His Excellency the Count of Lemos ordered that the thirteen battalion companies of this city of Lima be restricted to quarters. They were quartered until the 22nd of May of the year 1671, which was four months minus two days. His Excellency ordered that the quartering of the troops be lifted with the stipulation that every month there had to be two formations to train the soldiers, under penalty of eight pesos fine for those who failed to show up at a formation.

Killing of Juan de Cequera, the Altarboy

Sunday, the 24th of May, day of the Holy Trinity, at seven at night two men killed the son of Francisco de Cequera. It happened at the small door of Santa Clara [convent], the one near the mule stables, and it was said that the quarrel was over twelve *reales*.

Funeral Rites for the Archbishop

Monday, the 25th of May, memorial funeral services for the archbishop, Don Pedro de Villagómez, were held at the cathedral with great ceremony. All the nobility of this city gathered there, and the vicereine was present. That day the viceroy went to the church of San Pedro; His Excellency was making a novena at that church. The vicereine was present at the cathedral for these funeral rites, along with all the *oidores* and the secular *cabildo*. The archdeacon, Señor Don Juan Santoyo, gave the sermon.

Proclamation about Formations

Saturday, the 30th of May of the year 1671, at eleven in the morning a proclamation was issued by His Excellency the Count of Lemos: that all the battalion companies of this city form a squadron in the plaza with all the men they had enlisted in each company, with half the mounted companies, half of which were four as there are eight companies counting the four rural companies. Penalty for those who did not appear was six pesos and four days in jail for the infantrymen; twelve pesos and eight days in jail for the cavalrymen; the same for the regiment of merchants and the rural cavalrymen. Each regiment, alternately, was to go out [for squadron formation] every fifteen days, which means once each month.

Correspondence from Spain

Sunday, the 7th of June of the year 1671, at seven in the evening the royal correspondence arrived from Spain, coming from Cartagena by way of the kingdom [of Granada] and Quito. In it were [papal] bulls for the [appointments as] bishops: Señor Don

Cristóbal de Quirós, canon of this holy church of Lima, for Chiapas [Mexico]; and the Very Reverend Father [Francisco] de Loyola [y Vergara] of San Agustín for Concepción in Chile.

The decree [for appointment] of the two canons for this cathedral of Lima also arrived, one for Señor Don Diego de Salazar, who took over his post Monday, the 8th of June of this year of 1671. The other canon is Señor Don Martín de Negrón, a creole also from Lima, who was still in Spain and was arriving on the first galleons to leave for this kingdom.

Funeral Rites for the Duchess of Veragua

Wednesday, the 10th of June of the year 1671, funeral rites were held for [Doña María Luisa de Castro y Portugal], the Duchess of Veragua and sister of the Count of Lemos, presently viceroy of these kingdoms of Peru. They were held in the cathedral of this kingdom with the greatest pomp and ostentation, befitting such a lady. The catafalque was grandiose, and it had many candles. Showing signs of their sorrow, the viceroy with the vicereine, as well as all the nobility of this city in their mourning attire, were present at the funeral.

Death of the Prioress of El Carmen

Monday, the 29th of June, at eight at night the prioress of the nuns of El Carmen [convent] died. She was buried Wednesday, the 1st of July of the year 1671. The viceroy, Count of Lemos, and the vicereine, the secular and ecclesiastic *cabildos*, and all the nobility of this city of Lima were present at her burial.

Arrival of the Nuns from Panama

The [forty-four] nuns who came from Panama went to the palace from the *chácara* of Azaña at two in the afternoon of Thursday, the 2nd of July of this year, the day of the Visitation of Our Lady, Holy Mary. That afternoon from the corridors of the palace they watched the procession pass. There were forty-four that arrived at this city, and they were lodged in the palace, where His Excellency graciously received them with very great affection. Forty were professed nuns and four were novices.

Saturday, the 4th of the month, the nuns went out in carriages accompanied by the vicereine and many other women, wives of the *oidores* and *alcaldes* of the court, and other illustrious ladies. They saw all the monastery of Santo Domingo, and they even entered the refectory.

Sunday, the 5th of the month, with the same accompaniment

and with the viceroy and the vicereine, they went to the church of San Francisco and the chapel of Brother Bernabé. They only walked through the cloister, leaving by the main door.

Panama Nuns Enter the Convent of La Concepción

Monday, the 6th of the month, at twelve noon they went to see the cathedral with the same accompaniment, and from there they went to see the barefoot nuns at San José [convent] and then returned to the palace. That same afternoon at four, Monday, the 6th of July, with all the above named accompaniment, His Excellency took the nuns to the convent of Limpia y Pura Concepción where they were received with the ringing of the bells and the cross raised. They all entered and remained there.

Death of Doctor Reyes

Wednesday, the 8th of July, 1671, at ten at night [Doctor José de los Reyes] was found dead in the corridor of his house with a rosary in his hand. On Friday, the 10th of the month, he was buried in the monastery of San Francisco. The viceroy and all the *oidores*, the ecclesiastic and secular *cabildos*, and all the nobility of the city were at his burial. The death of Doctor José de los Reyes was deeply regretted by the citizens. He was prime professor of law.

Strife of the Nuns at La Encarnación

Sunday, the 12th of the month, at ten at night the mounted company paid from the guard [company] of His Excellency went to La Encarnación, and all that night they rode around the enclosure of that convent.

Proclamation to Pacify the Nuns

At eleven in the morning of Monday, the 13th, the said mounted company and that of the mercenary infantry from the palace went there along with a hundred rank and file men with their arms. A ban was placed on the convent: no person of any kind could leave or give help; eminent persons involved would receive a penalty of four years in Chile, and the others six years at Valdivia; mulattoes, Negroes, and women, two hundred lashes. It [the strife] lasted until ten at night when a president was elected, [and it began] because they wanted to take out four nuns and put them in different convents. Because of the vacancy left by the death of the archbishop, Don Pedro de Villagómez, the judges of the nuns were the archdeacon, Don Juan Santoyo [de Palma], and the canon, Doctor Don Diego de Salazar. There was great dissension the night before and all day Monday with a great pealing of the Angelus bells rung by the nuns. Peace was restored with the president they selected.

Proclamation of Peace with England

Friday, the 17th of July of the year 1671, at eleven in the morning a proclamation was made of the royal decree issued by the king, our lord, may God protect him, and the queen, our lady, dated in Madrid the 29th of October of the year 1670. [It stated] that peace had been made between the kings of Great Britain and our Spain, and informed all vassals of this kingdom of Peru that it had been made.

My Son Came from Cuzco

At four in the afternoon of Saturday, the 15th of August, day of the Assumption of Our Lady, my son Fray Francisco arrived at this, his home, from Cuzco. He had been gone three years and twelve days from the day he left this city of Lima until his return.

Consecration of the Bishop of Chiapas

Monday, the 24th of August of the year 1671, day of the glorious apostle Saint Bartholomew, Señor Don Cristóbal de Quirós, former canon of this holy church of Lima, was consecrated bishop of Chiapas, New Spain [Mexico]. In this same cathedral Don Francisco de Loyola y Vergara of the order of Saint Augustine was consecrated as bishop of Concepción, Chile. And this day at ten in the morning the two bishops went in procession from San Agustín [church] to the cathedral with the crosses of all the parishes held high, and with all the clergy and all the religious orders. Don Cristóbal de Quirós was presently the vicar general, and it [the procession] was unlike any seen before in this city of Lima.

The Ship that Departed for Acapulco

The new ship that His Majesty purchased set sail on Wednesday, the 9th of September of the year 1671, at two in the afternoon. It fired seven pieces of artillery as it left on its trip to the port of Acapulco. Captain Francisco Ruíz Lozano was in command of the ship, sent by the viceroy, Count of Lemos. It was said that the ship was going to bring firearms from the kingdom of Mexico. (It returned to the port of Callao after eight months with great quantities of clothing from China and many other materials.)

On Thursday, the 22nd of October of the year 1671, ten com-

Companies for Valdivia

panies of the regiment of merchants went forth to recruit men of this city of Lima. Juan de Beingolea was colonel of this regiment, and Francisco de Alduaín, sergeant major. The colonel and the sergeant major went with another eight merchants, among whom was Felipe de Zavala. The recruits were to be taken to Valdivia, kingdom of Chile. These companies set out from the headquarters of Colonel Juan de Beingolea in order to fly recruit flags in their quarters, except the company of Captain Felipe de Zavala, who used the palace guard corps for his headquarters.

Death of Fernando de Silva

This good man [Fernando de Silva] died Friday, the 23rd of October of the year 1671. He was buried Saturday, the 24th, at the Dominican monastery wearing the habit of that same order.

Departure for Callao of my Son Fray Francisco

My son, Fray Francisco, went to Callao to the monastery of San Francisco on Monday, the 21st of November of the year 1671, to become a resident of that monastery.

Voyage of the Flagship

On Saturday, the 4th of April, the royal flagship of this South Sea [Pacific Ocean] left the port of Callao as escort vessel with aid and other munitions for Panama. After having been in Panama not quite forty days, it set sail for Callao and arrived at this port the 25th of November of the year 1671, having taken seven months and twenty-one days for the whole trip from the time it left Callao to the day it anchored back in this port. Don Francisco de Baños y Herrera went as chief of all the men.

General Reform of all the Officers

At ten in the morning of Saturday, the 19th of December of the year 1671, senior and junior officers of the militia that went to the aid of Panama when it was captured by [Henry] Morgan, the English [buccaneer] admiral, were reformed [to inactive duty] by [order of] His Majesty.

Maritime General's Staff to Juan de Beingolea

Tuesday, the 22nd of December of 1671, the viceroy, Count of Lemos, went to Callao and presented the staff of maritime general to Juan Beingolea. Present were the viceroy, *oidor* Don Diego Mesía, *oidor* Don Lope de Munive, the *alcalde* of the court Don Diego de Ovalle, the *fiscal* Don Diego de Baeza, and many colonels and captains. All the artillery was fired [in salute] from the escort vessel and from land. (Juan de Beingolea died Wednesday, the 20th of March of the year 1675.)

Death of Dean Don Juan de Cabrera

Dean Don Juan de Cabrera, Marquis de Ruíz and [member] of the order of Santiago, who served this cathedral of Lima more than sixty years as canon, twice as vicar general, and dean and commissary of the Holy Crusade for many years, died at almost ninety years of age. His death occurred on Saturday, the 26th of December of the year 1671. He was buried in the afternoon of the 27th of that month at the hospital of Saint Bartholomew, as patron of the hospital where he spent and left all his fortune. Memorial funeral rites were held Wednesday, the 30th of the month, with the attendance of the viceroy, Count of Lemos, and the ecclesiastic and secular *cabildos*. The *oidores* did not attend either his burial or the funeral rites. All the religious orders and all the nobility of the city of Lima were present at the hospital. His executor was Francisco Tijeros, the present superintendent of the hospital of Saint Bartholomew, who attended to everything with care and punctuality.

The Year 1672

Friday, the first day of the new year 1672, Don José de Vega and Don Alonso Lazo, who were previously ordinary *alcaldes* and *regidores*, were elected as ordinary *alcaldes*.

Blessing of the Church of the Desamparados

Saturday, the 30th of January of the year 1672, the new church of the Desamparados was blessed, and the Count of Lemos gave support by attending [the ceremony]. The church was completed in all its grandeur in two and a half years.

It was blessed by Don Cristóbal de Quirós, bishop of Chiapas, with the presence of the viceroy, Count of Lemos, and the *oidores* and many *caballeros*. (He later received appointment as bishop of Popayán, where he went, leaving Callao the 11th of June of the year 1672 in a ship going to Guayaquil with the armada for Panama.)

This same day, Saturday, at eleven in the morning the dispatch ship arrived from Spain with [news of] the canonization of the holy King Ferdinand, and of Saint Rose [of Lima], and Saint Peter of Alcántara, and Saint Francis of Borja; and that the treasury official Moreto was [appointed] *oidor*; and other things.

Monday, the 1st of February of the present year, at seven in

Bonfires and Festive Lights

the evening there were great bonfires and festive lights. That night an arch that Don Sebastián de Navarrete had ordered made for this celebration was burned. It was made of cotton, very interesting, and very costly, and one of the festive lights caught it afire, burning the whole arch.

Procession of the Church of the Desamparados

Tuesday, the 2nd of February of the year 1672, day of the Candlemas, at four in the afternoon a procession unlike any seen in this city left from the royal chapel of the palace. The Holy Sacrament and [an image of] the Virgin of the Desamparados, accompanied by [statues of] many saints of the Society of Jesus were brought out. All the streets were hung with rich decorations and the flower-filled streets were partitioned off with boards and reed fences. The plaza fountain was well adorned and full of flowers. At the door of the palace there was an arch [put up by] the university; at the entrance of Bodegones Street and the nearby corner, a grandiose altar of the fathers of the Society [of Jesus]. All of Plateros [silversmiths] Street on both sides had a thousand items of worked and gilded silver, and many other curiosities. On the following corner there was another marvelous altar of the fathers of San Agustín. Mercaderes Street was hung from top to bottom with decorations, and on the balconies and windows there were rich fabrics and brocades. In the middle of the street there was an impressive arch, and the area it encompassed was laid with bars of silver. At the entrance of Las Mantas Street there was another altar of the fathers of La Merced, where they outdid themselves; and at the door of the *cabildo* [there was] another arch put up by the city.

The procession was magnificent. In front was [a statue of] the baby Jesus which belonged to the scribes, all of them lighting its way with candles in their hands. [The statue of] Saint Ignatius followed with all the fathers of the Society of Jesus with their surplices and candles. And so it continued with all the rest of the saints. Behind them followed representations from the four parts of the world, Europe, Asia, Africa, and America, which consisted of four triumphal floats, very well decorated and with angels singing. In the last float, which signified America, were the three sons of the viceroy, Count of Lemos, seated on their little chairs under a canopy. At the end were [images of] Saint Francis of Borgia and the Holy Virgin, and then the Holy Sacrament which that same evening was placed in this new church called the Virgin de los Desamparados. The viceroy with four other *caballeros* led the procession.

Procession of Saint Francis of Borgia

Thursday, the 4th of the month, a procession set out from the palace in the same manner described above and with all the illumination of the streets, altars, and arches. At the end was [the image of] Saint Francis of Borgia that was placed in this new church. The viceroy carried the banner, and only the *caballeros* of the order of Santiago, wearing their white cloaks, lighted the way, because the saint was of the same order.

Celebration for Saint Francis of Borgia

Wednesday, the 10th of February, His Excellency held a celebration in honor of Saint Francis of Borgia[50] in the new church, with a pontifical Mass sung by the bishop of Chiapas, Don Cristóbal de Quirós. All the nobility of this City of Kings was at the celebration.

First Play Presented in the Patio of the Palace

Thursday, the 11th of the month, the great play "Noah's Ark" began at eight at night and ended very late, with stage scenery like that used at the Retiro [park] in Madrid, never before seen here. It was attended by His Excellency with all his family and the *oidores* as well as the ecclesiastic and city *cabildos*. All the fathers of the Society of Jesus, and all their community saw it.

The Day the Executioner was Killed

Friday, the 12th of February of the year 1672, while trying to take a Negro out to flog him for having been caught with a dagger, and upon attempting to get him on a horse, the Negro killed the executioner with the same dagger. It happened within the court prison, and [he died] without [time for] confessing.

Races and Bulls

Saturday, the 13th of the month, there were races in the plaza which was barricaded with boards used for this purpose. Many *caballeros* raced; all were splendidly dressed. His Excellency also appeared on horseback, and on his chest he wore a jewel of

[50] The vicereine, Countess of Lemos (Doña Ana de Borja), was related to the new Spanish saint, Francis of Borgia (1510–1572). Francis had served in Emperor Charles I's court and later as viceroy of Catalonia. In 1546, after the death of his wife, he entered the Society of Jesus and nineteen years later was elected general of the Jesuit order. He was beatified in 1624 and canonized in 1671. *New Catholic Encyclopedia*, II, 709–10.

great value. Bulls were run with lassoes which made it a joyful afternoon.

Drama for Other Religious Orders

Sunday, the 14th of the month, the same play was held for the fathers of Santo Domingo and San Francisco [monasteries]. Monday, the 15th of the month, the same play was held at the palace, as on the first occasion, for the fathers of San Agustín and Nuestra Señora de las Mercedes, and for the fathers of San Juan de Dios.

The celebration of this play at the palace continued until Tuesday, the 2nd of March, which was Shrove Tuesday, and it was seen by the whole city. There were few who did not see it except for the nuns.

Departure of the Nuns for Panama

Sunday, the 21st of the month, at two in the afternoon the thirteen nuns [returning to Panama] left the convent of La Concepción, and went to Callao. The viceroy, Count of Lemos, accompanied them, and they stayed at the palace of Callao until Tuesday, the 23rd of the month of February. At four that afternoon they went aboard ship and set sail for Panama.

His Excellency, the Count of Lemos, had embarked at nine in the morning, and he did not disembark until all the armada set sail. This day he did not dine on land. As soon as he disembarked, he entered his carriage and returned to Lima with the vicereine. Many pieces of artillery were fired from land and sea, in a great gun salute.

Death of Captain Alonso Luján

Tuesday, the 23rd of February of the year 1672, at three in the morning Captain Alonso Luján died at the hospital of San Andrés. He was buried Wednesday, the 24th, at the monastery of San Francisco of this city of Lima.

The Bad Hour Spent by Francisco de Ochoa

Friday, the 26th of the month, at eight at night in the house of Palacios, while playing cards with the licentiate Don Angel de Pastrana, Francisco de Ochoa went through a difficult hour, [a pain] gripping the right side of his body. (He died the 14th of March of 1675.)

The Sawmill

Saturday, the 27th of the month, the water-powered sawmill started to saw wood. When the saw was in the beam they left it, and it [slipped and] pinned Diego de Oliva, blacksmith, against the wall, injuring him badly.

Death of the Comptroller Domingo de Barambio

Saturday, the 27th of February of the year 1672, my *compadre* Domingo de Barambio died. He was buried Sunday, the 28th of the month, at the Magdalena Recollect of the fathers of Santo Domingo. He professed to the monastic vows of this Dominican order.

The Brothers that Came from Mexico

Thursday, the 4th of March of the year 1672, at four in the afternoon the viceroy, Count of Lemos, went to the convalescent home for the natives, which is beyond El Cercado. He accompanied the six Capuchin brothers who came from Mexico to take care of the convalescing Indians who were moved from the Indian hospital of Santa Ana. They took over this convalescent home at the order of the vicar general, Don Esteban de Ibarra, and with the authority of the viceroy, who was present.

Death of Sergeant Major Francisco de Alduaín

Wednesday, the 9th of March of the year 1672, at twelve noon Francisco de Alduaín, presently sergeant major of the regiment of the seven companies of merchants, died. On Thursday he was buried with his arms[51] at the monastery of San Francisco. A company of his regiment [was present] with muffled drums, the flag lowered, and arms rendered. He died violently when an abscessed tumor broke which he immediately expelled through the mouth. He had made his will in the year 1670.

Childbirth of the Countess

Tuesday of Holy Week, the 12th of April of the year 1672, the Countess of Lemos gave birth to a son at eight-thirty at night. The following day, which was Holy Wednesday, at eleven in the morning the viceroy, Count of Lemos, went to the Society of Jesus [church] giving thanks to Our Lord.

The Infant is Baptized

Thursday, the 21st of April of the year 1672, the infant son of the Count of Lemos was baptized [and named Francisco de Borja Ignacio Castro y Portugal] at the cathedral of this city of Lima. There was great acclaim from the *caballeros*, and a great number of persons went as much to see the people as the chapel of the baptistry so grandly decorated. His godfather was Father Francisco del Castillo of the Society of Jesus, and he was baptized by

[51] Burying a man with arms was to give him the honor of a *caballero* or gentleman.

Señor Don Esteban de Ibarra, commissary of the Holy Crusade and the presently acting vicar of the vacant post.

Dispatch Ship from Spain

Thursday, the 5th of May of the year 1672, at noon the dispatch ship arrived from Spain, advising that a fleet and galleons would leave from Cádiz during the month of January of that year 1672. This dispatch ship brought news that Don Juan Moreto, Don Diego Baeza and Don Pedro de Ovalle were [appointed] *oidores* of this royal *audiencia*. Señor Don Cristóbal Bernaldo de Quirós, who was bishop of Chiapas, [was appointed] bishop of Popayán, and the bishop of Popayán [appointed] archbishop of Las Charcas; and as treasurer of the cathedral, the canon Balcázar. Don Esteban de Ibarra was named schoolmaster, and the 6th of that month, Friday, he assumed that position.

Proclamation Regarding the Armada

Thursday, the 5th of the month, a proclamation was issued that the armada would leave [Callao] for Panama without any delays on the 20th of that month of May with the treasure of His Majesty and of private individuals.

The Countess goes to the Mass of Purification

Friday, the 13th of May of the year 1672, the Countess of Lemos went to her first Mass after childbirth [Purification Mass] with a great following of *caballeros* on foot and in carriages, and the viceroy, accompanied by the *oidores*. The vicereine traveled in a sedan chair, and her daughter-in-law carried the baby in another chair.

Promoted to Infantry Captain

Saturday, the 4th of June of the year 1672, they gave me the [official] decree [of promotion] to captain of the Spanish infantry at the presidio of Callao, my appointment having been granted by the Count of Lemos. Of those [companies] that were at this presidio, a formation was made by the company of Ramos. I refer to the credential that I obtained from the government in which all the circumstances and honors that the viceroy granted me, Captain Josephe de Mugaburu y Honton, are listed.

At eight in the morning of Tuesday, the 7th of June of 1672, I assembled the guard in the guardroom of Callao, with my whole company and my ensign, Juan de Salazar, and sergeant Cristóbal de la Rocha, because it was pay day for the two companies embarking for Panama on the flagship and escort vessel. The guard sallied

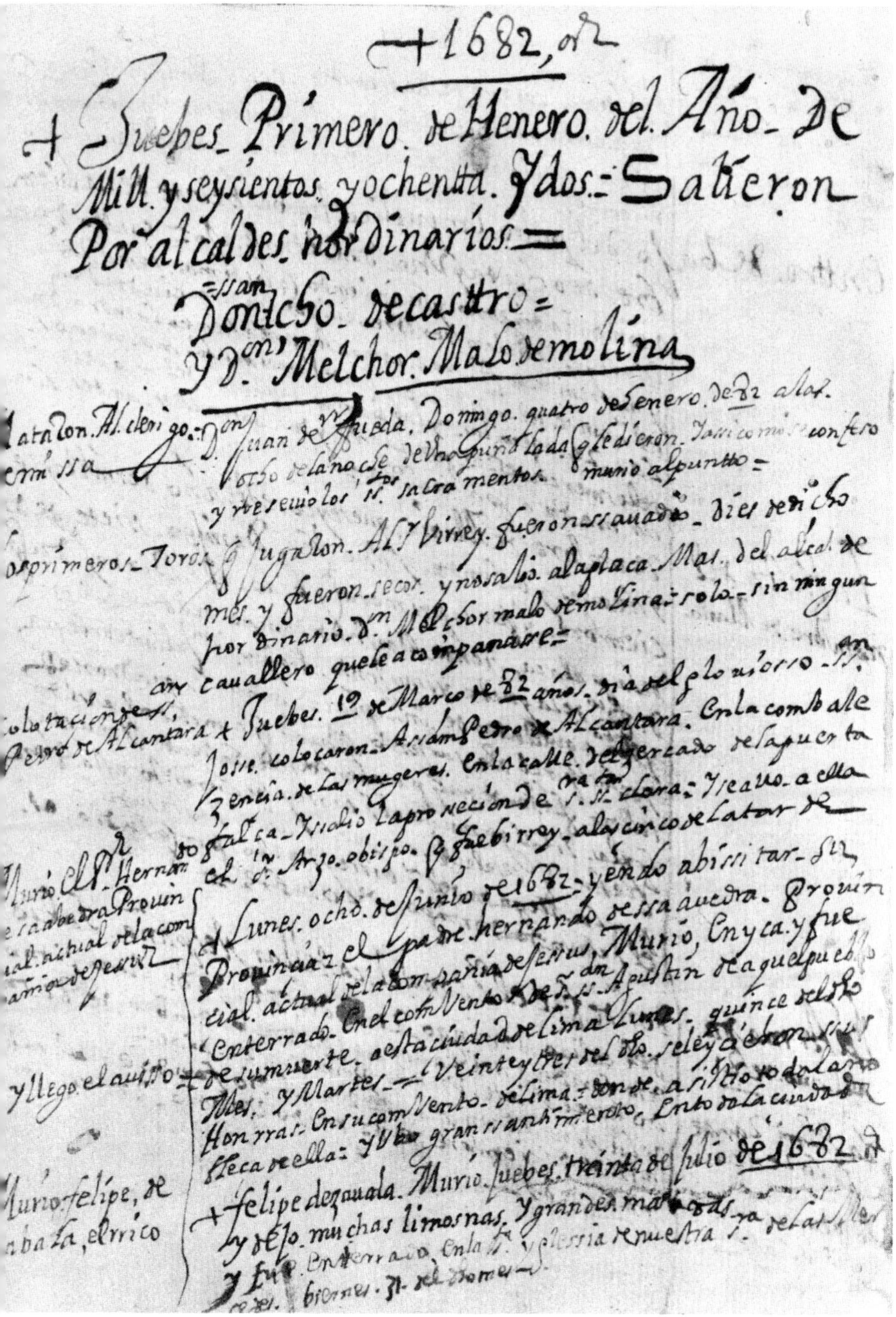

+1682, as

+ Juebes Primero de Henero del Año de Mill y seysientos y ochentta y dos: Salieron Por alcaldes hordinarios =

Don Juan Doncelo de castro =

y Don Melchor Malo de molina

Photocopy of a Folio of Mugaburu's Manuscript Diary.

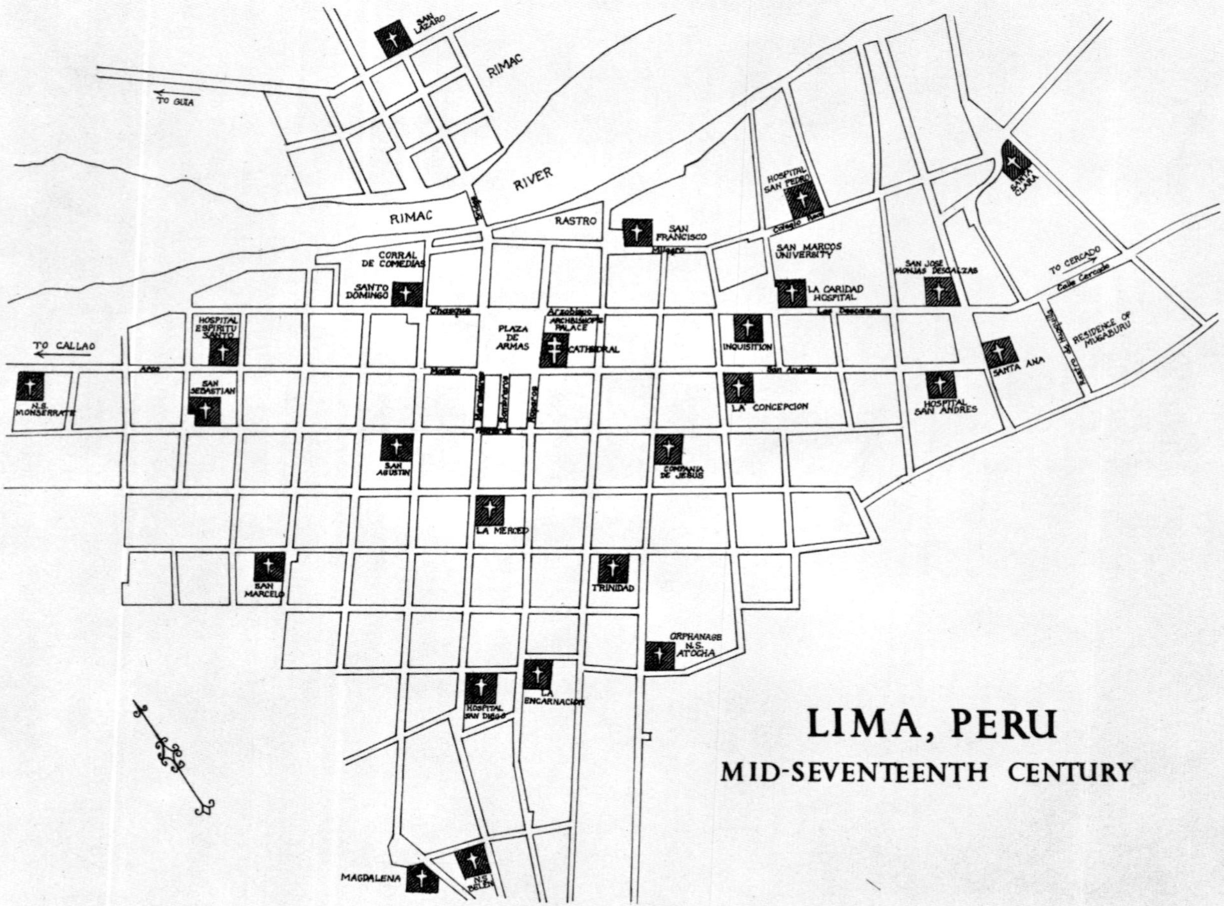

LIMA, PERU
MID-SEVENTEENTH CENTURY

Inquisition Procession in Lima, Seventeenth Century.

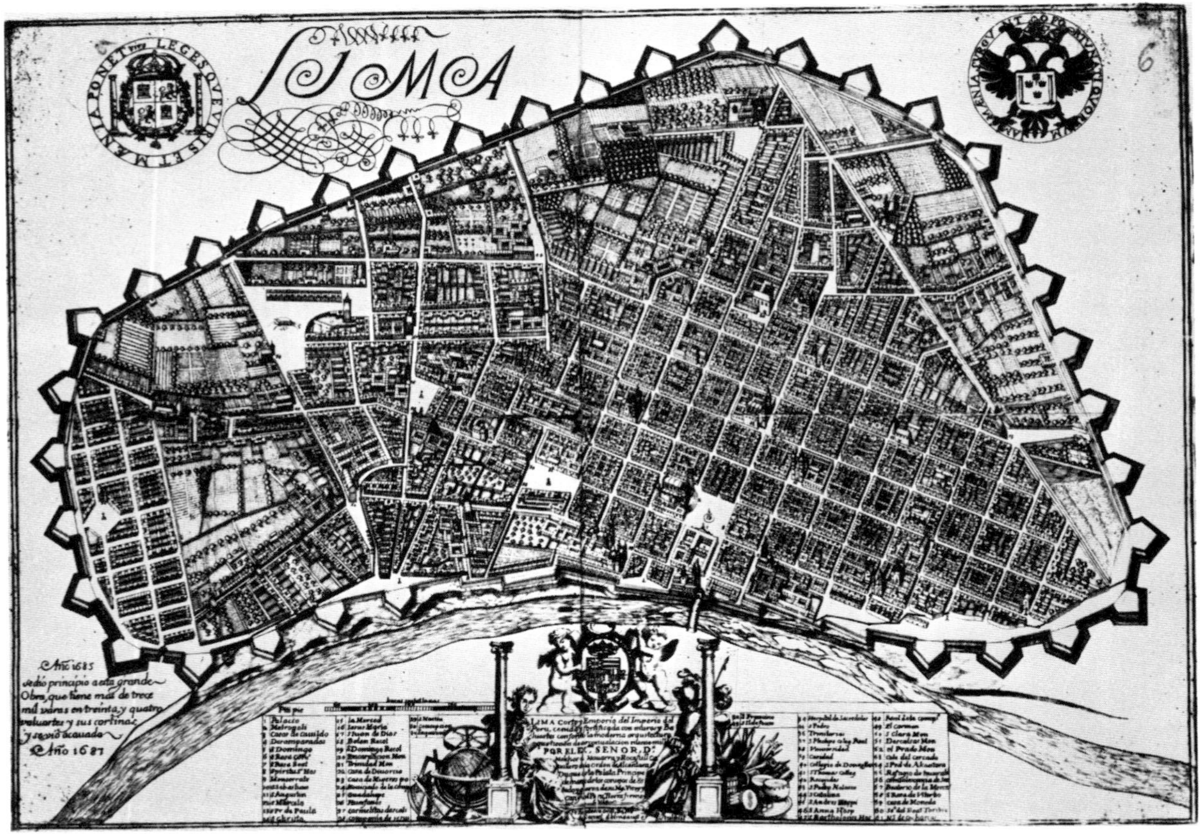

Bird's-eye View of Lima, 1687.

Bull of Canonization of St. Rose of Lima, 1671.

Viceroy Don Pedro de Toledo y Leyva, Marquis of Mancera (1639–48).

Viceroy Don García Sarmiento de Sotomayor, Count of Salavatierra (1648–55).

Viceroy Don Luis Henríquez de Guzmán, Count of Alba de Liste (1655–61).

Viceroy Don Diego Benavides, Count of Santisteban (1661–66).

iceroy Don Pedro Fernández de Castro, Count of Lemos (1667–72).

Viceroy Don Baltasar de la Cueva Enríquez, Count of Castellar (1674–78).

Viceroy Don Melchor de Liñán y Cisneros, Archbishop of Lima (1678–81).

Viceroy Don Melchor de Navarra y Rocaful, Duke of La Palata (1681–89).

Viceroy Don Melchor Portocarrero, Count of Monclova (1689–1705).

Don Pedro de Villagómez, Archbishop of Lima (1670–74, 1678–83).

Don Fray Juan de Almoguera, Archbishop of Lima (1674–76).

Don Melchor de Liñán y Cisneros, Archbishop of Lima (1676–78).

with more than one hundred thirty soldiers counting those invited by my son [-in-law], Colonel Don Diego Pardo, who went forth as [my] shield bearer. We paraded through all of Callao, and a pot of gunpowder was used, donated by my son [-in-law] Don Diego Pardo. The adjutants on active duty, Zamalvide from the escort vessel and Marcos [blank] from the flagship, acted as sergeants. And I marched with a lance and dressed in suede, very resplendent.

Departure of the Armada for Panama

Saturday, the 11th of June of the year 1672, at five in the afternoon the armada of flagship, escort, and other ships left from the port of Callao for Panama, with the treasure of His Majesty, may God protect him, and of individuals. Juan de Beingolea went as general, and Juan Zorrilla de la Gándara as admiral. Twelve sails set forth that afternoon in the convoy of that armada: the flagship and escort vessel, the king's lighter, that of Orejuela, and that of Farfalladas, all these five for Panama; two for Guayaquil in one of which went Bishop Don Cristóbal de Quirós, bishop of Popayán; the others to the valleys [of northern Peru] for provisions.

Imprisonment of Licentiate Tomás Gago

Friday, the 13th of July of the year 1672, at ten in the morning the inquisitors Don Juan de Huerta and Señor Doctor Don Bartolomé de Poveda imprisoned the licentiate Tomás Gago Vadillo, presbyter, who was spiritual father of the doctrine of Jesus Christ in the hospital of Saint Bartholomew of this city of Lima. (He was imprisoned in the Holy Inquisition until Tuesday, the 8th of November of this year of 1672, which made three months and twenty-three days. This same day, Tuesday, two ministers of the Holy Office took him to the hospital of Saint Lazarus, where they left him with the obligation that he stay at this hospital for four months without saying Mass, and [be] exiled fifty leagues from this city of Lima and that of Quito for six years.)

Death of Diego de Aldana

Saturday, the 20th of August of the year 1672, day of the glorious Saint Bernard, Diego de Aldana and Juan Rodríguez, cavalry soldiers, challenged each other to a duel on the plain behind the convent of the nuns of [Nuestra Señora del] Prado. It was over some words the two had in the palace. Juan Rodríguez suffered a wound in the face, and he inflicted two [wounds] at the same time on Diego de Aldana, one on the left arm with the dagger, and the other a sword thrust in the abdomen from which he died the following Sunday. He was buried Monday at the monastery of Nuestra Señora de las Mercedes.

Death of Gregorio de Torres

Gregorio de Torres, city meat supplier, died at the beginning of August of 1672, with barely time to make a will. Juan García Chico died Wednesday, the 24th of August of the same year, being barely able to make a will. Both were *compadres* and overwhelmingly in debt. May God forgive them.

Death of the Vicar General

Don Esteban de Ibarra, schoolmaster of the cathedral of Lima, present *provisor* and vicar general of this archbishopric in the vacancy [created by the death] of Archbishop Don Pedro de Villagómez, and general receiver of the Inquisition, died Tuesday, the 6th of September of the year 1672, at three-thirty in the afternoon. He was buried in the cathedral on Wednesday, the 7th, at five in the afternoon. A solemn burial was held with the attendance of the viceroy and Señor Don Alvaro de Ibarra, brother of the deceased and president of the royal *audiencia*, and all the *oidores*, the ecclesiastic *cabildo* with their long capes, as well as the secular [*cabildo*]. All the *caballeros* of this city of Lima with mourning capes, all showing great reverence, and all the doctors of the university [were also present]. May God keep him in His holy glory.

Saturday, the 10th of the month, day of the glorious Saint Nicholas of Tolentino, memorial funeral rites for Señor Don Esteban de Ibarra were held at the cathedral, where there was a magnificent catafalque with twelve stages of movable platform, highly adorned with fabrics, laces, and velvet on the twelve steps, and four hundred candles weighing a pound each, and many torches burning. All attended as on the day of the burial.

Vicar General of the Archbishopric

After the funeral rites for Señor Don Esteban de Ibarra, [in] the vacancy and absence of a dean by the death of Señor Don Juan de Cabrera, [and] Juan Santoyo de Palma being archdeacon, Señor Don José de Avila, professor of [blank] and canon of this cathedral, was named *provisor* and vicar general of this archbishopric of Lima.

Death of Doña Ana de San Martín

Doña Ana de San Martín, who was the wife of Captain Juan Pérez de Armas, died on Tuesday, the 13th of September of the year 1672, at eight at night. She was buried in the church of the convent of the nuns of Our Lady of Carmen at noon on Thursday, the 15th of the month, with a funeral Mass. On placing the body on the catafalque, which was well adorned with wax candles and many lit torches, [and] upon lifting the body, the foundations of the catafalque failed, having been badly placed. Those who were carrying it, who were some mulattoes and Negroes, stopped it [from falling]. She was buried with great praise from many illustrious persons and the secular *cabildo*, all well deserved by the deceased, who was a matron of great judgment and conduct.

The Mass in the presence of the corpse was said by her son, Father Fray Francisco of the order of Saint Francis, and the Gospel by another of her sons, a Mercedarian friar called Fray Nicolás. Another, her grandson, a friar of the Mercedarian order, Fray Francisco de Padilla, chanted the Epistle.

Open House of the Church of San Francisco

On the morning of Monday, the 3rd of October of 1672, all of the new church of San Francisco of this illustrious city of Lima was unveiled, with all the altars very well decorated as well as all of the cloister. The church was completely finished in every aspect with the exception of the doors and the towers. The blessing of the church and choir loft was given this same morning by the Very Reverend Father Francisco Delgado, present father provincial. The Reverend Father Fray Luis de Zervela, commissary general of that [Franciscan] order who came from the province of Santiago in Galicia, was responsible for all this, because with his fervor, assistance and care he was able to bring it to the state in which it can be seen today. Father Fray Fernando Bravo was guardian of this monastery. The Count of Lemos, present viceroy of this kingdom of Peru, and the countess were present on this day. The viceroy went up to the choir loft with all the religious community, accompanied by the *fiscal*, while the vicereine remained in the chapel of Brother Bernabé. After they descended, the viceroy and the countess, in the company of the father commissary, the *fiscal*, and Father Fray Juan Báez of La Merced, went to the cloister, entering from the garden, and while the vicereine gathered carnations in this garden, all the women who had entered the cloister went up to the choir loft.

That same afternoon there were many solemn vespers for the arrival of [the feast day of] Saint Francis [of Assisi], and at night there was a reading of the martyrology which lasted until eleven. In the small plaza there were great fireworks, and many festive lights were on the roof of the cathedral. Tuesday, the 4th of October, Masses were said at all the altars of this new church, and the high Mass was chanted by the very reverend father provincial of Santo Domingo, Fray Hernando de Carrasco, and the very reverend father definitor[52] of San Francisco, Fray [blank] de Loyola. Present were the viceroy, Count of Lemos, all the *oidores* and the secular *cabildo*, and a very great number of people, women as well as men, so many that they did not fit in this new church. The vicereine with all her children and family was also present.

Dispatch Ship from Spain

Wednesday, the 5th of October of 1672, the dispatch ship from Spain arrived at this city of Lima, bearing eleven boxes [of correspondence]. It was brought from Panama by the adjutant Gatica.

The Monstrance from Cuzco

My nephew, Fray José de Honton, a Franciscan religious, arrived at this city of Lima on Friday, the 7th of October of the year 1672, with an interesting monstrance that he brought from the city of Cuzco for the very reverend father commissary general of this order, Fray Luís de Zervela. (He left this city for Cuzco the 15th of this month and year in the company of the very reverend father provincial of Lima, Fray Francisco Delgado, who departed to visit his province. May God guide them safely.)

Ringing of the Animas *[Souls] Bells*

Monday, the 10th of October of 1672, day of the glorious Saint Francis of Borja, the bells of the churches began to ring at nine at night for all to commend [the souls of] all [those in a state] of mortal sin [to God]. This same night the cathedral sounded nine pealings of the bells, and all the other churches did the same.

Fiesta *in my Son's Parish*

My son, Don José de Mugaburu y Honton, presbyter, priest and vicar of the parish of Yanaoca of the bishopric of Cuzco, in the province of Canes y Canchis, held a *fiesta* to celebrate the completion of his new church. He had ordered it to be built from

52 *Definidor* (definitor) is an individual of a religious order who is a member of the governing committee or *definitorio*.

the very foundations with much splendid adornment, as grand as any seen, placing all his care and diligence [in supervising its construction]. The *fiesta* was held Sunday, the 6th of November of the year 1672. Many persons were present at this feast, and all the priests of that province and a great number of people, *caballeros* and learned religious, of the city of Cuzco, and my nephew the Very Reverend Father Fray Buenaventura de Honton, and his brother Doctor Don Diego de Honton, priest and rector of Santa Ana of the city of Cuzco. The celebration lasted three days. There were many fireworks, bulls, dances, tidbits, snacks, speeches, an acrobat, [paper figures of] giants and dwarfs, things which the Indians of that country had never seen before, and much other entertainment. There was plenty of food for all those who were at the *fiesta*. There were more than three thousand Indians at the *fiesta* who gathered from the province, but they were not included in the food which was for the many Spaniards present who were invited by him to the celebration.

Death of the Oidor *Alcocer*

Don Sebastián de Alcocer, *oidor* of this royal *audiencia*, died Friday, the 2nd of December of 1672. He was buried Saturday, the 3rd, at the church of San Agustín.

Death of the Marquis of Villar

[Don Manuel Joaquín Toledo Portugal Córdoba Monroy Ayala Pimentel,] the Marquis of Villar, who lived in the house of Captain Galiano on the street of Santa Clara in this city of Lima, and who had been *corregidor* of the provinces of Tarma and Chinchaicocha, died on Sunday, the 4th of December of the year 1672, at three in the afternoon. That same morning he professed as a religious of the order of Saint Francis in the hands of the commissary of that order, the Very Reverend Father Fray Luís de Zervela. As soon as he expired, the friars of San Francisco carried him to their monastery where he was buried. Because the friars of San Francisco buried him without carrying the cross of the parish at his burial, there were excommunications by the vicar general and also by the commissary.

Illness of the Count of Lemos

Monday, the 5th of December, at five in the afternoon the Holy Sacrament was brought publicly to the palace, where the Count of Lemos, viceroy of these kingdoms received it because of his illness, which was very grave. It was brought by the archdeacon,

Don Juan Santoyo de Palma, and the poles of the canopy were carried by the canons. That same night at one o'clock they anointed him.

Death of the Count of Lemos

Tuesday, the 6th of December of the year 1672, at eight-thirty at night the viceroy, Count of Lemos, died in his upstairs room in the palace. Immediately the signal was given by all the bells of all the churches and convents of this city; the first was the cathedral. At midnight they brought the body down to the large salon where it was embalmed, and his heart was taken to the church of the Desamparados, which was what His Excellency had ordered. His heart was placed at the feet of the [statue of the] Mother of God, and [later] his body was also buried in that church. When the Countess returns to Spain she will take his bones and have them buried at Monforte de Lemos in Galicia, where his father and grandfathers are buried.

After the embalming they took him up to the room where he had died, and they placed the body on a brocaded bed. He was colorfully dressed, very gallant, and wearing boots and spurs with his staff of captain general and with his colored hat with plumes. He looked like Saint George. He governed this kingdom five years and fifteen days.

Bishop for Cuzco

The bishop destined for Cuzco, Señor Don Manuel de Mollinedo y Angulo, arrived at this city of Lima on Friday, the 9th of December of the year 1672. He visited the vicereine and then went with the father commissary general of San Francisco, Fray Luis de Zervela, to the salon where the body of the deceased viceroy, Count of Lemos, lay, and the bishop said a responsory. Then he took his leave. (He left for Cuzco Monday, the 14th of August of 1672.)

Burial of the Count of Lemos

The day of his burial, after four normal [work] days, was Saturday afternoon, the 10th of December of the year 1672. At four in the afternoon the cortege began to leave the palace in the same manner as for the Count of Santisteban. There was no artillery at this ceremony of the burial of the Count of Lemos; only nine small iron cannons were fired at the nine funeral stops. From the palace gate to Mercaderes Street there were three stops, and the other six were from there to the small plaza of the Society of

Jesus. All the platforms were very high and very well adorned with brocades and other materials, with many torches and candles on them. Archdeacon Don Juan Santoyo de Palma, in the vacancy of the archbishop and dean, celebrated the high Mass. Four [Capuchin] brothers of the convalescent home for Indians carried the deceased on their shoulders, and the gentlemen *oidores*, tribunals, and others placed their hands on the bier.

The catafalque at the Society of Jesus was of majestic and grandiose architecture. The entire main chapel from top to bottom was hung with brocades, and the whole of the church, from top to bottom, with black taffeta, and there were many candles on the catafalque. The gentlemen of the *cabildo* went with their black capes dragging, and they were dragged with great mourning. The rapier was not carried at the burial. None of the children of the count were at the burial as they were very young.

Señor Don Alvaro de Ibarra and the *oidores* went to the burial except for Don Bernardo de Iturrizara and Señor Don Pedro de Velasco who did not go because they were ill.

The Mass held in the presence of the body was held Monday, the 12th of the month, and everyone, the gentlemen as well as all the accompaniment and all the family of the deceased viceroy, left the palace in carriages for the Society of Jesus where the Mass was said, and returned in the same way to the palace.

Señor Don Alvaro is Chosen as Captain General

On Wednesday, the 14th of December of the year 1672, in a council held that same night, all the *oidores* unanimously named Don Alvaro de Ibarra, who was presently the senior *oidor* and *visitador* of this royal *audiencia*, as captain general upon the death of the Count of Lemos.

Funeral Rites for the Viceroy

Memorial funeral rites for the viceroy, Count of Lemos, were held on Monday the 19th of this month, at the church of the Society of Jesus, and all the gentlemen and the accompaniment left the palace in carriages. The church was all hung with black, except the transept of the church [which was] in brocade, and [there were] many sonnets. Father López of the Society of Jesus gave the sermon.

Thursday, the 29th of December of the year 1672, at five in the afternoon, Señor Don Alvaro de Ibarra went to the port of

Staff of Captain General Callao where he was given the captain general's staff of command. It was delivered to him at the plaza of arms of that port by the battalion commander, Don Antonio Sancho de Avila y Guevara, *caballero* of the order of Santiago, who presently holds that post by [appointment of] the king, our lord. There was a great crowd of people, and a squadron that had been formed in that plaza. All the flags were lowered to him with a great gun salute of muskets and arquebuses, and the forts fired a gun salute with artillery. He then retired to the palace where he had his lodgings. His standard bearer was the son of General Juan de Beingolea.

Muster Friday, the 30th of the month, he reviewed the infantry, artillery, sailors, and seamen.

The Year 1673

Election of Alcaldes The first day of the new year was Sunday. This day Señor Don Fernando de Velasco, *caballero* of the order of Santiago and *oidor* of this royal *audiencia* of Lima, went to the offices of the *cabildo* with a guard of halberdiers to elect the *alcaldes* because Señor Don Alvaro de Ibarra was in Callao as captain general passing review of the men of sea and war at the fortress of Callao. Elected *alcaldes* were Colonel Don Francisco de la Cueva, *caballero* of the order of Calatrava, who was presently at his *chácara* in the valley of Pachacámac, and Don Fernando de Córdoba, Marquis of Guadalcázar, both illustrious *caballeros* of this kingdom.

Consecration of the Church of San Francisco The consecration of the new church of San Francisco of this city of Lima was [held] Sunday, the 22nd of January of the year 1673. It was consecrated by Bishop Don Manuel de Mollinedo y Angulo, cleric who came from Spain to be bishop of Cuzco. The consecration began at seven in the morning of that Sunday and ended at twelve noon, as everything was recited. The bishop did not say Mass but instead [it was said by] Father Fray Fernando Bravo, who was presently guardian of that same monastery because the father provincial, Fray Francisco Delgado, was absent [from Lima] on his visit. The Very Reverend Father Fray Luis de Zervela was commissary general of that order, and on this day the bishop ate in his cell [that of Fray Luis de Zervela], and he gave him a breastplate very rich in emeralds, and three very costly miters.

(The consecration of the cathedral of Lima was [held] in the year 1625, consecrated by Archbishop Don Gonzalo de Ocampo, and the event ended at four in the afternoon of that same day, which was Sunday, the 19th of October of the year 1625. The ceremony ended at that hour because it was sung. I make this notation so that it may adjoin that above.)

Staff of Lieutenant General

The staff of lieutenant general was given to Don Pedro Montoya, *caballero* of the order of Santiago, on Monday, the 30th of January of the year 1673. The *oidor* Don Fernando de Velasco y Gamboa presented it to him at eleven o'clock of that same day before many captains, lieutenants, sergeants, and a great number of *caballeros*. Don Felipe Romana, servant of the Count of Lemos, had held this staff from the day he arrived at this city until the death of His Excellency, which was five years and fifteen days.

I Became a Captain in the Palace Company

On Saturday, the 18th of February of 1673, I took over the post of captain in the [palace] company of Captain Don Martín de Marquina in the review held the same day at the palace of this city before Señor Don Bernardo de Iturrizara, who officiated because Señor Don Alvaro de Ibarra was ill. The battalion commander of Callao, Don Antonio Sancho Dávila y Guevara, *caballero* of the order of Santiago, was present. From the 23rd of March of 1672, when I was promoted from sergeant, His Majesty owes me 685 pesos, for thirty months and twelve days, and that which will accumulate from the 18th of February, 1673. (Sunday, the 11th of June of 1673, I was paid 342 pesos of the above, and they owe me another 342 pesos.)

Death of Father Castillo

Father Castillo of the Society of Jesus died Tuesday, the 11th of April of the year 1673, four months and five days after the death of the viceroy, Count of Lemos. He was twice godfather [for the children of the viceroy]. He was buried the following Wednesday at the main building of the Society of Jesus.

Death of the Precentor

The precentor, Don Francisco Calvo, of this holy church of Lima died on Monday, the 17th of April of the year 1673. He was buried the following Tuesday afternoon in the cathedral.

Don Bartolomé de Azaña, of the order of Santiago and *regidor*

Death of Don Bartolomé de Azaña

and *alcalde* of the [judicial] brotherhood of this city and a great man of this country, died. Dawn of Tuesday, the 20th of June of the year 1673 found him dead in his bed.

Death of Licentiate Fernández

The licentiate Nicolás Fernández, presbyter, died the 21st of June of 1673. He was found in his bed at dawn. At twelve noon that same day Cristóbal Romero, the city supplier of meat and bread, died of dropsy.

Dispatch for Spain

The dispatch sent to Spain [via Panama] by the *oidores* who governed this kingdom on the death of the viceroy, Count of Lemos, left the port of Callao on Thursday, the 22nd of June of the year 1673. This dispatch ship carried Don Felipe Allende del Agua. The gentlemen who governed due to the death of the [*audiencia*] president of Panama also chose as *oidor* Don Miguel Francisco Marichallar, who is *oidor* of this royal *audiencia*. He was presently in Panama because he had gone [there] to take the *residencia* of Juan Pérez de Guzmán, who had been president of Panama.

Another Dispatch via Buenos Aires

On Sunday, the 2nd of July of the year 1673, the [*audiencia*] president and *oidores* sent off another dispatch to Buenos Aires with the *chasque* that left that same day for Cuzco and Potosí. [At Buenos Aires] a ship from Spain awaited to take the dispatch in which they notified the queen, our lady, of the state of affairs in this kingdom. May God safely guide them.

A Merchant Kills his Wife

Friday, the 7th of the month, a merchant killed his wife at midnight while she was quite peacefully [sleeping] in her bed. He stabbed her three times. The killer was called [blank], and the deceased was the daughter of Diego Gómez Moratto, who lived next to the convent of Santa Rosa.

A Memorial of Certain Caballeros

Tuesday, the 11th of the month, certain *caballeros* submitted a petition to the royal council, the president and *oidores* governing this kingdom, that the post of *corregidor* and other offices not be given to the sons of the conquerors of this kingdom but [instead] to the worthy. The Viscount of Portillo was exiled fifty leagues from Lima for three years, and Don Nicolás de Anglós y Ribera and Don [blank] Manrique to Valdivia [Chile]. Until a ship was available they were put aboard the escort vessel.

Death of a Lay Friar

At eight that same evening a lay friar was killed behind the inn of the Huaquilla [ancient burial mound] of Santa Ana. He was slain by a friend who brought him to that spot by ruse, saying that he had a very good mule to sell cheaply, and he gave him a sword thrust from the back that came out through his chest. He confessed, received Our Lord [Eucharist] and extreme unction, and then died. May God keep him in His glory.

Professorship of Arts

The professorship of arts was given to Father Fray José de Zavala who competed for it with Don Francisco de Córdoba, professor Don José Morán Collantes, and Doctor Don Cristóbal de Castro, who was the last to lecture on Monday, July 17, 1673. The following Tuesday, Father Fray José Zavala, religious of the order of Our Lady of Merced, was elected after many votes; and there was much excitement.

Provincial of San Agustín

Friday, the 21st of July of the year 1673, at ten in the morning Father Maestro Fray Francisco Birúes was elected provincial of San Agustín to the great satisfaction of the whole Augustinian order.

Provincial of Santo Domingo

Monday, the 24th of the month, at eleven in the morning Father Maestro Fray Antonio de Morales was elected provincial of Santo Domingo. Of the ninety-two votes, he received eighty-seven; three were blank and two [he] lost. Present at the election were Señor Don Bernardo de Iturrizarra, Señor Don Tomás Berjón, and Señor Don Lope de Munive, *oidores* of this royal *audiencia*. Everyone was pleased with the election.

The Large Bell of San Francisco

The large bell of San Francisco was cast at the foot of the tower on Thursday, the 10th of August of the year 1673, day of Saint Lawrence. It was cast by the lientiate Andrés Meléndez, presbyter. It weighs eighty-six quintals. (Saturday, the 26th of the month, it was placed in the tower.)

The Bishop of Cuzco

The bishop of Cuzco left this city of Lima for Cuzco on Monday, the 14th of August of 1673, with a large following in carriages. All the canons of this city accompanied him until they were past Guadalupe [hermitage]. The commissary general also accompanied him from San Francisco [monastery] as far as Villa, the rural house of the Jesuit fathers.

This same day Don José de Alzamora, who was captain of the ship for Chile, was selected maritime general, and Florían de Luzuriaga as admiral.

General Don Diego de Martos, present governor of Chucuito, was named general battalion commander.

My nephew Don Pedro de Legorburu, who came from Spain for a second time, arrived at this city of Lima on Monday, the 21st of August of the year 1673. He entered at five in the afternoon and lodged at the house of Señora Doña María de Recalde.

The Infantry Company that Went to Callao

On the afternoon of Monday, the 4th of September of the year 1673, the infantry company that had been on guard at the palace of this city for a long time went to Callao at the orders of the president and *oidores* who governed this kingdom upon the death of the Count of Lemos. Don Martín de Marquina was captain of the company. That same afternoon Captain Don Fernando Carillo with his men on duty went on guard. He was the first to enter the palace and the guard compound since receipt of news from Spain that the English enemy was coming to these parts with a large armada under [Henry] Morgan. May God never bring him!

Imprisonment of the Prebend Aguilar

Tuesday, the 5th of September of the year 1673, the gentlemen of the Inquisition ordered that Don Sebastián de Aguilar, prebend of this cathedral of Lima, be detained. It concerned information he gave that tribunal that he had been sent from Spain because of his family relationship with someone in the Inquisition, which [information] appeared to be false. (He left the prison for his house on Friday, the 6th of October. The 10th of November of that year he left his house, by decree of the inquisitors, so that he could exercise his post as prebend at the cathedral.)

Proclamation Regarding Horses

Monday, the 11th of September of the year 1673, a proclamation was issued by the president and *oidores* that no person of any category whatsoever, and no one of this vicinity, either being in or living in the city of Lima, could ride on a mule, but [must ride] on horseback. Those violating this rule would be dealt with in accordance with their category, and a deadline was set for the end of the month. Also [everyone] had to declare the arms and horses that belonged to them, under grave penalties.

Preeminence of the Musketeers

Saturday, the 16th of the month, another proclamation was issued that all those of the company battalions of this city who wished to carry muskets would have the same preeminence as those of the mercenary [companies]. Many other orders were referred to in this proclamation.

Death of Doña Tomasa de Aguilar

Doña Tomasa de Aguilar, sister of the prebend Don Sebastián de Aguilar, died on Tuesday, the 19th of September of the year 1673. She was buried in the vault of the third order of Saint Francis, and the prebend was not present at her burial because of litigation with the inquisitors.

Parade of the Students

On the afternoon of Thursday, the 21st of the month, day of the glorious apostle Saint Matthew, about seventy-four students of grammar, [adorned] with many jewels of great value, set out on their well-harnessed and decorated horses. They had a number of pages dressed in fine livery, and a number of flutes and flageolets. In the midst of the said students was a bust portrait of Saint Francis of Borja, painted by brush. The ceremony was held in front of the palace gate, and the last one [of the group] who carried the banner was Don García Manrique de Lara, oldest son of the Count of Amayueles. His father had died before reaching Paita, enroute as *corregidor* of Cajamarca, and his son, Don García, went forth with the banner, as referred to above, on a splendid and high-spirited horse [named] Grifo [Griffin] that had belonged to the Count of Lemos, may God take him into His holy glory. Were he alive he would have held many great celebrations and plays for the glorious Saint Francis of Borja.

Received as Brother of the Third Order

Thursday, the 5th of October of the year 1673, at four in the afternoon I was received as a brother of the third order of Saint Francis. Present were Father Miguel Flores who was the rector, and Francisco Romero; and my patron was the licentiate Don Bartolomé de Allerza, presbyter. As of this day I begin my year as novice. (I professed on Sunday, the 14th of June, 1676.)

Sunday, the 22nd of October of the year 1673, at four in the

Formation for the Name of Mary afternoon an impressive formation was assembled in the plaza, made up of many persons of the thirteen companies of the battalion of this city. Don Francisco de Cueva was battalion commander, and Julián Corbeira, sergeant major, with Roque Rosales and Rueda as adjutants. At five in the afternoon the procession passed by the plaza, as is customary, in which five companies of merchants marched with their sergeant major, the deaf one, and there were great vollies of muskets and arquebuses fired. The president and all the *oidores*, [who governed] because of the death of the Count of Lemos, may God keep him in His holy glory, and Don Diego de Marbos, general battalion commander of all the kingdom and governor of the cavalry, were in the procession.

Don Juan de Cervantes Kills his Wife Don Juan de Cervantes killed his wife Doña Victoria at daybreak on Tuesday, the 14th of November of the year 1673, because he found her with his great friend, a lay brother. The latter he left badly wounded, and then he sought refuge in the hospital of San Andrés. [He went there] also to cure his wounds.

Miracle in the Jesuit Noviciate [It happened on] Monday, the 13th of November of the year 1673, day on which the fathers of the Society of Jesus celebrate the feast of Saint Stanislas. A novice, a brother called Francisco Javier, was in the noviciate, paralyzed to the waist without being able to move from his bed. On this same day another novice of the same society said to him, "Brother Javier, today is the day of our Saint Stanislas, who was a novice like ourselves. Commend yourself with fervor to this saint whose engraved portrait I bring you, and offer him something." And the sick one replied, "Take these two bouquets of flowers and place them on his altar, and place his image on this crippled arm." As soon as it was placed on his arm he was able to move it; and it was also placed on his legs, and he arose healthy and well and on foot he went to the celebration in his church. The information was reported to the vicar general of this city, Doctor Don José de Avila, canon of this cathedral of Lima. I, Josephe de Mugaburu, saw this novice at the cathedral, and he came with the rector of the noviciate of the Society of Jesus, and all the people of this city saw him. This novice is a fourteen-year-old creole from Las Charcas.

Don Agustín Bracamonte was killed by a pistol shot late on the night of Tuesday, the 21st of November, 1673. It happened at the very door of his house as he was getting out of the carriage in which he was returning with his wife. [He died] without confessing, and he was buried wearing the habit of Saint Francis in the monastery of Nuestra Señora de las Mercedes on Thursday the 23rd. The president and *oidores*, the ecclesiastic and secular *cabildos*, and a great crowd of *caballeros* were present at the burial. Friday, the 24th, funeral rites for him were held in this monastery with the same accompaniment except for the ecclesiastic *cabildo*. There was much mourning, and the canon Zegarra, as uncle of the widow, showed great sorrow.

Don Agustín Bracamonte Killed

That same day, Friday, the 24th of November of the year 1673, Don Melchor Malo de Molina, chief constable of the court and [member] of the order of Santiago, was brought prisoner in a carriage by the *alcaldes* of the court, Don Diego de Baños and Señor Don Gaspar de Cuba. They placed him in the city prison at the orders of the president and *oidores*, for the death of Don Agustín Bracamonte.

Imprisonment of Don Melchor Malo

A proclamation was issued at the same time that the chief constable was taken captive, which was at eleven in the morning. The proclamation stated that at the hour referred to, Don Agustín Bracamonte had been wretchedly killed, and it was advisable to take the proper proceedings; thus the president and *oidores* ordered that whoever discovered and reported the whereabouts of Don Melchor Malo de Molina, the younger, and Don Francisco de Medina, and the mulatto Cisterna, would be given [a reward of] a company [of soldiers] in Callao if they fell in that [*caballero*] category; and if they were slaves, their liberty; and if it were a free Negro or mulatto, a thousand pesos; and for an Indian, release from enforced service and [from paying] tribute. For persons who concealed it [information], the penalty would be their life.

Proclamation

Don Fernando de Balcázar, canon and treasurer of this holy church of Lima and doctor of the university, died Tuesday, the 28th of November of the year 1673, at nine at night, and at eleven [was carried off by] the fathers of the Society of Jesus. He was bishop-elect of Paraguay. When his body was about to be buried

Death of the Bishop-Elect of Paraguay

on Thursday, the 30th of the month, day of the apostle Saint Andrew, there was a disagreement between the ecclesiastic *cabildo* and the university as to whether the *cabildo* and the cloister should attend and be seated. The council determined that the doctors of the university were not to attend the burial, only the ecclesiastic *cabildo*. And so he was buried Friday, the 1st of December of 1673, at the Society of Jesus.

Death of Licentiate Pulido

Licentiate Francisco Pulido died Sunday, the 3rd of December of 1673. He was buried on Monday, the 4th, at the chapel of The Souls in the church of Santa Ana, where he had been serving for many years as interim priest.

Juan Bautista de Amesquita Killed

Juan Bautista de Amesquita, head administrator of the customs and excise taxes of His Majesty, who served in the port of Callao, was killed. At the pottery shop of Callao on Wednesday, the 6th of December of the year 1673, he was challenged to a duel by a man called Don José Martínez de Urrea, and the wounds that his opponent inflicted on him caused his death the 8th of that month. He was buried on the 9th at the Franciscan monastery of Callao. The other one [his opponent] was gravely wounded.

Night of the Alarm

At dawn on Friday, the 8th of December of the year 1673, the day of the Pure and Immaculate Conception of Our Lady, the whole city rose in arms because of the news that the *corregidor* of Cañete had sent to the president and *oidores* that some ships, more than eight, had been seen in the basin of Cañete [eighty miles south of Lima]. A search was made and there were three ships: one from Chile, another from Nazca, and the other from Pisco. [Meanwhile,] all the infantry and cavalry companies, with a great number of very well equipped men, were quartered for eight days. At the end of the week it became known that the ships were our own.

Don Andrés de Beingolea Killed

Don Andrés de Beingolea, collegiate of San Martín, was killed at eight at night on Tuesday, the 26th of December, the second day of Christmas, when he was on his way to see a Nativity [scene] at the house of Don Alonso Hurtado. The deceased had been born in the same house.

Dispatch Ship from Spain

The dispatch ship arrived at this city of Lima from Spain at ten in the morning of Wednesday, the 27th of the month, with fourteen crates, one leather saddle box, and all the letters.

The Counterfeiter

Saturday, the 29th of December, the ordinary *alcalde* Don Francisco de la Cueva, *caballero* of the order of Calatrava and battalion commander of the regiment of this city by appointment of the king, our lord, arrested a young man because he made false money. He was a Spaniard, named Gabriel de Palacios, [who lived] in the street called San Jacinto. They caught him with all his tools and a number of patacoons he had made.

The Year 1674

Monday, the first day of the new year, Don Gil de Cabrera and Juan de Castilla were elected ordinary *alcaldes* of this city. Because of the death of the viceroy, Count of Lemos, Señor Don Alvaro de Ibarra was present at the election as captain general.

The Habit of Santiago

On the afternoon of Monday, the 1st of January of 1674, Don Juan Merino took on the habit of Santiago at the monastery of Santo Domingo, with all the nobility of this city present.

Steward of the University

Saturday, the 27th of January of 1674, Don Francisco de Saldivia, present deputy of the main post office of this city of Lima, was elected steward of the university.

Review of the Seven Companies

Saturday, the 3rd of February of this year, day of Saint Blaise, more than five hundred men in seven companies appeared in this city of Lima on horseback. In the four duty companies there were three hundred and fifty men with their captains, lieutenants and ensigns, all very resplendent. The rest were also with their officers. These eleven mounted companies were governed by the general battalion commander, Don Diego de Martos, present governor of Chuquiago. Don Miguel de Loroña, present *corregidor* of Cuenca, came out into the plaza as governor of the cavalry. Three hundred musketeers of the battalion companies, and Don Francisco de la Cueva and his sergeant major, Don Julián de Corbeira de Ocampo, also sallied. Three times the cavalry advanced toward the musketeers who were well placed in six sections with six duty captains, and they drove back the cavalry. The president and the *oidores* were watching from the windows of the council hall. It was a very happy afternoon with much to see, as this plaza had never before been seen with such resplendent people and so much staring and so much finery. With everyone in shirt sleeves it seemed like a garden of flowers with so much variety of dress, coats, and red sashes.

Dispatch Ship from Spain

Shrove Tuesday, the 6th of February of 1674, the dispatch ship arrived from Spain at ten at night [bringing news] that Señor Don Baltasar de la Cueva [Enríquez], Marquis of Malagón and Count of Castellar, was coming as viceroy of Peru. [Named] as archbishop of this city was Señor Don Fray Juan Ramírez de Almoguera, present bishop of Arequipa.

Death of Señor Don Andres de Vilela

Señor Don Andrés de Vilela, retired *oidor* of this royal *audiencia*, died on Wednesday, the 7th of February of the year 1674, the first day of Lent, at three in the afternoon. He was buried Friday, the 9th, at the hour of the Ave Maria in the church of the monastery of San Francisco Solano. The president and *oidores* and all the nobility of this city attended his burial.

Death of Father Francisco de Herrera

Father Maestro Fray Francisco de Herrera, a worthy subject of the order of Saint Augustine, died on Wednesday, the 28th of February of the year 1674, and they buried him at six o'clock that same day since he had been dead for fourteen hours.

Flagship goes to Panama for the Viceroy

Thursday, the 1st of March of the year 1674, at five in the afternoon the flagship and another ship of His Majesty left the port of Callao for the port of Perico in Panama to bring back Don Baltasar de la Cueva, Marquis of Malagón and Count of Castellar, who was coming as viceroy of Peru.

The admiral was Florián de Luzuriaga, who presently held that post having been appointed by the president and *oidores* [who governed] upon the death of the Count of Lemos.

Death of Doña Sancha de Castro

Doña Sancha de Castro, legal wife of Don Diego de Carbajal y Altamirano, *caballero* of the order of Alcántara and postmaster general of these kingdoms, died on Sunday, the 11th of March of 1674. She was the legitimate daughter of Don Sancho de Castro, and she did not bear any children during her marriage.

She was buried in the church of San Francisco on the morning of Monday, the 12th of this month, with a great attendance by all the nobility of this city of Lima. The president and *oidores* went to the burial and funeral services since the postmaster general was a grandson of Señor Don Blas Altamirano, who had been *oidor* and president of this royal *audiencia* of Lima.

Death of Don Felipe de Pineda

Felipe de Pineda, merchant, who had very recently come from Spain, died very suddenly during the night of Saturday, the 17th of March of 1674.

Death of Don García de Híjar y Mendoza

Don García de Híjar y Mendoza, Marquis of San Miguel and constable of this city of Lima, died Tuesday, the 27th of March of the year 1674, the day after the Easter holiday of the Resurrection. He was buried Thursday, the 29th of the month, in the monastery of San Agustín of this city.

Death of Doña Antonia de Salazar

Doña Antonia de Salazar, legitimate wife of the treasurer of the funds of Lima, Don Sebastián de Navarrete y Amezcua, *caballero* of the order of Calatrava, died suddenly on Friday, the 30th of March of the year 1674. She was buried in the church of the Pure and Immaculate Conception, the convent of the nuns.

Notification to the Prebends

Tuesday, the 3rd of [April of] this year the president and *oidores* forwarded a decree in which the ecclesiastic *cabildo* was notified not to sit on chairs but on benches when they all met together with the gentlemen in togas [*audiencia*] and in particular at the memorial services for the deceased Doña Antonia de Salazar. They requested certification [that this decree would be complied with], and the ecclesiastic *cabildo* was not present [at the funeral services].

Don Baltasar Pardo is Killed

Wednesday, the 4th of April of the year 1674, after nine at night, while General Don Baltasar Pardo, *caballero* of the order of Santiago, was riding in his carriage near La Encarnación convent, he was stabbed in the eye and received two lighter thrusts in the body. He died Thursday, the 5th, at one-thirty in the afternoon.

Death of Don Matías Lisperguer

Captain Don Matías Lisperguer de Batanbergue died Thursday, the 5th of the month.

Death of Felipe de Mieses

That same day the councilor Felipe de Mieses died.

Counterfeiter is Burned

On the afternoon of Monday, the 16th of April of the year 1674, Gabriel de Palacios was burned for making false money. The ordinary *alcalde* and sergeant major was Don Gil de Cabrera who was the one that sentenced him to walk through the public streets, and they applied the garrote at the place where convicts were burned and then burned his body. And so he was executed, and the chief constable of the city, Don Nicolás de Torres, went with him along with a scribe of the *cabildo* and its ministers. The convict went dressed in the white habit of charity.

Killer of Don Baltasar Pardo is Hanged

Saturday, the 21st of April of the year 1674, at four in the afternoon the bells of all the churches began to ring the interdiction. At this hour the *alcaldes* of the court, who were Señor Don Andrés Flores de la Parra, Señor Don Diego de la Rocha, and Señor Don [blank], as well as two fathers of the Society of Jesus were already inside the prison. Before dusk they had garroted him inside the prison without having taken his confession nor giving him more than a half hour's time, as it was so agreed. The sentence was that he be garroted and dragged [through the streets]. He was removed from the jail and dragged on a rawhide pelt, and at eight at night he was hanged at the scaffold where he remained until nine o'clock the following Sunday morning. A decree to his mother [ordered] that he be buried only at night with [the light of] four torches and without funeral altar stops or any kind of public display. In the statement given in his justification by the convict it was ordered that he be called Don Pedro Noguera, the surname of his mother, and not that of Carbajal.

At nine that same night all the bells rang the suspension, and at ten that same night the judges who had condemned him were absolved, with which peace was restored.

Arrival of the Archbishop

Monday, the 30th of April of the year 1674, Señor Don Juan Ramírez de Almoguera, archbishop of this city of Lima, disembarked at the port of Callao en route from Arequipa. He is also a religious of the Holy Trinity order and was bishop of Arequipa, where he governed thirteen years, more or less. Upon his disembarkation at Callao he was received with a great artillery salute.

Tuesday, the 1st of May, having stayed the day before in Callao at the house of the vicar where he ate and slept, His Grace went to the *chácara* of the sergeant major Don Pedro Merino, *caballero* of the order of Santiago, who is married to a niece of the archbishop. The *chácara* is located near La Legua, between Callao and Lima, and his Grace stayed there until Sunday morning, which was the 6th of May of 1674. It was there that all the priests of this ciy of Lima gave him a luncheon.

Reception of the Archbishop in Lima

Sunday, the 6th of May of the year 1674, at five in the afternoon Archbishop Don Juan Ramírez de Almoguera left the noviciate of the Society of Jesus on a mule with purple trappings. He rode between the two *oidores*, Señor Don Diego Messía and Señor Don Diego Baeza. The other *oidores* and *alcaldes* of the court were in front, and the comptrollers and royal officials of the *cabildo* and of the city, and all the doctors of the university with its rector, Don Diego Bermúdez, and many clerics and collegiates of all the colleges [following]. The crimson train of the archbishop was carried by Don Alvaro de Torres, who was precentor of Buenos Aires, and his nephew.

The Gentlemen who Stayed in the Council Hall

Señor Don Alvaro de Ibarra, president of the council; Señor Don Bernardo de Iturrizarra; Señor Don Tomás de Caviedes; Señor Don Fernando Velasco—these four gentlemen, as the most senior *oidores*, did not accompany the archbishop on the day he was received, because they stayed in the council hall.

His reception was grandiose and ostentatious. The prebends received him in the cathedral with the cross held high and a canopy under which he went as far as the main altar. There they chanted [Mass] for him and he gave the papal blessing. Then he removed his pontifical vestments and left by the door of the Naranjos for the palace. That night there were many fireworks, festive lights, a great ringing of bells, and many other [demonstrations of] festivity. Never before had such a crowd of people been seen in the streets and in the plaza; and in the cathedral, so many that they could not get in. May God grant him excellent health so that he may govern well, and that it all be for His service! Amen.

Death of Canon Don Juan de Montalvo

The canon of this holy church of Lima, Don Juan de Montalvo, died at eight at night on Tuesday, the 15th of May of the year

1674, the third day of Pentecost. He was buried in the cathedral of this city, and the archbishop received the body at the entrance of the cathedral.

Bullfights for the Archbishop

Saturday, the 9th of June of this year, bulls were fought for the arrival of Archbishop Don Fray Juan de Almoguera in this city of Lima. They began to run them at four-thirty in the afternoon. None of the *oidores* appeared at windows of the palace council hall to watch them, and there were no ordinary *alcaldes* strolling through the plaza, nor a single *caballero* in the plaza because of the displeasure of the *oidores* who wanted to go to the *cabildo* to see them. The *alcaldes* and *regidores* had sent word that there was no room, the excuse that they gave.

Dispatch Ship from Spain

Friday, the 13th of July of 1674, at two in the afternoon the dispatch ship arrived from Spain in which notification was brought to the archbishop that his sacred [pallium] would arrive in the first galleons. Saturday, the 14th, His Grace was received in the council hall.

That same day the archdeacon, Don Juan Santoyo de Palma, was received as dean of this holy church.

Sunday, the 15th, the archbishop was received anew at the cathedral with great praise and with all the crosses of the parishes raised high. The clerics, communities of the religious orders, secular *cabildo*, and many *caballeros* accompanied him from the archbishopric palace to the cathedral, where there was a ceremonial seat placed on a platform at the entrance of the cathedral in the middle of the main door. His Grace sat there with his canons, and after that ceremony in the church was over, he descended and under a canopy went to the chorus where he sat in his chair. And much silver was dispersed. From the chorus he went to the main altar where they chanted for him. He sat in a chair, and there each prebend gave him the benediction, and he gave the papal blessing. From there His Grace went home in a sedan chair, as he had a bad leg.

Entrance of the Viceroy's Ambassador

Tuesday, the 24th of July of 1674, at four in the afternoon the ambassador of Señor Don Baltasar de la Cueva, Marquis of Malagón and Count of Castellar, the viceroy who was coming to this kingdom of Peru, arrived at this city and presented his credentials to the president and *oidores* [who governed] on the death of the Count of Lemos. He entered amidst great applause of the people and *caballeros* of this city. This ambassador belongs to the order of Santiago and is a young man of barely twenty-two years.

Bullfights for the Ambassador

Saturday, the 28th of this month, bulls were run in this plaza of Lima for the ambassador of the viceroy. The archbishop did not come out to see them.

The Commissary of San Francisco

Sunday, the 29th [of July] at four in the afternoon the Very Reverend Father Fray Alonso Garrido Melgar, Franciscan commissary general, entered this city of Lima.

Dispatches About the New Viceroy

[Six months ago on] Shrove Tuesday, which was the 6th of February of the year 1674, at ten at night a dispatch arrived from Spain [with the news] that Señor Don Baltasar de la Cueva, Marquis of Malagón and Count of Castellar, was arriving as viceroy. Then another dispatch arrived with news that he had arrived at Puerto Bello [Panama] the 14th of April with two galleons, and that His Excellency had left Panama the 12th of May, arriving at Paita [Peru] on the 9th of June.

Arrival at Callao

His Excellency arrived at the port of Callao on Sunday, the 5th of August of the year 1674. At four in the afternoon the [new] Count of Lemos, a boy of seven or eight years of age, left Callao in his carriage with all his family to receive the new viceroy at Bocanegra, where there were great courtesies. The viceroy embraced the young boy as did the vicereine [Doña Teresa María de Saavedra, Countess of Castellar and Marchioness of Malagón], giving him many kisses. At that place [Bocanegra] their Excellencies descended from their litters and got into the boy's carriage, going in it as far as the palace of Callao. Men of the six mercenary cavalry companies had been posted on the plain at intermittent distances one from the other, and as the carriage of His Excellency went along, the flag [at each post] was lowered and a gun salute fired; and the same was done by the other cavalry companies. In the meantime all the artillery of the port of Callao was fired in salute.

Upon entering the gate of the region of Callao, they ordered

Presentation of the Keys the carriage to stop where the battalion commander of the fortress stood holding a golden platter with the keys [to the city]. He gave them to the little count in his post as general of that port, and the boy presented them to the viceroy, and His Excellency to the battalion commander. The entire wall of Callao was covered with women in gala dress, and it was so crowded that it looked like a bouquet of varied flowers. That same night there were many fireworks, displays, and festive lights.

The following Monday all the tribunals went in succession to bid him welcome. Tuesday, the 7th, at two in the afternoon the new viceroy came from Callao to Lima to visit the Countess of Lemos. First he went to visit [the chapel of] Our Lady of Solitude and the monastery of San Francisco where he was received by all the community and the two commissary generals, the previous one and the one who had just arrived from Spain. From San Francisco His Excellency went to the house of the Countess of Lemos and was there more than two hours with Her Excellency. Leaving there he went to Santo Domingo and visited five altars, and then to the chapel of Santa Rosa. From there he returned to Callao that same afternoon.

Bullfights at Callao Saturday, the 11th of the month, there were bullfights, and they were not good. Sunday, the 12th, there was a play put on by the soldiers, and Monday, the 13th, bulls were run, and they were worthless.

Arrival of His Excellency at Lima Tuesday, the 14th, His Excellency came publicly to Lima with the countess and all his family. Fifteen cavalry companies went as far as La Legua to receive him; six companies were paid soldiers and nine were reserves, five rural and four of the city. That night he slept in the palace.

Reception of the Viceroy The day on which the viceroy was received in Lima was the greatest reception day ever seen since Peru was discovered.

Wednesday, the 15th of August of the year 1674, the day of the Assumption of Our Lady, at four in the afternoon all the tribunals went to the arch that is set up for this event below Espiritu Santo [hospital], as is customary. His Excellency was on a city platform where he received them, and before [this stand] passed all the cavalry companies, the *colegios*, the university, and all the tribunals. As soon as they passed, His Excellency mounted his horse and went under a canopy, the *regidores* carrying the poles. The two ordinary alcaldes, who were Don Gil de Cabrera and Don Juan de Castilla, carried the reins of the horse, and all [were dressed] in carmine red velvet clothing. Captain Don Nuño de la Cueva, of the order of San Juan [de Jerusalén], went with the lance company, ancient guard of the viceroys, as rear guard of the viceroy.

The vicereine was in the balcony at the corner of Mercaderes Street which faces Espiritu Santo. The oldest and youngest sons of the Count of Lemos, may God have received him in His holy glory, were with Her Excellency when His Excellency arrived under a canopy, and there were great courtesies. While he was [occupied] with these, from another balcony of a different house they threw a quantity of silver at the feet of the horse on which His Excellency rode; and it was a matter of some time before peace was restored among those who ran to pick up the silver which had been thrown.

Arch at Mercaderes Street

There was a very decorative arch in the middle of Mercaderes Street where there was much to see. The whole area adjacent to the arch was paved with bars of silver, the majority of which were more than two hundred marks [one hundred pounds], which pleased His Excellency upon seeing them.

Twenty-four lackeys and twenty-four pages went with His Excellency. The lackeys were mulattoes, free men who had been chosen in this city. [There were] three carriages with six mules, and six coachmen with boots and spurs, and all wore identical livery of red, silver and blue. Behind all this were twenty-four mules, covered with silk cloths bearing the coat of arms of the viceroy, and loaded with pastries. Each mule, with silver baskets and silk ropes and halters, had three large silver [escutcheon] plates with the coat of arms of His Excellency, one on the forehead and two hanging from the ears, and each mule was led by an Indian. This entrance into Lima was like his entrance into Germany as ambassador; [it was] a grand event, no such other having been seen in Lima.

Artillery

In the plaza at eight o'clock the same day the lieutenant general of artillery, with all the artillery sergeants and artillerymen of

Callao, brought out from the palace two tents in two carts with flags and insignia of arms of our king and lord, and ten pieces of artillery. They placed them next to the bronze fountain that is in the plaza, which they had cleverly decorated that day. In the time that it took His Excellency to mount his horse until he entered the palace, five vollies were fired. There were fifty pieces of artillery fired, which shook the whole city.

Infantry Squadron

There were also two infantry squadrons in the plaza, one of merchants and the other of the rank and file of the city, in which there were eighteen companies of Spaniards, and four more companies, two of mulattoes and two of creole Negroes, and another two of free Negroes from Guinea. There were all kinds of people in the plaza, more than one thousand two hundred infantrymen and more than eight hundred of the cavalry, and there was such a battering of the enclosed [artillery] charges which were fired upon the descent of His Excellency at the steps of the cathedral, that the city was stunned.

His Excellency remounted his horse, and the *oidores*, upon seeing such a volley of muskets and arquebuses, went on foot to the palace, to which His Excellency went under a canopy as far as the stairs. Upon descending from his horse he gave many thanks to the *alcaldes* and *regidores*, and [later] appeared at the balcony of the plaza, whereupon the infantry and cavalry gave him another gun salute.

As the bells rang the Ave Maria, His Excellency went in, and all was disbanded. That same night there were many fireworks and festive lights throughout the whole plaza.

Decoration of the Balconies

For the day of the entrance of the viceroy, Don Baltasar de la Cueva, Marquis of Malagón and Count of Castellar, all the balconies of the plaza were decorated with greenery, and all the decoration was done at the expense of the owners of these buildings.

The Play of the Jesuit Fathers

The fathers of the Society of Jesus gave a play in their monastery for the archbishop of this city, Fray Juan de Almoguera, which was entitled "The Prince of Fez," a magnificent thing to see. This was on Monday, the 13th of August of 1674.

Thursday, the 16th, near the hour of the Ave Maria, the

Countess of Lemos went to the palace in a sedan chair to pay her [courtesy] visit on the Count of Castellar, and the Countess remained until after eight o'clock at night. *Visit of the Countess of Lemos*

That same day, the 16th, news reached this city of Lima that the Duke of Veragua, recently received as viceroy of Mexico, had died five days after his reception.

That same day news arrived that *Corregidor* Don Francisco Luján Sigonés had died in his district.

Don Cristóbal de la Cuba, relator [prosecutor] of this royal *audiencia*, died this same day. *Death of Don Cristóbal de la Cuba*

The archbishop visited the viceroy on Friday, the 17th, at ten in the morning and stayed until eleven. *Visit of the Archbishop*

On the afternoon of this same day the relator, Don Cristóbal de la Cuba, was buried. He had a son, the present court *alcalde* of the hall of crime.

Monday, the 20th, a proclamation was issued that no mulatto, Negro, quadroon, or mestizo could carry a sword or dagger except for active officers of the militia, under penalty of one hundred lashes and fifty pesos [fine] for the first offense. For the second, [offense] two hundred lashes and four years in the galleys. *Ban on Mulattoes*

Saturday, the 1st of September of 1674, His Excellency went to Callao and that same day reviewed the infantry, artillery, and seamen; and he embarked on the tender and went to inspect the ships of His Majesty. There was a great gun salute of artillery from land and sea, and while on board he viewed the whole sea wall. He disembarked at Piti-Piti and saw the nine lighters in dry dock. There he entered his carriage and returned to Lima. *Review in Callao*

This same day he ordered a proclamation issued in Callao: that no captain on active duty or reserve, nor any soldier or other person receiving a salary from the king, could come to Lima without permission of the viceroy and the battalion commander of Callao. *Ban on Leaving Callao*

Sunday, the 2nd of September, at four in the afternoon His Excellency went with great ostentation to the plaza, without a cape, *Viceroy Goes to the Plaza* very gallant and resplendent. He took a turn around the entire plaza on the horse [named] Grifo which had belonged to the Count of Lemos until the countess, widow of Lemos, presented it to him. There were ten sections of musketeers in the plaza with more than two hundred and fifty musketeers, and ten cavalry companies, four of them mercenary, and the other four of the rank and file. The cavalry skirmished against the musketeers, firing ten vollies, and during all of them the viceroy on his horse was in the midst of the musketeers. The afternoon was very gay and worth seeing, and at prayertime it all ended.

The Company from Callao

Monday, the 3rd, Francisco Ruíz de la Cueva, captain of the mercenary infantry company of Callao, came from Callao with fifty soldiers. The 4th of the month made one complete year since the rank and file companies entered guard duty in the palace.

Visit of the Viceroy to San Francisco

Wednesday, the 5th of September of the year 1674, the viceroy and the vicereine, [Count and] Countess of Castellar, visited the monastery of San Francisco. Alone, they saw all of it; then they entered the chapel of La Soledad, and in a large salon the superiors had provided a great number of sweets and other items, and they enjoyed everything.

Imprisonment of General Alzamora

Thursday, the 6th, His Excellency ordered the detention of Maritime General Don José de Alzamora and the present sergeant major of Callao, Don Francisco Delzo, because they came from Callao to Lima without permission from His Excellency.

On the afternoon of Friday, the 7th, His Excellency went to visit the hospitals with the treasury official.

Memorial Funeral Rites for King Philip IV

Monday, the 17th [of September] the archbishop, Don Fray Juan de Almoguera, held memorial funeral rites for our king, Don Philip IV, at the cathedral of this city with the presence of the viceroy, Marquis of Malagón, the gentlemen of the royal *audiencia*, the secular *cabildo*, and all the nobility of this city. Father Rodrigo de Valdés of the Society of Jesus gave the sermon. The catafalque was made up of eight sections; on top there was a very expensive red ebony bed with crimson damask; in the middle a crucifix on a sideboard; and an imperial crown and sceptre on a pillow. [Representatives of] all the religious orders were present. This day, the 17th, was the day the king had died, nine full years ago, day of the wounds of Saint Francis.

Ban Regarding Indians

Saturday, the 22nd of the month, at eleven in the morning a proclamation was issued by His Excellency that no person, soldiers, or anyone else of the city [could] go out on the roads and take from the Indians the provisions that they bring to sell in the city, under penalty of four years in Valdivia; and that any ordinary magistrate could apply the law. [It also ordered] that no one carry a long sword or one with a needlepoint, with the same penalty.

Placement of Our Lady of the Waters

On the afternoon of Sunday, the 30th of September of 1674, they brought out in procession the image of Our Lady of the Waters that a man called Don Alonso Cortés de Monroy had had for many years at the fountain house. Monday, the 1st of October of that year, this image was in the cathedral, where a sung Mass was held with great solemnity. It was sung by the vicar general Don José Dávila, and a Mercedarian father gave the sermon. After the Mass was over, [the image] was taken in procession with a great accompaniment to the Sagrario chapel, and there this holy image of Our Lady of the Waters was placed.

Saint Rose of Viterbo

At four in the afternoon of Friday, the 5th of October of the year 1674, [the statue of Saint Rose of Viterbo] was taken in procession to the convent of Santa Clara with all the religious of San Francisco and [the statue of] their holy father, Saint Francis. From there they returned to the monastery of San Francisco with [the statue of] Saint Rose of Viterbo. Saturday, the 6th, after the sermon and when the high Mass was over, they placed it on the altar of Saint Louis, King of France, and Saint Isabel, Queen of Hungary. Saint Rose was of the third order of Saint Francis.

Mourning of the Viceroy and all His Family

That same day, Friday the 5th, the viceroy and the Countess with all their family put on long mourning robes for the death of the Duke of Veragua, brother-in-law of the viceroy, Marquis of Malagón, as the duke had married his sister. He died while he was viceroy of Mexico, five days after he had been received as viceroy.

Reception of the Viceroy at the University

On the afternoon of Sunday, the 14th, the viceroy, Marquis of Malagón and Count of Castellar, accompanied by all the *oidores*, was received in the learned Minerva [goddess of wisdom] and royal university of this city of Lima. He entered by way of the cloister and the lecture hall. All was decorated with wonderful draperies and great paintings, and Doctor Don Andrés de Paredes gave a eulogistic speech, tracing the royal blood [line] of His Excellency, and His Excellency [reciprocated] extending great honors. There were many prizes of silver platters, vessels, and other objects of value, and for His Excellency, a gold medal of Our Lady of Solitude and Saint Rose, amber-colored gloves and four doubloons. For the *oidores*, a gratuity of a doubloon to each one. The present rector was Doctor Don Diego Bermúdez, of the order of Santiago.

Fiesta *for Mary*

Sunday, the 21st of October of the year 1674, the celebration of the holy name of Mary [her divine motherhood] was held with the usual solemnity. In the afternoon there was a procession through the plaza, with a squadron made up of many infantrymen and ten companies on horseback, the six mercenary [companies] and the four of the rank and file of the city. On this day the rural mounted companies did not parade because there was not enough space in the plaza because of the formation of native Indians. The reason this feast was postponed eight days was the reception of the viceroy at the university.

Imprisonment of the Frenchmen

Saturday, the 3rd of November of the year 1674, at eleven in the morning all the *oidores* and chief comptrollers left the palace in their carriages, each one with his scribe, and they dispersed to the areas corresponding to them, in accordance with the order that they bore from His Excellency. They seized some well-known Frenchmen and confiscated all their goods. That same day they also visited all the merchants who had come from Spain that year and reviewed their books containing the entries of the materials they had imported, to ascertain if they had brought any materials from Spain for the French merchants. For those on whom they could find nothing, they only embargoed their books.

Tuesday, the 6th of November of the year 1674, the day that our king and lord Charles II was thirteen years of age, His

Excellency went to the cathedral in colorful gala attire, with all the *oidores*, to hear the pontifical Mass said by Archbishop Don Fray Juan de Almoguera. The viceroy, Don Baltasar de la Cueva, Count of Castellar and Marquis of Malagón, inaugurated the new carriage that he had brought from Spain.

First Bullfights for the Viceroy

That same afternoon the viceroy and vicereine left the palace in the new carriage, with a sedan chair behind and a large accompaniment, and made a tour around the plaza which was surrounded with planks [to sit on like bleachers] and lined with boards as used in the court [in Spain], and filled to the top with people. They went to the gallery of the *cabildo* to watch the bulls run. Don Miguel de Oruña and Captain Don Francisco de León entered the plaza of Lima in a carriage with fourteen horses following, eight of Captain León and six of Oruña, and their wide swords and many *rejones* [bullfighting spears].

Oruña gave two very good clean thrusts of the spear on the first bull that came out, and in the course of the afternoon he placed another six spears. The bulls badly injured two of the horses.

Don Francisco de León planted four spear thrusts, and the bulls crippled four of his horses. With his broadsword he injured another horse that he was riding while thrusting at the bull. Late [in the afternoon] a bull unseated him and he went towards the bull on foot with his broadsword in hand. Face to face he attacked it, but the bull threw him to the ground and mauled him, the clash injuring his face.

Don Rodrigo de Mendoza entered the plaza alone, as an adventurer, on his horse with two grooms and two spears that he employed quite well. He came out of it very commendably without changing horses and with many cheers.

Death of Francisco de Jurre

Francisco de Jurre, the one who used to tell about things that had happened thirty or forty years ago, and who was regarded as insane, died of diarrhea in the hospital of San Andrés on Tuesday, the 13th of November of 1674. He was buried in the Calvary [chapel] of this hospital by his friend, Francisco Tijeros.

Unfortunate Death of Laureano Gelder

Wednesday, the 21st of November of 1674, day of the Presentation of Our Lady, while returning from Guía at five-thirty in the afternoon, Laureano Gelder went along carefully because he had received a note instructing him to leave four hundred pesos in the hands of a religious, otherwise he would be killed. For protection he took along a Negro who carried a blunderbuss loaded with two balls and four mold shots. Arriving at his house and shop, he said to the Negro, "Put the blunderbuss on that table," where the Negro placed it, releasing the safety catch, as he had seen his master do. A long time later, while Laureano was playing in the patio with a spirited dog that he had, the blunderbuss fell on the table and fired, lodging three pieces of lead in his [Laureano's] shoulders and legs, and he died two days later. The bullets went past the doors of the carriage shed which open to the patio and the street, and lodged more than a span into the wall in front. A piece of artillery could not have done more damage. He gave legal power to his wife to make a will and act as guardian and executor of the estate. He left two daughters and admitted having in his possession 350,000 pesos, without [counting] silverware, and slaves and household effects. He was preparing to go to Spain. He was a son-in-law of the sergeant major Felipe Zavala.

Death of the Cathedral Priest

Licenciado Don Sebastián Islao, priest of the holy cathedral of this city of Lima, died suddenly on Wednesday, the 5th of December of the year 1674, at nine in the morning. He was buried on the afternoon of Thursday, the 6th, in this cathedral.

Professorship Won by Doctor Astorga

Thursday, the 6th of December of 1674, Doctor Don Pedro de Astorga was awarded the professorship in law which he won by one hundred and twelve extra votes. In competition for the title were Doctor Don Juan de Zamudio, Doctor Don Juan de la Cueva, collegiate of San Martín, [and] Doctor Don Pedro de Astorga. He carried off the professorship, amidst the applause of all, for being learned and very poor. And this day he took possession of the chair.

Play for the Viceroy

Friday, the 21st of December, day of the apostle Saint Thomas, the collegiates under the direction of their professors presented a play at the college of San Martín entitled "The Phoenix of Spain: Saint Francis of Borja." The viceroy, Marquis of Malagón and Count of Castellar, attended. The play began at five in the afternoon and lasted until eleven at night due to the many scenes it contained. It was written by Father Pedro López of the Society of Jesus in Lima.

Bullfights and *cañas* were held on the afternoon of Saturday the 22nd. There were four quadrilles with eight [persons] to a quadrille, which made thirty-two *caballeros*, all very resplendent and gallant, with a great number of pages, all in splendid livery. They jousted with *cañas* very well. At dusk a man came out from the enclosure on a very brave bull, astride his back and wearing spurs, and the bull bucking wildly, and he on top of the bull without shifting. The bull did not stop until they killed it with a sword thrust. The viceroy and the vicereine and the gentlemen in togas [*audiencia* members] were watching it all at the *cabildo* where the man who rode on the bull went to dedicate the bull.

Bulls and Cañas *in the Plaza*

The plaza has never been so clean, swept, and sprinkled as on this same afternoon, without the nuisance of Negroes or Indians, because the soldiers, on the one hand, had cleared it, and the sergeant major, Don Julián Corveira, with his two aides, Roque Rosales and Rueda, and all the battalion sergeants [saw to it] that the plaza had been cleared to the point where the bull scarcely had anyone to charge. They were very brave [bulls].

The Year 1675

Tuesday, the first day of the new year, Don García de Híjar y Mendoza and the royal ensign Don Pedro Lazcano were chosen ordinary *alcaldes* in this city of Lima for the year 1675. The viceroy, Marquis of Malagón and Count of Castellar, was present at the election.

Friday, the 11th of January of the year 1675, a dispatch ship arrived from Chiloé [Island, Chile,] sent by the man who governed that post. [He said] that he had received information from an Indian of those islands that the enemy was laying siege to the islands near the Strait [of Magellan] at fifty-one degrees [South Latitude].

Dispatch Ship from Chiloé

Tuesday, the 15th of January of the year 1675, the viceroy, Marquis of Malagón, issued the third proclamation, that the armada should leave the port of Callao for Panama by the 28th of this month without fail with the treasure of His Majesty and individuals.

Third Decree for Dispatching the Armada

That same day, at six in the afternoon His Excellency left this city for Callao with all his family. (He returned with all his family the 29th of the month, without sending the armada off.)

Archbishop of Las Charcas Arrives

The archbishop of Las Charcas [Upper Peru], Don Melchor de Liñán, who had been bishop of Popayán and *visitador* and president of Santa Fé [*audiencia*] in the New Kingdom [of New Granada], arrived at this city on Thursday, the 17th of January of the year 1675. He went from the *chácara* of Don Bartolomé de Azaña, without entering Lima, to Callao to see the viceroy, Marquis of Malagón, who was at that port to dispatch this year's armada. The archbishop of this city, Don Fray Juan de Almoguera, with all the canons and prebends went to receive him at the *chácara* of Don Fernando de Castro. From there the archbishops returned in the carriage of the archbishop of Lima, and the canons in their carriages. Then they accompanied him to the *chácara* of Don Antonio de Murga, where he was lodged.

Death of Don Alvaro de Ibarra

Saturday, the 19th of January of the year 1675, Señor Don Alvaro de Ibarra died, and he was buried on Sunday at four in the afternoon in the church of the Society of Jesus of this city of Lima. The viceroy was not present at the burial as he was in Callao to dispatch the armada, nor did the ecclesiastic *cabildo* attend the burial because of certain differences, for which they took revenge on the deceased after his death. Being a son of the earth, and having occupied so many honorific posts that were given to him by His Majesty, they were of no value to him at his death. And so it is that the only thing of value is to serve Our Lord Jesus Christ, as everything else is but mockery.

Funeral Rites for Señor Don Alvaro

Memorial funeral rites for Señor Don Alvaro de Ibarra were held on Tuesday, the 22nd of January of said year, at which the viceroy was present, having come from Callao the day before. The *oidores* were also present, and the viceroy brought the two nephews of the deceased to the church and returned them to their house in his carriage. The secular *cabildo* and all the nobility were [also] present. In the afternoon His Excellency returned to Callao.

Monday, the 28th of January of 1675, at five in the afternoon the lookout ship left the port of Callao for that of Valdivia with the governor of that area, Don Francisco Delzo. He had been sergeant major of that post and [later] of the fortress of Callao when they granted him the post of governor. The sergeant major and fortress commander of that post, worthy men who had served in Chile, also went on this occasion. Many men who had been exiled also went, and without any [financial] aid. Exiles leaving without aid had never been heard of before except in this government of the Marquís of Malagón.

Lookout Ship Sails for Valdivia

On Wednesday, the 6th of February, exactly at noon His Excellency, the Marquis of Malagón and Count of Castellar, issued a proclamation with all the other orders, that no one dare to throw trash next to the [Mercedarian] Recollect of Our Lady of Belén and the noviciate of the Society of Jesus, and in other places, under penalty of fifty patacoons. He gave the responsibility of the execution of this edict to the ordinary *alcaldes* and the water commissioner.

Ban on Trash

Friday, the 8th of February of 1675, His Excellency returned to Callao with the countess and his family to send off the armada. He returned from Callao on Saturday, the 23rd of the month, the same way he went, without dispatching the armada.

Dispatch of the Armada

Fray Nicolás Collazos, a Mercedarian religious, died at a *chácara* on Thursday, the 21st of February of the year 1675. He was buried in his monastery at midday on Friday, the 22nd.

Death of Fray Nicolás Collazos

Sunday, the 17th of March of 1675, Don Lorenzo de Gárate died and he was buried on Monday afternoon at Santa Clara [church].

Death of Don Lorenzo de Gárate

[They flogged] Don Juan de Villegas, as it was so stipulated in the decree, for having falsified the seal of the viceroy, Marquis of Malagón and Count of Castellar, and the signature of his secretary, and for the falsified decrees that he gave some soldiers and they took silver from the royal cash box which was due them from their salary. For this offense he was condemned to two hundred lashes and ten years in the galleys in Spain. It [the flogging] was done Monday, the 18th of March of the year 1675, between eleven and twelve in the morning.

Don Juan de Villegas Flogged Through the Streets

Gabriel de Mora Died

[He died] on Tuesday, the 19th of March of the year 1675, and was buried at the convent of Nuestra Señora del Prado. He was chief constable of the royal treasury of Lima.

Don José de Bolívar Died

[He died] on Wednesday, the 20th of March of 1675. He was a *caballero* of the order of Santiago and chief comptroller of the tribunal of accounts. He was buried at the convent of the Magdalena Recollect of the Predicadores order. The viceroy and all the *oidores* and *caballeros* of the city of Lima were present at the burial.

General Don Juan de Beingolea Died

[He died] on Wednesday, the 20th of March of 1675, from an abscess in the neck, and was buried Thursday, the 21st, in the Franciscan monastery of Lima.

First Sermon of my Son Francisco

The first sermon that my son Fray Francisco gave was in his Franciscan monastery at Callao. It was on the morning of Holy Thursday, which was the 11th of April of the year 1675.

Viceroy at the Stations of the Cross

The viceroy, Marquis of Malagón and Count of Castellar, with all the *oidores*, visited the stations of the cross on the night of Holy Thursday of the year 1675. The Countess of Castellar, on her part, [did the same] with the eldest son of the Count of Lemos and his younger brothers and with a very resplendent accompaniment.

His Excellency accompanied all the *oidores* at the candlelight procession of Our Lady of Solitude which left the monastery of San Francisco on the night of Holy Friday of this year of 1675.

Three Indians Arrive with News of the Enemy

While His Excellency was participating in this procession, a Spaniard and three Indians arrived in this city, sent by the governor of Chile. They were to explain to His Excellency how the English enemy was settling near the Strait [of Magellan], and how they had constructed a fortress and fenced off a town. They were located in two parts in that region, one on land and the other on an adjacent island, and they had four vessels, two large and two small, and a large one under construction.

Thursday, the 18th of April of the year 1675, His Excellency issued another proclamation: that all the merchants from Spain

Proclamation for the Dispatch of the Armada

and all the businessmen of this city prepare to embark. They were to deliver the silver to the silver masters aboard the flagship and escort vessel because the armada had to sail for Tierra Firme at the end of this month of April without fail and without permission for a delayed ship. Those responsible for the armada not leaving Callao by this time would have to pay all the costs resulting from the time [the Spanish ships] would be [waiting] at Cartagena.

Hoisting of the Dominican Bell

Wednesday, the 24th of April of the year 1675, the large bell of Santo Domingo was hoisted to its tower. The provincial was Father Maestro Fray Antonio de Morales.

Dispatch of the Armada

Saturday, the 27th of April of 1675, at five in the afternoon His Excellency left this city for Callao. [On the way] he first went to visit Our Lady of Solitude at San Francisco [church] and from there to [visit] the Countess of Lemos. From there he left for Callao with all his family, and he was not [going] to return to Lima without first having dispatched the armada and having it leave the port for Panama with the treasure of His Majesty and private individuals. [Because of uncertainty about European wars, the armada did not sail until six weeks later.]

Edict for a Review of the Merchant Companies

Saturday, the 4th of May of the year 1675, a proclamation was issued in this city of Lima by the viceroy, Count of Castellar and Marquis of Malagón: that Monday, the 6th of the month, the five companies of the merchants of Callao, those presently enlisted and those that had been in them, were to pass review before His Excellency. The penalty was reserved for His Excellency [to decide] in accordance with the category of each one of those who did not appear at the review. Monday, the 6th, at eight in the morning Captain Don Luis Calvo de O'Monte was to pass review with his company, and at four in the afternoon Antonio Padilla with his company. Tuesday, at eight in the morning Captain Montejo with all his company, and at four in the afternoon Captain Oyaga with his company. Wednesday, the 8th, Captain Vélez at eight in the morning.

The same day, the prior and consuls went to Callao to speak with His Excellency about the proclamation, and he ordered it suspended, [stating] that the companies were not to pass review until further orders.

Return of His Excellency to Lima

Monday, the 20th of May, at midday His Excellency arrived from Callao in his carriage, in shirt sleeves with his staff [of command in hand], and with only his nephew, the Marquis of Rivas. [He returned] to attend a council meeting with the togaed gentlemen of the royal treasury regarding the dispatch of the armada for Tierra Firme. They were very apprehensive about whether the armada should be sent or not, since they had received no news or dispatch ship from Spain.

Tuesday, the 21st of the month, at one in the afternoon a soldier named Juan Moreno arrived on horseback. He had been in Paita awaiting news of the dispatch ship, having been sent by His Excellency, and he brought news that the boxes [of mail] would arrive at Paita shortly. An *hidalgo* colleague who came on the dispatch ship had disembarked at Puna [Island, Ecuador], and he came with him to the palace bringing a folder of letters for His Excellency in which there was a very important piece of news for the viceroy as well as for the whole city. Señor Don Andrés Flores de la Parra, *alcalde* of the *court* of this royal *audiencia*, was to be precentor of this holy church.

Wednesday, the 22nd, the vicereine with all her family returned from Callao, and His Excellency went out with a large retinue to meet her on the road.

Two Dispatches Arrive from Spain

Wednesday, the 29th of May of the year 1675, two dispatches arrived at this city. One was that referred to above; the other was dispatched from the Canary Islands by the general of the fleet and galleons [with news] that they had left Cádiz the 13th of February of that year 1675. They brought much news of bloody wars of the emperor and Holland against France, and [news of the appointment] through competition of Don Pedro de Cárdenas as canon of this holy church.

Three Rebel Indians Hanged

Thursday, the 30th of the month, three Indians who were chairmakers and barbers by trade were hanged and two were flogged. They had said they were going to create an uprising in this city and call together all the other Indians to join forces with the English enemy situated in the Strait [of Magellan], killing all the Spaniards of this city, leaving only all the women, and they would become masters of the armory. The two that were flogged were given two hundred lashes and ten years in the galleys of Spain.

Friday, the 31st of May of the year 1675, the prebendary, Don Diego Portachuelo, entered this holy cathedral of Lima as a religious of the monastery of San Agustín. This same day he took on the habit of a religious.

The Prebendary Don Diego Portachuelo

Wednesday, the 11th of June of the year 1675, on the eve of Corpus [Christi], the armada left the port of Callao for Panama with the treasure of His Majesty and individuals. Nine ships went in the armada: the flagship, escort vessel, and the *San Lorenzo*, which were His Majesty's, and six merchant ships. Twenty-two million pesos went [with this armada] which was the silver of three years. Don José de Alzamora went as general, and Florián de Luzuriaga as admiral.

Departure of the Armada

The Countess of Lemos, widow of the Count of Lemos, left in this same armada with her entire family for Spain. May God deliver them safely! (This armada returned to the port of Callao on the 11th of October of that year 1675.)

The Countess of Lemos

In this same armada, which left Callao the 12th of June of 1675, my nephew Don Pedro Legorburu embarked for Spain, in good health, after having been in this city one year, nine months, and twenty-two days. He took with him to Spain Perote de Recalde and the daughters of Captain Fernando de Avila and their children. One [daughter] was married to Don Diego de Avila, and the other was the wife of Captain Don Miguel de Vergara, who was in Seville.

My Nephew Don Pedro Legorburu

At ten o'clock in the morning of Tuesday, the 18th of June of the year 1675, the [papal] bull of the beatification of Saint Francis Solano arrived at this city of Lima by *chasque* from Quito. Immediately thereafter the bells rang and all the people of the city became excited and went to the church of San Francisco, along with the archbishop, Don Juan de Almoguera, and the viceroy, Count of Castellar and Marquis of Malagón. The box containing the bones of the saint [he died in Lima in 1610] was brought out and opened at the main altar. After viewing the bones, they immediately ordered it closed, and the religious returned the box to its original place.[53]

Arrival of the Papal Bull

[53] Saint Francis Solano was born in Spain in 1549 and died in Lima, Peru, on

Staff of General of Callao Saturday, the 22nd of June of the year 1675, in a military formation the staff as general of land and sea was presented [by the viceroy] to the Marquis of Rivas, his nephew, with great solemnity. There were many *caballeros* of this city of Lima who went there for the event, and all that were in the formation carried their pikes. The infantry fired three musket salutes, and all the artillery also fired.

Horse Races His Excellency returned to Lima on the 23rd of the month, and on the afternoon of the 24th there were great races in the plaza of Lima and roped bulls in honor of the vicereine's birthday.

New Franciscan Provincial Fray Antonio de Oserín was appointed provincial of the order of Saint Francis on Saturday, the 29th of June of the year 1675, day of the glorious apostle Saint Peter.

Incident in the Theater Sunday, the 11th of August of the year 1675, two soldiers had words with a Negro slave of an *oidor* [Don José de la Cueva], son of the present battalion commander of Lima, Don Francisco de la Cueva. A city magistrate, Don Pedro Lazcano, by his authority wanted to imprison the two soldiers, but because there was such a great ruckus and differences between the two, the soldiers were turned over to the general battalion commander, Don Diego de Martos, and he dismissed the matter, permitting the soldiers to leave. When this was told to the viceroy, Marquis of Malagón, he ordered Don José de la Cueva arrested, fined two thousand pesos, and sent to Callao for imprisonment in the house of the battalion commander of that fortress until there was a ship for the kingdoms of Chile or Valdivia. If the imprisonment were violated, the fine would be ten thousand pesos. He was also demoted from his cavalry company and the post was given to Don Juan José de Acuña. (The military auditor took his wife's jewels to meet the two thousand peso fine.)

[She died] on Saturday, the 17th of August of 1675, at six in

July 14, 1610. He served as a missionary in Tucumán, Paraguay, and Peru for twenty years, mastering many Indian dialects while baptizing the natives. Later he was guardian of the Franciscan monastery in Lima. Beatified in 1675 and canonized in 1726, his feast day is July 24th. *New Catholic Encyclopedia*, XIII, 414.

the morning. She was a nun of the convent of San José de las Monjas Descalzas of this city of Lima, and she was well known as a great servant of God. At the time of her death it was sixty years since she had professed. She was buried in her convent Monday, the 19th of this month and year. The archbishop of this city, Don Fray Juan de Almoguera, and the viceroy, Count of Castellar, and the vicereine were present at the Mass. The archbishop and the viceroy and the countess entered the chorus within the convent before the Mass, and the vicereine remained with the nuns in the chorus until the deceased had been buried. The viceroy and the archbishop left the church for their seats where they remained until the services were over. The doctor and canon of this holy cathedral, Don Diego de Salazar, chanted the Mass, and all the most noble of this city of Lima were present at the burial. *Ana of the Holy Spirit Died*

(Memorial rites for this holy nun were held Wednesday, the 2nd of October of this year 1675. Father Maestro Fray Cipriano de Herrera, present prior of San Agustín [monastery], gave the sermon and mentioned many things about her exemplary life as a great servant of God. The viceroy and his wife, the archbishop, and all the nobility of Lima were present.) *Memorial Rites for the Holy Nun*

Wednesday, the 4th of September of the year 1675, the dispatch ship from Spain arrived at this city with eleven boxes of letters that the general of the galleons and fleet had brought to Puerto Bello. It also brought the pallium of the archbishop of this city, Don Fray Juan de Almoguera. There was great rejoicing this day. *Arrival of the Dispatch Ship from Spain*

Sunday, the 8th of September of this month and year, day of the nativity of Our Lady, the archbishop put on the pallium. It was presented to him by the dean of this holy church, Don Juan Santoyo de Palma, who also held the sung Mass. After it was over he placed it [the pallium] around the neck of the archbishop, after much ceremony. Father Fray Cristóbal Jaramillo of the order of Saint Francis gave the sermon. The viceroy, Marquis of Malagón, the president and *oidores*, all the secular *cabildo*, and the nobility of this city were present. *The Pallium of the Archbishop*

Sunday, the 15th of September of the year 1675, in the chapel of the palace, Don Cristóbal de la Cueva and his son Captain Don

Habit of Santiago to Don Cristóbal de la Cueva

Pedro received the habit of Santiago. The viceroy, Don Baltasar de la Cueva, Marquis of Malagón, was the sponsor of both; and Señor Don Fernando Velasco, *caballero* of the order of Santiago and *oidor* of this royal *audiencia*, as the most senior [member] assisted at all the other ceremonies that this act required. There was a small formation inside the patio of the palace, where all the captains on active service in the battalion regiment came out with their arquebuses, as well as those of the cavalry of the company of Captain Don Pedro de la Cueva, which is presently one of those on duty in this city. Everyone congratulated him.

Memorial Rites for the King our Lord

Tuesday, the 17th of September of the year 1675, memorial funeral rites were held in the cathedral of this city for the [former] king, our lord, Philip IV. They were ordered by the viceroy, Marquis of Malagón. A very large and expensive catafalque was erected, very luminous, where there were one thousand two hundred candles of every kind. The archbishop of this city, Don Fray Juan de Almoguera, gave the sermon at these [rites]. His Excellency attended with all the gentlemen of the royal *audiencia*, the chief comptrollers, secular and ecclesiastic *cabildos*, and all the nobility of the city. At the top of the catafalque there was a large box made of solid silver, and in the middle a crucifix of Christ, and at his feet a crown and sceptre. The four pillars were covered with black silk damask. It was ten years ago today that our king and lord, Philip IV, died.

A Ship Sailed for the Strait of Magellan

At four in the afternoon on Saturday, the 21st of September of the year 1675, day of the glorious apostle Saint Matthew, a large ship left from Callao with eighty infantrymen, ten artillerymen, ten pieces of artillery, six navigators, thirty seamen and cabin boys, all of them Spaniards. Two chiefs went along, one of whom was Pascual de Iriarte and the other Don Antonio de Beas Navarro. They went to reconnoiter the spot where the English enemy was holding forth. All the soldiers and sailors were given eight months pay. The Marquis of Malagón boarded the ship the day it sailed, and as soon as he disembarked the ship set sail. That same afternoon His Excellency returned to Lima.

On the afternoon of Monday, the 4th of November of the year 1675, day of the glorious Saint Charles, the Marquís of Malagón went on horseback to the Alameda [promenade] with a great accompaniment of *caballeros*, also on horseback. The vicereine in her new carriage and the wives of the *oidores* [also went]. Six white horses pulled the carriage, all very handsomely decorated. They greatly enjoyed themselves at the Alameda, and at evening prayer time all returned to the palace, where their Excellencies entertained everyone, offering them food, thin rolled wafers, and cold drinks.

His Excellency goes to the Alameda

Wednesday, the 6th of the month, on the fourteenth birthday of our king and lord Charles II, roped bulls were run in the plaza. Twenty-four very resplendent *caballeros* raced within a barricade set up for that purpose. The first to run was Don García de Hijar y Mendoza, presently ordinary *alcalde* of this city of Lima, who ran alone. Everyone put on a very good show in the six races. The last to run were the Marquis of Rivas, nephew of His Excellency, with the present captain of the cavalry troop, Don Antonio de Aguirre.

Bulls and Races

At night there was a comedy at the palace written by the licentiate Don Juan de Urdaide and entitled "Love in Lima is Fortuitous." After the play all the *caballeros* and *oidores* and their wives were feasted with dinner, thin wafers, much chocolate, and cold drinks.

Comedy

Mass was held in the cathedral the morning of the same day in thanksgiving, and it was said by Dean Don Juan Santoyo de Palma. His Excellency appeared in color, with a great chain of gold, and [with] all his family and all the *caballeros* of this city.

Thanksgiving Mass

Don José de Ortega, *caballero* of the order of Santiago and grandson of Doña María de Recalde, was married because he so wished and because the bride, called Leonor, was extremely beautiful. She was the daughter of Don Alonso Hurtado, *regidor* of Lima and present assessor of the viceroy, Count of Castellar. The wedding was held Monday night, the 11th of November of the year 1675.

Don José Ortega Weds

Antonio Moreno, the first provost general of war to hold this post at the fortress of Callao, whose salary was sixty pesos a month, died Saturday, the 9th of December of the year 1675. He was buried Monday, the 11th, in the chapel of La Soledad. The viceroy, Count of Castellar, ordered the royal treasury officials to release one hundred and fifty pesos for his burial.

A Horse in the Guardroom

That same day, Saturday the 9th, at nine o'clock at night while Captain Don Marcos de Lucio was on guard with his company, a horse ran into the palace through the gate leading to the plaza. With a saddle hanging around its paunch and dragging the stirrups, making a great noise, no one was able to stop it, and it entered the guardroom and went under a platform that was more than three spans and two fingers high.

Muster Edict

Thursday, the 12th of December of the year 1675, the viceroy, Marquis of Malagón, ordered a proclamation issued: that on the following Thursday all persons [men] who could bear arms should locate their [military] headquarters in accordance with the blocks in which they lived, to receive arms from their officers. Able-bodied *caballeros* were to mount on horseback, under penalty of one hundred and fifty patacoons and eight days in jail [for those who did not].

This decree was issued exactly at noon of that day because of the repeated news from Spain that the English enemy had taken up fortifications and established themselves in this sea beyond the Strait [of Magellan]. This general formation was to reconnoiter the men available in this city to take up arms and resist the enemy. No exception was made in the edict for any of the tribunals of the Crusade or the Holy Office [Inquisition], and all had to present themselves at the general formation as was ordered.

Exceptions

Later His Excellency exempted the warden and constable of the Holy Inquisition, all the learned [men] and the lawyers, owners and supervisors of bakeries, ordinary *alcaldes* and *alcaldes* of the hall of crime and their agents so that they could continue making rounds in the city, students in *colegios*, and students enrolled in the university.

The Formation

The muster [was on] Sunday, the 22nd of December of the year 1675, on an extensive plain on the land of the Augustinian lime quarry, bordering the native convalescent home.

Their Excellencies dined that day at this convalescent home, as did the *oidores*, separately, and many other important people and *caballeros*. The senior brother of this convalescent home, a priest called Fray Andrés de San José, attended this meal and all was very clean and complete. At three o'clock they planned to inspect the field. The archbishop of this city, Don Fray Juan de Almoguera, was also included, then followed [the group of] *oidores*, the bishop of Paraguay, followed by the gentlemen of the Inquisition and the Holy Crusade. At three o'clock the men in groups started to file into their rows in the squadrons. There were three squadrons of Spanish infantry, the reserves, the rear guard, and the substitutes. These three were lined up alongside the cavalry, and in the battalion the artillery pieces [were readied]. There were another three squadrons of *naciones* [races] composed of free mulattoes, *morenos* [Negroes], and Indians, at the sides and at a distance from the Spaniards, along with two carriages that were covered with canvas and with their flags [and] with everything necessary for the manipulation of the artillery. In the center was the captain general's tent with the flag and arms of the king our lord, from where the orders of the captain general were to emanate.

After all the squadrons had been formed, which must have been around five in the afternoon, His Excellency mounted Grifo, the horse that had belonged to the Count of Lemos, the page carrying his banner before him, and the *caballeros* and *encomenderos* following behind His Excellency. He posted himself, mounted, before the squadrons, and as he ordered the lances to be hoisted, a closed charge of artillery was fired of which there were ten pieces, [and] all the muskets and arquebuses [fired], which caused the whole camp to tremble. After this His Excellency started reviewing each squadron individually, saluting them and lowering the flags in front of the squadron.

More than five thousand Spanish men were present in this formation, four thousand on foot and a thousand on horseback, and five hundred more [who were] free mulattoes and Negroes, and Indians. This was the best day that [the people of] Lima had had to see the other camp where they [the reserves] were quartered, away from the royal one. They had large tents made of ships' sails which His Excellency had ordered to be brought for shade because they started to take up quarters at six in the morning, and where all the captains, each one in his quarters, had a splendid meal with gifts, chickens, wine, and many ices, each one trying to outdo the others. With all the regalia and trappings it looked like a field with a great variety of flowers; instead of war it seemed more like a celebration with tables where everyone was eating. And there were a great number of women present who came to enjoy the celebration.

The cavalry company of His Excellency's guard, whose captain was Don Antonio de Aguirre, and the other [company] also a mercenary [company] under Captain Don Francisco de León, skirmished twice before His Excellency and the other gentlemen.

These formations were organized by the battalion commander of this city Don Francisco de la Cueva, *caballero* of the order of Calatrava, battalion sergeant majors Hernando de Rivera and Julián Corbeira, battalion adjutants Roque Rosales and Juan de Rueda, and the adjutant of the merchants company, Ignacio de Heredia.

As night was closing in they terminated abruptly as all the squadrons broke up, to the great satisfaction of the captain general [as to their performance] and without any unfortunate occurrences.

The Year 1676

Wednesday, the first day of the new year of 1676, Don José de Castro and Don Luis Bejarano became *alcaldes*, and Don José de Aguero, *alcalde* of the water [commission].

Loss of the Ship Destined for the Strait

Friday, the 10th of January of the year 1676, at ten o'clock at night the dispatch ship arrived from Chiloé [Island, Chile]. [It brought news] that the ship that left from Callao to reconnoiter the area where the English enemy was situated had been damaged as it entered that port [Chiloé]. The wind had failed, and being calm, the currents carried the ship to a low spot, but God was served in that no one was hurt as they made it to land in Chiloé. They removed everything carried in the ship, even the pieces of artillery, and in the small ships, which were three, and twelve flat boats they proceeded on their journey. May God grant them good luck.

His Excellency Attends the Fiesta *at Callao*

Saturday, the 11th, at five in the afternoon their Excellencies left with all their family for Callao to see the three-day celebrations held by the soldiers. It consists of three days of theater and bullfights in honor of the Pure and Immaculate Conception of Our Lady. Good bulls were run, without any misfortune occurring.

On the afternoon of Monday, the 20th of the month, their Excellencies returned from Callao with all their family.

Death of Licentiate Salvador de Acuña

Licentiate Salvador de Acuña, presbyter, died on Thursday, the 16th of January of 1676. He was buried Friday, the 17th of the month, at the church of Santa Ana.

Devotees of San Pedro Enter Their Cloister

Sunday, the 19th of January of the year 1676, at five in the afternoon the [women] devotees entered the house of devotion, having chosen to wear the habit of the Holy Savior. The founder was the licentiate Alonso Riero, a presbyter of the clergy and a father of the school of Jesus Christ Our Lord in the church and hospital of San Pedro of this city of Lima.

The archbishop of this city of Lima, Fray Juan de Almoguera of the order of the Holy Trinity, was present at the entrance of the first devotees into the cloister. Many persons saw them enter, but the viceroy was not present as he was in Callao.

Death of the Comptroller Felipe de la Puente

Chief comptroller Felipe de la Puente, [member] of the order of Alcántara, died on Monday, the 20th of January of the year 1676. He was buried Tuesday, the 21st, at the monastery of San Francisco. The viceroy, *audiencia*, and the *caballeros* of this city of Lima were present at his burial.

Iron Chains of the Court of Justice

Friday, the 28th of February of the year 1676, they finished putting iron chains in the court of justice of the *alcaldes* and on the door of the jail. The *alcaldes* were Don Julián de Castro and Don Luis Bejarano, and the latter ordered these made at his expense and placed where they are. (His Excellency ordered that they be removed on Wednesday, the 11th of March of that year, because they had not requested permission of His Excellency to install them.)

Death of the Archbishop of this City

The archbishop of this city, Fray Juan de Almoguera, died on Monday, the 2nd of March of 1676, at eleven in the morning. He governed this holy church of Lima one year and ten months less five days. May God keep him in His holy glory.

His burial was held on Thursday, the 5th of March, at five in the afternoon. There were eight platforms placed around the plaza for the funeral stops, and counting another platform that was at the foot of the stairs of his palace, there were nine. The dean of this holy church, Don Juan Santoyo de Palma, officiated the high Mass. The viceroy, Count of Castellar and Marquis of Malagón, with all the gentlemen of the royal *audiencia*, the *cabildos*, and the university and colleges went to the burial, and twenty-one [members] of his [the archbishop's] family appeared in long mourning capes. The plaza could not accommodate all the people; even at the windows and rooftops there were a great number of people.

Friday, the 6th, the prebends held a Mass in the presence of the body, and the catafalque appeared the same as on the day of the burial, with the same number of candles. Neither His Excellency nor the gentlemen of the royal *audiencia* were present at this Mass.

Dispatch from Chile

News [from Chile] arrived at this city, brought by Captain Don Leoncio de Ureta, that they had gotten as far as forty-two degrees or more [South Latitude] and had found no trace of fortifications of the English enemy. The captain arrived Monday, the 9th of March of the year 1676, at eleven in the morning, and the next day His Excellency awarded this captain, Don Leoncio de Ureta, the post as *corregidor* of Yauyos.

Memorial Rites for His Grace

Saturday, the 14th of this month and year, memorial funeral rites for the Very Illustrious Fray Juan de Almoguera were held in the cathedral of Lima with the catafalque and the same candles and grandeur as the day of his burial. Present were the viceroy, the gentlemen of the royal council, the chief comptrollers, royal officials, the two *cabildos*, and all the nobility of this city. The Very Reverend Father Fray [blank] of the Mercedarian order gave the sermon at the funeral rites.

The Precentor Faints

On Palm Sunday, the 29th of March of the year 1676, while the canon Don Diego de Salazar was giving a sermon and the canons were seated in their benches, the present vicar general and precentor, Don Andrés de Flores de la Parra, had a strong attack of dizziness in the head and fell face downward to the floor, hitting his face against some rails that were near the chorus. He received a cut over his left brow which required four stitches and he was unable to speak for a long while. The viceroy, who was present, ordered him taken to his house and ordered the sermon to continue.

Unfortunate Death of the Canon Dávila

The doctor and canon of this holy church and present rector of the university and prime professor of canon law, Don José Dávila, died Monday, the 30th of March of the year 1676. Tuesday at dawn the Augustinian Recollect friars of Our Lady of Guía took charge of the body, and that same afternoon he was buried in the church of Guía. All the ecclesiastic *cabildo*, all the clergy, and all the nobles of the city attended because he deserved it for his nobility, his Christianity, and his learning. He died so suddenly that he was not able to make a will, and he gave proxy to another person. May God keep him in His holy glory.

Arrival of the Ship that Went to the Strait

Monday, the 20th of April of the year 1676, the ship that went to reconnoiter the Strait [of Magellan] to see if the English enemy had settled there, arrived at Callao. The captain of that ship was Captain Pascual de Iriarte, a native of Vizcaya, who had made a reconnaisance of all the islands as far as fifty-four and two-thirds degrees [South Latitude], checking everything. He sent his son with sixteen soldiers and a navigator to put a bronze plaque with the arms of our King and lord at that spot, but upon their setting out in a launch that they took for that purpose, a great storm arose. For more than four days Captain Iriarte attempted to find his son and the other soldiers, but being unable to find trace of them, they returned with the others to Callao. He reported to the viceroy that no trace of the enemy was found in all the area they inspected.

That same day His Excellency with the *oidores* and the other tribunals went to the cathedral at eleven in the morning to give thanks to Our Lord.

Masquerade and Races

At eight o'clock that same night there were races by *caballeros* carrying lighted torches. Many races were held inside the palace grounds and throughout the plaza.

Bulls in the Plaza

Tuesday, the 21st, there were twenty-one bulls roped in the plaza, all in honor of the good news brought by Pascual de Iriarte that there was no fortification of the English enemy in all the area he inspected. Praise the Lord that it is thus, and may His Majesty [the Lord] never want the enemy to come into this South Sea [Pacific Ocean], as thus we will have peace and quiet!

The Indian From Chiloé Flogged

Wednesday, the 22nd, at eleven in the morning the Indian who came from Chiloé was taken through the usual streets and given two hundred lashes for the bad and false news that he had brought [concerning English ships on the coast of Chile]. A tall mangrove pole was set up in the plaza in front of the palace next to the fountain, and at the height of a tall man a board was secured to it. After he was flogged they stood the Indian on the board, tying him to the pole with a thong. He remained there until the Ave Maria [dusk], when they took him to the court prison, and the following day he was taken to the island of Callao to haul rocks for six years.

Papal Bull

Friday, the 1st of May of the year 1676, day of Saint Philip and Saint James, at the orders of the king, our lord Charles II, and the queen his mother, a papal bull was made public in the cathedral of Lima. The holy pontiff who today rules [Clement X] ordered that in all Christendom the day of the holy King Ferdinand, which is the 30th of May, be celebrated as though it were a Sunday.

Death of the Prebendary Don Sebastián de Aguilar

Friday, the 1st of May of the year 1676, day of the glorious apostles Saint Philip and Saint James, at five-thirty in the morning [my step-son] Doctor Don Sebastián López de Aguilar, prebendary of the holy church of Lima, gave up his soul to his creator, Jesus Christ Our Lord. Saturday, May 2nd, at five in the afternoon he was buried in the cathedral with great splendor and with the attendance of all the *caballeros* and clergy of the whole city.

Memorial funeral rites were held Monday, the 4th of the month, in the cathedral with the same people [attending] as the day of his burial.

My [step-] son, the prebendary Don Sebastián, had the following characteristics: his face, happy for everyone; his eyes, loving; his words, pliant and smooth; and his person, pleasing, as he was tall; his color, white; his face, handsome; his dealings and conversation, of great honesty; and loved by all of this city of Lima. In everything, my [step-] son, Don Sebastián López de Aguilar, was endowed by God. May God keep him in His holy glory. He died at fifty years of age.

Death of the Precentor

Don Antonio Flores de la Parra [died] at five in the afternoon on Thursday, the 14th of May of this year 1676, day of the glorious Ascension of Our Lord Jesus Christ. He died in the garden called La Zapata, this side of Cercado, where he had gone to convalesce from his illness.

He was buried at the cathedral on Saturday, the 16th of the month, with an impressive attendance of people. The viceroy did not accompany the body, but awaited in the cathedral and was present at the offices of the dead.

Memorial funeral rites were held Monday, the 18th, with the viceroy, all the gentlemen of the royal *audiencia*, and all the nobility of this city of Lima present.

I Professed in the Third Order of Saint Francis

Sunday, the 14th of June of the year 1676, I, Josephe de Mugaburu, professed in the third order of Saint Francis to the honor and glory of God and of my lady the Virgin Mary, and the glorious Saint Francis. In charge was Father Fray Miguel Flores, who was present rector of the third order, and my sponsor was the master gunner of the artillery of Lima, Juan de Ortega.

Celebration for the Holy King Ferdinand

Sunday, the 21st of June of the year 1676, a celebration was held for the holy King Ferdinand and Saint Hermenegildo, martyr, in the monastery of Santo Domingo of this city of Lima, with great praise as much for the splendor as for the illustrious [attendance] of this city. The viceroy, Marquis of Malagón, attended in the morning as well as the afternoon with all the secular *cabildo*, and all wore gold chains around their neck. Maestro Fray Juan de Francia of the order of Predicadores gave the sermon at this celebration. The adjutant and commissary general of the paid cavalry, Don Francisco de León, a native of the great city of Seville, held this celebration at his cost and in his name.

Arrival of Mail from Potosí

Friday, the 17th of July of the year 1676, at eight at night the mail arrived from Potosí, sent by the president of Chuquisaca [*audiencia*] and the archbishop and *oidores* and all the miners of Potosí. [They told] how silver probes proposed by Don Juan del Corro had revealed so great an increase of the metal and ore located there that no one could estimate their value. At that same hour of the night all the bells of all the churches of Lima rang out, and all the people of this city rejoiced.

Saturday, the 18th, His Excellency went with all the *oidores*, the *cabildo* of the city, and all the *caballeros* to the cathedral where a sung Mass was held in thanksgiving.

Night Masquerade That same night at eight o'clock His Excellency, the Marquis of Malagón and Count of Castellar, left the palace, very resplendent with a lighted torch in his hand, and behind His Excellency were many *caballeros* with their torches. They paraded through many of the streets, and all the city rejoiced at such good news and for the parade which they liked. Thanks be to God for everything.

Departure of the Author from Lima [Having retired from the army,] I left the city of Lima with my wife and children [step-daughter Damiana and her husband; sons Francisco and Antonio] the 12th of September of the year 1676, and Sunday, the 1st of November, All Saints' Day, entered the city of Cuzco with all my family after fifty days of traveling, without having any misfortune occur, thanks be to God. I remained in the city of Cuzco nine days, where we were much feasted and visited by all the *caballeros* and ecclesiastic and secular *cabildos*.

We left Cuzco on Tuesday, the 10th of November, with a large accompaniment. At four in the afternoon of the same day, God having been served, we arrived at our destination in Lucre, the hacienda of my son Don José de Mugaburu y Honton.

The Year 1677

Antonio Real left Lucre for Potosí on the first Friday of Lent which was the 5th of March of the year 1677. He did not go by way of Yanaoca but by way of the road to Tinta, and he remained in Cuzco four months enjoying himself.

My Son Antonio Enters the Seminary Antonio de Mugaburu, my son, left Lucre for the college of San Bernardo in the city of Cuzco on the second Friday of Lent of the year 1677 which was the 12th of March of that year, exactly six months after we had left Lima. He went very well equipped with bed, clothing, and linens which were given to him by his brother Don José de Mugaburu, vicar and priest of the parish of Yanaoca. He looks out for his brother and takes care of him as though he were his father, [being a father] for him and for everyone. May God repay him!

My son Don Antonio de Mugaburu y Honton was received at the college of San Bernardo of the city of Cuzco on Thursday, the 25th of March of 1677. In the chapel of that college, the guardian father of the Franciscan monastery of Cuzco, the Very Reverend Father Fray Juan Negrón, said Mass, gave him holy communion, and put the collegian's sash on him. In attendance were his two cousins, the Very Reverend Father Fray Buenaventura de Honton, and Doctor Don Diego de Honton, the present curate of Santa Ana [church] of Cuzco; his brother, Fray Francisco de Mugaburu y Honton, preacher of the order of Saint Francis; as well as the father custodian and many lectors and important fathers of the Franciscan monastery.

As he was about to receive communion from the hand of the guardian father, with the presence of the father rector and the prefect and all the collegiates, he took a vow on the Holy Scripture to defend the purity of Holy Mary, obey the prelates, and support his fellow students in things licit and honest. His sponsor was Don José Romero, collegiate of the same college and a virtuous man who is much loved and esteemed by the bishop of the city of Cuzco. That same afternoon he went to visit him [the bishop] with the abovementioned sponsor, and His Grace received him with many attentions, and all the nobility of the city offered him a thousand felicitations. May God Our Lord protect him, granting him many years of life with which to serve Him, and also [protect] his brother Don José de Mugaburu y Honton, the appointed priest of Yanaoca, who is the one who takes care of his advancement, as well as his parents and brothers.

We comply With Our Church Obligation

Holy Wednesday and Holy Thursday [my son-in-law] Don Diego Pardo and I, Josephe de Mugaburu y Honton, with the servants of our house went to the church of Oropesa to comply with our obligation to the holy church. The two of us also went to hear Mass at Oropesa the first day of Easter; on the second and third day my son Fray Francisco de Mugaburu said Mass for us in our chapel at the hacienda. The 1st day of May was Saturday, day of the glorious apostles Saint Philip and Saint James, and the following Sunday Doctor Don Diego de Honton came from Santa Rosa and said Mass for us these two days in the chapel of our hacienda in Lucre. Monday, day of the Holy Cross of May, all of us, including my son, the *bachiller* Don José de Mugaburu, who had arrived the night before from his benefice, went to Santa Rosa, which is the hacienda of Señor Don Diego de Honton, and he said Mass in his chapel for us. With permission that the priest of Oropesa gave him, he gave confession and communion to [my wife] Doña Jerónima and her daughter Doña Damiana in this chapel; and all complied with the obligation to the holy mother church. God be praised.

This same day Doctor Honton invited us to dine, and he feasted us handsomely. May God grant him a long life and health. That night we all returned to Lucre. We also went to see the outdoor holy cross since this was the feast day [of the holy cross]; and the holy cross was very well adorned with flowers and small carnations.

Bad News that my Son José was Very Ill

Saturday, the 24th of July of 1677, at eight in the morning an Indian arrived at Lucre [with news] that my son, Don José, was very ill at his parish. At that hour I asked the superintendent Juan de Gamboa for a mule, and with one of the Indians from here I arrived at Yanaoca on Sunday, the 25th, at ten in the morning, day of the apostle Saint James. I found my son very ill, both from hemorrhoids and a high and malign fever. He had already had two bleedings [done] on his ankle. Don Diego Pardo and Doña Damiana had left Lucre for Yanaoca twelve days before I arrived, and had attended him constantly during his illness; if his sister had not been there the invalid would have had a much more difficult time.

Wednesday, the 28th, at eight at night he suffered with a pain in his right side so that he could not rest all night from the pain. He asked for confession; we called the priest from Tinta, and he arrived Thursday, remained all day and night with the invalid, and gave him confession. Friday, the 30th, the priest from Tinta said Mass and gave the invalid the Holy Sacrament with much solemnity. This day and Saturday there was great doubt as to what it was. Some said it was flatulence; others a great pain at his side, as it was, and he showed it by emitting a little blood through his nose.

Sunday, the 1st of August, two bleedings were performed on the right arm; Monday, another on the same arm and two on the left arm; and Tuesday, two in the same arm. The blood that came out was putrid. With these bleedings God was served in that he was alleviated from pain and fever.

Doña Damiana [Jerónima?] left Lucre with all the family and Fray Francisco, and Antonio, who had come from his college in Cuzco the previous Saturday, day of the glorious Saint Ignatius Loyola. They arrived at Yanaoca on Tuesday, the 3rd of August. From Andapata until reaching Yanaoca she went with a guard of fourteen Indians that her son the vicar had sent for that purpose. Don Antonio, my son, and I left Yanaoca on Tuesday, the 10th of August, day of the glorious Saint Lawrence, and we arrived safely at Lucre on Wednesday at five in the afternoon. Thursday my son Don Antonio went to the celebration of his patron of the college of San Bernardo. I remained alone without company, without even anyone to talk with in this Lucre. Who would believe it! Praise be to God, forever and ever. Amen.

My Son José Died

My beloved son Don José de Mugaburu y Honton, priest of the town of Santiago de Yanaoca and vicar of Los Canes, died the 18th of August of 1677. [He was thirty-six years old]. He was buried in this town and church which he had built at his expense, as appears in the construction book of the church. It cost my son nineteen thousand thirty-two pesos and three *reales* which he graciously donated for this church before the bishop of Cuzco, Don Manuel de Mollinedo y Angulo on the 26th of September of the year 1675, as appears in the book of visits that His Grace kept that year. And he gave many other items as ornaments, as well as a rug twelve yards long and eight wide with the [insignia of] arms of Mugaburu y Honton, and the habit for [the statue of] Santiago [Saint James] which was finished only one day after his death, which amounted to seven hundred and fifty-five pesos. The rug, Maldonado [elsewhere given as Jerónima Maldonado y Flores], his parents, donated to this church the 20th of September of that year 1677. The *bachiller* Don Juan de Vargas Machuca became interim [priest] of this church.

The Year 1678

On the morning of Tuesday, the 15th of October of the year 1678, Bishop Don Juan de Mollinedo y Angulo at his house conferred the post of prebendary on my nephew Doctor Don Diego de Hon-

Doctor Honton Appointed Prebendary

ton y Olarte. About four o'clock on the afternoon of the same day he took over his post in the chorus of the holy cathedral of this city of Cuzco, with all the gentlemen of the ecclesiastic *cabildo* of this church present. Today marked fifteen years that he had been priest and vicar of the parish of Santa Ana of this city of Cuzco.

Death of Father Gregorio de Acevedo

My godson, Father Gregorio de Acevedo, ordained in the gospel of the Society of Jesus, died at the age of twenty-three years and some months at five in the afternoon of Friday, the 22nd of April of 1678, the second Friday of Pentecost. His death was caused from influenza. All the religious orders of this city of Cuzco held a sung Mass and responsory for him.

The Franciscans of this city of Cuzco buried him. The guardian of the order, Father Fray Juan Negrón, said the Mass and Father Fray Francisco de Mugaburu y Honton, the Gospel, and the proctor, Father Fray Juan de Santa Gadea, the Epistle, all three of them creoles of Lima. [Members of] all the religious orders of this city were present, in great mourning, at the Mass held with the body present that same day of the burial, Friday the 22nd. May God keep him in His holy glory.

New Mercedarian Provincial

Saturday, the 7th of May of 1678, at five o'clock in the morning the Very Reverend Father Fray Gonzalo de Peralta became provincial of the Mercedarian order in the city of Cuzco.

Habit of Santiago to Luis de Pimentel

This same Saturday, the 7th of May, at four in the afternoon Don Luis de Pimentel was presented the habit of [the order of] Santiago at the Society of Jesus of this city of Cuzco, and it was given to him by Don José Pardo, son of Don Baltasar Pardo. His sponsor was Don Tomás de Mollinedo of the same order, ordinary *alcalde* of the city and nephew of the present bishop, Don Manuel de Mollinedo y Angulo. His Grace was present as well as all the *caballeros* of the city. It [the ceremony] was [held] with great ostentation and accompaniment; and there were horse races and *alcancías* games in which apples were thrown. Roped bulls were also run. His brother-in-law, Luis de Córdoba, gave him the cape, and he went forth very gallant that day.

Captain Don Luis de Córdoba, brother-in-law of Don Luis Pimentel, died in the city of Cuzco on Wednesday, the 1st of June of the year 1678, at the age of twenty-eight. He died of the great affliction, as it is called in this city, which is a pain in the side. He was buried in the monastery of San Agustín the following Thursday; all the nobility of the city attended the burial.

Death of Don Luis de Córdoba

Tuesday, the 12th of July, the *chasque* arrived at Cuzco from Lima [with the news] that on Friday, the 17th of June, at seven forty-five at night there had been a great earthquake that lasted a long time, and it was very strong, the likes of which had not heretofore been heard in that city. It damaged all the buildings of that city and [the church of] Our Lady of Guía, as well as the chapels of the cathedral of that city. May God Our Lord guard them from all hazards!

News of the Earthquake in Lima

Sunday, the 3rd of July of the year 1678, Don Manuel de Mollinedo y Angulo, bishop of Cuzco, gave [the sacrament of Holy] Orders in which only priests, clerics, friars and fathers of the Society of Jesus and the colleges of San Antonio and San Bernardo were ordained. There were thirty-eight as priests and more than another fifty for the Gospel and the Epistle. His Grace gave these sacraments at his house, and all invested [with their new authority] went from there to the Society of Jesus.

Ordination by the Bishop of Cuzco

Tuesday, the 26th of July of the year 1678, day of Saint Ann, at one in the afternoon there was a great uproar over the [selection of] alternates in the monastery of San Francisco in the city of Cuzco. The vice-commissary was the Very Reverend Father Fray Francisco Delgado of the province of Lima.

Uproar over Alternates in San Francisco

Tuesday, the 2nd of August, day of the *Portiuncula* [Franciscan Jubilee] the Very Reverend Father Fray Cristóbal Daza de Avalos was elected provincial of the province of Cuzco.

Election of the Franciscan Provincial

Saturday, the 27th of August, at ten in the morning the Reverend Father Fray Francisco Delgado, vice commissary general, left for Lima with a large following.

Saturday, the 12th of November of the year 1678, Father Fray Buenaventura de Honton, Father Fray Miguel Quiñones, and Father Fray Clemente de Heredia, left Cuzco for Lima at the orders of the archbishop and present viceroy of Peru, Don Melchor de Liñán [y Cisneros,] because of the uproar that occurred Tuesday, the 26th of July, over the alternates.

The Year 1679

Chácara *at Lucre Auctioned Off*

The *chácara* at Lucre [which belonged to my son José] was sold by auction on Thursday, the 23rd of March of 1679, at forty thousand pesos to Don Antonio de Lea, ordinary *alcalde* that year. In a petition I have appealed this settlement to the royal *audiencia* of Lima.

Ordination Held by the Bishop of Cuzco

Tuesday, the 4th of April of the year 1679, third day of Easter, the bishop of Cuzco, Don Manuel de Mollinedo y Angulo, gave the sacrament of ordination. This day at eleven all the invested came in procession from the house of the bishop to the cathedral of this city.

My Entire Family Departs from Cuzco for Lima

On Monday, the 9th of October of the year 1679, [two years] after the death of [my son] the licentiate Don José de Mugaburu y Honton, who had been curate of Yanaoca, I left the city of Cuzco for Lima with my entire family and with my son[-in-law] Don Diego Pardo, in the pack train of José Ruíz Barúa. We arrived at this city of Lima on Monday, the 4th of December of that year, without any unfortunate experiences on the way, nor any snowfalls, nor rain storms. The rivers were dry with the exception of the Apurímac and Uramarca [Urubamba], which we crossed on their bridges.

From the day we left [Lima] until the day of our return, three years and three months had elapsed.

Beginning on the back of this sheet, I resumed recording events that occurred in Lima from Monday, the 1st of January of 1680.

The Year 1680

New Alcaldes

Monday, the first day of the new year 1680, Don Juan Roldán, *caballero* of the order of Alcántara, and Don Francisco de Perales, water commissioner, were elected *alcaldes* in Lima.

On the afternoon of this day the archbishop-viceroy [Don Melchor de Liñán y Cisneros] went with all the *caballeros* of Lima to ride to the cane fields and through the Alameda.

The present inspector general of the royal armadas of the South Sea [Pacific Ocean] and the fortress of Callao [died] suddenly on Tuesday, the 6th of February of the year 1680, at six in the afternoon. He was buried Thursday, the 8th of the month, at San Francisco [church].

Death of Don Pedro de Urrutia

Holy Wednesday, the 16th of April of the year 1680, the dispatch ship arrived at this city of Lima from Spain. [It brought word] that our king, Charles II, had wed [Marie Louise of Orléans], a cousin of the king of France, and that peace had been made between Spain and France, and many other items of news.

Dispatch Ship from Spain

Wednesday, the 24th of the month, a proclamation was issued in this city of Lima by decree of His Majesty, ordering that the merchants of Seville would be obligated to send two dispatch ships to this kingdom of Peru and another two to Mexico every year at their own expense, without any expense to His Majesty, may God protect him. Nor were the viceroys to send any captain with a dispatch ship, but rather a private individual should take them to Panama, delivering the letters to the [*audiencia*] president, which he then would deliver to the governor of Cartagena, and he to the captain or chief that came in the galleon from Spain.

Proclamation Regarding Dispatch Ships

This same day the *residencia* of the viceroy, Marquis de Malagón, was approved as being good and being free [of appeal] and without cost [without deficits or fines]. That night there were many bonfires, festive lights, and many torches lit.

Residencia *of the Viceroy Count of Castellar*

Thursday, the 25th of the month, day of the holy evangelist Saint Mark, a royal decree of His Majesty appeared which said that another royal decree had been sent to the Marquis of Malagón dated October 14, 1678, in which he was instructed and ordered to depart immediately for Mexico, and he had not complied with the order of His Majesty. He was sending another royal decree to the same effect as the abovementioned to the archbishop-viceroy to have the orders contained in the decree executed immediately.

This same day Don Tomás Berjón, president and *oidor* of this royal *audiencia*, was notified that he was to leave this city of Lima within twenty-four hours and embark for Mexico at the first opportunity, where he was to assume the post as the junior *oidor*.

Decree Naming Don Tomás Berjón

Dispatch Ship for Spain

Saturday, the 8th of June of 1680, the dispatch ship for Spain sent by the archbishop-viceroy left the port of Callao. It was captained by the brother of the present general of the South Sea, who was *corregidor* at Ica.

News From Panama of the Enemy

At dawn on Friday, the 28th of June, the eve of [the feast day of] the prince of the apostles Saint Peter, a dispatch from the [*audiencia*] president of Panama arrived, brought by Gadea the defender of Guayaquil, and at five in the afternoon another auxiliary arrived from Panama. The dispatches were identical; in them the president of Panama advised that the English enemy had entered this South Sea [Pacific Ocean] by land and by way of the site of Andarriel, having been given entrance and a great number of canoes and shown the way by the Indians. They burned the town of Chepo, and the president of Panama sent two hundred men in canoes who fought with the enemy. Having [obtained] their [the enemy's] surrender, they requested good treatment, but our chief did not wish to accept the request and our men, in firing a small bronze piece [of artillery] at them, caused their canoe to be rent apart and sunk. Then the enemy resumed its attack on our men killing more than one hundred and fifty men. As they now found themselves the victors they sailed toward Perico [Island in the Bay of Panama], where they found five large ships and burned three, one of which belonged to Ascarruz and the other two to other owners, because they were unmanned except for Negro cabin boys. On this occasion they captured a small yawl with fifty thousand pesos as it arrived from Lima. In the two ships and other small vessels the enemy is going about causing a thousand damages.

As soon as he received the news, the archbishop-viceroy issued a proclamation informing the whole city of Lima of what had occurred, and [ordered] that no person of any kind whatsoever leave this city without permission of the government, under penalty of six years [imprisonment] at Valdivia.

Another proclamation was issued the same day, the 28th, that everyone [in military reserves] abandon their profession, join their squadrons and companies, and go to their quarters.

Wearing his hooded clerical cape and carrying his staff as captain general, His Excellency went to the large salon where there were more than five hundred men. He appealed to them, saying that if he could, he would leave the [archbishop's] habit he wore and go to punish the great audacity of the enemy. He said that he had ordered the three best ships that were in Callao to be outfitted with artillery and munitions and to go with five hundred mercenary soldiers [to meet the enemy]. All the nobles and *caballeros* willingly offered to embark, and His Excellency thanked them profusely.

Sunday, the 30th of the month, all the companies were ready in their quarters. His Excellency called all the generals, colonels, and sergeant majors and gave them orders to have all the companies of natives, mulattoes, and Negroes posted outside the city at all the high spots overlooking it, in the surrounding countryside.

His Excellency Visits the Quarters

Monday, the 1st of July, at eight in the morning His Excellency left the palace in his carriage with the whole accompaniment of generals, colonels, and sergeant majors and went visiting all the quarters until after eleven.

Election of the Franciscan Provincial

That same day at four in the afternoon the election for provincial of San Francisco was held, and Father Oserín became provincial. It was an afternoon of great uproar where there could have been many deaths. The fathers from Spain did not want to pledge him obedience, and so priests as well as lay brothers all went to the hermitage of Guadalupe, leaving the main monastery empty with only the creole fathers [remaining].

His Excellency Reviews the Troops

On the morning of Tuesday, the 2nd, day of Saint Elizabeth, at the palace guard house His Excellency the archbishop-viceroy reviewed the infantry companies which were to be taken to Panama.

Dispatch of the Armada

At dawn on Wednesday, the 3rd, His Excellency left Lima for Callao to dispatch the three ships that carried six hundred men to the aid of Panama with much gunpowder, balls, and fuses, and equipped with all kinds of armaments. The soldiers were given four months pay.

The Armada left for Panama

Saturday, the 6th of July, at four in the afternoon [the armada] left the port of Callao. There were three merchant ships, the best ones to be found in the port, and five government ships: the flagship, consort vessel, another ship, a large frigate, and the launch, well-outfitted with artillery and foot soldiers. Montejo, who was *corregidor* of Ica and *caballero* of [the order of] Alcántara, went as general.

Imprisonment of Fathers Delgado and Oserín

Wednesday, the 14th of August of 1680, at three in the afternoon the Reverend Fathers Fray Francisco Delgado, who was [Franciscan] provincial and vice commissary of this province of Lima, and Father Oserín, who had been provincial of this same province, left the palace for Callao in a carriage drawn by four mules. They were exiled at the orders of His Excellency and his priest, the commissary general Fray Marcos Terán, who presently lived in the palace with His Excellency. One was embarked on the flagship and the other on the king's tender, each with a guard of six lay brothers who could not speak to anyone.

That same night all the choristers left the monastery of San Francisco and went to [that of] Santo Domingo.

Tuesday, the 27th of this month of August, the ship for the kingdom of Chile left the port of Callao. Aboard were the Reverend Fathers Fray Francisco Delgado and Fray Antonio Oserín, exiled by the father commissary general, Fray Marcos Terán.

My Son Fray Francisco

The deposition of my son Fray Francisco was taken at Guadalupe [hermitage] on Tuesday, the 3rd of September of 1680, to justify nullification of his habit.

Death of Juan del Castillo, Surgeon

Juan del Castillo, surgeon, died Friday, the 6th of September of the year 1680. He was buried Saturday in San Francisco [church], and the gentlemen of the Inquisition went to the burial.

Arrival of the Enemy at Barranca

News reached this city that the enemy had been at Barranca [about 130 miles northwest of Lima] the 24th of September of 1680 and had captured a ship that had left Guayaquil for Callao with a cargo of wood, clothing from Castile, and a great quantity of cocoa.

His Excellency, [Viceroy-]Archbishop Liñán, immediately issued a proclamation that all those who wanted to enlist as soldiers should do it. Each one was given four months pay to embark in search of the enemy.

Muster

At the guard company His Excellency held a muster of all the people brought by the merchant captains, who were seven. Among them was Juan de Garay, who was stationed at the wall of Callao, as well as six other captains, each of whom offered to pay fifty soldiers four months wages for the above-mentioned [enlistment].

That same Tuesday, the 1st of October, His Excellency went to Callao to arrange for the dispatch of the tender *San Lorenzo*, which was to leave in search of the enemy.

This same day the large boat which the Count of Lemos had ordered to be constructed was launched, and the second lighter was set afloat Thursday, the 3rd of October, with the archbishop-viceroy present.

The San Lorenzo *Sails from Callao*

The *San Lorenzo*, tender of the king, our lord, carrying eighteen pieces of artillery, set sail on Friday, the 4th of October, at twelve at night; Pantoja went as captain of sea and war, and a Franciscan religious, said to have been raised among the Turks, as chief. There were also one hundred fifty infantrymen chosen from among more than five hundred soldiers, thirty artillerymen, and thirty soldiers. All were chosen by the referred-to Franciscan religious, with Don Juan Hurtado and Don Francisco Salazar as captains of the infantry. All went in good spirits to see if they could meet up with the enemy. May God Our Lord grant them victory and confound the heretic dog that has come to infest this pacific South Sea.

The Viceroy-Archbishop Names Corregidores

Tuesday, the 5th of November of 1680, at five in the afternoon twenty-eight [members of] municipal councils were named to posts as *corregidores*; there were more than two hundred aspirants.

On the morning of Wednesday, the 6th, His Excellency went with a large accompaniment to the cathedral to hear Mass in thanksgiving for the birthday celebrated by our king and lord Charles II, and may he have many heirs. Amen. In the afternoon there were horse races and bull roping.

Celebration for Archbishop Saint Toribio

This City of Kings had a *fiesta* for the beatification of the sainted archbishop, Don Toribio Alonso de Mogrovejo, who had been archbishop of Lima.[54] The eight day celebration at the cathedral,

[54] Saint Toribio Alfonso de Mogrovejo was a famous archbishop of Lima from 1581 to 1606. Born in Spain in 1538, he went to Peru in 1581 where his

where all the famous preachers gave sermons, began on the eve of Monday, the 11th of November of the year 1680. First to preach was the canon Don Pedro de Cárdenas; the second the canon Don Juan de Morales; the last the licenciado Don Antonio Garcés. On Sunday, when the *fiesta* was sponsored by the vicar general Don Pedro de Villagómez, Father Vicar of the Mercedarian order gave the sermon. Toward evening the patronage of the glorious patriarch Saint Joseph was celebrated, and Father Maestro Sotomayor of the same order gave the sermon.

All the altars, chapels, and sacristy of the cathedral and baptistry were adorned and decorated with hangings during the eight days. They extended as far as the three doors leading into the plaza. Never had such interesting details and valuables been seen as were in those adornments which had been made by various individuals. Every night there were different fireworks with many innovations [consisting] of three and four pieces of fireworks. Only on the night preceding the *fiesta* of the university were there no fireworks.

There were also seven beautiful altars set up in the [plaza] entrance streets, and much to see. The first altar was that of the Franciscans, at the entrance of Pescadería Street; the second, at the post office corner, set up by the clergy of this city, which was the one that was the most outstanding of all; the third, on the corner of Santo Domingo; the fourth, belonging to San Agustín, on the corner of Las Mantas; the fifth, on the corner of Mercaderes Street, of the Mercedarians; the sixth, at the entrance of the alley of San Juan de Dios; the seventh, on the corner of El Jamón, of the Society of Jesus.

Tuesday, the 19th of the month, at four in the afternoon a procession began with all the luster of the religious orders, all the clergy of the city, all the brotherhoods with their patron saints, and the archbishop-viceroy and all the togaed gentlemen [of the *audiencia*], who [also] attended Mass and sermon during the eight days. Upon leaving the cathedral in the procession, the large statue of Saint Toribio fell from its litter and could not be taken in the parade. At the feet of [the statue] of Saint Peter, who appeared as the pontiff seated in a chair, they placed a painted

---

ecclesiastical reforms were so well received that they were subsequently adopted in all of South America and Asia. He was beatified in 1680 and canonized in 1727. *New Catholic Encyclopedia*, IX, 999–1000.

portrait of the glorious Saint Toribio. All the procession continued until it ended successfully at six in the afternoon, to the honor and glory of God. Amen.

Procession from the Cathedral to Santa Clara

Monday, the 25th of November of 1680, at four in the afternoon a very large procession for Saint Toribio de Mogrovejo left from the cathedral for [the convent of] Santa Clara. There was much to see including a float with many little girls singing and wearing habits of the sisters of Saint Claire, and with their abbess and their organ. All the religious orders marched, each with its [statues of] saints. The nuns [of Santa Clara] held the celebration for the saint because he had founded that convent. And the viceroy and *oidores* attended the Mass and sermon during those days that the *fiestas* of that church lasted.

Celebration held by the Viceroy-Archbishop

Sunday, the 8th of December, began the eight days of devotion for the Pure and Immaculate Conception of Our Lady that the archbishop-viceroy ordered to be held at the cathedral. They were for the honor and glory of God and his Holy Mother, and success of our king and lord Charles II, and victory for his arms against the enemies of the faith and the [English] pirates who are presently in this ocean. Eight of the best representatives of the religious orders of this city gave sermons.

Arrival of the Dispatch Ship from Spain

Wednesday, the 11th of the month, eighteen boxes of letters arrived in the dispatch ship from Spain, bringing much news. The inquisitor Queipo [was appointed] bishop of Huamanga, and Don Pedro de Cárdenas, canon of this holy church, as bishop of Santa Cruz de la Sierra.

Death of the Adjutant Gaspar de Savariego

Saturday, the 28th of December, the last day of the Christmas holidays of the year 1680, my friend Gaspar de Savariego died. He was buried Sunday, the 29th, at the church of San Francisco, and he was given a very good burial. It was this night when they set fire to the cell of the father commissary, Fray Marcos Terán.

Uproar at San Francisco and What Occurred

Sunday, the 29th of December of 1680, at eleven at night the bells of [the monastery of] San Francisco and those of the cathedral were rung violently. All the people of the city rushed to San Francisco and saw that the cell of the commissary general was burning. The choristers had set fire to it to trap the father commissary because of the ill will they bore him for imposing the alternate [provincial] on them. But he escaped through a small skylight in his cell, exited through the chapel of La Soledad, and went to the palace. There he was defended by the Spanish priest who said he had been raised in Africa with the Moors and had been a great corsair. The latter went among the choristers with a round shield and a rapier calling them scoundrels, vile scaps of humanity, and [saying] that he ought to kill all of them. One among the choristers stood up to him and with a stick or stone knocked him to the ground, [and he fell] asking for confession, wherein they inflicted three or four wounds. He could not receive the Eucharist due to the great amount of blood that gushed from his mouth. They gave him Extreme Unction, and so he remained [died].

On Monday morning His Excellency ordered that five of the merchant companies enter the monastery, but the fathers resisted, not opening the doors of their convent until His Excellency, the viceroy-archbishop, ordered a piece of artillery brought. It was placed in front of the entrance, and with two *alcaldes* of the court and the *oidores* they opened the doors and entered with these [merchant] companies. They closed the doors of the monastery and those of the church, and Mass was not said on Monday or Tuesday, day of the glorious Saint Silvester.

Nine Religious Prisoners

At five in the afternoon of this same day, Tuesday the 31st of the month, nine [Franciscan] religious were taken in two carriages as prisoners to the escort vessel in Callao. [They were:] Father Contreras, provincial; Father Superior Garrido; the father [who was a] brother of Father Contreras; Father Guadalupe; the definitors [governing committee]; Father Fray Juan de Cáceres; and the remaining ones. As they were taken through the streets there were a great many outcries and clamoring to God by men and women, and there was great compassion.

Father Manrique Killed

Less than a quarter of an hour after the fathers had left for Callao, a soldier shot one of the religious inside the noviciate. At that point the creole fathers who saw the mishap took the Holy Sacrament and went through the streets lamenting to God for the unfortunate death of the religious. They took the body to Santo

Domingo [church] and then to the Holy Sacrament [chapel] adjacent to the Society of Jesus, where it was left with more than seventy religious and some lay brothers. May God grant us mercy!

The Year 1681

Wednesday, the 1st of January of 1681, Ordoño de Zamudio, *regidor*, and Don Melchor Malo Bique were elected ordinary *alcaldes*.

The Comet

A comet appeared at the beginning of the month of January of this year of 1681. At six in the afternoon as the sun was setting, a very bright star appeared in the West, and from this same star a long tail appeared, the color of ashes, which reached a great length. It disappeared towards the West. It was something abnormal; only God Our Lord knows what it might be.

Departure of the Friars from San Francisco

On the 6th of January all the religious of San Francisco [monastery] were ordered to leave by the father commissary, Fray Marcos Terán, who was at the palace. All those from Spain, priests as well as lay brothers, were given permits to leave the main monastery, some to go to [Nuestra Señora de Los Angeles] the Descalzos [monastery], and others to other monasteries of the province. The lay brothers sacked all that they could, taking more than eight hundred chickens, twenty-four bedsteads, a number of mattresses, sheets, pillows, blankets, and as much as they could carry, leaving the pharmacy without supplies and without spatulas, pans, and other things that they took, all belonging to the infirmary. The lay brothers claimed they had sought and solicited alms for that infirmary, [and with] their commissary giving them safe conduct, they left the poor creole religious with nothing and without food. This was authorized by the commissary [since], as the lay brothers said, it was only because they had asked for them that the seculars gave alms. Thus the lay father Fray Carlos, who was a workman, sold six Negroes, saying that they were ones that he had bought and that they were being sold to pay what was owed.

Consecration of the Bishop of Misque

Sunday, the 12th of January of 1681, the archbishop-viceroy, Don Melchor de Liñán y Cisneros, consecrated Doctor Don Pedro de Cárdenas, present canon of the cathedral of Lima, as bishop of

Misque and Santa Cruz de la Sierra. All the *oidores* and secular *cabildo* were present as well as all the *caballeros*, noblemen, and illustrious of the city, and with much applause from all. It was a very enjoyable day for everyone.

Dispatch Ship Departed for Spain

At five in the afternoon of Sunday, the 19th of January of that year, the ship *Goyonete* left the port of Callao with twenty pieces of artillery and eighty soldiers and twenty sailors. It was going as dispatch ship to Panama with letters for Spain. For its protection other ships accompanied it to Guayaquil and the other [Panamanian] coast in apprehension of the pirate that cruises in this South Sea. The Franciscan commissary general, Fray Marcos Terán, embarked on this ship with other religious of his faction. By order of His Excellency, the archbishop-viceroy, this ship is to visit all the ports and bays there are from Callao to Panama. Two large launches also went with their pieces of artillery and soldiers. Each launch had ten oars on each side, and all the oarsmen were Indians from Callao. Each soldier and oarsman was paid four months salary.

The archbishop-viceroy had ordered the imprisonment of Francisco de León on the 5th of June of 1680, and he was held prisoner on the escort vessel, guarded so that he could speak to no one, with serious penalties [if he were to do so]. He was held prisoner on that ship from the abovementioned day until Sunday, the 19th of January of the year 1681, when they transferred him to the ship *Goyonete* which departed as dispatch ship for Panama. He went to Spain at the orders of the archbishop-viceroy.

Great Earthquake

A great earthquake occurred Monday, the 20th of the month, at one in the afternoon.

The Englishman Garroted

Wednesday, the 26th of March of 1681, at eleven in the morning the little [insignificant] Englishman whom they had caught at Barbacoas [southwest coast of modern Colombia] was garroted at the court prison. He died a Christian, as they had baptized him, and later they hanged him from a scaffold in the plaza.

Procession of the Rosary

On the afternoon of Saturday, the 24th of May of 1681, a procession left the monastery of Santo Domingo with the statue of Our Lady of the Rosary which was the fourth time it was taken out of its niche. [The statues of] Santo Domingo and Saint Rose accompanied her [Our Lady of the Rosary] to the cathedral with the grand accompaniment of the archbishop-viceroy and the ecclesiastic and secular *cabildos*. The court *alcaldes* and treasury officials carried the holy image, attended by the whole city, men as well as women. Extensive penances were ordered by the viceroy-archbishop to pacify God Our Lord for the evil and robbery that the English enemy perpetrated in this sea. [During] the three days of Pentecost there was full jubilation with many indulgences [granted] by the archbishop-viceroy, and a sermon all three days with the attendance of His Excellency and the *oidores* and all the religious orders. On the last day of festivity the image was returned with all the accompaniment as on the day it was taken out.

News of the Viceroy

The evening of this same Saturday, the 24th of May, a letter arrived from the [*audiencia*] president of Panama advising the viceroy-archbishop that a convoy fleet and galleons had arrived [from Spain] at Cartagena on Good Friday. Also [aboard] was the new viceroy for this kingdom. Don Melchor de Navarra y Rocaful [Duke of La Palata].

Proclamation of the Armada

Monday, the 26th of May, the second day of Pentecost, a proclamation was issued for the dispatch of the armada that is to leave the port of Callao the 20th of July of the year 1681. Two mounted soldiers were immediately sent out, one for Potosí and the other for Arica, to forward the silver in all the kingdom and the letters.

Childbirth of the Marchioness of Malagón

Thursday, the 29th of May of 1681, the Marchioness of Malagón [and Countess of Castellar, former vicereine] gave birth to a son at five in the afternoon in the [nearby] town of Surco, where she had been living for more than two years.

Tuesday, the 3rd of June, and Friday, the 6th, bullfights were held and bulls ran free. The Count [of Castellar] did not go out to see them, but all the people of Lima did.

Visit of the Archbishop-Viceroy

Monday, the 2nd of June, the viceroy-archbishop went to Surco to congratulate her [the Marchioness of Malagón] on the new infant to which she had given birth. He placed a very lovely and expensive pectoral [cross] with a gold chain on the chest of the newly born, as well as [leaving] other valuables. He also placed a gold chain on the nurse that cared for the infant.

The reception given the archbishop-viceroy by the Marquis of Malagón was impressive. After more than an hour visiting, the viceroy-archbishop returned to Lima, very pleased.

Arrival of the Marquis of Malagón from Surco

Wednesday, the 4th of June, the Marquis of Malagón came from Surco with a large accompaniment of *caballeros* and great ostentation to pay a visit on the archbishop-viceroy. After spending a long time with His Excellency he returned to Surco, and both men were very pleased.

Arrival of the Gentleman Sent by the New Viceroy

The gentleman sent from Porto Bello by the new viceroy, Don Melchor de Navarra y Rocaful [Duke of La Palata], arrived at this city of Lima with a box of letters for the viceroy-archbishop on Saturday, the 7th of June of 1681, at nine at night. At that hour His Excellency called a council meeting of all the *oidores* and *alcaldes* of the court, which resulted in the imprisonment of Sebastián de Navarette, official of the Royal Treasury of Lima. He was put in the court jail and they confiscated all his property. Don Diego Inclán, court *alcalde*, with six soldiers on horseback and the secretary of the council, carried out the order for imprisonment.

Baptism of the Son of the Count of Castellar

Sunday, the 8th of June of 1681, at five in the afternoon [Don Fernando] the only son and heir of the Marquis of Malagón and Count of Castellar, who had been viceroy of these kingdoms, was baptized in the church of the town of Surco, two leagues from Lima. His godfather was the present provincial of Santo Domingo, the Very Reverend Father Fray Juan de los Ríos, and the one who baptized him, Juan de la Cantara, an inquisitor in Lima. He was baptized with such grandeur that had he been a son of the king there could not have been more ostentation. There were tapestries decorating the cloister of the convent as well as adorning the church; three different altar tables in gilt silver; and items of great value. The baptismal font was in the body of the church and it was of solid silver; the cradle had brocade curtains; the sheets were edged in white lace that looked like snowflakes; the pillows all had the same edging, and the buttons were all diamonds. [It was] grandiose and something never seen before. That same day there were more than four hundred guests, persons of great influence and *caballeros*. The tables were very well laid out around the cloister and with many plates of food; all [the guests] had good appetites as it was both bountiful and good. Everyone left well pleased.

People and Festivity

All the people of Lima went to see such grandeur, with men as well as women in the finest and most gala attire which had ever been seen, even at the entrance of new viceroys. A great sum of silver had been spent.

Death of the Father Superior of Surco

Tuesday, the 10th of this month of June, the father superior of Surco, Fray [blank] de Sotomayor, died suddenly. Because of his death they did not run the very brave bulls brought from Maranga nor those of Cristóbal Chamorro. Everyone came away without seeing the bulls.

Miguel de Medrano died suddenly before dawn of that same day.

Arrival from Surco of the Count and Countess of Castellar

Saturday, the 5th of July of 1681, the countess returned to Lima from the town of Surco where she had been [living for] more than two years and where she had given birth to her son. There was a great accompaniment of *caballeros* and ladies who came in more than thirty carriages. Before going to the house where they were to live, they [the count and countess] went to the chapel of Our Lady of Solitude.

Death of Diego de Arepachateaga

Don Diego de Arepachateaga, *caballero* of the order of Santiago, present general of the port of Callao, and *corregidor* of Sana for His Majesty, died rather suddenly, on Wednesday, the 16th of July, at nine at night. He was eighty-one years old, and the doctors said it was apoplexy. His burial was Friday, the 18th, with great mourning, at the Society of Jesus in Lima with a great accompaniment of *caballeros* as well as the attendance of the whole city. The body was buried with his armaments, and a horse with pared hooves [following the body]. There was a formation in the plaza where there were three funeral stops. Artillery pieces were fired at each stop, the flags were dragged, and at the responsory they draped them over the body. At the moment he was being buried nine pieces of artillery were fired in the small plaza of the Society of Jesus.

The archbishop-viceroy awaited the deceased at the church of the Society of Jesus, and he was present until the divine offices were over, which lasted until eight at night.

Augustinian Provincial

Monday, the 21st of July of 1681, Fray Martín de Híjar was elected provincial of San Agustín.

Second Proclamation Regarding the Armada

That same day a second proclamation was issued for the 15th of August, that the armada should leave the port of Callao for Tierra Firme with the treasure of His Majesty and individuals without further delay.

Dominican Provincial

Thursday, the 24th of this month of July, the Very Reverend Father Fray Diego de Espinosa was elected Dominican provincial, and he did not lose a single vote. This election was held at the Recollect of La Madalena, with great approval of all the voters and all the city.

Ban on the Military

Monday, the 29th of the month, a proclamation was issued by royal decree of His Majesty: that the viceroys were not to give permission to any military person to go to Spain to apply [for a promotion or transfer], but rather [such applicants] should submit a memorandum to the viceroy, who would remit the memoranda to Madrid giving an account of the persons and submitting information as to the time they had served so that His Majesty, may God protect him, could give [proper] retribution for the services of each one. If they were to go there, their petitions would not be admitted. The government was to take note of the royal decree of His Majesty.

Death of Don Alonso de Orellana

Don Alonso de Orellana, [member] of the order of Santiago and *oidor* for Chile, died Monday, the 28th of July of 1681. He was buried Wednesday, the 30th, at Santo Domingo [church]. The archbishop-viceroy and the ecclesiastic and secular *cabildos* attended his burial, and the gentlemen of the royal *audiencia* did not go. I do not know what the reason was.

Death of the Dean Santoyo de Palma

The dean, Don Juan Santoyo de Palma, died Tuesday, the 29th of July of 1681. His burial was held at the parish of San Marcelo, where he had been the curate for many years, on the afternoon of Thursday, the 31st of that month, with a great accompaniment of more than four hundred clerics wearing surplices. Señor Don Melchor de Avendaño, a canon who was acting as commissary of the [Holy] Crusade, went between Señor Don Diego Mejía, senior *oidor*, and the *contador* Don Martín de Zavala. The viceroy awaited the body at San Marcelo.

The Large Bell of Santo Domingo

The bishop of Misque, Don Pedro de Cárdenas, blessed the large bell on the afternoon of Thursday, the 31st of the month. It was hoisted into position on the morning of Friday, the 1st of August of 1681. It weighed two hundred and twenty quintals.

The Count of Castellar Departs for Spain

Departure from Lima for Callao of the Marquis of Malagón and Count of Castellar. The archbishop-viceroy, having been in Callao for many days to dispatch the armada with the treasure of His Majesty and individuals for Spain, returned from Callao on Saturday, the 13th of September of 1681. Sunday, the 14th, he left his archbishopric palace on horseback with a great retinue, and went to the residence of the count in the house of the treasurer of the Holy Crusade, Don Luis de Cabrera, facing the church of San Pedro. From there they both rode together, the two viceroys on horseback, preceded by many *caballeros* and collegiates, [officials of] the university, all the tribunals, and two rank and file companies marching ahead with the battalion commander Don Francisco de la Cueva. They passed in front of the church with all the accompaniment, and in the small plaza of San Diego there was a formation of battalion infantry that fired a closed charge. The sergeant major of that battalion, Don Julián Corbeira, was there with his aides Rosales and Rueda. The viceroy-archbishop bade farewell to the count at [the Recollect of] Belén which he then entered. The count took his leave of all the accompaniment, and entering his carriage, took off for Callao. The [former] vicereine had gone to Callao on the morning of that same day. The count and the countess were lodged at the house of the curate of Callao. The countess awaited at La Legua and from there they went together.

The viceroy-archbishop, after having been in the monastery of Our Lady of Belén for a long while, also took off for Callao with the retinue that accompanied him.

Because the Count of Castellar had so ordered, no artillery

salute was fired upon his entrance into Callao. But when the archbishop-viceroy arrived at eight at night, he ordered that all the artillery be fired.

Departure of the Armada

The armada left the port of Callao with the treasure of His Majesty and individuals at six in the afternoon on Sunday, the 21st of September of the year 1681, day of the glorious Saint Matthew. The armada was composed of a flagship, escort ship, and five other merchant vessels. Don José de Alzamora went as general, and Manuel de Pantoja as admiral or chief. More than twenty-four million pesos went [in that shipment] for Spain and for purchases at Puerto Bello. May God keep them well and guide them safely to Spain!

The Count of Castellar, having been deprived of his post as viceroy to Peru three months [years] ago, embarked on the escort ship with the countess and their son who was born at Surco, and all the family.

As the escort ship set sail, a bright star appeared in the West, and all who saw it marveled at it.

Armada of the Year 1681

(The armada in which the Count of Castellar went to Spain left Callao on Sunday, the 21st of September of 1681. The escort ship anchored back at Callao the 12th of November of 1682; the [round] trip [to Panama] took one year, one month, and twenty-two days. And the flagship *San Lorenzo* anchored at Callao the 17th of December of 1682; it took one year, two months, and twenty-six days.)

News from Paita

Wednesday, the 24th of September, news arrived at this city from Paita that the [new] viceroy [Don Melchor de Navarra y Rocaful], Duke of la Palata, had arrived at Paita on the 13th of this month aboard the *Goyonete*. That ship had left Callao with artillery and infantry at the orders of the viceroy-archbishop to reconnoiter all the ports as far as Panama because of the enemy who is infesting this ocean.

Entrance of the Ambassador

Friday, the 10th of October of 1681, at five in the afternoon Don Diego de Villa Alvarado, the ambassador sent by the viceroy, Duke of la Palata, entered Lima between the two ordinary *alcaldes*, Ordoño de Zamudio and Don Melchor Malo Bique, and all the *regidores*, and with a great accompaniment of *caballeros*. The archbishop-viceroy received him in his archbishopric palace where he gave him lodging. He entered very splendidly, extending great courtesies to all the people.

Bullfights for the Ambassador

There were bullfights for the ambassador on Friday, the 17th of the month, with no *caballero* going out into the plaza. The bulls were very balky and sluggish.

Entrance of the Viceroy in Callao

Sunday, the 19th of October of 1681, at eight at night the viceroy, Duke of la Palata, entered the port of Callao with his wife [Doña Francisca Toralto y Aragón] and all his family in twenty-seven litters. From Bocanegra they crossed over to Callao.

On the same day at ten o'clock the viceroy-archbishop left Lima and went to Callao, where he awaited him at the house of the vicar of that port. As soon as he arrived he surrendered to him the staff of captain general and all the guard, and at ten at night he returned to Lima.

Arrival of the Duke in Lima

Tuesday, the 21st of the month, at twelve noon the viceroy, Duke of la Palata, entered this city from Callao with six *caballeros* of his [official] family. They came in inquisitor Cantera's carriage drawn by four mules. First he entered the palace to see the arrangements being made, where he remained until two in the afternoon. At that hour he went sightseeing with His Excellency [the archbishop-viceroy] in his carriage until three in the afternoon. Both going and returning the two gentlemen received great courtesies. Then he went a second time to see the palace, and he enjoyed looking at the garden where he was served some sweets and cold drinks. At four o'clock he headed for Callao in the archbishop's carriage with six mules, and there was a great crowd of men and women to see him.

Bullfights at Callao

The soldiers of the presidio at Callao ran bulls three days for His Excellency. They were very brave because the soldiers went on their own to different places to buy them.

Entrance of the Viceroy in Lima

Wednesday, the 5th of November of 1681, at six in the morning His Excellency left the port of Callao, and at his departure for Lima all the artillery of that port was fired. At nine he arrived at this city in the archbishop's carriage and with a great following. In the carriage was the mother of the vicereine and her granddaughter, the child of the viceroy. The vicereine was in the back seat and the Duke in front. Since there were a great number of people in the plaza, in carriages, on mules and on foot, their Excellencies with all their family entered [the palace] through the garden gate.

Thursday, the 6th, their Excellencies left for the sung Mass which was given at the cathedral in celebration of the birthday of our king and lord, Charles II. The archbishop attended as viceroy, accompanied by the *audiencia* and secular *cabildo*.

Reception of the Duke of La Palata

Friday, the 7th of the month, at ten in the morning the Duke of La Palata was received in the council hall as [*audiencia*] president and viceroy, with the attendance of all the togaed gentlemen and a great number of *caballeros*. This reception was [held] before his public entrance under a canopy. After the viceroy's reception, the archbishop went in a sedan chair, with a great accompaniment, to visit him at the palace.

First Proclamation Issued by the Duke

Friday, the 14th of November of the year 1681, a proclamation was issued by His Excellency, the Duke of La Palata, that he was to be received in public on Thursday, the 20th of the month.

He made his public entrance under a canopy Thursday, the 20th of November of 1681, a workday, with all the accompaniment and splendor that the other viceroys have usually received in this city. I refer to an earlier page where the entrance of the Count of Castellar is described in its entirety. This was the same except for the twenty-four pack mules and the [lack of] bars of silver in the arch at the street of the Mercaderes, which [silver] had been sent two months previously with the armada to Panama.

Celebration for the Name of Mary

The *fiesta* for the name of Mary, which was the first [*fiesta*] that the viceroy, Duke of La Palata saw, was held this year of 1681, on Sunday, the 7th of December. The battalion commander was Don Francisco de la Cueva and the sergeant major Don Julián Corbeira. That afternoon there were four squadrons in the plaza formed by the sergeant major, and there had never before been such a day as this. The afternoon was very much worth seeing with many people and great festivities, and the viceroy enjoyed himself very much seeing this great *fiesta* which is celebrated every year.

It had been delayed for the arrival of the new viceroy, its usual day being the second Sunday of October.[55]

The Year 1682

Thursday, the 1st of January of the year 1682, Don Sancho de Castro and Don Melchor Malo de Molina were elected ordinary *alcaldes*.

Secular Priest Killed

Don Juan de Rueda [was killed] Sunday, the 4th of January of 1682, at eight at night by a knife thrust. He died immediately upon confessing and receiving the holy sacraments.

Bullfights

The first [bulls] that were run for the viceroy were on Saturday, the 18th of the month, and they were spiritless. Only the ordinary *alcalde* Don Melchor Malo de Molina went out into the plaza, alone, without any *caballero* accompanying him.

Placement of [the Statue of] Saint Peter

Thursday, the 19th of March of 1682, day of the glorious Saint Joseph, [the statue of] Saint Peter of Alcántara was placed in the women's convalescent home on Cercado Street. [They entered] through the small door. The procession left from Santa Clara [convent] at five in the afternoon, and the archbishop who had been viceroy was present.

Father Castillo Broke His Leg

Licentiate Pedro de Castillo broke his leg on Wednesday, the 6th of May of the year 1682, near the drainage ditch of La Peña Horadada. He was thrown from a mule while watching a bull being lassoed. Running from the bull, he broke a leg and the bones broke through the torn skin. It happened at four in the afternoon on the eve of [the *fiesta* of] the Ascension of the Lord. (He died on Friday, the 15th of this month of May, at nine in the morning.)

Don Carlos and Another Englishman Garroted

Friday, the 8th of May of the year 1682, they garroted Don Carlos in the court prison. They had caught him twelve years ago at Valdivia on a ship that had come from England, and he had said that he was a Recollect Franciscan friar and a priest.

[55] See note 14 for Mary's *fiesta* dates.

Under torture he said that he was not, but at the moment that they were about to tighten the collar, he confessed that he was in truth a friar and had said Mass, and he cited the judges [to be themselves judged] at the tribunal of God. At four in the afternoon another Englishman was also garroted, and they hanged him on the scaffold in the middle of the plaza as they had the eight previous ones who had been captured at Arica.

My Son To Huamanga

My son, Fray Francisco of this city of Lima, left for Huamanga Wednesday, the 13th of May of 1682, to continue the litigation for nullification [of his vows]. He went in the company of three priests of the clergy in great comfort. This day he was thirty-five years old.

Father Hernando de Saavedra Died

Monday, the 8th of June of 1682, having gone to visit his province, Father Hernando de Saavedra, present provincial of the Society of Jesus, died at Ica. He was buried in the Augustinian monastery of that town.

News of his death arrived at this city of Lima, Monday, the 15th of the month, and Tuesday, the 23rd, funeral rites were held at his monastery in Lima. All the nobility of the city attended, and there was deep sorrow felt throughout the whole city.

Death of Felipe de Zavala, "the Wealthy"

Felipe de Zavala died on the 30th of July of the year 1682 leaving a substantial legacy and bequeathing large sums to charity. He was buried in the church of Nuestra Señora de las Mercedes on Friday, the 31st of the same month.

Fortress Built in the Plaza of Lima

A [mock] fort, made of wood and covered with canvas and surrounded by rocks piled one upon the other in simulation of a stone wall, was built in the plaza of Lima with the fountain in the center. The construction took eight days, and it was designed by Don Rodrigo Martínez who had come from Spain as aide to the combat sergeant major.

On Saturday, the 15th of August of the year 1682, the day of the Assumption of Our Lady, at four in the afternoon a company of one hundred men, resplendent in battle dress, marched in with great solemnity to take possession of the fort. The procession was headed by Captain Diego Hurtado and his groom, Captain Juan de León, camp master for combat training. There was great celebration that evening with festive lights and masquerading that lasted throughout the night. At dawn on Sunday, the 16th, the day of Saint Roch and Saint Hyacinth, the fort was magnificent, and there were sonnets in praise of the viceroy, Duke of La Palata, and his brother-in-law, General Tomás Paravisino. On this same day at three o'clock in the afternoon the troops started entering the plaza through Archbishop Street. They were headed by General Tomás Paravisino in his most imposing splendor and immediately followed by his chiefs of staff. Unsheathed sword in hand before the viceroy, who was at the ceremonial seat in the balcony of the palace accompanied by all the *oidores*, he extended the proper courtesies which consisted of thrice kissing the unsheathed sword, and he repeated the homage to the vicereine who stood at a distance with her court. Various detachments followed on horseback, the captain of each company executing the same courtesies as his general. And thus the mounted companies took up their respective posts.

Entrance of the Infantry into the Plaza

Battalion Commander Don Francisco de la Cueva being ill, the sergeant major Don Julián Corbeira followed suit with all the infantry troops extending the same courtesies to the viceroy and the vicereine as had the general and his captains. After all had taken up their respective posts, ten pieces of artillery, that were in the plaza with their campaign tent, were fired. And there were many other campaign tents in the plaza.

The General's Orders

The general sent trumpeters to the fort commander ordering him to surrender or else the castle would be blown up. But the fort commander replied "that he would not surrender; that he had men, gunpowder, balls, and provisions." Finally, all the requirements having been fulfilled, the general ordered a musket charge and two or three [bursts] of artillery, and there was an attack on all sides of the fortress. They did not wish to surrender until two parts of the castle were damaged and the fortress torn in half. Then the general ordered firewood to be brought, and all the foot-soldiers and cavalrymen entered the palace yard where there was a great quantity of branches that the Indians had brought some days before. Everyone carried [wood] as though they were in a live war. As soon as those in the fort saw such a great force of men, the fort commander called the other four captains who were in the fort to a council, and they surrendered. They were permitted to leave with their arms unloaded and with the arms and flag with which they had come forth. Another company went into the fort and put up the flag, with which the war [game] was over and they proceeded to leave the plaza in the same manner that they had entered. There was also a cavalry company of Indians and another of mulattoes, as well as another of Negro and mulatto footsoldiers. This was Sunday, the 17th of August of the year 1682, day of the greatest rejoicing seen in Lima, because everyone who lived there went to see it. The Lord be praised!

The sergeant major Don Julian Corbeira with his adjutants Roque Rosales and Juan de Rueda, who came forth resplendent, organized the squadrons of the battalion infantry in which not a single mercenary soldier appeared. Only the day before twenty mercenary soldiers joined the company that is at the palace under Captain Don Fernando Bravo.

Masquerade of Mulattoes for Saint Rose

Saturday, the 9th of August of 1682, at nine at night a masquerade of more than eighty mulattoes in costumes and silly attire set out with two floats. Many of them went dressed as women, dancing with much gaiety to the rhythm of harps and guitars. Bearing many lights, they went completely around the plaza. The viceroy and vicereine with all their family were in the balconies, and all the people were in the plaza and in the streets through which the masquerade passed.

Altar of Saint Rose in the Cabildo

Sunday, the 30th of the month, the day of Saint Rose, a procession left the cathedral at four in the afternoon. It went around the plaza, with all the accompaniment of the *oidores*, the two *cabildos*, and all the illustrious of Lima except for the viceroy as he was ailing and was watching the procession pass from the balconies. An altar was set up in the *cabildo*, where [the statue] of Saint Rose was located. It was of such magnificent architecture, where there was much to see of interest, and never before had such a well-decorated altar been seen in Lima. Because of this, and so that everyone could see it, it was not dismantled until the following day at four in the afternoon. Don Sancho de Castro, present ordinary *alcalde* of this year of 1682, had ordered this altar to be made.

Death of Francisco del Molino

Licentiate Francisco del Molino, son of my *compadre* Pedro del Molino, died Saturday, the 12th of September of the year 1680. He was buried in the cloister of the monastery of San Agustín, where his father Pedro del Molino is buried, as is his wife, Doña Juana de Ratera. He had one daughter, who is a professed nun in the convent of the Pure and Immaculate Conception of this city of Lima, to whom he left as heir more than eight thousand pesos, with Eulogio del Salto as his executor. He was buried on Sunday, the 13th, at the convent and in the sepulchre that his father had bought before dying.

Celebration for the Name of Mary

The *fiesta* of the holy name of Mary was [held] on Sunday, the 25th of October of the year 1682.[56] It was celebrated that morning in the church of Santo Domingo where this celebration has always been held, with great solemnity, attended by the viceroy, *audiencia*, and secular *cabildo* with all the nobility of this city. The sermon and high Mass were given by the fathers of the Society of Jesus.

In the afternoon there were four squadrons in the plaza with a great number of very resplendent people. The companies of Indians, mulattoes, and free Negroes also came forth.

The procession was at five in the afternoon at which time it went through the plaza, and three salutes of arquebuses and muskets were fired with great noise in honor of the Holy Mother of God. The fathers of the Society [of Jesus] officiated as priests, and in the procession the Jesuit fathers and the Dominican religious went intermingled.

The viceroy with his retinue walked along behind the image [of Mary] as customary. The vicereine with her mother and daughter and her family watched from the balcony of the corner of the palace.

General Don Tomás Paravisino, brother of the vicereine, came forth very resplendent on a horse. He made a fine appearance while circling the plaza, assisted by a great number of cavalrymen and the adjutant Don Rodrigo Martínez, who positioned the cavalry at their posts.

The sergeant major Don Julian Corbeira with his two adjutants, Roque Rosales and Rueda, set up the squadrons because the battalion commander Don Francisco de la Cueva was ill.

[56] See note 14 for Mary's *fiesta* dates.

It was an afternoon where there was much to see and great rejoicing as it was the feast of the Holy Mother of Our Lord, Jesus Christ, and defender of all the human race, and of Catholics. God be praised!

Death of General Urdanegui

General Don Juan de Urdanegui died at dawn on Monday, the 16th of November. The following Tuesday he was buried in the Society of Jesus [church] as a religious of that Society, [which he had become] with a dispensation from His Holiness, since the general was currently married and had a daughter. As soon as he died the fathers of the Society took his body [to the monastery]. He was a very rich man and left much for charity. In his homeland [Spain] he was from the city of Orduña in the province of Vizcaya, where he ordered a college to be built, and he left sufficient money for upkeep as well as many other pious works. He was a *caballero* of the order of Santiago, and he had taken on the habit Thursday, the 18th of August of the year 1667, fifteen years and twenty-nine days before he died. May God keep him in His holy care.

Death of the Battalion Commander

Don Antonio Sancho de Avila, *caballero* of the order of Santiago and present battalion commander of the presidio of Callao for His Majesty, died suddenly at eight in the morning of Thursday, the 3rd of December, after having been ill for a long time. He was buried on the afternoon of Friday, the 4th, at the monastery of San Francisco. His body was dressed in the chapter cloak, as *caballeros* of the order were buried, and with his staff of battalion commander. Four rank and file companies [attended the funeral] as there were no other mercenary companies in Lima except the one that is always on guard at the palace. At each funeral stop during the responsory a flag was thrown over his body. A horse with pared hooves also went behind the body, and all the cavalry of the city accompanied it [the cortege]. May God keep him in His holy glory! Amen.

Staff of Battalion Commander of Callao

At his headquarters the general of Callao, Don Tomás Paravisino, presented the staff to Don Francisco de Zúñiga, the deaf one, *caballero* of the order of Santiago. This was Monday at noon, the 7th of December of the year 1682.

Monday, the 21st of December of 1682, day of the apostle Saint Thomas, the bull of the Holy Crusade was made public at the cathedral of Lima. It was brought from the monastery of San Francisco by Doctor Don Melchor de Avendaño, commissary of the Holy Crusade and canon of that church. The viceroy, Duke of La Palata, was present along with all the togaed gentlemen, the secular and ecclesiastic *cabildos*, and all the other people of this noble city of Lima. Archbishop Liñán, who had been viceroy, was not present at this noble function.

Publication of the Papal Bull

Don Sebastián de Navarrete, *caballero* of the order of Calatrava and official of the royal treasury of Lima, who was exiled to the kingdom of Mexico at the order of His Majesty, was embarked on the ship named *El Popolo*. It left the port of Callao at four in the afternoon on Wednesday, the 23rd of December of the year 1682, with quicksilver that was being sent to Mexico.

Captain Juan de Monsurieta went as chief and governor of that ship carrying forty infantrymen as well as artillery and artillerymen. May God guide them safely! (This ship named *El Popolo* that went to Acapulco returned to the port of Callao and anchored there on Wednesday, the 9th of March of 1684.)

The Year 1683

Friday, the 1st of January of the year 1683, Don Alonso Lazo, present *regidor*, and Don Diego Manrique, *caballero* of the order of Santiago, were elected ordinary *alcaldes*, and José de Agüero, water commissioner.

José de Armendáriz Kills his Wife

[The murder] happened at five in the afternoon on Saturday, the 23rd of January of the year 1683, in his house and garden at Cercado. Without the dead woman being guilty of anything, he stabbed her more than twelve times with a wide dagger type knife and then he disappeared. It was a great shame to see her cut to pieces and leaving four children. The following Sunday she was buried in the church of Santa Ana.

Don Pedro Merino de Heredia, *caballero* of the order of Santiago, died Sunday, the 31st of January of the year 1683.

Don Tomás Berjón, who had been *oidor* of this royal *audiencia* and was to go to Mexico as *oidor*, died on Monday, the 1st of February of this year of 1683. He was buried the following day at San Francisco [church]. The viceroy, Duke of La Palata, with all the *oidores* and all the city went to his funeral.

Regular Ensign Killed

He was killed at eight at night on Shrove Tuesday, the 2nd of March of 1683, near the rubbish heap at the minor entrance of Santo Domingo [monastery]. They stabbed him more than twenty-four times after which they threw him in the river, which had a lot of water. Three days later the body was discovered near the mill of La Pastrana.

José de Aguirre Died

Licentiate José de Aguirre, lawyer of this royal *audiencia*, died suddenly at two in the afternoon on Friday, the 1st day of Lent, which was the 5th of March of the year 1683. He was a young man of twenty-six years of age, [and he died] just after eating. May God keep him in His holy glory!

General Montejo was arrested on the morning of Saturday, the 6th of March of 1683. The adjutant, Captain Rodrigo Martínez, and four soldiers on horseback went to arrest him, and they brought him to Callao.

Four Soldiers Dishonorably Discharged

The four soldiers who had come from Quito bound for Chile, [and who were in prison] for the mutiny they instigated on the ship, and for the deaths [they caused], and for fleeing in Paita with the pay and deserting the flag, were taken from the court prison by a guard of mercenary soldiers, and they were put in the infantry guard house. Then shackled and under the same guard they were taken out to the plaza where there was a formation made up of men of the battalion. Accompanied by a fife and two muffled drums they read each one his sentence of discharge [stating] that at no time could they hold an honorable post in a military or any other kind of profession. The instigator of this flight, since he was chief of the group, was exiled for all the days of his life to Valdivia, without salary, only with rations. The other three received ten years. The mounted soldiers and the provost took them to Callao the same day for embarkment on the ship that was soon to leave for Chile.

Captain Don Sebastián de Carranza Arrested

That same night, Saturday, the 6th of March, Captain Don Sebastián de Carranza was arrested at the order of His Excellency and taken to Callao and turned over to the guard company of that fortress. He is a nephew of licentiate Vallejos, secretary of the previous archbishop-viceroy of this kingdom. He was arrested by the cavalry soldiers who took him to Callao.

My son the *bachiller* Francisco de Mugaburu returned from Huamanga on Tuesday, the 23rd of March, 1683. He is now a layman, the litigation [to annul his religious vows] having been settled in his favor. In order to appeal he was obliged to leave this city of Lima for Huamanga on Wednesday, the 13th of May of 1680.

Ensign Francisco de Rojas died of diarrhea in the hospital of San Andrés at midnight on Monday, the 26th of April of 1683. He was buried on Tuesday, the 27th of the month, in the hospital church.

Bullfights

Bulls were run in the plaza for the *fiesta* of Saint John the Baptist by the mulattoes, [who were] keepers of that chapel [of Saint John] in the church of Santa Ana. They were run the first day on Wednesday, the 8th of July of 1683; the second bulls were Thursday, the 5th of August; the third, that were very brave, were provided by the carpenters, [and run] Saturday, the 7th of August.

The first celebration that was held in the new chapel of Saint Cajetan was Sunday, the 8th of August of the year 1683, and that day Father Fray Francisco Machuca of the Mercedarian order gave the sermon.

Viceroy and His Wife to Amancaes

On the afternoon of Sunday, the 8th of August of the year 1683, the viceroy, Duke of La Palata, and the vicereine went to Amancaes. They were invited by Don Diego Manrique, *caballero* of the order of Santiago and present ordinary *alcalde*, who offered a celebration in his honor, with many dogs and game birds. The whole city, and the viceroy in particular, went to that spot that afternoon to watch the falcons and partridge fly, and the running of greyhounds with deer, and also to see the tents and picnic lunches; there were any number of things. All the expenses of this afternoon were paid for by the ordinary *alcalde*, who would do better to spend silver on pious works in the service of God.

The Viceroy Goes to Surco

At eleven in the morning of Wednesday, the 8th of September of this year, on the day of the nativity of Our Lady, the Holy Virgin, His Excellency left with his family in carriages for Surco. A great number of *caballeros* and private individuals accompanied them; [they were] colorfully dressed and very gallant. He returned to Lima from Surco on Friday, the 17th of the month.

Death of the Canon Cartagena

The canon Cartagena died Friday, the 1st of October, and he was buried on Saturday at the cathedral.

Ordoño de Zamudio, *regidor* of Lima died that same day.

Miguel Núñez de Meagadas, a very rich man, died that same day.

Sunday, the 3rd of this month, Father Maestro Fray Fernando de Araujo, of the order of Saint Augustíne, died.

Fiesta *at San Francisco Church*

At four in the afternoon of Sunday, the 3rd of October of the year 1683, [there was a *fiesta*] as is customary each year on the eve [of Saint Francis' day]. As the statue of Saint Dominic approached the corner of the plaza, a large serpent fireworks was set off, and for the glorious Saint Francis, as soon as his statue appeared at the plaza, another device was set off, a very large lion that fired many rockets. When the [statues of the] two glorious saints reached the palace gate, reverences were made and then they set off another fireworks. [Made of paper] it was two men representing those who were explorers of the promised land, and they carried a cluster of grapes on their shoulders which was another device that fired many rockets and burned a long time. There was a great crowd of people. The procession continued to San Francisco [church] where there were two more large pieces of fireworks, and a flying kite of fire which floated down from the tower throwing off great quantities of fire.

The whole city went to see the novelty, never seen [before] those days. At night there were other pieces of fireworks constructed very artistically. The two towers were hung with many and interesting things, and there was much to see. All of the church was admirably decorated from the door to the main altar, not with daisies or greenery but all of very rich plumes of the type brought from Spain. Suffice it to say that from the time this city of Lima was founded to this day there has not been another [event such as this], as it has been a wonder of delight and rejoicing.

Dispatch Ship from Spain

Friday, the 8th of October of 1683, brought much news. The first was a royal decree that a mint should be established in this city for many reasons; and, at the stipulation of our king and lord, no silver bars were to be sent to Spain, as they were going to foreign kingdoms. Many other official communications for this kingdom and the government of Chile arrived on this dispatch ship. The present sergeant major of the battalion of this city, Don Julián Corbeira de Ocampo, [was to take over] the post as sergeant major of the kingdom; and the precentor of the church, Don Luis Merlo, [to be made] dean of that church; and much other news that I do not list. [Elections for] alternates of the Franciscan religious of Cuzco and Lima were not to be held, being suspended until the litigation in Rome is completed.

The [papal] bull [naming] the Very Reverend Father Fray Antonio de Morales of the order of the Predicadores as bishop of Concepción, kingdom of Chile, [also] arrived on this dispatch ship. It was more than four years since this bishopric had been granted to him.

Franciscan Provincial Vicar

Father Fray Pedro Castrejón was received as provincial vicar of all the religious of San Francisco [monastery], with cross held high, at five o'clock on Saturday, the 17th of this month of October. They pledged him obedience as their own prelate, and he, being one of the three fathers that had been named from Spain, [officiated] until the arrival of the new commissary general. And with this they were pacified since Father Castrejón was from Spain. The same [news of assignment] arrived for the province of Cuzco. May God grant peace to all of them!

New Convent

The three nuns that left [Our Lady of] Carmen to found a new convent in the city of Huamanga left at dawn on Tuesday, the 19th of October of the present year of 1683, with a large accompaniment.

The *fiesta* for the great name of Mary, which is celebrated every year, was on Sunday, the 24th of October of this year.[57] And it was a very wonderful afternoon with a [military] formation and much to see.

Tribute Paid by the Indians

Monday, the 25th of this month of October, a royal decree of His Majesty was published that all the Indians be registered, as well as the towns they were from, so that they would pay tribute to their superiors or else leave this city of Lima for their lands.

[57] See note 14 for Mary's *fiesta* dates.

Sack of Veracruz, Mexico

Bad news was received that the French enemy [pirates] had sacked the city of Veracruz and more than two thousand of our men had been killed. They took more than six million in silver and jewels that had been brought there to trade, because all the commerce of Mexico was through that port. And the silver for Spain arrived at that port on the second or third day of the sacking. The enemy spent five days there.[58] This dispatch arrived at this city of Lima on Tuesday, the 26th of October of 1683.

Residencia *of the Archbishop-Viceroy*

At noon on Saturday, the 30th of October of 1683, the *residencia* of the archbishop for the time that he governed as viceroy was made public, heralded with kettle drums. The *residencia* went before Don Rafael de Ascona, *alcalde* of the court of this city of Lima, by royal decree dispatched by His Majesty to this Señor.

Duplicate Dispatches for Spain

At four in the afternoon of Wednesday, the 17th of November of the year 1683, the ship sent by His Excellency, the Duke of La Palata, with news for Spain left the port of Callao. The dispatches were in duplicate, both copies going in the same ship as far as Panama. One was destined for Puerto Bello, awaited there by a large ship that would take it [to Spain]. The other dispatch went [from Panama] to Mexico where the viceroy of that kingdom would dispatch it for Spain as soon as possible. This dispatch ship went on behalf of the *consulado*. May God guide it safely!

Consecration of Bishop of La Concepción

Fray Antonio de Morales, of the order of Saint Dominic, was consecrated as bishop of La Concepción, Chile, on Sunday, the 21st of November of the year 1683. The archbishop of Lima, Don Melchor de Liñán y Cisneros, consecrated him. The Viceroy Duke of La Palata, the gentlemen of the royal *audiencia*, the secular *cabildo*, and all the *caballeros* of the city as well as all the people of the city were present. After the consecration the archbishop and the bishop left the cathedral together and then embraced and said farewell. The bishop went to his monastery in a procession with the cross held high and with all the community of his religious order.

[58] For details of this pirate raid on Vera Cruz, Mexico, in May of 1683, led by two Dutchmen, Laurens de Graaf and Nicholas Van Horn, see Clarence H. Haring, *The Buccaneers in the West Indies in the XVII Century* (New York: E. P. Dutton, 1910), pp. 242–43; and Francisco Santiago Cruz, *Los piratas del golfo de México* (Mexico: Editorial Jus, 1962), pp. 134–40.

Pedro López, [member] of the Society of Jesus and present rector of the college of San Martín, an expert in sermons and brilliant in all respects, died the 22nd of November of the year 1683. May God keep him in His holy glory. He died at sixty years of age.

Death of Father López

Friday, the 3rd of December of the year 1683, a ban was published by royal decree of His Majesty ordering that no ingot or worked silver, even though the royal fifth [of taxes] had already been paid on it, could go to Panama or Spain, but that all of it be made and worked into *reales* in the new mint established in this city of Lima. To this effect, grave and very severe penalties were prescribed for those who dared to break this ban. Anyone who wanted to know in detail the contents of this ban could find out in the office of the government. And so that he could keep his eye on these things, the viceroy, Duke of La Palata, put the *oidor* Lobatón in charge of all that this ban contains, and of the mint in Lima.

Ban Regarding Silver

Sunday, the 12th of December of 1683, the first stone of the new church being built for the nuns of Saint Theresa was placed where the main altar was to be located. In it were placed the customary coins of [the reign of] our king and lord Charles II, governing all Christiandom [*sic*]. The Duke of La Palata as viceroy of all these kingdoms and the archbishop of Lima, Señor Don Melchor de Liñán y Cisneros, the ex-Viceroy of these kingdoms of Peru, as well as all the nobility of the city, were present at the placing of this stone. May it be for the honor and glory of God Our Father and his Holy Mother. Amen. In Jesus.

Cornerstone for the Convent of Santa Teresa

The Year 1684

Saturday, the 1st of January of the year 1684, Don Nicolás de Avalos, and Don Juan de la Celda, *regidor*, were elected ordinary *alcaldes*.

Doctor Don Diego de Baños, who had been *alcalde* of the court and was retired enjoying a full salary, died. He died suddenly on Thursday night, the 6th of January, day of the Epiphany, of the year 1684. He was buried in the church of San Francisco on Saturday at eight in the evening.

The New Money

Friday, the 7th of January, money began to be coined in the new mint.

The New Meat Market

The new meat market selling meat by weight began on Saturday, the 1st of January of 1684. Formerly, from the end of July until the first of January, a quarter of mutton, large or small, cost three *reales*. In this new system there are quarters that weigh at least five or six pounds, because the two contractors purposely brought mutton from Callao by the pound that looked like donkeys, and thus the poor people suffer. And in order to do good business, they sold a head and scraps for half a *real*; and none of this are the poor people able to buy.

At the petition and clamoring of the entire city, on Saturday, the 8th of the month, the viceroy ordered that the weight system be stopped and that meat be sold as usual at three or three and a half [*reales*] a quarter. This evil did not last more than eight days because the entire city beseeched God and the viceroy, who immediately ordered it terminated.

Death of the Canon Bernabé de Villacorta

Don Bernabé de Villacorta, canon of the holy church of the cathedral of Lima, died Thursday, the 27th of January of this year of 1684, at twelve noon. He was buried in the cathedral on Friday, the 8th, at five in the afternoon. He was about forty-eight to fifty years of age.

Death of the Licentiate Roque de San Martín

Licenciado Roque de San Martín, one of the original chaplains of the convent of Nuestra Señora del Carmen since its founding in this city of Lima, died Saturday, the 5th of February of 1684, exactly at noon. He was buried at five in the afternoon of Sunday, the 6th, in the church of the convent. He was more than ninety years old.

Death of Don Alvaro Navamuel y Rios

Monday, the 7th of February of 1684, Don Antonio Navamuel y Rios, *caballero* of the order of Alcántara and presently lieutenant general of the cavalry, died suddenly on Monday, the 7th of February of 1684. As soon as he died the religious of San Francisco took him, and Tuesday, the 8th, buried him as a Franciscan religious.

The staff was given to Don Nuño de Espínola Villavicencio,

caballero of the order of Alcántara and son-in-law of General Don Baltasar Pardo. The said Don Nuño had been *corregidor* of Cuzco five years, by [order] of His Majesty, may God protect him, and the staff was presented to him Wednesday, the 9th of this month of February.

The Staff of Lieutenant General

Monday, the 8th of February of 1684, the dispatch ship from Spain arrived at this city of Lima, bringing much news: war of the [holy Roman] emperor with the sultan of Turkey, and the victory of the emperor, which was tremendous; and also the galleons of Malta and many other good events.

News from Spain

The royal decree of His Majesty, may God protect him, also came appointing Don Gaspar de la Cuba, presently president of the hall of crime, as *oidor*.

[News of] the granting of the habit of [blank] to Don Luís de Oviedo, Count of La Granja, also arrived, as well as much other news that was brought by this dispatch ship.

Habit for the Count of La Granja

The Count of La Granja received the habit in the Society of Jesus on Sunday, the 5th of March of 1684, and his sponsor was the Count Don Luís Ibáñez.

The dispatch ship sent by the governor of Chile arrived on Saturday, the 11th of March of 1684, at two in the morning [with news] that four large enemy ships had been seen in two parts of that kingdom sometime in February. On Sunday, the 12th, His Excellency issued a proclamation that all the mercenary [soldiers] go to Callao, and also the mercenary company of Don Fernando Bravo that was in the palace. And Monday, the 13th, the rank and file guard company under Agustín de la Cueva entered [the palace] on duty.

News from Chile about the Enemy

Saturday, the 6th of May of 1684, a squadron of six battalion companies of Lima was formed on the plain of Juan Simón. The mercenary palace cavalry company and the infantry skirmished, General Don Tomás Paravisino supervising. All the people of the city of Lima went to see it.

Maneuvers on the Plain of Juan Simón

Sunday, the 11th of June of the year 1684, a second squadron of eight rank and file companies, eight of the cavalry, and the

The Second Squadron

mercenary cavalry company of the palace was formed on the plain of Juan Simón. The cavalry skirmished with the infantry, under the supervision of General Don Tomás Paravisino. The Viceroy, Duke of La Palata, and the vicereine with all the family were present as well as all the people of the city of Lima. It was a very enjoyable afternoon with a great variety of gala attire and plumes. The battalion commander, Don Francisco de Cueva, marched before the squadron with his spear, and after having executed the [appropriate] courtesies to the captain general, he mounted his horse to direct the squadron.

Death of Bartolomé de Barañano

My friend and fellow countryman Bartolomé de Barañano, present manager of the [playing] card concession, died Monday, the 12th of June, at nine at night. He was buried on Tuesday afternoon in the church of the monastery of Nuestra Señora de las Mercedes. May God keep him in His holy glory.

Death of Don Rafael de Ascona

Dawn of Thursday, the 15th of June, found Rafael de Ascona dead. He was currently an *alcalde* of the court and had died suddenly. He was buried on the afternoon of Friday, the 16th, in the vault of the chapel of the Pure and Immaculate Conception at the cathedral. The viceroy, Duke of La Palata, with all the gentlemen of the royal *audiencia*, secular and ecclesiastic *cabildo*, and all the nobility of the city were present at the burial.

The deceased was the one who took the *residencia* of Archbishop Don Melchor de Liñán for the time that he was viceroy of these kingdoms of Peru.

The Walls of Lima

At four in the afternoon of Friday, the 30th of June of 1684, the day of the holy apostle Saint Paul, they began to enclose and wall this city of Lima with adobe blocks. Beginning at Monserrate [hermitage], the first foundation was laid by the chief engineer and battle sergeant general, Don Luís Venegas Osorio, who for this project was sent by our king and lord, Charles II. The viceroy, Duke of La Palata, and many gentlemen were present.

Outing at Amancaes

The viceroy, Duke of La Palata, left the palace on Monday, the 3rd of July, at one in the afternoon with the vicereine and all his family and went to the hill of Amancaes for lunch. In the afternoon deer were run with many dogs, and falcons flown, and there was much to see. This celebration was given by the ordinary *alcalde* Don Nicolás de Avalos. All the city, the women in gala dress and the gentlemen handsomely attired, attended.

Two very large culverins [cannons] which were cast for Callao by José de Cubas were finished the 11th of July of 1684. They are larger than any of those encountered in Callao, and it took more than a year to make them.

The Negroes who Worked on the Wall

Tuesday, the 11th of July of 1684, His Excellency issued a proclamation regarding the Negroes hired by the day. They had quit because they had only received five *reales* a day for the days they worked on the project, and they wanted six. His Excellency ordered that they only be paid five *reales* a day, and if [they did] not [accept this] that they be sent to [San Lorenzo] Island, off Callao, to carry rocks for a year without pay.

Don Manuel Rapossa Killed

Thursday, the 20th of July, at nine at night the merchant Tomás de Zabugal killed Don Manuel de Rapossa, merchant and shipper of dry goods. He was unable to confess [his sins], having received three mortal wounds. The following Friday he was buried at the cathedral in the chapel of All Saints, [and interred] in the vault of the Menachos. The archbishop and prebends, as well as all the nobility of Lima, were present at his burial. The aggressor was not found at his home, which will cost him one hundred pesos [fine] when he is brought to justice.

Sergeant Roque Rosales Killed

At eight at night on Tuesday, the 15th of August, the day of the Assumption of Our Lady, in the year 1684, Sergeant Roque Rosales was killed. He was the son of Captain Roque Rosales, battalion adjutant.

Open House of the Church of San Bartolomé

Thursday, the 24th of August of the year 1684, day of the glorious apostle Saint Bartholomew, all of the church of the hospital of San Bartolomé was completed except for the dome of the main chapel. The viceroy, Duke of La Palata, and Archbishop Don Melchor de Liñán y Cisneros were present at the first Mass chanted by a religious of San Agustín [monastery] and the sermon given by Father Aguilar of the Society of Jesus. The first stone of that hospital of San Bartolomé had been placed in the year 1661 in the presence of the Count of Santisteban, who was viceroy in that year.

Ban on Leaving the City

Saturday, the 2nd of September of 1684, the viceroy, Duke of La Palata, issued a decree like those issued during wartime. It forbade any person of any kind whatsoever to leave the city of Lima without permission from the government, under penalty of loss of life and all his possessions. The order was sent to all the *corregidores*, lieutenants, and other dispensers of justice of all the kingdom that they [offenders] be arrested and brought to this city.

Another Proclamation

That same day and at that same hour he issued another proclamation: that all those who would enlist as soldiers would be given four months pay.

Death of Don Alonso Bravo

Don Alonso Bravo, chief comptroller of the supreme tribunal of accounts, died that same day, Saturday the 2nd. He was buried at the monastery of Nuestra Señora de las Mercedes on Sunday. The viceroy, all the *oidores*, all the *caballeros* of the city, and the two *cabildos*, ecclesiastic and secular, were present.

Proclamation of Amnesty

Sunday, the 3rd of the month, the viceroy, Duke of La Palata, issued another proclamation: that all delinquents who had criminal charges against them present themselves. All those who appeared would be given amnesty and pardoned if they enlisted [as soldiers] to reinforce the fortress of Callao against the enemy that had entered the South Sea [Pacific Ocean]. The exceptions were those of flagrantly wicked sins and those who had been accomplices [to these nefarious acts], those who had committed a premeditated crime, and other offenses reserved for Rome. Except for these, all the rest would be granted amnesty and pardoned.

Dispatch Ship from Spain

The dispatch ship from Spain arrived at Lima on Friday, the 8th of September, the birthday of Mary, Our Lady, bringing much news. First, [the appointment of] Canon Oserín who had been confessor of the Marquís of Malagón, ex-viceroy of these kingdoms, as commissary general of San Francisco. Señor Barreto y Novoa was [named] prebend, and Castelbi [appointed] canon of Cuzco. He had competed with Doctor Carrasco, who was in first place, but it was awarded to Castelbi. (He was received [as canon] on Sunday, the 3rd of December of 1684.)

Much other news was brought regarding habits [of the military and religious orders]; the victory of the [holy Roman] emperor against the sultan of Turkey in 1683; other things which I do not list here; and royal decrees of His Majesty, may God protect him.

Procession of Our Lady of the Rosary

Saturday, the 16th of September of the year 1684, at five in the afternoon a resplendent procession left the monastery of Santo Domingo with the statue of Our Lady of the Rosary. It was accompanied by all the religious orders, the viceroy, Duke of La Palata, all the togaed gentlemen, the ecclesiastic and secular *cabildos*, and all the *caballeros* lighting the way with their torches. It entered the plaza by way of Las Mantas Street, and in the plaza there was a very large and impressive formation of infantry and cavalry. The procession went along the [street of] scribes to the palace, and from there to the cathedral, where the statue of Our Holy Lady of the Rosary was left for three days with many candles and the main chapel highly adorned. On Sunday, the 17th, as an offering of thanks the father confessor of the viceroy, who was of the Society of Jesus, gave a sermon about the victory of the emperor over the sultan of Turkey.

Monday, the 18th, Father Sotelo of the order of Saint Dominic preached on the same topic; and Tuesday, Maestro Marín of the Mercedarian order gave a sermon on the same [topic]. The viceroy and the gentlemen referred to above attended all three days. Tuesday at five in the afternoon, with the accompaniment and squadron that had been formed, the Holy Virgin [statue] was returned to her home by way of the palace, the street of the *chasque*, and from there to the monastery. Many women went along saying the Rosary in loud voices. It was an act of thanks to Our Lord for the intercession of his Holy Mother in the fortunate outcome of the empire. And so we all beseech Him that He grant [victory] in this South Sea against the enemy pirate who entered about the month of March of 1684.

Fiesta *for the Holy Name of Mary*

Sunday, the 8th of October of the year 1684, the *fiesta* for the name of Mary was held.[59] In the afternoon a procession went forth, very resplendent, accompanied by the viceroy, Duke of La Palata, all the gentlemen of the royal *audiencia*, secular *cabildo*, and all the nobility of the whole city. The bishop of Concepción,

[59] See note 14 for Mary's *fiesta* dates.

Chile, Fray Antonio de Morales of the order of Predicadores who had been provincial of that order, also walked in the procession. In the afternoon there was a squadron made up of a great number of infantry and cavalrymen, very impressive.

Bishop of Concepción Leaves for Chile

Monday, the 16th of October of 1684, the ship carrying the bishop of Concepción, Chile, Fray Antonio de Morales of the order of the Predicadores, left the port of Callao. On the day he left this city, [Archbishop] Don Melchor de Liñán accompanied him in his carriage as far as [the Recollect of] Our Lady of Belén. May God deliver him safely and free of bad tempests and the enemy that is in this South Sea. Amen.

Proclamation Regarding the French

At noon on Wednesday, the 25th of the month of the year 1684, a proclamation was issued that all the French who were in this city of Lima and in all this kingdom must declare themselves, and the property of all those of this city was confiscated. Anyone who held goods in safekeeping for the French would receive very grave penalties. This was by royal decree sent by His Majesty, may God protect him, in retribution for the king of France having done the same with Spaniards in all his kingdom. The viceroy, Duke of La Palata, ordered this proclamation be made public that same day in the same manner used during wartime.

Proclamation About the Armada

The viceroy, Duke of La Palata, issued a proclamation on Tuesday, the 31st of October, that the armada was to leave the port of Callao for Panama on the 1st of January of 1685, without fail, carrying the treasure of His Majesty, may God protect him many years.

Holy Sacrament Placed in the Sagrario Chapel

A procession with all the religious orders left the cathedral at four in the afternoon on Sunday, the 12th of November of 1684, going around the plaza as on the day of Corpus [Christi]. The Holy Sacrament was carried by the archbishop, accompanied by the viceroy, the *audiencia*, and all the nobility of this city; and many altars [were set up along the way]. The Holy Sacrament was deposited that same afternoon [in the cathedral] at the new Sagrario chapel which was adorned magnificently to receive such an important host.

Monday, the 13th, the viceroy, Duke of La Palata, held the

celebration of the Holy Sacrament, and his confessor gave the sermon. Tuesday, all the curates of the cathedral held the celebration, and Father Medina of the Dominican order gave the sermon. The viceroy, *audiencia*, and secular *cabildo* attended the three days. Archbishop Liñán held the celebration on Wednesday, and a religious of the order of Saint Augustine gave the sermon.

There were many fireworks and many dances. All the mulattoes formed an infantry company and had a float that went behind the procession, and there was much to see.

New Steps at the Cathedral

The new steps and railing that lead out into the plaza were finished for the day of the celebration of the placement [of the Holy Sacrament] at the new [chapel of the] Sagrario.

The Year 1685

Don Fernando de Espinosa and the *regidor* Don Domingo de Vilela were elected ordinary *alcaldes* on Monday, the 1st of January of the year 1685.

Display of the Standard

At four in the afternoon on Friday, the 5th of January, 1685, the resplendent royal ensign, Don Pedro Lezcano, carrying the standard set out for vesper services at the cathedral. The viceroy, Duke of La Palata, left the palace on horseback, without a cape, and with all the *oidores* wearing togas, and many *caballeros* in shirt sleeves. After vespers they promenaded through the usual streets. On Saturday, the 6th, day of Epiphany, he went from the palace to the cathedral with the same accompaniment to hear the Mass and sermon.

Decree Regarding Volunteers

By order of the viceroy, Duke of La Palata, a decree was issued the 8th of January that the company of volunteers with its men and flags go to Callao. Any soldier who stayed in Lima and did not follow his flag [would be punished by] two rope treatments (*tratos de cuerda*),[60] and without exception the same penalty to anyone leaving Callao without permission of the camp master.

A Soldier was Maimed

Thursday, the 25th of January, at five in the afternoon one of

[60] *Trato de cuerda* was a torture or punishment inflicted by tying the victim's hands behind his back and then hanging him up by them.

the five soldiers that had been sentenced, having come under the above-mentioned decree, was maimed. His Excellency ordered that lots be drawn [among the five] and the unfortunate one be given two rope treatments. There was a great row by some of the clergy and Mercedarian religious because they wanted to take him down at the second hanging.

Theft of Three Bars of Silver

At dawn of Wednesday, the 31st of January, it was discovered that during that night thieves had stolen three bars of silver valued at four thousand pesos. They climbed the street wall onto the roof where they made a hole and descended to where the treasure was located. There were more than fifty [bars of silver there], and the previous afternoon there had been more than thirty thousand pesos which had just been minted that were taken out by Don Gregorio de Salamanca, the owner of the three bars.

Edict of the Viceroy

Thursday, the 1st of February, the viceroy issued a proclamation promising anyone who revealed who the thieves were, five hundred pesos if they were free and liberty if they were slaves. And even if they were involved in the theft they would be granted amnesty, given the five hundred pesos, and their offense would be pardoned. The stolen three bars, and two other bars, wrought silver, *reales* of eight pesos, and dry goods were discovered at a house adjacent to San Francisco de Paula [church], where the thieves lived with some women.

News of a Shipwreck

Thursday, the 15th of February of the year 1685, news arrived that the ship on which Fray Antonio de Morales, bishop of Concepción, Chile, was traveling, was lost in sight of that port, and forty-one persons were drowned including the bishop. The ship struck a shoal and the navigator, the boatswain, an orderly of the bishop, and six Negro seamen escaped in a boat. The loss caused a great deal of compassion in this city, and it was a full four months from the time that it had left Callao until receipt of the bad news. May God keep all those who drowned in His holy glory. Amen.

Chasque *for Santa Fé de Bogotá*

Thursday, the 22nd of February of the year 1685, at the decree and orders of the viceroy, Duke of La Palata, the *chasque* was to make a run every month from this city of Lima to Quito, [Ecuador], and from there to Santa Fé [de Bogotá, New Granada or

Colombia]. This run of the *chasque* began today, Thursday, the 22nd of February of the year 1685.

New Chapel for Our Lady of Cocharcas

At five in the afternoon of Saturday, the 24th of February of the year 1685, day of the glorious apostle Saint Matthew, a procession left the church of Santa Ana with statues of Saint Joseph, Saint Joachim, and Our Lady of Cocharcas. With great solemnity [the latter] was carried to its new chapel, where it was placed. Don Francisco Colmenares, official of the royal treasury of His Majesty, carried the banner, and the *cabildo* of the city with all its ordinary *alcaldes* marched with their lighted candles. All the streets were hung with flags, and the ground was strewn with many flowers.

Arrival of the Fleet at Cartagena

Saturday, the 3rd of March of 1685, news arrived at this city that the fleet and galleons [from Spain] had arrived at Cartagena on the 28th of November, 1684. Also the ship bringing dispatches from Spain was lost near Barbacoas in this South Sea [Pacific Ocean], while fleeing from the enemy, and more than eight Spaniards drowned. This news came via [runner from] Quito.

Proclamation About the Armada

Sunday, the 4th of this month, a proclamation was issued that the armada for Panama with the treasure of His Majesty and of individuals was to leave the port of Callao on the 1st of April of 1685, without fail.

Proclamation on Tax Exemption

Tuesday, the 27th of this month of March, a proclamation was issued by the viceroy, Duke [of La Palata], stating that he pledged the word of the king, our lord, that no more than seven per cent would be taken by the royal treasury of this city [as a royal tax] on funds sent to be used [for purchases] in Puerto Bello. The [*audiencia*] president of Panama confirmed that he would follow to the letter the decree issued by His Excellency after a council meeting. And if perchance something different should arise in connection with this exemption [from any tax] higher than seven per cent, it would be paid from the royal funds which he pledged in backing the royal promise.

Duke of La Palata to Callao

The viceroy, Duke of La Palata, went to Callao on Monday, the 9th of April of 1685, to send off an armada in search of the enemy that sailed along the coast of Panama waiting for our armada with the treasure of His Majesty and individuals. It was agreed in council that the armada was to go without any silver in search of the enemy.

Edict About the Muster

A proclamation was issued on Tuesday, the 10th of the month, in which His Excellency ordered that all the new soldiers who had enlisted in the volunteers heretofore mentioned, appear to pass muster on Palm Sunday, the 15th of the month. The death penalty for being considered traitors to His Majesty [would apply to those who did not appear].

In this muster they chose the soldiers that were to make up the new infantry companies destined to embark on the ships in the following manner. The consort vessel with forty pieces of artillery and as many artillerymen; the flagship with the same; the ship *San Lorenzo* with much artillery, and many artillerymen and seamen; the same for the ship named *Popolo* and the ship called *Goyeneche*; and the fireship and the king's tender with six pieces of artillery, and soldiers and seamen. These ships all go with superb men and well outfitted with all types of munitions for combat.

The Viceroy Visits the Ships

Wednesday, the 17th of the month, His Excellency boarded all the above-named ships on a visit, and they gave His Excellency a great artillery salute. He was very pleased to see them so well-outfitted and prepared for combat.

Death of the Canon Barreto

The canon Barreto died Tuesday, the 1st of May of 1685, and he was buried in the cathedral.

Death of Bishop Cárdenas

Bishop Don Pedro de Cárdenas died suddenly at his bishopric in Misque. This news reached Lima with the *chasque* on the 4th of May, 1685. He had been consecrated as bishop on Sunday, the 11th of January of 1681.

The Armada Sailed for Panama

At four in the afternoon of Monday, the 7th of May, 1685, the armada set sail from the port of Callao under orders from the viceroy carried out by his brother-in-law, Don Tomás Paravisino, marine general who went in this armada. The admiral was Don Antonio de Beas. The armada carried the treasure of His Majesty, may God protect him, and of individuals who had not wanted to embark nor send their silver for fear of the enemy that was waiting at Isla del Rey [Pearl Islands] near Panama.

The following ships went in this armada in search of the enemy for battle. The escort vessel, carrying twenty-four pieces of artillery and very splendid men and good soldiers, artillerymen, and seamen, and many munitions of war; the flagship with the same munitions, artillery, and good men; the government ship *San Lorenzo* that belongs to His Majesty, with twenty pieces of artillery and a great number of munitions of war, and a good chief, and good artillery soldiers and seamen. A privately-owned ship named *Popolo* carried the same; and another called *Rosario* did likewise. A small tender of His Majesty carried six pieces [of artillery], twelve blunderbusses, and fifty soldiers chosen to the satisfaction of the chief. This man paid the fifty soldiers with his own silver; he is from Vizcaya and has fought many times with the enemy in the Atlantic Ocean. The fireship carried twenty seamen and artillerymen and six pieces of artillery. There were two fireships available, and [since] one was already outfitted for fire, it was the ship that sailed for the government. The other one, belonging to a man from Vizcaya named Don Mende de Antunduaga, was armed for war. Thus seven ships with the tender and the fireship left the port of Callao that same afternoon. May God deliver them safely and may we have very good news and victory against those perverse heretics.

Procession of the Holy Cross

That same day a procession left the cathedral [of Callao] with [statues of] the holy crucified Christ and Saint Francis Xavier. The Viceroy carried the standard, accompanied by many clerics and all the religious of Callao, and they placed [the statues of] the holy Christ and Saint Francis Xavier in the fortress of that city. When they were in position on an ornate platform, the escort ship fired all its artillery and the flagship did the same, followed by all the rest of the ships that were going on this venture. Then all the forts on land fired their salute for the captain general of heaven and earth [Jesus Christ] and his admiral Saint Francis Xavier.

As soon as the referred-to [ceremony] was over, the escort ship set sail, firing many pieces of artillery in salute as [did] the flagship and the other ships that followed. The firing of the artillery pieces in turn as the ships set sail lasted from two in the afternoon until the hour of the Ave Maria; and the viceroy was at the sea wall with the standard in his hand during the whole time. As the ships left the port it was getting dark and the same procession returned to the cathedral, all the music playing, and night closed in.

All the people of the city of Lima were in Callao and the city was empty.

Fourteen Hundred Men in the Armada

In this armada went eight hundred soldiers and six hundred artillerymen and seamen paid for eight months, and all went with great enthusiasm and very content.

The Staff of General

The viceroy presented the staff as maritime and land general and governor of the arms of the presidio of Callao to Señor Don José de Alzamora y Ursino on Thursday, the 10th of May of 1685. It was received with a formation and a great artillery salute.

The soldiers, artillerymen, and seamen were paid on Friday, the 11th of the month. With the year and one month partial payment that they gave us of seven pesos and four [*reales*], it leaves fourteen months [unpaid]. Without deducting these payments all the old soldiers received one hundred and sixty patacoons that day.

The viceroy returned to Lima from Callao with all his family on Sunday, the 13th of the month, after the dispatch of the armada. The archbishop, Don Melchor de Liñán, went out to the countryside to receive His Excellency near the *chácara* of Don Sancho de Castro. As soon as they came upon each other they descended from their carriages and, after many courtesies between the two gentlemen and to the vicereine, the viceroy ascended the carriage of the archbishop and the two gentlemen went together to the palace, accompanying the vicereine as far as the large salon. After a long while the archbishop came out with a great accompaniment of *caballeros* and all those of the family of His Excellency. The whole city was very pleased to see the principal gentlemen [the archbishop and the viceroy] in such good humor and friendship.

Funeral Rites for Father Fray Francisco Delgado

Thursday, the 17th of May of 1685, funeral rites were held over the bones of Father Fray Francisco Delgado, former provincial and commissary general of the order of Saint Francis. He had died in the kingdom of Chile and [his remains] were brought back by the Very Reverend Father Oserín, who had been provincial of the same order, both of whom had been exiled by the commissary Fray Marcos Terán. All of the religious orders went to the funeral rites, and all the nobility of the city of Lima were also present.

The Penitent Procession

Friday, the 25th of the month, a procession with [penitent] blood[61] left [the monastery of] San Juan de Dios at four in the afternoon and went through the whole city. [The procession was held] for the successful outcome of the armada that went to Panama, that God may liberate them from the enemy that awaited at Isla del Rey, and that good news be received. Amen, in Jesus.

Men and Munitions of the Armada

General statement of everything provided for the armada that left the port of Callao on the 7th of May of the year 1685 for Panama to fight with the English enemy that awaited at Isla del Rey [Pearl Islands]. The men and munitions included in this armada are one thousand four hundred and thirty-one posts, without counting the men who embarked on their own, with which the total would amount to one thousand seven hundred men; one hundred and thirty-four pieces of brass artillery; forty-eight slings [for fire balls]; forty-three thousand five hundred and sixty-three pounds of fine and regular gunpowder; four thousand five hundred and sixty-six artillery balls of different calibers; one hundred seven quintals of fuse cord; nine hundred grenades; more than four hundred and fifty *alcancías* [fire balls]; arquebuses and muskets with the guns corresponding to the [number of] men as well as spares. So it appears in the books and lists of the paid officials, from which I have taken this accounting.

Proclamation Heralded at the Street Corners

Friday, the 1st of June of the year 1685, a proclamation was heralded throughout the city at the orders of the viceroy, Duke of La Palata. All those [men] between the ages of fourteen and sixty who were not signed up, must enlist in accordance with the blocks they lived in, and pledge allegiance to the flags in their quarters. All those who did not enlist and were missing would be punished, and they would serve in the port of Callao for two years without salary.

Santiago Concha, general purveyor of the armada of the port

[61] Procession *de sangre* (with blood); see note 30.

Death of Santiago Concha

of Callao, died on Monday, the 4th of June of the year 1685. He was buried Tuesday, the 5th, at the church of the Society of Jesus.

Death of Don Pablo de Lucén

Don Pablo de Lucén, a merchant with wife and children, died on Sunday, the 10th of this month. He had professed as a religious of Saint Dominic, and they buried him as a religious of that order.

Proclamation About Preferential Treatment

A proclamation was issued Monday, the 18th of the month, at the order of the viceroy, Duke of La Palata. All the soldiers that serve in the rank and file companies of this city of Lima would have the same preeminence as the mercenary soldiers if they serve as musketeers. Their captains should have the names of each one, and he should give each soldier his [the captain's] signature so that he may carry it with him. Each captain was to submit a list of those that serve with muskets in his company to the auditor so that he can have them on file; those that were not on the lists of the auditor would not enjoy any rights.

Augustinian Provincial

Saturday, the 21st of July of 1685, the Very Reverend Father Fray Juan de Sanabria, who was prior at Cochabamba this year, was elected Augustinian provincial.

Dominican Provincial

Wednesday, the 24th of the month, the Very Reverend Father Fray Ignacio del Campo was elected Dominican provincial.

News that Arrived via Buenos Aires

A proclamation was issued in this city of Lima on Monday, the 6th of August of 1685, by decree of His Majesty, Charles II, dated in the month of November of last year, 1684. It had come via Buenos Aires and said that a twenty year peace treaty had been signed by our king and lord, His Catholic Majesty Charles II, and the Christian King of France [Louis XIV], to the honor and glory of the Holy Trinity and all of Christianity, and with many agreements between these kings that they will hold and observe all promised, as gentlemen that they are in everything. May God Our Lord protect them, that the faith of Jesus Christ be increased in all the universe. Amen. And there were many other items contained in the peace agreement.

On the corner of the plaza a fire that lasted more than two hours began at four in the afternoon of Saturday, the 18th of August

Fire in the House of Don Pedro de Sosa

of 1685. [It started] in the tallow storeroom of Sergeant Pedro de Sosa, a storekeeper who made candles. More than three hundred quintals of candle grease and more than two hundred jugs of wine were destroyed.

From his windows Archbishop Don Melchor de Liñán ordered that all the clothing and linens that were thrown out of the windows and doors be taken to his palace; even so, much was looted. The one who lost the most was Sergeant Pedro de Sosa as all the melted grease ran out into the street as though it were water, and the fire caused a lot of damage to the buildings. The archbishop kept shouting that no one steal anything or they would be excommunicated under [the provisions of] a papal decree as well as by His Grace, but it was to no avail with the number of all types of people that were around. May God Our Lord grant us His grace and keep us out of such confusion as there was that afternoon.

Placement of the Statue of Saint Rose

At four in the afternoon of Sunday, the 2nd of September of the year 1685, a very solemn procession left the main monastery of Santo Domingo with [statues of] Saint Rose and many saints of the [Dominican] order, and with the Holy Sacrament. In accompaniment were the viceroy, all the *oidores*, the archbishop, and all the people of the entire city. All the streets were neatly hung [with decorations] and the ground covered with orange blossoms. They went to her new church that was marvelously adorned.

That same afternoon the Holy Sacrament and the [statue of] the glorious Saint Rose were installed. There were very solemn vespers, and that night many fireworks and great rejoicing.

Monday, the 3rd, the [Dominican] father provincial, Fray Ignacio del Campo, held the sung Mass, and Father Fray Alvaro de Francia gave the sermon. Viceroy Duke of La Palata and all the *audiencia* were at the Mass and sermon, and it was His Excellency who sponsored the celebration. Archbishop Don Melchor de Liñán y Cisneros was also present.

An octave is being held for the celebration of Saint Rose; on Tuesday the archbishop will hold the celebration; Wednesday, the *oidores*; and the rest of the tribunals follow [in sponsoring celebrations the remaining days of the octave].

Tuesday, the 4th of September, at three in the afternoon news arrived at this city that our flagship, escort, and the other ships,

News of the Battle with the Enemy

after having disembarked the silver in Panama, left in search of the enemy and encountered them at Isla del Rey, where they fought. They defeated the enemy and the latter did not wait, but fled. Although there were eight enemy ships with sails, only two had come into this sea; the others were ships that they had pillaged and large canoes. They left all of the latter as they were loaded with supplies, and with their two ships they fled, one of them being badly damaged and listing.

That same afternoon there was great rejoicing and ringing of the bells and at night many fireworks and festive lights.

Masquerade

The night of Wednesday, the 5th, there was a masquerade of many *caballeros* and ordinary *alcaldes* of the city.

The viceroy went to Santo Domingo [church] the same afternoon the news arrived to give thanks to Our Lord and his Holy Mother, the Holy Virgin of the Rosary, for the successful arrival of the treasure at Panama.

Proclamation

Thursday, the 13th of September of 1685, His Excellency ordered a proclamation issued that all those [merchants] who were assigned to go to Puerto Bello be ready by the 1st of October, because another small armada was to leave the port of Callao on the day mentioned, without fail, as a result of an agreement reached in council.

Loss of the Escort with Four Hundred Men

At ten in the morning of Wednesday, the 19th of September of the year 1685, news reached this city that at four in the afternoon on the 5th of this month, the royal escort ship of this South Sea that had gone to Panama with the treasure of His Majesty and of individuals, had been consumed by fire. After having fought and repelled the enemy, who fled, it went to Paita, and while General Don Tomás Paravisino was on land with some of his retinue, [apparently] through some carelessness, the powder magazine caught fire and blew up the ship with more than four hundred men who were aboard. May God keep them in His holy glory. This has been the greatest and saddest loss to occur in this Southern Sea, which probably will not be likened in a lifetime.

Saturday, the 22nd of the month, funeral rites were held in the cathedral for the deceased who died in the burning of the escort ship at Paita. They were very solemn and held at the expense of His Majesty, with the viceroy and all the *oidores*, secular *cabildo* and other tribunals, and all the nobility of the city present, as well as the archbishop and his *cabildo*. The catafalque was very ostentatious with many candles. There were many Masses prayed and two hundred pesos were given to all the monasteries so that an additional number of Masses would be said for the deceased.

Funeral Rites for the Deceased

Monday, the 24th of the month, a proclamation was issued by decree of His Majesty, may God protect him, that no one going in this second armada to trade in Puerto Bello could take bars of silver, nor unrefined silver, nor any flat silver without paying the *quinto real* [twenty per cent royal tax]. Penalty would be confiscation [of the silver], half of the violator's property, and ten years in Valdivia.

Proclamation on Silver Bars

Nor could those who went to Puerto Bello to trade buy any gold or silver needlepoint, nor laces, under penalty that all [contraband] would be burned, and other severe punishment, by order of the new decree of His Majesty, May God protect him.

Wednesday, the 10th of October, at three in the afternoon His Excellency left the palace with his whole family for Callao in order to dispatch the second armada of merchants. These were the ones who had remained behind, not wishing to embark in the first armada that left the 7th of May, for fear of the English enemy who awaited at Isla del Rey.

The Viceroy to Callao

Wednesday, the 24th of the month, a proclamation was issued by His Excellency that no silver sent in boxes could be embarked unless it was aboard the flagship or escort, which were designated as assuring more safety in reaching the port of Paita, where the royal armada awaited to go to Panama and Puerto Bello for duty. Penalty [for disobeyance] would be four thousand pesos for the masters of the ships and the captains, loss of all their goods, and four months exile at the presidio of Valdivia.

Proclamation about Shipment of Silver

Tuesday, the 6th of November, His Excellency ordered the prior and consuls and all the merchants to go to Callao. He gave them a long speech about the harm that resulted from their not having embarked in the armada that left Callao the 7th of May

Departure of the Consulado *for Callao*

of that year 1685, and the burning of the escort ship in Paita, and he asked them for five hundred thousand pesos for damage and expenses that they had caused His Majesty. Until they were collected, His Excellency ordered that no merchant nor consul leave Callao, and that posts be set up at all the entrances of Callao with soldiers and sergeants on active duty. The merchants would be obligated to give one hundred thousand pesos on the return of the armada from Panama; if not, they would have to build, at their own expense, two large warships in Guayaquil. As soon as His Excellency gave the order, the posts at the gates of Callao were set up.

Death of the Canon Olea

Wednesday, the 7th of November of 1685, as the Holy Sacrament was being taken to the canon Don Melchor de Avendaño, present commissary of the Holy Crusade, and while carrying one pole of the canopy, the canon Don Bernardo Arma de Olea died. He had just been made canon twenty days before; previously he had been a fully endowed prebendary. He was buried at the cathedral on Thursday, the 8th.

The Second Armada

The second armada to leave Callao in the year 1685 left on Friday, the 17th of November, at seven in the morning, with all the merchants that did not go in the previous armada that sailed from Callao the 7th of May of that year 1685. In this last armada, on which Don García de Hijar y Sarmiento went as chief, well over twenty million [pesos] left for Spain and for purchases in Puerto Bello. Five ships left Callao with the flagship and escort, and only the latter two with artillery. There was no military guard because the merchants were to act as soldiers until they reached Paita where they would join the first armada that had left in search of the enemy. Don Tomás Paravisino went as general.

Viceroy Returns from Callao

His Excellency with all his family returned to Lima from Callao on Sunday, the 18th of November, after having dispatched the second armada with all the merchants for Panama.

Law Books Sent by His Majesty

Monday, the 19th of November of 1685, the six large boxes of books sent by His Majesty, Charles II, may God protect him, were opened in a royal council meeting. Each *oidor* was given four of those law books, which contain a brief treatment of all types of litigations.

The Day of the Sweet Name of Mary

Sunday, the 12th of December of the year 1685, a *fiesta* was held for the sweet name of Mary. It is [normally] held every year on the second Sunday of October,[62] but this year it was delayed because His Excellency was in Callao dispatching the second armada that left for Panama with all the treasure and those who were to trade at Puerto Bello. In this celebration Don José de Alzamora Urzino appeared in the plaza as general of Callao, his present position.

The Year 1686

Tuesday, the 1st of January of the year 1686, elected as ordinary *alcaldes* of Lima were Don Domingo de Zúñiga y Torres, who had been *alcalde* in the year 1668, and Don Diego Tebes Manrique.

Provincial Chapter of San Francisco

Saturday, the 5th of January of the year 1686, a general chapter was convened in the main monastery of San Francisco, and this same day the establishment of provincial alternates was confirmed. In this first chapter the Very Reverend Father Fray Diego Felipe, present superior of the Spanish Descalzos [barefoot monks], was elected provincial. In another chapter a creole provincial [will be elected]. The Very Reverend Father Fray Félix Como, who was confessor of the viceroy, Marquis of Malagón and Count of Castellar, was the commissary general.

All the religious were quite pleased and very much in accord, because for the last seven years the religious from Spain and the creoles [from America] had had a great number of disagreements and there was much discontent. May God keep them in peace and in agreement for His honor. Amen.

Ensign Horseshoer Killed

The ensign horseshoer of the regular company of Captain Don Pedro Córdoba was killed at noon on Monday, the 28th of January of the year 1686. It happened in his own shop where he was working, and he did not have time to confess. May God grant him forgiveness. Amen, in Jesus.

Ban on Mutton

Tuesday, the 19th of February of the year 1686, His Excellency issued a proclamation that no landowner of *chácaras* could sell meat or have more than one hundred sheep for sustenance, and when they were gone, another hundred. If more were found, he

[62] See note 14 for Mary's *fiesta* dates.

[the landowner] would be subject to stiff fines which would be applied towards the cost of the construction of the wall [around Lima].

That same day, the 19th of February, a proclamation was issued that no mulatto woman or Negress could resell meat, under penalty of one hundred lashes and fifty pesos to be paid by her master. Butchers who sold meat to these women retailers [would receive] one hundred lashes and six years on [San Lorenzo] Island, off Callao, carrying rocks for the wall of Callao. So that these penalties would be severely executed, the chief constable of the city, Don Nicolás de Torres, was appointed judge of these cases.

Death of the Canon Avendaño

Don Diego de Avendaño, doctor, canon, and present commissary of the Holy Crusade, died on the night of the 25th of February of 1686, the last Monday before Lent. He was buried on Ash Wednesday, the 27th of the month, at the cathedral. Funeral rites were held on Thursday, the 28th.

Juan Infante Trujillo Died

He died on Wednesday, the 27th of the month, and left more than four hundred thousand pesos in *reales*, and a very large hacienda that he had in Huaura, the greater part to his nephew. He left another one [hacienda] of considerable value that he had in Chancay to the fathers of the Society of Jesus who assist at the church of the Desamparados, where he was buried on Thursday, the 28th of the month.

Oidor *Don José Calvo Died*

He died on Friday, the 1st of March of the year 1686. He left many children and all very poor. He was buried Saturday, the 2nd, in the monastery or church of San Francisco with a large attendance of the viceroy, *audiencia*, and the two *cabildos*.

Proclamation Regarding Soldiers

Saturday, the 16th of the month, a proclamation was issued that soldiers who had a designated post should confirm it within four days and they would be given their pay. Action would be taken against all who did not do so.

Decree to Work on the Wall

Sunday, the 17th of the month, a decree was issued that all bricklayers and laborers go to work on the wall [around Lima] to complete it as soon as possible, under penalty of twenty pesos [fine for those who did not obey]. All [other] construction work in the city was to cease.

Call to Arms

At ten on the night of Friday, the 19th of April of the year 1686, the general of Callao, Alzamora, advised His Excellency that there were two large ships behind the island [of San Lorenzo, off Callao]. His Excellency immediately came from the palace, and a call to arms was quickly executed. Accompanied by many soldiers, he visited all the [military] quarters on foot, but at dawn it was ascertained that the two ships were [Spanish] ones coming from Chile. Since the enemy had sacked the city of Saña only a few days ago, everyone was very apprehensive.

The Enemy Entered Chérrepe

At the beginning of Lent of the year 1686 the enemy entered the port of Chérrepe [in northwestern Peru]. From there they marched five days with soldiers to the city of Saña, which is seven leagues away, and entering it sacked what they could with no one to prevent them. The present *corregidor* of that city was Don Luis Venegas Osorio, the man who came [from Spain] as battle sergeant major. The viceroy, Duke of La Palata, ordered that he be brought as a prisoner [to Lima], but he remained in Trujillo as he was ill.

Later, at the beginning of April, [the enemy] left for Paita where they captured two ships that had just arrived from Panama two days before, one loaded with more than three hundred recently-imported Negroes and many Spanish passengers and Franciscan religious that were coming from Spain. The enemy demanded ransom for the seculars and religious.

In Colán they broke open many bales and sold the clothing to the Indians very cheaply telling them they did not want clothing, only silver. And they ravaged any number of the Indian women, married and single, without respect for their age, young or old. May God remedy the situation with His divine power. Amen.

News arrived Tuesday at midnight, the 14th of May, that the enemy had entered Huacho and had burned the town on Monday, the 13th of that month. Then they marched on to Huaura and entered that town on Tuesday, taking up lodgings at the Franciscan monastery of the Descalzos. They imprisoned everyone they found, which totaled eighteen families.

Aid for Huacho

Wednesday, the 15th, His Excellency dispatched more than two hundred soldiers for Chancay and Huaura, one hundred musketeers and a hundred cavalrymen of the mercenary soldiers of the guard of His Excellency. His Excellency ordered that each soldier be given two patacoons apiece. Thus they left Lima at ten o'clock on May the 15th with good commanders, who were Don Nuño Villavicencio, [member] of the order of Alcántara and son-in-law of Don Baltasar Pardo, as lieutenant general of the cavalry; and as general of the infantry, Don Blas de Corral, present captain of the infantry of the presidio of Callao and appointed sergeant major of the battalion of Lima by His Excellency. He was a good soldier and an expert in formations. Don Julián de Corbeira, former sergeant major of this battalion, was given the staff of lieutenant to the general battalion commander; and Don Pedro de Mendoza, who had been general battalion commander, was retired and granted the same salary [he had been earning] for the many services that he and his father had performed for His Majesty.

Loss of the Ship Headed for Panama

Thursday, the 16th, news arrived that the ship His Excellency had dispatched with four thousand *fanegas* [or 64,000 bushels] of flour for aid to the armada that was in Panama as well as for that city, had been lost at La Herradura, near Huaura. Before the succor sent by His Excellency arrived, the enemy withdrew its ships.

Sunday, the 19th, news arrived that Domingo de la Carrera had fought at Huaura with the enemy, and [he and his men] had killed four Englishmen and the ensign. Since our men were few, they [the enemy] took the said Domingo de la Carrera and many other persons as prisoners and requested eighteen thousand pesos ransom for them. Two thousand three hundred [pesos] were forwarded, but in return they sent the head of the said Domingo de la Carrera and his superintendent, who was a large landowner of Huaura, and [advised] that if the adjusted eight thousand pesos were not sent they would do the same with all those held prisoner.

Wednesday, the 22nd of this month, the cavalry company of the guard of His Excellency and the rest of the infantry that had gone as relief arrived back at this city of Lima. They left the enemy at La Barranca with their two large ships and three small ones.

Proclamation to Enlist Men

Wednesday, the 22nd of May, His Excellency issued a proclamation throughout the whole city and San Lázaro. All persons who were able to take up arms in the defense of this city and their homes and property, exempting no one, should enlist by Sunday, the 26th of the month. All those who offered their services would be enlisted in the same company and kept apart so that His Excellency could assign their posts. Those who did not obey would be given grave penalties in accordance with their positions, and those who were not such [of a certain prominence or position], two years exile in the fortress [of Valdivia].

Another Proclamation to Search for the Enemy

Wednesday, the 29th of the month, a proclamation was issued stating that His Excellency was preparing two ships and a tender to go in search of the pirates that were robbing the ports and the valleys. All those who wished to embark on this mission would be granted, in the name of His Majesty, may God protect him, all that they captured in the vessels of the pirate with the exception of the ship and the pieces of artillery which would be divided among the commander, whoever he was, and all the soldiers. In the proclamation he did not designate any salary for those who embarked.

Another Proclamation Granting them Salary

Friday, the 31st of the month, His Excellency had another proclamation issued: that those who enlisted as soldier, sailor, or artilleryman would be given four months pay. [It would be given] only to those who embarked for the purpose of going in search of the enemy.

This same day a dispatch ship arrived with news that on Sunday, the 26th of the month, the pirates had entered the town of Huarmey, and the *corregidor* was shot in the leg, but he escaped. The pirates did not find anything in this town as everyone had withdrawn to the mountains.

Sunday, the 27th of May, the archbishop ordered all the priests to enlist [in the army] and more than five hundred enlisted, not counting the ones assigned to the church [cathedral]. His Grace named nine of the priests as captains; the first was the licentiate Jáuregui, chaplain of the city jail chapel; [the second,] the licentiate Don Gonzalo de Zavala; and another seven whose names I do not know. Each captain was assigned fifty of the enlisted priests to take up the flag at the guard posts they were assigned, for the guard and custody of the convents of nuns.

Proclamation to Pass Muster Thursday, the 4th of July of the year 1686, the viceroy ordered a proclamation issued that all soldiers, artillerymen, sailors, and shipboys would pass muster at Callao on Saturday, the 6th of the month, for the trip to be made in search of the enemy pirates. Penalty for those who failed to appear would be three rope treatments[63] and four years in Valdivia.

Departure of His Excellency for Callao At three in the afternoon of Sunday, the 7th of the month, the viceroy left the palace and went directly to see the archbishop in his palace. After a long while His Excellency came out from his visit and departed for Callao.

At ten in the morning of this Sunday, the 7th of the month, all the soldiers, the Spaniards [officers], and the companies of mulattoes were embarked on the ships that were to go in search of the enemy.

Departure of the Small Armada At four in the afternoon of Tuesday, the 9th of July, the small armada of flagship, escort vessel, and another ship, with a great number of infantry and well outfitted with artillery, left the port of Callao in search of the enemy. Don Francisco de Zúñiga, *caballero* of the order of Santiago and present battalion commander of Callao, went as chief and commander. Don Gaspar de Manzanilla, present infantry captain of the presidio, went in the flagship for His Majesty, and Pedro García San Roque, with eighty courageous mulatto soldiers, was aboard the tender. On this day they gave all the soldiers who embarked an advance of ten pesos.

His Excellency returned to Lima the same afternoon that he dispatched the small armada.

The Enemy Entered Coquimbo Saturday, the 13th of the month, news arrived from Coquimbo in the kingdom of Chile that the enemy had entered that town. Many of them had gone ashore to kill, and the inhabitants, who could not have been even twelve, attacked two [of them]. They caught one who was a Catholic from France, and they sent him to Lima to His Excellency.

That same Saturday at three in the afternoon news arrived that the enemy had entered Pisco on Thursday, the 11th of July. They

[63] For penalty of rope treatment, see note 60.

seized the fort along with five pieces of artillery, fifty mercenary soldiers, and the women that were inside the fort.

The Procession

At four in the afternoon of that same day, Saturday the 13th of July of the year 1686, a procession left the cathedral for [the church of] San Pedro with [a statue of] Saint Philip Neri and the image of Our Lady that was dedicated to the church. It was a painting brought from Rome and donated by [Innocent XI], the highest pontiff who governs the church this year of 1686. Father Alonso Riero brought it from Rome, and it was placed on the altar of the church of San Pedro that same day.

Sunday, the 14th, His Excellency sponsored the *fiesta* and that day his confessor gave the sermon. Monday, the 15th, the archbishop held the celebration, and Father Fray Matías Lisperguer of the order of Saint Augustine gave the sermon. Tuesday, the 16th, the celebration was held by a married matron, and this day the Very Reverend Father Fray Bartolomé de Sotomayor of the Mercedarian order gave the sermon.

News from Pisco

Thursday, the 18th of the month, the viceroy received news that the enemy had taken over the fortress at Pisco along with five pieces of artillery and many persons, and had imprisoned them, asking ransom for the prisoners. A *caballero* and sergeant major of that port, Don Ventura de Ysásiga, sent three men with a ransom of twenty thousand pesos for all the prisoners. They received the twenty thousand pesos and beheaded those that brought the silver. At this point the men from the district of Cañete under Martín de la Cueva arrived, and the men from Ica with Don Pedro Zigarra, and our men attacked the fortress killing forty-seven Englishmen. They left through a breach they had opened in order to get into the fortress. In this encounter with the enemy nine of them were wounded very badly, and the number of deaths ascended to fifty-one. On our side twenty-five Spaniards, Negroes, and mulattoes were killed. After this they sent the prisoners, except four that they held as hostages, asking two thousand jugs of water [ransom] for them. This is what has happened up to the present time.

Image of Christ Placed in the Society of Jesus Church

That same day at four in the afternoon a procession left the Desamparados [church] with [an image of] Christ to be placed in the church of the Society of Jesus. A great number of people participated.

Procession of the Jesuits Saturday, the 20th of July of 1686, at eight at night the fathers of the Society of Jesus went forth with [an image of] Christ and many lights, preaching through the city of Lima and advocating penance and avoidance of sin.

News from Spain Sunday, the 4th of August, letters arrived from Spain saying that the inquisitor Bruna was coming as bishop of Huamanga and the one in Huamanga was going to be coadjutor of the bishop of Quito.

Habits The habit of Santiago [was granted] to the present sergeant major of the merchant [company], Don Francisco de Oyague. It was also given to Don Santiago de Urdanegui, who is in Puerto Bello, having gone there to trade; and to Pedro Baquero, present treasurer of the holy Inquisition.

Don Luis Venegas Osorio, battle sergeant general, died at the port of Callao where he was imprisoned. He was in prison at the orders of His Excellency for having allowed the enemy to enter the city of Saña while he was *corregidor* of that city for His Majesty, may God protect him. He died Tuesday, the 13th of August of the year 1686, and was buried the following Wednesday as a prisoner and private individual. He was buried in the church at Callao.

President of Las Charcas Señor Don Diego Messía, *oidor* and former president of this royal *audiencia*, left this city to become president of Las Charcas. With a large number of followers, he departed at three in the afternoon of Saturday, the 17th of the month of August, with all his family including his daughter who was going to marry the court *alcalde* and present governor of Huancavelica, Don Juan Luís López. That same afternoon they stopped to rest at San Juan, the *hacienda* of the fathers of the Society of Jesus.

Inquisition Auto-da-fé Saturday, the 28th of September of this year, eight men were sentenced in the chapel of the Inquisition for being married two, three, four, and five times; and others for other offenses they committed. Among them was one called Jorge Varillas, which was an assumed name, for being married twice. Of these eight, only three were flogged through the streets.

Arrival of General Paravisino in Lima

Wednesday, the 2nd of October of this year, Don Tomás Paravisino, who was general of the armada that left the port of Callao on Monday, the 7th of May of 1685, with the treasure of His Majesty, may God protect him, and individuals, arrived back at Lima coming overland from Paita. Because of ill health, he left the armada, which was returning from Panama with many ships loaded with dry goods, in charge of Admiral Don Antonio de Beas. The day that the general returned to this city there was much rejoicing for his arrival.

Bullfights for the King's Birthday

Saturday, the 9th of November of the year 1686, bulls were run in the plaza of Lima. Before they started, General Don Tomás Paravisino with the receiver general, Don Diego Hurtado, and Don Sebastián Franco, rode around the plaza three times on the footboard of a carriage. It was a very happy afternoon.

Second Bullfights

Wednesday, the 13th of this month and year, the second bulls were run in the plaza, with the same ride [around the plaza] of the general. They were better bulls than on the first day.

[Subsequent notations in this journal were made by Francisco de Mugaburu, son of Josephe de Mugaburu y Honton.]

Death of my Beloved Father, Captain Mugaburu

My beloved father, Captain Don Josephe de Mugaburu y Honton, having been taking a cure for two months to get rid of his ailments, died on Tuesday, the 12th of November of the year 1686, between six and seven in the morning. After [suffering] pain and a burning sensation in the kidneys, a throbbing from stomach to chest overtook him, and on the night of the 11th of November he expelled some blood clots. He calmed down and then at five in the morning started to expel them again, with which, finally, between six and seven he emitted [blood] through his mouth and nose until he expired. In his infirmity he received the viaticum twice and holy oil once. He confessed many times, leaving sure hopes for his salvation, as much for his good life as by his moral death. He died at the age of eighty years minus two months more or less.

His Burial

Wednesday, the 13th of the month, between nine and ten in the morning he was buried in [the chapel of] La Soledad with a Mass with the body present and as much decorum as my strength allowed. I buried him at this hour because it was an afternoon of bullfights. We attended the funeral wearing long black mourning cloaks.

Memorial Funeral Rites

Thursday, the 14th of this month, I held memorial funeral rites for my father in the convent of [Nuestra Señora del] the Prado. Nineteen prayed Masses were held for him.

Election of the General Procurator

Sunday, the 3rd of November, an election was held in the Jesuit Society for general procurator for Rome, and Father Nicolás de Olea was elected, to the satisfaction of all. He was the present secretary of the Very Reverend Father Provincial, Martín de Jáuregui; and in second place, Father Juan de Sotomayor, present rector in Cuzco.

Election of the Abbess of La Encarnación

Thursday, the 14th of November of the year 1686, Doña [blank] de Becerra was elected abbess of the convent of La Encarnación. La Cabrera was slighted, and her following staged a large demonstration against the one elected, even breaking her chair and tearing apart her cushion. His Illustrious Grace excommunicated her and [threatened] punishment if they continued in disobedience.

General Paravisino Departs for Callao

At dawn that same Thursday news arrived that the flagship, escort vessel, and other ships were about to enter the port. That same morning the general went to receive them and pay the men.

Death of Doña Agustina de Vega

Doña Agustina de Vega, wife of Don Sebastián de Colmenares, present inspector general of these kingdoms who had been secretary of the Count of Lemos, died on Thursday, the 7th of November of the year 1686. This lady died just after returning from Spain with her husband and family, where they had looked after her mother. She was buried in [the church of] La Merced.

Payment of the Armada

Wednesday, the 20th of November, payment was begun for the seamen who had just arrived, and also for the infantry of the presidio. The payment went on for several days with stopping due to the delayed arrival of *El Popolo*, a ship of mercenary soldiers.

Fiesta *for Father Martín de Porres*

The 23rd of November of the year 1686 the file of information on the servant of God, Fray Martín de Porres, was closed. Between one and two in the afternoon the closed file was taken from the cathedral to the monastery of Santo Domingo, accompanied by all the Dominican order, the chief constable of the city, and many illustrious persons. All the mulatto women came out with banners, dancing ahead in great joy and taking among them in a prominent place a little mulatto girl who was a relative of the glorious servant of God. With this file of documents his beatification can begin.[64]

This same day without prior notification the Very Reverend Father Fray Ignacio del Campo arrived, to the great joy of the whole community. At night lights burned throughout all the streets of Lima and there were bonfires at Santo Domingo for the glorious servant of God, by order of a proclamation issued by the ordinary *alcaldes* Don Diego Tebes and Don Yñigo de Zúñiga, with grave penalties [for non-observance].

The Lima Mint

From the 1st of December of 1683, when the Lima mint was inaugurated, until the end of October of 1685 there have been minted 7,762,878 pesos. Of those, His Majesty received as seigniorage 115,864 pesos. The rights of mintage have yielded 212,026 pesos of which His Excellency only collected 60,745 pesos because the remaining 151,281 pesos were distributed in operating costs and salaries to officials of the mint. Thus for both items [seigniorage and mintage rights] the royal treasury has collected 179,609 pesos, and the total profit of the works up to the end of October, 1685, amount to 327,890 pesos.

Parade of the Flag

Saturday, the 23rd of November of the year 1686, Don Francisco de Oyague, *caballero* of the order of Santiago and sergeant major of the merchant [company], brought out the flag in the parade for the beatification certificate for the two glorious servants of God, Fray Pedro de Urraca and Fray Gonzalo [illegible].

[64] Martín de Porres, son of a Spanish nobleman, Don Juan de Porres, and a free Negress, Anna Velásquez, was born in Lima in 1579 and he died in that city in 1639. His piety and service as a Dominican friar led to his beatification and, three centuries later, his canonization in 1962. *New Catholic Encyclopedia*, XI, 595–96.

There was a large crowd. All the religious of the Mercedarian order paraded, and on the right side of the flag was the Very Reverend Father Maestro Fray Juan Beas, prime professor of the royal university, and the Very Reverend Father Maestro Fray Vera on the left, both very solemn.

That night there was much rejoicing. Four fireworks pieces were exploded in the large plaza and two at La Merced [church]. The parade was held in the late afternoon.

Death of Don Nuño de la Cueva

Don Nuño de la Cueva, *caballero* of the order of San Juan [de Jesusalén], died suddenly on Friday, the 22nd of November. He was buried in San Agustín [church].

Father Soto's Finger is Cut Off

Wednesday, the 13th of November of the year 1686, a chorister and cellmate cut off a finger of the Very Reverend Father Sotomayor, present prefect of [the Mercedarian Recollect] Belén. It was a grevious offense, as much for his being a prelate as for being a learned and important man. He cut it off because the Father Maestro, missing a number of pesos from his trunk, wanted to catch him to find out [if he was the culprit], but he [the chorister] took out a machete and attacked him. The chorister is a son of Don Alonso Lazo, *regidor* and former *alcalde* of this city. The amount [involved] was nine hundred pesos, and the finger cut was the index finger.

Proclamation About the Excise Tax

Thursday, the 28th of November, a proclamation was issued by the viceroy, Duke of La Palata, exacting a penalty on all those who left Lima with dry goods without having paid the excise tax.

Second Proclamation

Friday, the 29th of this month and year, the viceroy, Duke of La Palata, issued a proclamation that no ship whatsoever leave the port, under grave penalty.

Death of the Marchioness of Rivas

The Marchioness of Rivas died on Tuesday, the 3rd of December of the year 1686, between eight and nine in the morning. She was the daughter of Coca and the brother of the Count of Salvatierra, Don Alvaro de Luna, and wife of the Marquis of Rivas who was a nephew of the Marchioness of Malagón and a former general of the port of Callao.

She was buried in San Francisco [church] on Wednesday, the

4th of the month. The body was carried in a carriage, and the viceroy, Duke of La Palata, who was already at the church, went out to the door and escorted the Marquis at his side. They seated him after the *alcalde* Tebes.

That same afternoon a young daughter of Tomás de Mollinedo, nephew of the bishop of Cuzco, was buried in the same monastery. The catafalque was black for the Marchioness, and then they removed these coverings and the catafalque [for the young girl] was covered with mirrors, which is as it was ordered. The abovementioned Tomás was married to a daughter of Azaña.

Funeral Rites for the Marchioness

Thursday the 5th, memorial funeral rites were held in the same monastery, attended by the viceroy and the archbishop, who on the day of the burial went to the house of the deceased but did not go to the church.

Death of Bishop Don Nicolás de Ulloa

News of the death [in Tucumán] of Señor Don Fray Nicolás de Ulloa, Augustinian religious who had been professor in this royal university and prior of his order, arrived on Tuesday, the 3rd of December of the year 1686.

Dispatch Ship from Spain

The dispatch ship from Spain arrived Sunday, the 15th of December of the year 1686, and brought news that the [*audiencia*] president of Panama had sent three hundred men in three ships, well equipped with arms, grenades, etcetera, to Coiba Island [in the Pacific Ocean off Panama]. When they encountered the enemy, one of the ships caught fire and the enemy captured the other two, destroying the lives of many men and imprisoning the others.

[News of the following appointments also came in the dispatch ship.] The Canon Don Agustín Negrón, appointed treasurer; the prebendary Doctor Don Bartolomé Velarde, present professor of arts in this royal university [appointed] canon; Don Francisco Garcés de Cartagena, who was a Jesuit and presently in Spain, [appointed] prebendary. Don Andrés de Paredes, lawyer of this royal *audiencia*, [appointed] as fiscal of the royal *audiencia* of Quito.

Procession of the Papal Bull

Friday, the 20th of December of the year 1686, the [papal] bull of the holy Crusade was taken in procession, and Saturday, the 21st of the month and year, the customary Mass and procession at San Francisco was celebrated. Don Diego de Salazar was commissary of the holy Crusade.

New Carmelite Convent

Saturday, the 21st of December of 1686, [four] Carmelite nuns left the old convent to found a new one near Chacarilla. Their departure was as follows. At three in the afternoon His Grace the archbishop of this city, Don Melchor de Liñán y Cisneros, arrived, and at the door in the presence of the entire community he requested to hear the contents of the decree stating that the four religious would leave to found the new convent. They were named Antonia María de la Santísima Trinidad, María Alberta de Jesús, and Francisca [blank], these three professed nuns, and Marina, a novice, all of whom were to be brought to Her Excellency, Señora Doña Francisca de Toralto, Duchess of La Palata and present vicereine, [who was] to take them to the new convent where they would be cloistered. Antonia María was to be the prioress; Alberta, [mother] superior; and Francisca, door keeper.

In the midst of this ceremony when the decree had been made known, the viceroy, Duke of La Palata, arrived with the vicereine and their daughter, Doña Elvira. There were many tears among the nuns that were leaving and those that were staying, and witty remarks and courtesies exchanged between the principal parties. [The four nuns] came out, and the vicereine took Antonia with her right hand and Alberta with her left hand, while her daughter took Francisca, and the novice went ahead alone. They entered the church to pray and upon leaving all of them bowed to the chorus, the weeping continuing. The vicereine took the four nuns in her carriage [seating them] in the best place. The vicereine sat on one footboard and her daughter on the other. The nuns kept objecting [to having the best seats] until the archbishop ordered them to obey. The viceroy took the archbishop in his carriage at his right, and they went to the Society [of Jesus] where the Holy Sacrament that was to be placed [at the new convent] was located.

All the fathers of the [Jesuit] Society and the community of Saint Francis came out to receive them as well as those of Saint Augustine, and many Mercedarians and Dominicans. There the archbishop put on his pontifical attire, took the monstrance, and the procession began. [The statue of] Saint Ann, whose patronage was chosen for the new foundation, was carried on a litter, and ahead of the holy mother, [the statue of Saint] Theresa de Jesús, then the canopy carried by the *oidores*, followed by the preceptress, then the nuns and the vicereine, and finally the viceroy. They went by way of Estudios Street, and from there directly to their convent. The walls were hung with an incredible grandeur of engravings, canvases [paintings], and tapestries. At the gate of the college of San Martín, the collegiates, whose rector was Father Oña, set up an altar that could not be improved upon in art and in grandeur. They arrived at their permanent quarters with the great rejoicing of the whole city that attended the celebration.

The following day, Sunday, the 22nd of this month and year, the archbishop sang the pontifical Mass in the new convent. Father Francisco López, confessor of His Excellency the viceroy, gave a fitting sermon; he praised the founder of the work and house, the inquisitor Don Pedro de la Cantera, whose personal work has been without equal and well known. And the viceroy gave a rich tapestry, a canvas, and other valuables for the main altar.

Procession of Saint Roche for the Plague

Monday, the 23rd of December of this month and year, [the statue of] the glorious Saint Roche was taken in a procession of supplication from the cathedral to [the parish church of] San Sebastián. The following day Mass was sung to him, with great solemnity, that he beseech Our Lord to liberate this city from the present great plague of smallpox affecting the little angels [children] as well as the adults. May God help us.

Death of the Licentiate Dávila

The licentiate José Dávila died at ten in the morning of Monday, the 30th of December of the year 1686, while he was setting up chaplaincies and doing private work for the convent of [San José de las Monjas] Descalzas at the Huaquilla of Santa Ana. He died with the reputation of being just.

The little son of Basualdo died this same day.

The Year 1687

Wednesday, the 1st of January of the year 1687, Don Pedro Zegarra, a private *caballero*, and the *regidor* Don José de Agüero were elected ordinary *alcaldes* of this city. Zegarra put into service a marvellous carriage and much livery.

Funeral Rites for Bishop Ulloa

Memorial funeral rites for Señor Fray Nicolás de Ulloa were held on Saturday, the 11th of January of 1687, in his monastery of San Agustín where he had been prior. Father Maestro Fray José de Prado of the same [Augustinian] order gave the sermon. All the *caballeros* of the city attended with long capes. All the prelates of the religious orders chanted the Mass. The present provincial of his religious order, the Very Reverend Father Maestro Fray Juan de Sanabria, sang the Mass. The catafalque was the most magnificent seen in these times because it was all in black velvet and lined in silver. The archbishop attended with his *cabildo*.

I do not want to omit recording here a very special theological text brought by the preacher to review how he [Bishop Ulloa] had died. It was about Nebuchadnezzar, who lived miraculously for seven years among the beasts after God had deprived him of his authority, grandeur, and power in the sciences, in which he was very learned. Then he [the preacher] said, "Our illustrious prelate was taken from this court, leaving behind his acclaim, and he was separated from his dealings in the [sciences and] letters and cast out to Tucumán [Argentina], where the most that can be found are mules. He lived there miraculously for seven years and finally died from being there. It should be known that he was a bishop for seven years."

Procession of the Rosary

Saturday, the 18th of January of the year 1687, at four in the afternoon [the statue of] Our Lady of the Rosary was taken in procession from Santo Domingo [church]. It went along Pozuelo and Las Mantas Streets, then entered the plaza, where a well-organized squadron was formed that gave a [gun] salute and the flags were lowered. Then it returned to the [mother] house along the post office street. The archbishop, the viceroy, and the *audiencia* attended the procession. The image was brought forth on a new litter of silver which had been made for it by the sodality; it was exquisite. The purpose of this procession was the debut of the new altarpiece of Our Lady and the placement of the holy image in its new chapel. It had been left on the main altar while the new chapel was being built next to the one of the Gospel; the previous one had been next to [that of] the Epistle. Four days of celebration were held. On the first day the Very Reverend Father Maestro Fray Diego Morato gave the sermon; the second [day] Father Fray José de Mora; the third [day] the celebration for the holy kings

Saint Ferdinand and Saint Hermenegildo was held, and toward evening, that for Saint Sebastián. The Very Reverend Father Maestro Fray Jerónimo de Salcedo gave the sermon in the morning, and the Very Reverend Father Maestro Fray Alvaro de Francia in the afternoon. On the fourth day, about evening, the divinity student, Father Fray [blank] López [gave the sermon].

Memorial Funeral Rites for Licentiate Dávila

Tuesday, the 21st of January of 1687, memorial funeral rites were held for the venerable licentiate Don José Dávila, founder of the small convent of the Descalzas [nuns], who died on Monday, December 3rd. They were held in the convent of Nuestra Señora de la Limpia Concepción, where his body was. The licentiate Alonso Romero, head of the Saint Philip of Neri [brotherhood] at San Pedro [church], gave the sermon. He said admirable things about the virtue [of the deceased] and the many graces given to him by God.

Corregidor *of Huanta*

At eight in the morning of Wednesday, the 12th of January of 1687, the stepson of the secretary of the Duke of La Palata took the decree of [appointment to] the *corregimiento* of Huanto to the house of the battalion commander, Don Juan Luís de Rassa, my dear friend and landlord. He had won it in competition with two other very powerful pretenders. There is no doubt that God gave it to him.

Death of Admiral Zorrilla de la Gándara

Friday, the 24th of January of the year 1687, Admiral Juan Zorilla de la Gándara died. He was the father-in-law of Don Juan José de Acuña, the Count of La Vega. He [the admiral] was buried Saturday, the 25th, in the church of San Agustín, and Monday, the 27th, his funeral rites were held in the same church with much grandeur at both events.

A Liar Sentenced

Saturday, the 1st of February of the year 1687, a young man who is said to have come from Barbacoas was sentenced to ten years at Valdivia. He arrived here saying that he was a gentleman and that he brought news from Spain, whereupon the *corregidores* gave him gifts and financed him. His Excellency, the Duke of La Palata, recognized that he was falsifying, and he sent two mounted soldiers along the highway where they captured him. Having determined his guilt, His Excellency exiled him as mentioned.

Earthquake at Huancavelica

Wednesday, the 5th of February of the year 1687, news arrived that there had been tremors from eight in the morning and [lasting] through most of the day at Huancavelica and all its district, Ocobamba, Huanta, Huamanga, etcetera. According to the news, it happened on the 28th of January.

Destined for Chile

That same day the son of General Don José de Alzamora y Ursúa left for Chile and Valdivia as chief of the two ships.

Shortage of Candles

In the evening of Thursday, the 13th of February of the year 1687, second day of Lent, His Grace and Excellency, Archbishop Don Melchor de Liñán y Cisneros, began the story which he was going to preach all during Lent. He finished by preaching about the lack of clothing and the cut in quality and scarcity of candle wax. The result was that on that same night no candles were to be found in the stores.

Entrance of the Enemy in Cañete

On the morning of the first Saturday of Lent, the 15th of February of the year 1687, news arrived at Lima that the day before, Friday the 14th, at four in the morning the enemy had entered Cañete. At the mouth of the river they seized more than two hundred bales of dry goods from Castile, destined for Cuzco, in which many people had a [financial] interest. They imprisoned most of the people of the town. Among the captives were the *bachiller* Matías Cascante, its present curate; the *corregidor* Don Martín de la Cueva; and many others. It is said that the licentiate [blank] de Armas was badly wounded and held captive. His Excellency immediately ordered that all the [military] quarters be opened [for enlistments]. May God give us strength and look on us with eyes of mercy.

Sunday, the 16th of February, the viaticum was given to Don Ignacio Casteluí, canon of this holy church and cathedral.

Proclamation About Candle Wax

Monday, the 17th of February of the year 1687, two proclamations were issued in the same morning. One ordered any persons who had candle wax hidden to declare it before Don José de Agüero, ordinary *alcalde*, under grave penalties [for those who failed to do so], and for the slave who denounced his master, it would be kept secret and he would be given a third part of the confiscated wax.

The other proclamation ordered that all the sailors, mates, shipboys, etcetera, that were in Lima, be in Callao within twenty-four hours, under penalty of four years in the presidio without pay and the arbitrament of His Excellency.

Death of Doctor Casteluí

That same day, Monday the 17th, Doctor Don Ignacio Casteluí, canon of this cathedral and professed in the Society of Jesus, died at seven at night. [He was buried] on Tuesday, the 18th of February, with the attendance of the university, ecclesiastic *cabildo*, and the archbishop. Funeral rites were held in the same church on Thursday, the 20th, because Wednesday was a day of sermon and they were postponed [to Thursday].

Second Proclamation on Candle Wax

This same day, Thursday the 20th of February, at twelve o'clock a proclamation was issued ordering that a quintal of candle wax sell at eight pesos and that all the stores be stocked with the necessary wax candles without mixing them with other ingredients. Grave penalties [were specified] both for those who did not include the proper ounces in the candles and for those who hid wax or sold it at more than eight pesos.

Habit for Don Santiago Urdanegui

Monday, the 24th of February, day of the apostle Saint Mathew, Don Santiago de Urdanegui put on the habit of [blank] at the church of La Encarnación.

Father Lisperguer's Sermon

Wednesday, the 5th of March, Fray Matías Lisperguer preached in the royal chapel on ecclesiastic immunity, the monopolies of the merchants, and on giving church offices to members of the [viceroy's] family. He horribly shocked the viceroy, Duke of La Palata.

Archbishop's Sermon

Thursday, the 6th of this month and year of 1687, the archbishop, Don Melchor de Liñán y Cisneros, preached at the cathedral in the evening, and continuing the sermons, he attacked the viceroy severely on ecclesiastic immunity. He also [complained] that on the previous Saturday a scribe had entered [the cathedral] to notify the canons, in the name of the government, to give more salary than that presently designated to the mulatto in charge of the dogs.

Dispatch Ship from Panama Friday, the 7th of March of the year 1687, at seven in the evening the dispatch ship from Panama arrived. It brought news that two pirogues and a galleon, well equipped for war, with four hundred restless men had set sail from Panama.

News also arrived that [Don Melchor Portocarrero Laso de la Vega], the Count of Monclova, had arrived at Veracruz as viceroy of Mexico. [We were] also advised that the Count of Trens sailed with thirty ships for these parts.

Death of Félix Guerra Monday, the 10th of March of the year 1687, Félix Guerra died just after having opened his store. He was buried on Tuesday, the 11th, in the church of San Francisco where he was alms treasurer.

Death of the Count of Cartago During the night of Monday, the 31st of March, second day of Easter, Don José Hurtado de Chaves, Count of Cartago, died of apoplexy. His death was lamentable, and even more so because it occurred at the house of his mistress.

He was buried at San Francisco [church].

Great Earthquake Tuesday, the 1st of April of the year 1687, last day of the Easter holidays, at eleven forty-five at night there was an earthquake so horrible for the fury with which it began, that it was comparable only to the force with which it terrified the whole city. More than a month earlier [someone] had been going about saying that through a revelation he knew about this [earthquake]. God look on us with eyes of mercy, that such a thing was not listened to. It was clear from the way it swayed that it was a slap from the hand of God. At that hour all the churches were opened, there were confessions, and many priests preached through the streets advocating penance.

On the evening of Wednesday, the 2nd, the Very Reverend Father Luís Galindo de San Ramón preached in the cathedral. Never had such a crowd of people been seen as that day in the cathedral, filling the whole church and even the steps; and there were also people in the halls. He preached that God was very angry about our faults, and that which has him most annoyed is the nefarious sin which is practiced between members of the same sex, women with women, and men with men. May God liberate us from such faults; with good reason is His Majesty [God] angry, and may He give us His grace so that we will offend Him no more.

That same Wednesday at seven in the evening the whole religious order of Saint Francis set forth, led by a priest carrying a holy crucifix of considerable size. They walked along the public streets, barefoot and with cords around their necks, even the Very Reverend Father Commissary Fray Félix Como. On each corner there was an act of fervent contrition. It [the procession] was accompanied by the greatest crowd ever seen. May it all be for the honor and glory of God.

Procession of the Franciscan Fathers

Monday, the 7th of April of the year 1687, the [Masses in] compensation for [offenses against] Our Redeemer began with the holy body and blood [sacramental bread and wine] uncovered, and a holy crucifix at the right side. On the evening of this day the Very Reverend Father Commissary Fray Félix Como gave the sermon with great fervor.

Tuesday, the 8th, at five forty-five in the morning there was an earthquake, but not very great. God grant us His mercy that we may love Him.

Another Minor Earthquake

Wednesday, the 9th, at three in the afternoon there was another earthquake.

Another Earthquake

This same afternoon Father Guadalupe gave a spirited sermon on the vindication for Our Redeemer.

Thursday, the 10th, the custodian from Cuzco who is going to Rome, Fray Pedro Saavedra, preached effectively.

Friday, the 11th, the Very Reverend Father Fray Nicolás de León gave an astonishing sermon. I will put down a part of his theme. "Cain sinned," he said, "and God told him that he who offends will receive a punishment seven times greater than that deserved. Wherefore, after Cain killed Abel he went to live in a land where there were earthquakes. We know then that with Cain being so bad, it would even be worse for one who dared to sin in a land where there are frequent earthquakes."

Saturday, the 12th, Father Fray Francisco Mexía, of those [Franciscans] who arrived from Spain, gave the sermon.

Sunday, the 13th, at ten in the morning there was an earthquake.

Earthquake

On that day Father Francisco del Risco gave the sermon.

Monday, the 14th, Father Fray José Delgadillo gave the sermon with the general approval of the whole city.

Tuesday, the 15th, the retired father lector and present guardian of Guadalupe [hermitage], Fray Gregorio de Quesada, preached with notable wit, subtlety, and spirit.

Arrival of the Small Armada

Saturday, the 26th of April of 1687, the escort vessel and tender of the small armada of mulattoes returned to the port of Callao. For nine months they had been giving assistance to Panama and looking for the enemy. Nothing is known about their flagship which disappeared one night.

Loss of the Flagship

Tuesday, the 29th of April, news arrived that the flagship in command of Captain Don Gaspar Márquez de Mansilla, a singular man and worthy of eternal memory, had arrived at Huarmey with a shortage of supplies and with the topmast badly damaged. There it encountered the French ship named *Tigre* which has thirty-six pieces [of artillery], and our flagship was a small frigate called *Santa Catalina* that had only four pieces. The enemy was loading gunpowder and meat. Our Don Gaspar attacked with considerable valor and without letting the advantageous strength of the opponent daunt him. They battled a day and a half, fighting steadily, and finally our Don Gaspar died like a Bayard [Pierre Terrail Bayard, a French military hero]. The enemy placed all their artillery on one side and directed [the fire] at our ship. Those that remained alive rowed the frigate to land, only fifty men escaping of the two hundred and ten that went thereon. The others died and the ones that jumped into the water were taken alive as prisoners by the enemy. Everything goes against us. May God have mercy on us and take our deceased into His Kingdom.

Don Francisco Pontejo Killed

Friday, the 2nd of May of the year 1687, on the eve of the [feast of] the Holy Cross, between seven and eight at night Don Francisco Pontejo, *caballero* of the order of Alcántara, who was going to the *corregimiento* of Cuzco to succeed Don Pedro Balbín, was shot to death. He was killed as he was entering the door of the house of La Concha, where he lived on the lower floor on the right. The bullet went through the large muscle of his arm and through his lung. He fell, and they carried him to his bed where he confessed, received the last sacraments, and made a will. While he was being cared for, he became nauseous and died. May God keep him in His holy glory.

He was buried on Saturday, the 13th, at the church of Santo Domingo.

Imprisonments for this Death

The same night that he was killed, Don José de Agüero, ordinary *alcalde* who had taken the declaration of the wounded man, arrested Don Ventura de Góndola, who had the contract here for importing Negroes [slaves], and another man. Both are uncles of the assassin, Góndola being an uncle on the father's side, and the other man on the mother's.

[Events leading to the murder] began as follows. On his way from Spain the deceased *caballero* stopped in Panama where he stayed in the house of Don [blank] de Góndola, who had a son and a daughter. The father tried to marry her to this *caballero*, and he [Pontejo] did not reject it [the proposition]. Later he backed down saying that while here [in Lima] he would try to fulfill his promise. Fearing some trickery, the father of the girl gathered together his estate and went to Spain, leaving enough for the girl's dowry with her brother, a young man about nineteen years old, and with the maternal uncle. In leaving he said to the son, "There is your sister, either see that she is married or consider what you should do." The young man came with his uncle and sister to Lima. Pontejo backed down. The young man spoke with Father Maestro Saldana, Dominican religious, to see if he could expedite it, and this priest spoke to Pontejo who answered that he was not committed. Asking Pontejo if he were afraid of any consequences, he replied that there was nothing to fear. Upon learning this, the young brother went to the viceroy and said to him; "Sir, if Don Francisco Pontejo does not marry my sister, she and I will be without honor, and I do not know what I am likely to do." The viceroy called the *caballero* and forcefully proposed the case, but the latter replied that he owed nothing. The viceroy said, "Then look out for yourself." He [Pontejo] then tried to marry the daughter of Don Gaspar de Zuazo, *caballero* of the order of Calatrava and secretary of the government. The young man learned that Pontejo had gone visiting at the house of Zuazo that afternoon and had had cold drinks and chocolate. Grieved and without any hope, the young man reached a decision and that night killed him [Pontejo]. The uncles are imprisoned, but the young man has disappeared.

Abbess of the Descalzas Convent

Monday, the 5th of May, Micaela de San Juan, who had just been assistant abbess, was elected as abbess.

Misfortune at Santo Domingo Church

At eleven thirty in the morning on Thursday, the 8th of May, which was the day of the Ascension of Our Redeemer, while the father instructor Fray José de la Peña was preaching at Santo Domingo, Pedro, my servant boy, went there to look for my friend Fray José de Avila. I had sent him on this [errand], and Migueli-to went with him. [Going] by way of the high cloister above the sacristy, Miguel kept close to the wall, but Pedro went very near the supports over the new meeting room that was being constructed for the chapter, and he fell into the cloister when supports and ceiling [gave way]. Miguel ran and was saved, but my Pedro fell and all the ceiling fell on top of him and crushed his leg to pieces, a piece of my heart. Miguel came to notify me, and with this sad news I went to Santo Domingo on the little mule of my friend Don Bartolomé de Uribe. I found him calling for me, and I had him taken to San Andrés [hospital] whereupon the surgeon, Don Pedro de Castro, cut off his leg. I did not have the heart to see it. May the will of God be done for him, for me, and in all matters affecting me.

Death of Don Alonso Balbín

Don Alonso Balbín, *corregidor* of Cuzco who had come down [to Lima] with a pack of mules, died before dawn of this same day.

This same day of the Ascension, Don Luis Calvo, who had been administrator of Callao died, suddenly.

A baker named Pozo also died suddenly on this day.

The Small Armada of Privateers

Saturday, the 10th of May, His Excellency went to Callao to dispatch the small armada of armed merchant ships [privateers].

Entrance of the Enemy in Guayaquil

Wednesday, the 14th of May, [news] arrived directly from Guayaquil advising that the enemy had entered that port, where they killed as many as eighty men and captured the two fortifications and other parts of the city. They say that the enemy landed four hundred and sixty men. Our small armada had not yet left Callao when this news arrived. May God assist them.

The small armada of corsairs furnished by the merchants was made up of two ships well equipped with artillery and four hundred men. It departed on Thursday, the 15th of May of the year 1687, and that afternoon the viceroy returned to Lima. May God deliver them safely. *Departure of the Small Armada*

Competitive examinations for the professorships that have been vacant more than ten years due to the litigation on the votes began on Tuesday, the 6th of May of the year 1687. On this day *bachiller* Don Antonio de Palacios of the royal college read the lecture. *Bachiller* Don Pedro de la Serna, lay brother, read on Saturday, the 10th, and the *bachiller* Don Pedro de Castro, lay brother, read on Tuesday, the 13th. Licentiate Don José de la Concha, collegiate of San Martín, read on Friday, the 16th, astounding all the cloister. *Lectures for the Competitive Examinations*

Thursday, the 22nd of May of the year 1687, news arrived from Guayaquil that seven enemy ships entered that port where they killed many of our men, burned the houses, and captured three hundred prisoners for whom they asked one hundred thousand pesos ransom. It was reported that they [the enemy] had carried off the artillery of the fortresses. [In Callao] the ship *San Lorenzo* and the ship *El Populo* were loaded to go to Arica, but His Excellency immediately ordered that they be unloaded, leaving them only with their artillery, to go out for combat in convoy of the small armada that is going in search of the enemy. *News from Guayaquil*

At noon this day a proclamation was issued that all those who had arrived battered from the flagship that fought with the enemy near Huarmey and ran aground should apply to receive aid. *Proclamation on Aid*

Saturday, the 21st of June of the year 1687, the extremely sage Doctor Don Diego Montero del Aguila lectured at the competition for the professorships. Taking chapter 15 *De Decimis,* book 3 *Decretalium* [compilation of canon law], point by point especially for this occasion, he gave the greatest lecture that has been heard, as lively in reciting as he was sharp in replying. The cloister, *audiencia,* and other persons listening were left in admiration. All agreed that it would be unjust not to give him the prime professorship. *The Professorships*

News of the Enemy Sunday, the 22nd of June of the year 1687, news arrived that an enemy ship was near Casma [200 miles north of Lima]. This news found present the ship *San Lorenzo*, which is the best in port, equipped with artillery and well prepared [for combat], and His Excellency immediately issued a proclamation that anyone who wanted to should enlist. Many applied, [and] to three hundred of those [who were chosen], His Excellency gave two months [pay] which is forty pesos. Monday, the 23rd, they embarked and that afternoon set sail.

Doctor Don Bartolomé Romero read [for the professorship competition] on Saturday, the 12th of July, and Doctor Don Pedro de la Peña on Wednesday, the 16th of July.

Departure for Conchucos On Tuesday, the 5th of August, I left Lima for Conchucos on a business trip accompanying the *bachiller* Don Francisco del Prado, who was going as curate of San Luís de Huari. I left my mother alive along with my sister Doña Damiana, who lived near the Prado and El Carmen [convents].

The Year 1690

At four in the afternoon of Friday, the 5th of January of 1689, the royal ensign, Don Pedro de Lescano, came forth with his standard [in the plaza] near the cabildo. And from the palace the viceroy, Duke of Palata, came out in shirtsleeves and on horseback, accompanied by all the *oidores* with their [illegible], and many *caballeros* appeared in a group near the cathedral and archbishop's palace. Honors were presented in the usual manner, then the group went from the palace to the cathedral to hear mass and a sermon. It was [the eve of] the day of the Kings [Epiphany].

Jerónimo Modesto Honton was born between nine and ten on the morning of Wednesday, the 15th of June of 1689. At the age of two months and twenty-one days he was baptized in Santa Ana [parish], and *bachiller* Don Diego Cequeira anointed him with oil and chrism. His sponsors were Laureano Tello and Doña Antonia Cívico. Holy water had already been sprinkled on him, in case of emergency, by the *bachiller* Don Andrés de Uribe, and the *bachiller* Don Juan de Landázuri held him on that occasion. He started school on Monday, the 31st of August of 1693, at the age of four years, two months and sixteen days. He did not begin to read until Monday, the 25th of January of 1694. Jerónimo Modesto was confirmed in the Prado convent on Thursday, the 3rd of March of 1695, by the Most Illustrious señor Don Fray Sebastián Pastrana, bishop of Paraguay. His godfather was Captain Antonio Prabalon.

The Year 1690

The Virgin of Solitude

Friday, the 16th of June of the year 1690, I placed the [statue of] the Holy Virgin of Solitude in her niche at the base of the holy cross in the cemetery of the Prado [convent]. The following day, Saturday, it was unveiled, and the appropriate *Salve Regina* antiphon and litany were chanted. It is the same statue that was found at dawn with the face burned.

The Year 1694

Agueda, daughter of my Negro [slave?] Francisca, was born at seven thirty at night on Thursday, the 5th of February of 1694. The *bachiller* Julián Lozano sprinkled baptismal water on her; her godfather was Juan de Peñaranda. She was baptized [in church] on Wednesday, the 31st of October of 1696, at the age of two years, eight months, and twenty-five days. Her godmother was Isabel Barragan. The *bachiller* Diego Munico Sotelo, [priest] of the parish of Santa Ana, anointed her with oil and chrism.

The Year 1696

Death of Don Gregorio Fernández de León

Don Gregorio Fernández de León Huaman Yauri died on Tuesday, the 21st of February of the year 1696. Along with his wife, I was named executor of his estate. She was left an inheritance for the rest of her life, after which it was ordered that one thousand pesos be set up as income for a chaplaincy, for which he named me, the *bachiller* Francisco de Mugaburu, as first chaplain and in charge of carrying it out. He executed the testament before the secretary Lorenzo de Herrera in the month and year referred to above. And he added a provision that if his wife [re-] marry, everything that Don Gregorio had [left her] should immediately be withheld, and that I should use it as income for the chaplaincy. [For details] I refer to the will.

The Year 1697

Margarita, my godchild, was let go [adopted]. She was born on the 20th of July of 1696, and the licentiate Roque Valcazar, presbyter, sprinkled water on her in case of necessity. At the age of ten months and twenty-five days she went to the church of San Lázaro where the licentiate Don Iñigo de Segura, interim priest of that church, anointed her with oil and chrism, and I, the licentiate Francisco de Mugaburu, was her godfather. She was put up for adoption at the door of my house on Saturday, the 15th of June of 1697.

[The original diary continues with notations about the births and deaths of Mugaburu's children; the data is summarized below.]

Antonio Marcela	(1637–1644)
Marcos	(1639–1655)
José	(1641–1677)
Juan Félix	(1643–1653)
Ana Josefa	(1645–1648)
Francisco	(1647–after 1697)
María Josefa	(1650–1656)
Juan Sebastián	(1652–1654)
Margarita	(1654–1655)
Antonio Ventura	(1656–after 1677)
Jerónima de la Cruz	(1658–1660)

Glossary of Spanish and Peruvian Terms

alcalde, magistrate or mayor of a town; usually two, elected by the *cabildo* on January 1; sometimes appointed.

alcalde mayor, royal governor of a frontier district or province.

alcancías, jousting games where charging horsemen hurl hollow clay balls at each other; fire balls used in warfare.

alguacil, a constable or peace officer.

audiencia, administrative-judicial courts for viceroyalties and provinces. The one in Lima served as supreme court and cabinet to the viceroy; outlying judicial districts were located in Panama, Quito, La Plata, Santiago, and Buenos Aires.

auto-de-fé or auto-da-fé, public ceremony of the Inquisition where sentences of the condemned were read and punishment of heretics executed.

bachiller, bachelor, or the holder of the lowest university degree; baccalaureate.

caballero, a mounted horseman, hence a Spanish knight or gentleman; an army officer.

cabildo, town or city council, or the building where they meet; also a cathedral chapter or council.

cañas, jousting games where mounted adversaries hurl canes or reed spears at each other.

chácara, Peruvian term for farm or rural estate.

chasque, Quechua and Peruvian term for post runner or postoffice.

colegio, seminary, college, or school.

comadre, godmother or mother of a person's godchild.

compadre, godfather, father of a person's godchild, friend, or benefactor.

consulado, merchant guild or board of trade; representing Spanish traders, it had considerable influence as a kind of chamber of commerce.

corregidor, royal governor of a province (corregimiento).

creole, a person of European descent but born in the New World; Mugaburu also used the term *creollo negro* for Negroes born in America.

definidor, definitor or member of the governing committee of a religious order.

encomendero, individual who for distinguished service received a royal grant of the tribute and/or labor of Indians within a certain boundary, with the duty of protecting and Christianizing them.

fanega, a grain measure equal to 1.6 bushels.

fiesta, a celebration of a public or religious holiday.

fiscal, a royal treasury official or public prosecutor.

garrocha, iron-pointed pole used as a weapon in bullfighting.

hidalgo, a nobleman.

lanzada, an old form of bullfighting where the bull is maneuvered so that it will be run through by a lance imbedded in the ground.

licenciado, licentiate, or the holder of a university degree ranking between bachelor and doctor.

mestizo, a person of mixed Spanish and Indian parentage.

oidor, a judge of the *audiencia* court.

provincial, the superior of a province of a Roman Catholic religious order.

quinto real, royal fifth or twenty per cent tax or tribute on jewels, treasure, gold and silver.

regidor, elected member of the cabildo or town council; alderman or councilor.

relator, a lawyer who prepares briefs of laws, decrees and proceedings in the high courts of justice.

residencia, review of an official's conduct at the end of his term of office.

Tierra Firme, or Castilla de Oro, the northern Caribbean shore of South America; Mugaburu sometimes used the term for Panama.

visitador, royal inspector with authority to execute justice.

zamba, a female offspring of Negro and Indian parentage; a male is called zambo or sambo.

Index